Religion and Education:
comparative and international perspectives

Religion and Education:
comparative and international perspectives

Edited by
Malini Sivasubramaniam & Ruth Hayhoe

Oxford Studies in Comparative Education
Series Editor: David Phillips

SYMPOSIUM
BOOKS

Symposium Books
PO Box 204, Didcot, Oxford OX11 9ZQ, United Kingdom
www.symposium-books.co.uk

Published in the United Kingdom, 2018

ISBN 978-1-910744-01-7

This publication is also available on a subscription basis
as Volume 27 Number 2 of *Oxford Studies in Comparative Education*
(ISSN 0961-2149)

Printed and bound in the United Kingdom by Hobbs the Printers, Southampton
www.hobbs.uk.com

Contents

Acknowledgements

We would like to thank all the contributors to this volume for their enthusiasm for this project, their encouragement, their belief in the value of this work, and most of all for the engaging chapters they have written. They have graciously responded to the comments and suggestions we have made throughout the editorial process. Each chapter makes a unique contribution in facilitating a comparative understanding of the role of religion in education and the diverse geographical and political contexts bring richness to the discussion on fostering deeper religious dialogue. This has been a long journey, but we believe it has been a worthwhile one. *Nisi Dominus Frustra* ('everything is in vain without God') has truly been our motivation for this work.

We thank the reviewers who provided feedback and comments on certain chapters. We thank Keith Watson, whose preface highlights the contributions the book makes to the field. We would also like to thank David Phillips, the series editor, who has been enormously encouraging and patient throughout this process. Similarly, we thank the publisher, Symposium Books, for their extended support of this project. We also gratefully acknowledge the support of our institution, the Comparative, International and Development Education Centre (CIDEC) at OISE/University of Toronto. Last but not least, we thank our families for their ongoing support.

Foreword

This book on 'religion and education from a comparative and international perspective' could not have come at a more timely moment. The issues concerning what religion, or aspects of religion, should be taught in schools, or whether religion should even be on the school curriculum, or whether religious teaching should be simply left to parents or believers in a particular faith, have recently come to the forefront of debate in many national settings, especially in the western countries. This is largely because of a realisation that multiculturalism has failed to integrate different ethnic groups, particularly Muslims, into mainstream society, but also because of the sudden and unprecedented scale of migration of Arabs fleeing the chaos and violence of the Middle East and of different African peoples seeking a better quality of life in the economically advanced countries (though with so many in refugee camps, these hopes are still a distant dream). How best to integrate the thousands of children involved so that both they and children in the host societies can learn to understand and respect each other's faiths and values is at the core of many of these debates. Yet, surprisingly, no such debate seems to be on the agenda of the important international bodies.

The United Nations (UN) documents 'Education for All', 'Millennium Development Goals' and, more recently, '2030 Agenda for Sustainable Development' pay scant regard to religion and how this impacts the lives of millions of people across the globe. Much of the literature emanating from the World Bank and the United Nations and its sub-organisations concerned with education and socio-economic development, such as UNESCO, hardly make any reference to religion, and certainly not with regard to education. For the past half-century or so the emphasis from international agencies has been on education for literacy and numeracy, increasing the opportunities for girls and women, skills development of one sort or another, with employment seen as the main, or even the only, purpose of education in the modern age. With the growth of technology and robotics, and the likely consequence that people may have more time away from paid employment, the need for a rethink about the purpose of education and schooling has resurfaced. Several of the authors in this book, such as Katherine Marshall (Chapter 1) and Ghosh and Chan (Chapter 16), stress that the time is ripe for a reconsideration of the place that religion should play. Indeed, as Marshall notes, the place of Catholic religious organisations and the role of the Aga Khan Foundation in providing schools in poorer countries should be praised because they teach not only basic skills but also attitudes of mutual understanding between different groups.

The importance of religion in societies goes back millennia, even to primitive societies, as the quote from Barnes (1989, p. 3), cited in the introduction to this book, reveals: 'Religion is the heart of culture, that collection of mores, myths and fundamental beliefs which holds a people together and gives a society a sense of coherence and identity.' We can see this in the history of the Jews with their scriptures, which not only tell the history of the Jewish people and their special relationship to Yahweh, but also contain the rules and laws by which people should relate to each other and by which society should be regulated. We can see this in the early developments of China as alluded to by Hayhoe (Chapter 6) where she discusses dialogues between Christians, Buddhists and Confucians over different historical timescales. Both the emperors of China and the patriarchs of Israel and Judah were able to exert order and control through citing their scriptures and teaching these to the young. It is also evident from the Hindu Vedas and the Sanskrit writings in India. Perhaps more than anything else was this sense that religion was/is the glue that holds a culture together. Even in more modern totalitarian societies such as Albania, North Korea, the People's Republic of China, Turkmenistan and the Soviet Union, where the authorities tried to abolish religion as 'the opium of the people', governments soon found that it was essential to establish some form of religion, usually the cult of the leader or the political ideology, as a means of holding society together. Inevitably this led to schools and other educational institutions being used for indoctrination purposes, as Lisovskaya (Chapter 15) so clearly points out. Even so, despite attempts to suppress all religion in Mao's communist China and President Xi's suppression of Christianity in many of China's provinces, the strong influence of Catholic teaching on people in a rural area of Western China has enabled young female migrant workers to resist the temptations of urban life and to find support from other Christians. This is amply shown by Seeberg et al (Chapter 5). Far from being problematic, it would appear that the morality instilled by the Catholic teachers has helped these young women to adjust to modern living without too much difficulty.

When religious belief fades away as a glue that holds a society together this is often the beginning of the decline of a country or even a civilisation. This was one of the main reasons for the decline of the Roman Empire, as Edward Gibbon argued in his massive *The History of the Decline and Fall of the Roman Empire*, which was written between 1776 and 1788. Similarly, Arnold Toynbee (1889-1975), in his masterly 10-volume *The History of the World*, written between 1934 and 1954, noted through his study of fifteen civilisations that have come and gone that the erosion of state religion was a key factor in the decline of those societies/civilisations. It was not only that, of course. Other factors included the breakdown of the family, an obsession with homosexuality, political corruption, a complacency about their achievements and an unwillingness to defend these achievements and values against aggressors. We are seeing this in the West today, especially in Europe, though the decline is caused by far more than simply a decline in religious belief. As Tulasiewicz and Brock (1988, p. 9) pointed out:

> The historical role of the Christian church in the development of European nations' political and education systems makes the Christian tradition a powerful agent in shaping cultural and national identity.

Davies 1997 (p. 9) goes even further when he quotes T.S. Eliot (1948, pp. 122-124):

> The dominant feature in creating a common culture between peoples, each with its own distinct culture, is religion ... I am talking about the common tradition of Christianity which has made Europe what it is... It is against a background of Christianity that all our thought has significance ... I do not believe that the culture of Europe could survive the complete disappearance of the Christian faith.

Because of the growth of secular humanism, which stresses that there are no absolutes to follow and that everyone's opinions are as valid as the next person's, and because of the European Union's (EU's) Lisbon Treaty's rejection of any reference to Europe's Christian roots, despite pleas from the Pope and other religious leaders, the EU is now finding itself unsure of what its values are. There is a politically correct sense of guilt about Europe's imperial past and an unwillingness to stress her achievements in the arts and sciences, in law and in the sense of justice and human rights, to say nothing of political theories such as democracy that have spread across the world. Because there is no longer a set of rights and wrongs that used to be taught in schools, there is now a moral vacuum where anything goes as long as it is pleasurable. The result is that there is no overarching belief holding together the nations of Europe. There is no longer a clear sense of common identity, and the political leaders seem unable to know how to respond to, or withstand, the massive influx of Muslims that is changing the traditional Christian, even secular, aspects of European societies. One author has called what is happening '*The Strange Death of Europe*' (Murray, 2017).

With the exception of some of the writers in the eighteenth-century Enlightenment and the French Revolution, the place of religion in education was hardly challenged in a serious way until the twentieth century, when two world wars shattered many of the old beliefs and certainties. The rise of communism in several countries and regions, most notably the Soviet Union and Eastern Europe, China and parts of Southeast Asia, and also several countries of South and Central America, was seen as a new way of achieving more equal societies, a sort of Utopia. Religion was regarded as a major constraint on progress, both social and economic.

However, it needs to be recognised that in nearly every society, before the State began to take responsibility for educational provision, the earliest forms of education were provided by religious figures, largely because they were the only people who were literate. Thus, education in Europe was provided by monks and priests in cathedral and monastic schools, by Buddhist monks in monastic schools in Southeast Asia, and by imams in private homes or mosques in the Islamic world. From different periods of the nineteenth century the State began to provide, or partially provide, schooling while leaving space for religious providers.

This is not the place to discuss the different approaches to religion in global politics and the different approaches to religion in education through different state attitudes and policies (see Haynes, 1998). Suffice it to say that since the end of World War II there has been a steady decline in religious practice, if not belief; there has been a growth in liberalism and secular humanism, what Sookhdeo (2016) has called '*The New Civic Religion*', in the western world since this has been seen as progressive and modern while traditional and institutionalised religion has been portrayed as conservative and backward. At the same time, there has been a growth in Islamic fundamentalism based on the Wahabist teaching and interpretation of the Quran in many parts of the Islamic world. This has been linked with the growth of Islamist extremist organisations, most notably Al-Qaida, Al Shabaab, and ISIL/Daesh. In many parts of the Islamic world, especially where there is a separate religious affairs ministry that is responsible for large areas of educational provision, there appears to have been little attempt to bring religious teaching up to date with today's world. Add to these trends the increase of migration across the world, including of people adhering to some of these extremist views, and many countries are confronted with how best to educate their children with a mixture of understanding, respect and tolerance of others with different beliefs and traditions.

There is a belated acknowledgement on the part of governments that there needs to be a re-examination of the place of religion in society and new approaches towards teaching religion in schools that can be both mutually beneficial as well as life enhancing. Many of the chapters in this book set out to do just that. For example, Li (Chapter 2) shows how Confucian thinking has been harnessed with African thinking to open up new approaches to development; Niyozov (Chapter 4) examines how Islamic education in Post-Soviet Tajikistan is being transformed so that what is being taught is more in line with what the State requires; Wu's analysis of recent reforms of state schooling for Hui Muslims in Western China (Chapter 8) makes similar points; Herzog and Adams (Chapter 10) show differing approaches to modernising Islamic teaching in two very different settings, Bangladesh and Senegal; and Kidwai (Chapter 14) questions whether the state governments in India are really serious about bringing madrasas into mainstream education or whether they are being hoodwinked into believing their policies are working. However, it must be acknowledged that in many parts of the

Islamic world there has been little appetite for any meaningful educational reform with regard to religious teaching. Some of the chapters explore religious education per se (Wong, Chapter 7; Katz, Chapter 12; Barnes, Chapter 13; and Ghosh and Chan, Chapter 16). A slightly different slant on this is Chapter 9 by Niyom et al, on the Buddhist underpinning of the Thai curriculum with its strong emphasis on an ethical approach to living.

While there are a few comparative studies in the true sense of the word – for example, Hwang (Chapter 3,) Herzog and Adams (Chapter 10), Ghosh and Chan (Chapter 16), Sivasubramaniam and Sider (Chapter 11) and Collet and Bang (Chapter 17) – the fact that all the chapters in this volume shed new light on what is happening in several countries across the globe is of great value. Some are based on empirical research; some are based on analyses of government documents, and others on observation and interviews. All of them make an interesting addition to our understanding of religion's place in the world and how it is, or should be, approached in today's uncertain political climate. I certainly commend this volume as an interesting way of approaching an age-old topic. My hope is that this volume will be a precursor to many more comparative and international studies on the role of education and religion.

Keith Watson

Emeritus Professor of Comparative and International Education,
University of Reading, UK

References

Barnes, M. (1989) *Religion in Conversation: Christian identity and religious pluralism.* Cambridge: Cambridge University Press.

Davies, N. (1997) *Europe: a history.* London: Pimlico.

Murray, C.D. (2017) *The Strange Death of Europe: immigration, identity, Islam.* London: Bloomsbury, Continuum.

Sookhdeo, P. (2016) *The New Civic Religion: humanism and the future of Christianity.* McLean, VA: Isaac Publishing.

Tulasiewicz, W. & Brock, C. (Eds) (1988) *Christianity and Educational Provision in International Perspective.* London: Routledge.

INTRODUCTION

Religion and Education from a Comparative and International Perspective: issues, tensions and possibilities

MALINI SIVASUBRAMANIAM & RUTH HAYHOE

> Religion is the heart of culture, that collection of mores, myths and fundamental beliefs which holds a people together and gives a society a sense of coherence and identity. (Barnes, 1989, p. 3)

We believe this book is timely. It comes at a critical period when religious tensions and fears of religiously rooted terrorism threaten to erode peace and national security in many regions of the world, particularly in the post-9/11 era in which we live. Instances of religious radicalisation and intolerance frame many ethnic conflicts in our political landscape. Contrary to philosophical and sociological debates that have anticipated the demise of religion, there is renewed awareness of how important religious faith is in the lives of many and how deeply religion impacts communities. The growing diaspora of minority faiths in many countries in North America and Europe has also fuelled the need to better understand 'the other' and has reaffirmed the importance of inter-faith dialogue.

We believe this book fills a void in the field of comparative and international education where discussions around religion, religious organisations and religious education have been somewhat muted. Contrary to seeing religion as inconsequential to humanity's broader development goals, we believe issues of religion and religious education should be given high priority. The Parliament of the World's Religions continues to be a strong advocate for the revival of inter-religious dialogue and the involvement of religious activists in mainstream development issues. It has recently established a United Nations Task Force, which takes the position that the world's faith communities have a crucial role to play in achieving the

Millenium Development Goals (Parliament of the World's Religions, 2017). This dialogue is crucial given that religious and cultural differences continue to give rise to conflict and concern in many countries.

Religious organisations and faith communities have had a long history of involvement in schooling and the delivery of a variety of services. As Watson (2010) points out, many of the modern education systems have been 'shaped by the interaction between religion ... and the state' (p. 308), yet the contribution religious groups could make to reaching global development and education goals has not been fully recognised or embraced. As we contemplate this post-2015 development compact, it is both timely and imperative to consider the role that religion, religious education and religious bodies may play in shaping both the policy and the political discourse.

The 2030 Agenda for Sustainable Development and its 17 Sustainable Development Goals (SDGs) provide an agenda for the global community to reach its goals post-2015 (UNESCO, 2014). While the SDGs reiterate the role of civil society actors as important partners in achieving global education goals, there is little mention of religious organisations and institutions and the contributions they can make.

Equally critical is the the newly proposed Sustainable Development Goal 4, which reads, 'Ensure inclusive and equitable quality education and promote life-long learning opportunities for all', and includes a set of associated targets.

One of the targets is as follows:

> By 2030, ensure that all learners acquire the knowledge and skills needed to promote sustainable development, including, among others, through education for sustainable development and sustainable lifestyles, human rights, gender equality, promotion of a culture of peace and non-violence, global citizenship and appreciation of cultural diversity and of culture's contribution to sustainable development. (Goal 4.7)

Here again, the role of religion, religious education or religious institutions in the post-2015 education agenda is glaringly absent. Clearly the salience of religion in promoting 'a culture of peace and non-violence, global citizenship and appreciation of cultural diversity and of culture's contribution to sustainable development' is important. Increased pluralism within societies through expanding migration patterns has created a need for a deeper understanding of religious diversity. A lack of religious or spiritual education within the curriculum of public schools leaves a moral vacuum that may then be exploited by religious extremism. This lack of attention to religious education in the public school system has given rise to what Watson (2010) draws attention to as a backlash from some minority faith communities, resulting in an increase in the number and significance of faith-based schools by communities wanting to preserve and teach their faith to the next generation.

David Baker's presidential address to the Comparative and International Education Society (CIES) in 2013 called for more comparative and international education (CIE) research on the 'affinity between religion and education' (Baker, 2014, p. 16), and we have been inspired to see this book as a response to that call. Baker (2014) points to the mounting evidence suggesting that in schooled societies, religion and spirituality do not necessarily decline, but may rather thrive. Subsequently, a number of the chapters in this volume were first presented at CIES annual conferences, in Toronto in 2014 and in Washington, DC in 2015, further contributing to the CIE scholarship on religion and education. The collection of chapters we have brought together in this volume explores both the possibilities and tensions around religion and religious education, and draws parallels across differing contexts to help enhance our collective understanding of the role of religious education and religious institutions in the post-2015 development agenda. Both theoretical and empirical work inform this discussion, with examples drawn from different contexts in Africa, Asia, Europe and North America.

We also acknowledge the limitations of this volume. Understandably, the book is not able to pursue all the major faith traditions and forms of spirituality, nor is it able to address all major religiously motivated conflicts in the Global North and South. We have structured and organised the book into three related, thematic sections: Internationalising/Globalising Religious Values; Curriculum, Pedagogy and School Leadership; and Religion in Policy Processes and Conflict Resolution. The sections and the chapters therein each bring unique perspectives to the issue of how religion can deepen and enrich our understanding of education in a globalised world.

Section One, 'Internationalising/Globalising Religious Values', contains six chapters. They provide an understanding of the impact of religion beyond the nation-state and of the role of religion and religious actors in the interaction between the global and the local. We begin the book with Katherine Marshall's chapter, 'Global Education Challenges: exploring religious dimensions'. In this chapter, Marshall examines the contribution religious institutions make to the global agenda for sustainable development by exploring six topics where religious actors are particularly involved: delivery of education and outreach to underserved populations; specific education approaches for refugees and displaced populations; curricular focus on pluralism and 'religious literacy'; addressing education challenges surrounding values in education and understandings of citizenship; training of religious leaders; and advocacy for education goals and reforms. As we contemplate the post-2015 development compact, it is both timely and imperative to consider the role that religious organisations may play in shaping the policy discourse and informing the global development agenda. Through each of these six encounters Marshall shows how religious institutions can positively shape and advance the SDGs.

Next, Jun Li, in his chapter, 'Confucius Institutes and Classrooms as Educational Partnerships in Africa: the 2030 agenda of sustainable development from a Confucian perspective', examines the development of Confucius Institutes and Classrooms in Africa, focusing in particular on educational partnerships between Chinese and African educational institutions and their implications for international development, in as much as they relate to the recent UN 2030 Agenda for Sustainable Development Goals. He identifies three key characteristics of Confucian educational partnerships – demand-driven, ethics-based and pragmatic – and sees these as the key to the success of such partnerships. With the ascendancy of China as a dominant economic power, cultural diplomacy becomes more crucial in promoting cross-cultural understanding. These Confucius Institutes invite us to consider the potential of educational development and partnership based on Confucianism, a moral philosophy that is also seen as having religious dimensions in some periods of its lengthy history.

A slightly different perspective is examined in the next chapter. Institutions of Christian higher education pursue a Christian vision for world mission as well as embracing internationalisation of their activities. Christina Hwang's chapter entitled 'The Internationalization of Religious Higher Education: a comparative study of Christian universities in South Korea and Canada' examines how this dimension of world mission that Christian universities espouse enriches their mandate for internationalisation. She uses the case studies of two Christian universities, one in South Korea and one in Canada, to show the commonalities that arise from the pursuance of their respective views of world mission, despite cultural and geographical differences. Each case brings to the discussion a richer understanding of religion within higher education.

Sarfaroz Niyozov's chapter, 'Islamic Education in Post-Soviet Tajikistan: a tool in creating and sustaining a nation-state', presents the continuities and changes, tensions and dilemmas, potentials and perils of Islamic education in post-Soviet Tajikistan. He argues that Islamic education has been and will continue to be be a field of contestation between various forces due to the centrality of Islam to the history and identity of the various peoples of Tajikistan. He suggests that the mode of their engagement could improve with efforts to be both more critical and more constructive.

Vilma Seeberg, Shujuan Luo and Ya Na's chapter entitled 'The Church and Religious Learning of Young Women Migrant Workers in Western China' draws on ethnographic research to demonstrate the vital role of incidental and informal religious learning for young Catholic rural women seeking a new life in the city as migrant workers in Western China. As the researchers track the lives of young women who come from a remote village lying in the Qinling Mountains, where all residents had 'always' been Catholic for as long as anyone knew, they find that the girls' deeply inculcated religious and moral values served to shield them from many of the social ills of urbanisation that they encounter.

Ruth Hayhoe's chapter, 'Inter-religious Dialogue and Education: three historical encounters between Christianity, Buddhism and Confucianism', concludes this first section. By viewing three pivotal encounters between China and Europe through a historical lens Hayhoe shows how how in each encounter Christianity has been impacted and enriched through engagement with Buddhist, Daoist and Confucian believers. Hayhoe's chapter offers a counter to what Huntington (1996) has termed the 'Clash of the Civilisations' by showing how these historical interactions, even during periods of geo-political threat, offer meaningful lessons for present-day inter-religious encounters and demonstrate the potential of respectful dialogue among religions. This chapter thus embodies one of the core themes of the book, and its central ethos.

The second section of the book, 'Curriculum, Pedagogy and School Leadership', has six chapters which concentrate mainly on issues of religious education in the school curriculum and the pedagogy of religious education, as well as leadership of faith-based schools. Mei-Yee Wong's chapter entitled 'Religious Education in a Multi-religious Context: an examination of four religious schools in Hong Kong' examines religious education for all students with religious or secular backgrounds in four government-subsidised religious schools (one Catholic, one Taoist, one Protestant and one Buddhist). It offers a unique perspective by exploring single religion-based curricula in a multi-religious setting through the study of moral and values education. Wong shows that in the four investigated religious schools, the schools did not focus on multi-religious learning but strictly adhered to their respective religious affiliations. Nevertheless, all schools included moral education in their religious education curricula such that the teaching of religious education had both religious and moral purposes.

Unlike the previous chapter on Hong Kong where a multi-religious context is dominant and protected, Xinyi Wu in her chapter, 'State Schooling and Religious Education for Muslim Hui Students in Northwestern China: changing perceptions and new developments', takes up the issue of rural Muslim Hui students from the Ningxia Hui Autonomous Region in a single religious context. Using a case-study approach, she examines how state schooling and religious education in China interact with each other. She shows how Muslim Hui students negotiate a secular school system with their belief systems and also how this generates complementary, rather than contradictory, possibilities for the students.

'The Buddhist Approach to a School-based Curriculum: the effective learning innovation that promotes human values to learners for sustainable living in Thailand' by Prapapat Niyom, Art-ong Jumsai Na Ayudhaya, Witit Rachatatanun and Benjamin Vokes offers a detailed description of how Buddhist values are infused and taught in the curriculum. Basing their work on a case study of three very distinct schools, the authors, who are practitioners, founders and teachers of these schools, provide rich, detailed examples of how Buddhist and other religious mindfulness practices in the curriculum, along with sustainable living, learning principles and values, can holistically transform learners in the Thai school system. The authors write from their own experience as teachers using an approach that Parker Palmer terms 'teaching with heart and soul' (Palmer, 2003). The chapter demonstrates how spritual considerations in education and teacher education offer the potential for a richer understanding of cultural diversity and holistic learning.

In 'Modernizing Islamic Education: Bangladesh and Senegal', Lauren Herzog and Nathaniel Adams explore the role and significance of Islamic school systems in Bangladesh and Senegal. As major education providers, these schools serve an important function by filling gaps in state-run education systems – for example, by reaching marginalised populations. The authors also highlight the many challenges these schools face in their efforts to modernise and integrate within broader national educational reforms as they struggle to reform and respond to contemporary needs. Yet, the contributions that the madrasas make in reaching otherwise unschooled children must be emphasised.

Malini Sivasubramaniam and Steve Sider's chapter entitled 'Faith-based Low-fee Private Schools in Kenya and Haiti: the paradox of philanthropy and enterprise' is the only chapter that examines school leadership practices in faith-based schools. The authors explore the role school principals are playing as social entrepreneurs in education, particularly in the private provision of faith-based education in low-fee private schools in Kenya and Haiti. They show how the changing leadership demands on school principals within a market-based educational context in these low-fee schools provide both challenges and opportunities, yet enable them to contribute to the betterment of the communities they serve. This chapter also gives examples of how faith-based low-fee school providers are uniquely positioned to meet the underserved school-going children as they negotiate the tension between profit and philanthrophy.

In the last chapter in this section, 'Religious Education in the Israeli State School System' by Yaacov J. Katz, we have a brief historical overview of how the religious and secular educational tracks have changed in Israel since 1948. Katz also shows how an integrated state educational system balances and manages the many demands of ensuring full legitimacy and autonomy for all tracks, including those preferred by the modern-orthodox and ultra-orthodox sectors of the religious population. He further examines how religious minority students – namely, Christian and Muslim students – are accommodated within the current Jewish education system.

The final section, 'Religion in Policy Processes and Conflict Resolution', includes five chapters which examine some of the politically sensitive issues inherent in religion and education discussions that involve the role of the state. These political discourses are often contentious and polarising. One such example is the long-standing religious conflict between Catholics and Prostestants in Northern Ireland. L. Philip Barnes, in his chapter 'Religious Education in Northern Ireland: conflict, curriculum and criticism', examines this conflict. In particular, Barnes examines the role that religious education has played in contributing to the ongoing peace process in the context of this conflict. He argues that religious education can be manipulated to serve the vested interests of authorities and thus may perpetuate conflict rather than assisting the process of conflict resolution. At the same time, he also suggests that forms of religious education that nurture genuine religious faith may be more effective for peace building and understanding than a purely academic exposure to knowledge about other religions.

Huma Kidwai's chapter entitled 'Mainstreaming Madrasas in India: resistance or co-optation?' explores the role that the state policies play in (re)structuring religious schools. Her chapter takes on the case of madrasas in the Uttar Pradesh province of India. She highlights ways in which madrasas have both resisted and adapted to the state policies to mainstream or 'modernise' them. Kidwai's chapter demonstrates ways in which religious minority groups seek to preserve their value systems and capacity amid broader state-driven reforms, as in the case of the madrasa system of education in Uttar Pradesh, a state that is Hindu dominant, with a minority Muslim population.

Elena Lisovskaya's chapter, 'Religion's Uneasy Return to the Russian School: a contested and inconsistent desecularization "from above"', has similarities with Niyozov's chapter in this volume (Chapter 4), as it examines the context of a post-Soviet revival of religion. Lisovskaya argues that the religious education course introduced by the State in 2012 is driven by a political agenda that is a result of the alliance between the Church and the State. She traces the historical process of what she terms 'desecularization' from above and shows how it is ideology driven rather than process driven. Similar to points made by Barnes in Chapter 13 of this volume, she shows how politically or ideologically driven religious education hampers the promotion of religious understanding.

A number of political tensions and conflicts are rooted in religion. Religiously motivated extremism fuels political rhetoric in a number of countries around the world. To counter the sprouting of religious radicalism, Ratna Ghosh and W.Y. Alice Chan in Chapter 16 posit that religious education may offer one counterbalance to the current terrorism fears in their chapter entitled 'The Role of Religious Education (RE) in Countering Religious Extremism in Diverse and Interconnected Societies'. They see this as more important than just a focus on a military response or tighter counter-terrorism strategies. However, they also rightly comment that RE alone is not a panacea, but rather requires critical pedagogy and an awareness of and respect for the vital role religion plays in human development. They also caution that when religious education is promoted without respectful understanding and dialogue, it may breed extremism instead.

The final chapter in this section and the book, 'A Multicultural Analysis of School Policies on Religion in 20 Western Democracies, and Their Challenges for Accommodating Migrant Religions: a cluster analysis' by Bruce A Collet and Hyeyoung Bang presents a comparison of public school policies as they relate to new immigrant students in 20 countries. Their analysis examines how these policies impact the religious accommodation of students in schools and how this affects their learning. Using hierarchical cluster analysis, the authors group the countries into five clusters: high religious freedom providers (Australia, Canada, and Sweden); moderate religious freedom providers (Austria, the Netherlands, Portugal, Spain, and Denmark); Christian-focused religious freedom providers (Finland, Germany, Greece, Ireland, Italy, Norway, Switzerland, the United Kingdom); committed secularists (France and Belgium); and sensitive religious freedom providers (New Zealand and the United States). Their chapter points to how differences between the clusters correspond to differences in how well supported immigrants are in the public school system and consequently how well they are integrated into the broader society. The chapter offers meaningful lessons in how cross-cultural dialogue can be fostered.

Despite the increased push towards secularisation in state schooling, issues of religion and spirituality that relate to education have become increasingly important. As comparative and international educators and researchers, it is imperative that we advocate for the opportunities for dialogue that religious education provides and urge for the reinsertion of religion into schooling as an important consideration in meeting the Millenium Development Goals. We concur with Miller et al (2013) that the study of religion should be more broadly conceptualised as a form of citizenship education as it plays an important role in equipping young people for living responsibly in societies that are increasingly pluralistic in terms of religion and culture. We would further contend that the study of religion must be considered a core competency within global education. The seventeen chapters in this book have reaffirmed the importance of religion within broader education and development goals. More specifically, they have demonstrated that to ensure equitable learning outcomes for all, we need to engage communities of faith and to consider the role of religion in shaping the SDGs. Several of the chapters have also shown the importance of the spiritual dimension of teaching and learning. However, some of the chapters have also introduced cautions over how religion can be exploited by state interests. Central to the book is the core idea that in equipping the next generation, religious education must be rooted in respect and must nurture the capacity for inter-faith dialogue and understanding of other religions. It is our hope that this book provides a timely and rich cross-disciplinary contribution to this underexplored area of study within the field of comparative and international education.

References

Baker, D. (2014) Presidential Address. Minds, Politics and Gods in the Schooled Society: consequences of the education revolution, *Comparative Education Review*, 58(1), 6-23. https://doi.org/10.1086/673973

Barnes, M. (1989) *Religions in Conversation: Christian identity and religious pluralism.* Cambridge: Cambridge University Press.

Huntington, S. (1996 T*he Clash of Civilizations and the Remaking of World Order.* New York: Simon & Schuster.

Miller, J., O'Grady, K. & McKenna, U. (2013) *Religion in Education: innovation in international research.* New York: Routledge.

Palmer, P. (2003) Teaching with Heart and Soul: reflections on spirituality in teacher education, *Journal of Teacher Education*, 54(5), 376-385. https://doi.org/10.1177/0022487103257359

Parliament of the World's Religions (2017) https://parliamentofreligions.org/

UNESCO (2014) Global Education for All, 2014 GEM Final Statement. The Muscat Agreement. https://sustainabledevelopment.un.org/content/documents/7170GEM%20Musca t%202014.pdf

Watson, K. (2010) Contrasting Policies towards (Mainly) Christian Education in Different Contexts, *Comparative Education*, 46(3), 307-323. https://doi.org/10.1080/03050068.2010.503743

SECTION ONE
Internationalising/Globalising Religious Values

CHAPTER 1

Global Education Challenges: exploring religious dimensions

KATHERINE MARSHALL

SUMMARY Education goals are at the center of global agendas for sustainable development and humanitarian action, but these agendas tend to deal glancingly, if at all, with religious dimensions. Religious institutions, however, play significant parts in national and international education systems and approaches in many countries. In some instances they are critical partners, in others significant critics. Understanding religious differences is increasingly understood as central to citizenship and peaceful societies. This chapter explores six topics where religious actors are particularly involved: delivery of education and outreach to underserved populations; specific education approaches for refugees and displaced populations; curricular focus on pluralism and 'religious literacy'; addressing education challenges surrounding values in education and understandings of citizenship; training of religious leaders; and advocacy for education goals and reforms.

Education as a Right and an Imperative: religious engagement?

In October 2016 a high-level international commission issued a report ('The Learning Generation') highlighting the large global challenges ahead for education: 'Unless we change course now, nearly 1 billion school-aged children will still be denied basic secondary-level skills in 2030. Even in 2050, one child in three in Africa will not be able to complete basic secondary education... If we transform the performance of education systems, unleash innovation, prioritize inclusion, expand financing and motivate all countries to accelerate their progress to match the world's top 25% fastest education improvers, we can build the Learning Generation' (International Commission on Financing Global Education Opportunity, 2016). The Commission's recommendations build on the global consensus reflected in the year 2000 Millennium Development Goals (MDGs) and their successors, the Sustainable Development Goals (SDGs) that were approved by United Nations (UN) member states in 2015. SDG 4 sets out the contemporary framework and bold objective: 'Ensure inclusive and quality education for all and promote lifelong learning' (see Appendix 1). 'The Learning Generation' report's emphasis on quality and equity likewise reflects contemporary concerns about the relevance of education and deep inequities between and within nations.

Education is widely acknowledged as a basic human right and a critical prerequisite for successful contemporary democracy and for thriving, sustainable and just economies and societies. The specific SDG education goals have grown out of a decades-long, strengthening international consensus calling for joined global efforts to assure 'Education for All' (EFA).[1] Broad commitments were launched formally at the global conference in Jomtien, Thailand in 1990 and both goals and monitoring systems have sharpened since then [2] – for example, from an earlier focus on primary education and increasing enrollments of girls to the current focus on full educational systems, lifelong learning and broad understandings of inclusion. Current objectives include not only access for all to primary and secondary education but also quality education, addressing glaring inequities, and early childhood education (Pritchett, 2013). Progress toward goals is measured regularly in various ways and debates about the quality and direction of education figure prominently at national and international levels. The goals are justified in ethical (fairness and equity) and material (preparation for employment and citizenship) terms. Education as a right and as a central link in the development chain thus ranks high on most global agendas.

The marginal treatment of religious aspects in the global discussions is striking and puzzling ('The Learning Generation' report cited above is a case in point). Religious institutions play major educational roles, and religious beliefs in relation to educational curricula and pedagogy are pertinent for core education goals and design. A central reason why religious aspects have tended to be ignored is that in framing global education goals, the state is seen as carrying the primary responsibility. The assumption is that the state itself will support, deliver and regulate education. While there is increasing recognition that many sectors of society are involved, notably private and civil society actors, religious actors are relatively neglected.

Reasons for this neglect include historical events that actively separated religious and secular approaches in education, concerns to assure impartial treatment of different communities in public educational systems, and special sensitivities around religious involvement in national affairs in various countries. This includes quite widespread fears that religiously run or shaped education cannot be separated from efforts to convert to a faith (fear of proselytism). The sheer size and complexity of religious communities, beliefs and educational roles present daunting challenges that range from poor and confusing data to the perils of sweeping generalizations about roles of religion and culture. Lack of engagement with religious actors can also reflect differences in approach, agendas and priorities among disciplines and communities; these differences can be perceived or actual. For example, the 'Learning Generation' report focuses squarely on four transformations seen as vital to achieving long-term goals: performance, innovation, inclusion and financing. The SDGs highlight quantitative targets and likewise focus on system performance and equity. Two topics that religious actors highlight often – cultural relevance and values as a goal of education – may be embedded in these agendas, but how is not obvious. The way goals for inclusion and innovation are discussed by secular and religious actors tend to sound very different even where at their core they address similar issues.

This chapter focuses on six dimensions of global educational challenges that are relevant for religious [3] actors and institutions. (a) Religious institutions run large education systems that provide a significant share of education in many countries. Parts of these systems are models of excellence, educating leaders and serving as exemplars of what can be achieved; others fall near the bottom of the heap in terms of quality and social benefit. Especially relevant for global development goals are their capacities for innovation, access and knowledge, especially for poverty-related access and achievement issues. Poor data and understanding of scope and performance often limit constructive engagement of these systems in national policies. (b) Widely varied actors linked to religious traditions play important roles in efforts to address contemporary challenges of assisting refugee and internally displaced populations with wide-ranging education programs. (c) Religious institutions often do and certainly should contribute to defining what is taught in national education systems about religion – across curricula. Increasing general understanding about religions deserves priority [4] because this is a fundamental part of identity and culture for the many world citizens who live in increasingly plural societies. Understanding religious approaches can be critical for social cohesion. (d) Religious institutions commonly highlight their roles in and concern for core social values. They play significant roles in preparing young people to be informed and proactive global citizens. These global citizenship challenges link at a fundamental level to ancient and broad questions of how educational approaches and systems address questions of values and how that translates into educational practice. (e) Training of religious leaders is a generally neglected topic for education policy, yet in today's era of globalization, future religious leaders and scholars need heightened awareness about living within dynamic and plural societies and understanding issues of social change cum development (gender equality, for example). And (f), religious institutions and leaders can be powerful advocates for social justice, including education for all, at global, regional, national and community levels. Likewise, their opposition or tepid support can slow progress. How far are advocacy roles appreciated and engaged?

With these six dimensions as the starting point, the chapter highlights briefly the extensive experience with schooling at all levels of many religious traditions, and long-standing, sophisticated and authentic religious commitments to learning and education. This experience and the moral underpinnings of religious support for education are important assets. There are many pertinent models, some well known (Jesuit education), some less so (the Aga Khan Network, for example). Various faith-inspired approaches address the central challenges for global education: service delivery for some of the world's poorest populations and shaping of elite values, for example. Religious institutions also influence opinions and politics on thorny issues for education policy – for example, standards for religious literacy, treatment of minorities in contemporary plural societies, gender norms, extremist teaching, and shifting expectations and norms on secular versus religious approaches in law and practice. The chapter's core argument is that, notwithstanding widely diverse situations and particular sensitivities, religious institutions should be engaged as significant players for achieving global education goals.

Education Delivery: access and integration of systems

Religious institutions and communities run schools, widely varied but covering virtually all types of education institutions from pre-kindergarten through post-graduate and adult education. There are no reliable estimates on the aggregate share of religiously run education (though some broad figures, up to 50%, are fairly commonly heard). World Bank economist Quentin Wodon's review of data from 16 sub-Saharan African countries found that 14% of primary school enrollment and 11% of secondary school enrollment was in faith-inspired schools (Wodon, 2013, 2014; Wodon & Lomas, 2015; University of Birmingham, 2015). This is indicative but a very partial view. The mixed guesstimates highlight serious shortfalls of data on quantity and quality. What is clear is that in some countries religiously run education is a significant part of the education system while in others (especially where religious schools have been nationalized or outlawed) it is relatively small.

Relationships between religiously run education and the state and more specifically public education systems vary widely. In some cases religious schools are well mapped and integrated within a national system, but elsewhere they may be highly decentralized and operate quite separately, without official sanction, certification or oversight. Catholic Church-run schools are among the largest and most significant. As an illustration, Catholic Church figures put the number of students in Catholic schools in Africa in 2012 at close to 23.5 million (Grace et al, 2007). Arrangements vary by country, but Catholic schools are commonly recognized by governments as private schools. A rather different situation applies in various countries for Islamic education (Adams et al, 2016). To illustrate, in Senegal, the large Quranic education system is highly decentralized and unregulated. In Bangladesh, part of the Islamic education system (Alia madrasas) is part of the State system, while another part (Quomi madrasas) is not.

Seen from the global perspective, and starkly clear in the monitoring reports of international progress toward education goals, the most difficult challenges ahead lie in assuring access in hard-to-serve regions and communities. That includes countries in conflict and those with sizable vulnerable populations. Religious communities are significant education providers in many such situations (Democratic Republic of the Congo and Sierra Leone are two examples). Nigeria and Pakistan may be the two most challenging countries today for education goals; in both cases religion is at the forefront of policy debates and religious institutions are significant providers.

For all these reasons, the extensive, complex networks of educational institutions run by religious communities should be part of deliberate efforts to work toward global education targets and goals. Reasons for the partial focus we see today are generally context specific and characteristically complex. In Senegal, debates about whether and how to integrate parts of or the whole of the Quranic education system into the very French-style public education system have continued since independence in 1963 and are still unresolved. The upshot is that in many countries representatives of what are often extensive educational systems with vast relevant experience (religiously run systems) are not party to policy reviews and discussions.

The limited attention paid to faith communities as education service providers stems in part from the tendency to focus on public education systems in framing global discussions about education. The presumption has been that, particularly where poverty is a central issue, private education has little relevance. This is under challenge, with mounting recognition of the substantial and growing phenomenon of private schools serving poor populations.[5] Research (*inter alia* by James Tooley, 2009) has highlighted the blinkers that public policy-makers have worn where private entrepreneurial education is concerned, that have contributed to poor understanding and data gaps. Religiously run systems can fall into similar traps.

The enormous complexity of development assistance today further complicates the matter. Dysfunctional patterns have evolved where numerous, uncoordinated actors operate in countries heavily dependent on development assistance. Many work with differing objectives and approaches, individual monitoring systems, and their own requirements for reporting. Intensive efforts to harmonize aid are reflected in agreements forged in Paris, Rome, Accra and Busan.[6] Many aid programs have, in response, moved from a 'project' approach to program- or sector-wide efforts involving multiple donors under a single umbrella, with a clear focus on government leadership and ownership for the respective countries. This trend toward better harmonization is evident in education programs in various countries.

Yet faith-run programs tend to be among the outliers in fragmentation in many, though by no means all, situations. With the focus on the imperative need for greater discipline and clear focus on program goals, assessments of progress, and policy instruments, religious actors who aspire to be part of national efforts to improve education quality need to be more actively represented at the aid harmonization tables.

Faith education programs may be marginalized because of the diversity of these systems and their general lack of mutual contact. Faith-run education systems vary widely in size, approach and significance, from region to region and also within countries. This author is aware of no effort to estimate their aggregate role in any systematic fashion, and, still less, to engage in comprehensive assessment of relative quality and impact. The situation is well mapped in some places and for some systems. Data on Catholic Church schools, for example, are well kept and quite readily available (the Catholic school system is the world's largest faith-based educational network, with some 120,000 schools and over 1000 colleges and universities).[7] There are, however, important gaps in the data (for example, schools run by the dynamic and growing Evangelical churches). Data about Muslim schools run the gamut from fairly detailed and reliable (Indonesia, India) to patchy and uncertain (Pakistan, West Africa). Information about Buddhist education and specific education programs within the enormous social movements with a religious impetus in South Asia is poor, though ambitious education programs are common. In short, the data available are appallingly weak. Gaps in knowledge are a significant explanation for the lack of attention to these important systems, especially at the global level.

Complexity of systems is another obstacle to thoughtful engagement, further compounded, in some instances, by their unofficial status. 'Hybrid' systems are not uncommon, meaning that schools fall somewhere between the public and private systems. This can apply to individual schools or to broad systems. For example, in Cambodia, both Buddhist- and Christian-run schools may receive some public support yet rely primarily on private funding, volunteer teachers and community resources. The Fe y Alegria system, a Jesuit-led federation of schools serving communities in 16 Latin American countries, supports schools which are generally part of the public education system yet count on extensive support from other sources (church, community, business, international organizations). It may be difficult in such instances to pinpoint the roles of religious actors.[8] In some cases where the roles are ambiguous or informal or where conflicts are involved, religious institutions and leaders may elect not to draw attention to their roles.

Where the roles of faith-run systems are the subject of expert or public debate, issues tend to echo broader questions about state/religious relationships or tensions. A dramatic case in point is tensions around schools run by the Turkish Hizmet or Gülen movement, seen by the current Turkish government as subversive. In some situations religiously run schools are seen as undermining state authority and provoking tensions among communities or accentuating marginalization. In contrast, they may also be seen as playing roles in meeting the needs of minority communities.

The complex and highly varied Islamic education institutions present particular issues; the enormous diversity of Muslim communities and of education systems in Muslim-majority countries complicates the picture. Systems run by Muslim leaders and communities range from small, largely community-led pre-school institutions to fully fledged systems extending from pre-primary through advanced education (for example, the Al Azhar system in Egypt). They also vary widely in quality, from outstanding institutions (for example, in Indonesia) to poorly resourced institutions where learning is confined largely to memorizing the Quran in Arabic, which students may well not understand.[9] Critiques focus on quality of education provided, for example highlighting the tendency to rote learning and weakness of science teaching, and the perils of exclusivity. Concerns about textbook content that promotes extremist views are another concern. The perceived link between Islamic education and terrorism, often amplified by media sources and various global leaders, distorts dialogue about the roles that Muslim-run educational institutions do and could play in advancing broad education goals. It is a factor, for example, in European debates about the desirability of allowing or supporting Muslim schools even in systems where the state provides long-standing support to schools run by Christian and Jewish denominations. Sensitivities were illustrated by florid debates about a Saudi-sponsored school in the Washington, DC metropolitan area. While most thoughtful analysts view such concerns as overblown and confined to a small minority of schools (see, for example, McClure, 2009), they complicate reform efforts in various situations.

An important and fairly specific challenge concerns faith-run education knowledge and networks where fragile or poorly performing states are involved, and for 'the bottom billion' of the world's population (Collier, 2007). The well-known irony is that these communities most need assistance, yet governance and conflict make that assistance hard to use well. Conflict and corruption together impede virtually all public services and education almost always suffers. Religiously run institutions are often major service providers, a force of continuity and a support to communities. However, actual and potential education roles are not mapped and analyzed in a systematic fashion. Promising programs build on deliberate partnerships in countries like Sierra Leone and Liberia, but practical steps to carry the recognition of faith roles and their on-the-ground experience into broader and active dialogues and partnerships are still quite limited. The upshot of the fractured analysis and dialogue is that much of the rich knowledge and experience gained in faith-run systems is poorly reflected in policy analysis and decision-making.

Three transnational educational programs with strong faith links illustrate the variety and potential roles that faith-inspired institutions play and their pertinence to global educational challenges. The Fe y Alegria system prides itself on its commitment to serve communities 'where the asphalt ends' – in other words, the poorest and least well-served communities across Latin America. Part of the large, complex and very varied system of Catholic Church education, it exemplifies the ancient Christian traditions of education and their contemporary manifestations. Fe y Alegria was begun and is run by priests of the Jesuit order (though its staff is now about 97% lay). It is thus a distinctive Jesuit-run system, though part of the broader Catholic network. It has a strong ethos of serving the poorest communities. Fe y Alegria's approach emphasizes excellence, commitment to strong values and community involvement, and the system, with its 53-year experience, shows impressive results. Fe y Alegria's pioneering work in vocational education and radio distance learning is relevant, and Fe y Alegria often runs the only schools available to the disabled.[10]

A very different example that illustrates the pitfalls of politics and religion is the network of private schools run by the Gülen movement. Originating in Turkey, and inspired by Fetallah Gülen, a Muslim Sufi leader, the system operates schools in some 120 countries. Each is entirely independent and largely financed by local resources, in many cases businessmen (for a general overview, see Hakan Yavuz & Esposito, 2003). The schools stress excellence and have achieved impressive results, with a strong emphasis on science. The schools are private, with some commitment to equity (some scholarships are offered), but above all they reflect a broad commitment to quality education as a general principle, in service to the society. With the 2016 controversy around the failed coup d'état in Turkey, Gülen and his movement were blamed and the future of many Gülen schools is in question.

The Aga Khan Development Network (AKDN) does not consider itself religious, although its leader and founder, the Aga Khan, is the spiritual leader and Imam of the Ismaili Community. Education is a long-standing passion for the Aga Khan and therefore a central focus of the work of AKDN institutions.[11] Their education work is seen in many quarters as 'best practice'. Projects include universities, academies and a system of pre-schools. The latter, and particularly a network of madrasa pre-schools in East Africa, offer a remarkable example of a sensitive effort to build on community initiatives, to engage with local faith communities, to work actively with women, and to engage local ideas and meet their needs at the same time as maintaining the highest-quality standards.[12]

Religious Roles in Humanitarian Emergencies: refugees and internally displaced populations

Religious communities and institutions (notably faith-inspired organizations like Caritas Internationalis, World Vision and Islamic Relief Worldwide) play large roles in humanitarian work, and education is often an important focus. Attention to education ranges from advocacy for refugees and internally displaced populations (IDPs) to, in protracted refugee situations, running schools and literacy programs. The focus of the Jesuit Refugee Service on education and creative efforts to address needs in extraordinarily demanding situations is an illustration (McPherson, 2016). In Kenya, faith-linked organizations, international and Kenyan, have developed widely varied education programs, including some that specifically address refugee parents' demands for religious education for their children (Stoddart & Marshall, 2015).

Understanding Religion, Understanding 'the Other'

Many public education systems in different world regions, including prominently the United States, France and China, have seen a dramatic shift in curriculum over the past decades, away from one where even the primers used for the youngest children were imbued with religion, to a situation where religion is almost totally absent from the curriculum (Prothero, 2008). Other countries may teach religion as part of the official public curriculum but dominated by a single denomination's perspective. Results include a sharp decline in 'religious literacy' among the population. This is of concern because plural societies are the norm today, increasing in significance, yet relations among communities suffer when there is poor understanding across different communities. Social tensions are an almost inevitable result. A further concern is that many people today lack even basic knowledge of their own cultural heritage, which can limit their appreciation of literary references and other elements of culture and identity.

Teaching about different religious traditions is a sensitive topic, easier said than done. Sensitivity in approach, across different topics and disciplines, is needed and there can be no single formula or curriculum. Even so, there is an emerging consensus that purposeful efforts to develop sound curricula, particularly at the secondary level, are needed. An example of interesting groundwork to develop appropriate curricula is the United World College (UWC) system, which piloted a world religions curriculum.[13] UWC schools generally offer a two-year program leading to the International Baccalaureate, draw students from some 120 countries, and are inspired by a philosophy to achieve international peace and understanding by educating future leaders, together. UWC is one among many examples of efforts to find effective and appropriate ways to develop curricula that ensure a level of religious literacy that modern plural societies need.

Professional exposure to 'religious literacy' is another priority, starting with higher education (note the Henry R. Luce Foundation's initiative on religion and international affairs [14]) and extending to professional organizations such as diplomatic services and United Nations institutions. Ignorance about religion can be a serious obstacle in many fields, ranging from education to business to public affairs to medicine. The challenge of redressing 'illiteracy' demands partnerships among secular and religious leaders and institutions. Contemporary efforts to develop religious literacy programs include those of the Harvard Divinity School and the Woolf Institute at the University of Cambridge.

Thorny Values, Questions and Social Cohesion

A vignette: a priest engaged in interfaith dialogue, a World Bank education specialist and I meet to discuss a forthcoming report on education in an important region, the Middle East. The priest launches into a description of obstacles blocking a small theological exchange program he wants to develop that will involve students from a Christian and a Muslim institution. The World Bank specialist's eyes glaze over, his unspoken question: 'What on earth does this have to do with the subject at hand?' I turn the subject, asking how the forthcoming report addresses the question of values in curriculum reform. The specialist says: 'What we want is values-free education.' The priest blanches. Impasse.

What the specialist had in mind, and explained cursorily, was that in his view education systems and curricula should be value neutral and impartial; students should learn to think for themselves. A curriculum or system structured around a particular set of values was by implication biased and excluded ideas and people. The priest blanched because to his mind nothing was more important in education than imparting basic values, a sense of right and wrong, preferably in conjunction with a grounding in teachings from one or possibly more faith traditions because they are grounded in rich ethical frameworks. This, he believed, allows an individual to contribute to the society.

This story offers a glimpse of debates that help to explain why the role of religious perspectives and institutions in education is often contentious. Whereas 100 years ago religious institutions dominated education systems in many places and religion was taught without compunction, the situation today is far more mixed. To complicate matters, questions about religion as part of education today are embroiled in broader debates, notably about the respective roles and responsibilities of public and private actors in education and about how public education systems address the religious pluralism that is a common characteristic of modern societies. The 'values' question described in the exchange between the priest and the technical specialist involves questions about 'whose values?' and 'how can values best be taught?'

Debates about values reflect important policy questions that can and should engage a wide range of educators. They obviously go deeply into questions about the nature of societies and governance systems. They go to the heart of questions about the core purposes of education and the rights of different parties. Education is sometimes seen and approached as a largely technical matter, presenting schooling as geared essentially to preparing students for the labor market (indeed, this is a common negative perception of education approaches expressed by religious actors in various consultations). Preparing students for jobs is plainly a vital function, but undue focus on labor markets and utilitarian goals can obscure other vital functions of education, notably in contributing both to social cohesion and to the civic understanding and attitudes that are vital to democracy.

School systems, public or private, can teach in ways that either ease or exacerbate ethnic and religious tensions. Religious leaders and communities see themselves as having a major stake in these issues. The examples of the Balkan countries and the former Soviet Union countries after 1989 include many situations where issues were framed around the social functions of education. The role of education in social cohesion takes on special importance in diverse, plural societies. Education specialist Stephen Heyneman (2008a) stresses that schools influence social cohesion through formal curricula, contributing to social norms, a school climate that conforms to those norms, adjudicating competing group views on what to teach, and convincing students and parents that the educational opportunities offered are truly fair. These questions involve understandings of nationalism and ideology. 'Throughout Europe the main challenges on school choice today come from the debates over whether Muslims have the same right to their own publicly funded schools as do Jews, Protestants, and Catholics' (Heyneman 2008a, p. 95).

Interestingly, there are echoes of these debates in the history of the framing of the Universal Declaration of Human Rights. Reflecting about rights to education, Eleanor Roosevelt commented that in retrospect she understood the reasons for, but nonetheless regretted agreeing to, the provision in the Declaration that specified that 'parents have a prior right to choose the kind of education that shall be given to their children' (Roosevelt, 1949). The insistence on including this provision, she said, came from Catholic countries, and was driven particularly by the fresh memories of totalitarian brainwashing of students before and during the Second World War. What she saw as the tension was between parents' rights and the rights of both children and society. Fear of religious and ethnic extremism can be so great that it can influence policy on school choice. One possible conclusion is that all schools should essentially teach the same core values – that citizens of all kinds are welcome; that all religions are welcome; that all ethnic groups are welcome; that in addition to the national language, all languages are welcome. But they also need to teach that the obligations on minorities are exactly the same as the obligations on majorities – that is, to conform to social norms. When this happens effectively, schools can add to every nation's social cohesion (Heyneman 2008a).

In an ideal world, schools are indeed neutral, not perhaps 'value free' but teaching students to think on their own, to respect difference in views and backgrounds, and to work to create new and better societies. There can, however, be significant differences in approach. An October 2016 note by the Holy See representative to the United Nations (Auza, 2016) offers an illustration, in its emphasis on the rights of parents in the content of education:

> The right to a quality and integral education must include religious education. This presupposes a holistic approach, which is ensured first and foremost by respecting and reinforcing the primary right of the family to educate its children, as well as the right of churches and social groups to support and assist families in this endeavour. Indeed, education, which etymologically means 'to bring out' or 'to lead out', has a fundamental role in helping people to discover their talents and potential for putting them at the service of mankind: each person has something to offer to society and must be enabled to provide his or her contribution. An authentic education should focus on relationships because development is the fruit of good relations.

Ignoring tensions surrounding differences in values, pretending that differences are unimportant, cannot serve the ends of dialogue and wider participation. Addressing questions that remain strong beacons of concern is as important as it ever has been.

Training Future Religious Leaders

Jewish, Muslim and Christian theological education in the past often included important segments designed to teach about other faith traditions. This, various observers contend, is less the norm today. Many religious leaders emerge from their advanced training programs with quite limited understanding of other faiths, far less the kind of personal contact that would contribute to real understanding. Given the importance of interfaith relations in plural societies, this is an important lacuna. Thus an area for action in education concerns theological training institutions of many kinds.

Promoting exchange programs among institutions and religious communities has significant potential, and important initiatives show what can be done. Examples include the World Council of Churches Institute at Bossey, interfaith programs at the Hartford Divinity School, the interfaith Claremont School of Theology [15] and multi-faith chaplaincy arrangements at leading universities (Georgetown University is among them). Global interfaith institutions like Religions for Peace, the Parliament of the World's Religions and the United Religions Initiative all have as a core mandate increasing interfaith understanding and action. There is considerable interest in reaching out beyond the boundaries of a single faith and in finding ways to strengthen networks and collaboration.[16]

Gaps in understanding among communities and between religious and secular leadership extend well beyond theology. Religious leaders pride themselves on their engagement in virtually every aspect of community life, from sex education and trade policy through housing, water and agriculture.

Debates and different approaches can matter: for example, priests or other religious leaders who preach against genetically modified crops (GMOs, or genetically modified organisms) can exacerbate tensions around this technical and ethical issue. Religious leadership on conservation of natural resources can make an enormous difference in shaping public attitudes. Action on child marriage and domestic violence can benefit from better understanding both of rights dimensions of the issues and of relevant religious teachings. Religious indifference or opposition can make it more difficult to tackle the problems. Broadening theological education to address such topics can enhance public and community dialogue and, in some instances, provide a foundation for interfaith cooperation that can have important spill-over effects. Various deliberate educational programs in African theological programs on health matters aimed to support religious leader engagement with HIV and AIDS, malaria and other health issues. In Bangladesh, various Imam training programs have centered on a range of development issues. Preparing faith leaders to address some contemporary issues such as sex education, market functioning and use of social media might well offer wide benefits.

Engaging Religious Actors in Advocacy and Policy Debates on Education

The right to education is viewed by many advocates both of human rights and of development as perhaps the single most important priority area for action on the global development agenda. It is fundamental to developing human capabilities, seen today as a primary means and end of development work (Sen, 1999), and weighs heavily in the United Nations Development Programme's (UNDP's) Human Development Index that ranks country performance.[17] Viewed from a religious perspective, development of the human person is seen in many scriptures and faith traditions as the core of belief and action; education is a central means to that end. The extraordinary progress that has marked global education over the past century builds on the foundations laid by religiously run and inspired schools and universities, both within their own societies and as missionary ventures. Thus a common shared interest in global goals on education seems a natural path to follow.

Protracted discussions that led up to the year 2000 definition of the MDGs and to periodic reviews of their implementation rarely engaged religious actors in any systematic fashion.

The MDGs and SDGs and associated targets, with their elaborate indicators and monitoring systems, global, regional and national, were led almost exclusively through public institutions – governments and international organizations above all. Today's discourse, however, assumes that civil-society and private-sector support for development generally, and for SDG targets more specifically, is essential. Dialogue about global education challenges and policies to achieve them thus takes in a widening range of actors outside official institutions. By 2013, with the SDGs in sight, active civil-society participation was seen as a norm. Religious institutions, especially those represented at the United Nations in New York and Geneva, engaged in the extensive consultations that resulted in the SDG framework. However, education issues have to date received somewhat less attention in these processes than topics like health, where there has been a longer history of engagement. Dialogue and advocacy on education issues has tended to be more focused at the national level.

Direct activism and advocacy among many faith institutions increased over the 15-year life of the MDGs and in the formulation and launch of the SDGs. This heightened interest can be witnessed in a variety of settings, ranging from global interfaith institutions to specific initiatives within denominations or at local level. The Religions for Peace focus on the MDGs (it was in the spotlight at the Kyoto 2006 Global Assembly and in partnerships with the United Nations), the ambitious poverty agenda of the Parliament of the World Religions (at its December 2009 meeting in Melbourne), and the Micah Challenge (an evangelical Church-initiated advocacy campaign) illustrate explicit commitments to mobilizing public support for action on the global goals.[18] A task force of United Nations agencies (Karam, 2015) has worked creatively both to highlight ongoing partnerships between religious groups and UN agencies and to explore new areas of cooperation. Various leaders – for example, Archbishop Desmond Tutu – have taken up the MDG/SDG cause as central planks of their ministries. Around the launch of the SDGs, various religious institutions and leaders agreed to support a 'moral imperative' to end poverty by 2030. But these important efforts can be seen as fairly limited when set against the fact that in countless congregations, many have heard little if anything about MDGs and SDGs, much less reflected on their importance and what their community might do to advance them. In sum, despite important efforts and initiatives, religious institutions have in practice been less active advocates and less central players in the global mobilization effort than might be expected.

Notwithstanding daily engagement on education issues at a practical level, broad religious advocacy directly linked to the global education agenda has been quite rare. Even looking to Catholic Social Teaching [19], often the deepest-ranging theological articulation of policy, global education issues have not had a central focus. Education was not a central focus of the (June 2009) Papal Encyclical *Caritas et Veritate* – the word education appears only 12 times in this long document, and it is missing any resounding statement as to its central importance for human welfare.[20] Education advocacy is less prominent than other issues for several global Muslim organizations, with the notable exception of the Aga Khan Development Network. Even where strong rhetorical support for education by faith leaders is in evidence, putting education at the center of ministries, at the global level, is quite rare.

The somewhat patchy support for global education goals in some faith and interfaith settings is something of a puzzle. Some reasons are not hard to discern. Finding effective tools to translate good will and intentions into practice has proved a difficult challenge; for many religious actors the path toward meaningful action on global issues is not well marked. Subtle but significant barriers block dialogue and engagement. The dominant paradigm of public provision of education can discourage active engagement of institutions whose focus may be on private provision of services, or where there is skepticism about the legitimacy and caliber of national governance itself. History comes into play in some situations, especially where the spread of modern education was closely tied to missionary efforts. Tensions around education in northern Nigeria, closely linked to the Boko Haram movement, reflect violent opposition to education that is perceived as coming with a western face. Ambivalence on faith roles in public education systems that are built around secular principles both dampens fervor in acknowledging direct religious roles in running schools and poses questions about how religion can and should be taught (witness France, but also Senegal and Bangladesh). In some communities, commitment to equity goals – for example, closing the gap in enrollment of girls – may not rank high among change priorities in religious communities.

Some solutions lie in addressing the perils of generalization – the nobility of the goals may appear self-evident, but tangible action steps need to be defined in plausible and understandable ways to mobilize energies and channel them to results. Focusing on obstacles to progress and on genuine areas of concern (for example, doubts as to the safety of girls' school attendance, poor quality of education in public systems) can help. Increasing transparency and clarity in international and national commitments and disbursements for education helps advocates to press for action more effectively since they can see where shortfalls are taking place. Various efforts are under way to address this challenge, some faith specific, others (like the ONE campaign) spanning a wider range of institutions. The MDGs/SDGs have provided an effective scaffolding to explore practical ways to engage faith energies and to address latent concerns through dialogue that has yet to be fully developed.

Inclusion, a key dimension of global education goals, is perhaps the most significant area where focused dialogue and advocacy with religious communities could be beneficial. Serving excluded communities and the disabled and meeting the education needs of people in conflict situations and among refugee populations are areas where experience, ideas, leadership and commitment are vitally needed. In all these cases, religious institutions play critical roles and have extensive networks of leaders, community groups and media channels that have long involvement in education.

There would appear to be significant potential for deliberately engaging religious communities more actively as partners in mobilizing support for education, both in international and in national settings. Their support can help identify and define new approaches to specific gaps and problems (innovation). This is not simply to advocate a 'cheerleader' function, however vital that role can be in sensitizing communities to global dimensions of issues and in practical mobilization (witness Jubilee 2000).[21] It is just as important to engage faith leaders in the global policy dialogue about the MDG/SDG mission, including its weaknesses and challenges, and future directions. Major global interfaith organizations and international religious bodies should be key partners, lending their voices and support, keeping tabs on progress, addressing shortfalls and thinking ahead to next steps.

Toward Conclusions

Humankind in a global age must balance and reconcile two impulses: the quest for distinctive identity and the search for global coherence. What this challenge will ultimately require of us is a deep sense of personal and intellectual humility, and an understanding that diversity itself is a gift of the Divine and that embracing diversity is a way to learn and to grow – not to dilute our identities but to enrich our self-knowledge. What is required goes beyond mere tolerance or sympathy or sensitivity – emotions which can often be willed into existence by a generous soul. True cultural sensitivity is something far more rigorous, and even more intellectual than that. It implies a readiness to study and to learn across cultural barriers, an ability to see others as they see themselves. This is a challenging task, but if we do that, then we will discover that the universal and the particular can indeed be reconciled. As the Quran states: 'God created male and female and made you into communities and tribes, so that you may know one another' (49.13). It is our differences that both define us and connect us (Aga Khan, 2008).[22]

The Aga Khan frames the central challenges facing contemporary education, in this age marked by forces of interconnectedness that flow from globalization and the increasing pluralism of today's societies. Challenges are 'quantitative', as exemplified by the access and equity facets of the SDGs, but even more they are qualitative: complex and nuanced with multiple dimensions. Culture and religion need to be seen as integral parts of the challenge and therefore religious actors belong at the policy tables where global and national educational issues are discussed.

Religious leaders and institutions in some situations and parts of the world can be 'part of the problem'. They represent doubters, even stalling the push for universal education, the most notable example being hesitations at equal opportunity for girls. Significant tensions around approaches to education and curriculum are common. But religious actors can and should, in many instances, be 'part of the solution', actively engaged in reflection and action. That is because religion (and its tightly linked companion, culture) is so vital to people, and because of the rich history and ethical contributions.

Among practical ways forward, information is essential. Better data and better ways to share research and information could change mindsets and mobilize energies. Research – for example, on the benefits of educating girls – provides such compelling evidence that it often counters reticence based on traditions and cultural norms. More positively, most religious traditions, scriptures and leaders have a deep commitment to education. Their history is the history of education, and the oft-stated commitment to human dignity and the development of human potential are what education is about.

There is plenty to debate: about the very purposes of contemporary education (for jobs or citizenship? Social or individual development?), how to teach difficult subjects, and so on. But the values of faith traditions, their extensive and often path-breaking work, and their commitment to human progress suggest that faith communities should be key allies in the global effort to bring education for all. Knowledge and dialogue can and should have global, regional, national and often local dimensions. Interfaith groups, whether bringing parties together to address educational policy matters or promoting active educational and community exchange, can play important roles.

Translating this ideal into practice cannot follow a simple blueprint. History and sociology are deeply imprinted with religious roles, perhaps nowhere more so than in the field of education. Respect for history is an important first step.

Notes

[1] http://www.unesco.org/new/en/education/themes/leading-the-international-agenda/education-for-all/

[2] See Heyneman, 2008b for a thoughtful critique of the background of Education for All, including its flaws.

[3] Definitions are contentious where religion is concerned. The terms 'religious', 'faith' and 'spiritual' are used often with specific significance but quite differently in different contexts. Frequently 'religious' suggests association with a specific religious institution while 'faith' and 'spiritual' may carry a broader and less institutional significance. But there is no consensus on the matter. This chapter uses 'religious' and 'faith' interchangeably, with an effort to reflect the preference of the relevant institution or community. The term 'religious actors' is used rather than 'religious leaders' to reflect a larger group of individuals and institutions, beyond those with formal institutional leadership roles. See also: Marshall & Van Saanen (2004), Marshall & Keough (2007), Marshall 2010, 2013.

[4] Two recent books make the point about the dearth of general knowledge about religion and its negative consequences particularly well: Albright (2007) and Prothero (2008).

[5] See Tooley (2009) and http://research.ncl.ac.uk/egwest/

[6] For background and relevant texts, see http://www.aidharmonization.org/

[7] See CARA (2015), for example.

[8] One organization described the Federation of Fe y Alegria, which served 1.3 million students, as 'the largest and most successful education provider in Latin America and the Caribbean outside of public education systems'. See http://www.magisamericas.org/donate/feyalegriabestpracticesvenezuela.pdf. The Harvard Business School has an interesting case study on the system; see: http://harvardbusiness.org/product/fe-y-alegria-one-or-many/an/SKE101-PDF-ENG

[9] Research on madrasa systems includes the following examples. The Religions and Development Research Program, undertaken with the Department for International Development support by a consortium of universities led by the University of Birmingham, has reviewed madrasas in Bangladesh, Pakistan, and India, with findings highlighting the diversity of experience (see first published working paper: http://www.rad.bham.ac.uk/files/resources module/@random454f80f60b3f4/1211530945_working_paper_13___for_web. pdf). The World Bank Development Dialogue on Values and Ethics also has a volume on madrasas (Wodon, 2014). The International Center for Religion and Diplomacy, a Washington, DC-based think tank, has worked to support reforms of Pakistani madras; see http://www.icrd.org/index.php?option =com_content&task=blogsection&id=10&Itemid=149

[10] Chapters in the author's two books about development and faith describe the Fe y Alegria system: *Development and Faith: where mind, heart, and soul work together* (with Marisa Van Saanen), and *Mind, Heart and Soul in the Fight Against Poverty* (with Lucy Keough), published by the World Bank, 2004 and 2007.

[11] Aga Khan Education Services (AKES), a network of educational institutions, combines operation of over 300 schools and management of programs to enhance the quality of teachers, academic resources and learning environments in Asia and Africa. AKES seeks to respond creatively to the educational needs of children in the developing world in a way that will enable those children better to shape their future. Its central premise is that all children must have access to good schools, effective teachers and the best learning resources possible. AKES aims for communities to take responsibility for ensuring that their children receive quality education. AKES is part of the Aga Khan Development Network (AKDN), a group of private development agencies established by His Highness the Aga Khan, the 49th hereditary Imam (spiritual leader) of the Ismaili Muslims. See http://www.akdn.org/akes

[12] For a short summary, see http://www.partnershipsinaction.org/downloads/briefs/Brief _MADRASA.pdf

[13] See http://www.uwc.org/

[14] http://www.hluce.org/hrlucerelintaff.aspx

[15] https://cst.edu/

[16] The World Council of Churches has taken leadership in one area, HIV/AIDS training. For one example, see http://www.oikoumene.org/uploads/tx_wecdiscussion/HIV-AIDS_1-_Teaching_and_Talking_about_Our_Sexuality.pdf

[17] See http://hdr.undp.org/en/content/human-development-index-hdi; also UNESCO Global Monitoring Report, http://en.unesco.org/gem-report/

[18] See http://www.wcrp.org/resources/toolkits/faith-in-action for a World Conference of Religions for Peace 'Toolkit' on advancing the MDGs; and the Micah Challenge mission and work is summarized on its website at http://www.micahchallenge.org/. The Micah Challenge originated as an evangelical Christian effort to highlight global social justice issues.

[19] For a brief introduction, see http://www.usccb.org/beliefs-and-teachings/what-we-believe/catholic-social-teaching/

[20] For text, see: http://www.vatican.va/holy_father/benedict_xvi/encyclicals/documents/ hf_ben-xvi_enc_20090629_caritas-in-veritate_en.html

[21] Jubilee 2000 was an international coalition movement in more than 40 countries that called for the cancellation of Third World debt by the year 2000. For more information, see: http:// www.jubileeusa.org/. CCED_A_503739.fm Page 285

[22] http://www.akdn.org/speech/his-highness-aga-khan/annual-meeting-international-baccalaureate

References

Adams, N., Herzog, L. & Marshall, K. (2016) *Modernizing Islamic Education: the cases of Bangladesh and Senegal*. Berkley Center and WFDD.

Albright, M. (2007) *The Mighty and the Almighty: reflections on America, God, and world affairs*. New York: Harper Perennial.

Auza, H.E. Archbishop Bernardito, Apostolic Nuncio and Permanent Observer of the Holy See to the United Nations (2016) Note of the Holy See on the First Anniversary of the Adoption of the Sustainable Development Goals. https://holyseemission.org/contents//statements/5806914667987.php

CARA (2015) Global Catholicism: Trends & Forecasts. Center for Applied Research in the Apostolate. file:///Users/katherinemarshall/Documents/Global%20Catholicism%20Release%2 0(1).pdf

Collier, P. (2007) *The Bottom Billion: why the poorest countries are failing and what can be done about it*. Oxford: Oxford University Press.

Grace, G. & O'Keefe, J. (Eds) (2007) *International Handbook of Catholic Education: challenges for school systems in the 21st century*. Dordrecht: Springer. https://doi.org/10.1007/978-1-4020-5776-2

Hakan Yavuz, M. & Esposito, J.L. (2003) *Turkish Islam and the Secular State: the global impact of Fethulla Gulen's nur movement*. Contemporary Issues in the Middle East. Syracuse, NY: Syracuse University Press.

Heyneman, S. (2008a) Education, Social Cohesion, and Ideology, in Emin Karp (Ed.) *Right to Education: policies and perspectives*, pp. 89-104. Ankara: Turkish Education Association.

Heyneman, S.P. (2008b) The Failure of Education-for-All as Political Strategy. Presented to the Annual Meeting of the Comparative and International Education Society, 20 March, at Columbia University Teachers College, New York City, USA.

His Highness the Aga Khan (2008) Lecture delivered at annual meeting of the International Baccalaureate, 18 April 2008. http://www.akdn.org/speech/his-highness-aga-khan/annual-meeting-international-baccalaureate

International Commission on Financing Global Education Opportunity (2016) The Learning Generation: investing in education for a changing world. http://report.educationcommission.org/report

Karam, A. (2015) Opinion. Religion and the SDGs: the 'new normal' and calls for action. Inter Press Service (IPS). http://www.ipsnews.net/2015/07/opinion-religion-and-the-sdgs-the-new-normal-and-calls-for-action/

Marshall, K. & Van Saanen, M. (2004) *Development and Faith: where mind, heart, and soul work together*. Washington, DC: World Bank.

Marshall, K. (2010) Education for All: where does religion come in? *Comparative Education*, August.

Marshall, K. (2013) *Global Institutions of Religion: ancient movers, modern shakers*. London: Routledge.

Marshall, K. & Keough, L. (2007) *Mind, Heart and Soul in the Fight against Poverty*. Washington, DC: World Bank.

McClure, K. (2009) Madrasas and Pakistan's Education Agenda: western media misrepresentation and policy recommendations, *International Journal of Educational Development*, 29(4), 334-341. https://doi.org/10.1016/j.ijedudev.2009.01.003

McPherson, G. (2016) *Providing Hope, Investing in the Future*. Jesuit Refugee Service, USA. https://www.jrsusa.org/Assets/Publications/File/Ed_Policy_web.pdf

Pritchett, L. (2013) *The Rebirth of Education: schooling ain't learning*. Washington, DC: Center for Global Development.

Prothcro, S. (2008) *Religious Literacy: what every American needs to know about religion (and doesn't)*. New York: HarperOne.

Roosevelt, E. (1949) Making Human Rights Come Alive. Speech to the Second National Conference on UNESCO, Cleveland, Ohio, 1 April 1949. Originally published in *Phi Delta Kappan*, 31 (September), 23-33.

Sen, A. (1999) *Development as Freedom*. New York: Anchor Books.

Stoddart, E. & Marshall, K. (2015) *Refugees in Kenya: roles of faith*. World Faiths Development Dialogue. https://berkleycenter.georgetown.edu/publications/refugees-in-kenya-roles-of-faith

Tooley, J. (2009) *The Beautiful Tree: a personal journey into how the world's poorest people are educating themselves*. Washington, DC: Cato Institute Press.

United Nations (2015) Sustainable Development Goals. http://www.un.org/sustainabledevelopment/sustainable-development-goals/

University of Birmingham (November 2015) The Role and Impact of Philanthropic and Religious Schools on Education in Developing Countries.

https://www.gov.uk/government/uploads/system/uploads/attachment_data/file/482700/Philanthropic-Religious-Evidence-Brief.pdf

Wodon, Q. (2013) Faith-inspired, Private Secular, and Public Schools in Sub-Saharan Africa: market share, reach to the poor, cost, and satisfaction. https://mpra.ub.uni-muenchen.de/45363/1/MPRA_paper_45363.pdf

Wodon, Q. (2014) *Education in Sub-Saharan Africa: comparing faith-inspired, private secular, and public schools*. Washington, DC: World Bank. https://doi.org/10.1596/978-0-8213-9965-1

Wodon, Q. & Lomas, K. (2015) *The Economics of Faith-based Service Delivery: education and health in Sub-Saharan Africa*. New York: Springer. https://doi.org/10.1057/9781137348463

APPENDIX. Education in the Sustainable Development Goals

SDG 4: Ensure inclusive and quality education for all and promote lifelong learning

1. Enrolment in primary education in developing countries has reached 91 per cent but 57 million children remain out of school
2. More than half of children that have not enrolled in school live in sub-Saharan Africa
3. An estimated 50 per cent of out-of-school children of primary school age live in conflict-affected areas
4. 103 million youth worldwide lack basic literacy skills, and more than 60 per cent of them are women

Targets

5. By 2030, ensure that all girls and boys complete free, equitable and quality primary and secondary education leading to relevant and Goal-4 effective learning outcomes
6. By 2030, ensure that all girls and boys have access to quality early childhood development, care and pre-primary education so that they are ready for primary education
7. By 2030, ensure equal access for all women and men to affordable and quality technical, vocational and tertiary education, including university
8. By 2030, substantially increase the number of youth and adults who have relevant skills, including technical and vocational skills, for employment, decent jobs and entrepreneurship
9. By 2030, eliminate gender disparities in education and ensure equal access to all levels of education and vocational training for the vulnerable, including persons with disabilities, indigenous peoples and children in vulnerable situations
10. By 2030, ensure that all youth and a substantial proportion of adults, both men and women, achieve literacy and numeracy

11. By 2030, ensure that all learners acquire the knowledge and skills needed to promote sustainable development, including, among others, through education for sustainable development and sustainable lifestyles, human rights, gender equality, promotion of a culture of peace and non-violence, global citizenship and appreciation of cultural diversity and of culture's contribution to sustainable development

12. Build and upgrade education facilities that are child, disability and gender sensitive and provide safe, nonviolent, inclusive and effective learning environments for all

13. By 2020, substantially expand globally the number of scholarships available to developing countries, in particular least developed countries, small island developing States and African countries, for enrolment in higher education, including vocational training and information and communications technology, technical, engineering and scientific programmes, in developed countries and other developing countries

14. By 2030, substantially increase the supply of qualified teachers, including through international cooperation for teacher training in developing countries, especially least developed countries and small island developing states

CHAPTER 2

Confucius Institutes and Classrooms as Educational Partnerships in Africa: the 2030 Agenda of Sustainable Development from a Confucian perspective

JUN LI

SUMMARY Based on broad observations of the development of Confucius Institutes and Classrooms in Africa over a decade, this chapter focuses on educational partnerships between Chinese and African educational institutions and their implications for international development, as they relate to the recent UN 2030 Agenda for Sustainable Development Goals. The chapter identifies a *Zhong-Yong* model of educational partnerships through Confucius Institutes and Classrooms, a pragmatic model for educational development centered on Confucianism. Three key characteristics of Confucian educational partnerships – demand-driven, ethics-based and pragmatic – are seen as the key to the success of such partnerships. The chapter concludes that the Confucian *Zhong-Yong* model of partnerships has the unique potential to re-envision education for international development in ways that may be of interest to such international agencies as the Asian Infrastructure Investment Bank, the World Bank and the United Nations.

Introduction

Whether Confucianism is a religion or not has been debated within China and globally. It cannot be denied, however, that the fundamental values and tenets of Confucianism have served religious purposes in history and in the contemporary world. Confucius temples are widespread not only in

Mainland China, Hong Kong, Taiwan, Korea, Japan, Indonesia, Malaysia and Vietnam, but also in many other parts of the world. Confucianism is also seen to have a more symbolic philosophical role in the recent worldwide flourishing of Confucius Institutes (CIs) and Classrooms (CCs).

Beginning in 2004, CIs have rapidly flourished around the globe as China's state initiative with a language and cultural mission. Two years later, CCs, a variation on CIs, became part of the global movement. In 2015 there were 500 CIs and 1000 CCs, with a total expenditure of US$800 million (The Hanban, 2015), constituting the largest project of language education and cultural exchange in the world today. Based on a mutual benefit and respect principle and responsiveness to demand, CIs and CCs have enabled educational institutions around the world to be matched with Chinese counterparts, with shared missions, funding, governance and standards for teaching and learning, as well as community networking, both local and global. In the African continent there were a total of 46 CIs and 23 CCs by 2015, with more applications submitted by African universities and schools waiting for approval from the Hanban (the CI headquarters) in Beijing.

What are these CIs and CCs doing in Africa? How far have their roles matched the principle of mutual benefit and respect claimed by China and what goals have they achieved over this short time period? More importantly, what do the efforts made jointly by China and African countries mean in relation to the UN 2030 Agenda for sustainable educational development? This chapter offers a snapshot of the roles played by African CIs and CCs based on observations made during multiple field trips in Africa since 2012, in addition to critical reflections on the *Zhong-Yong* (Middle Way) model of educational partnerships based on Confucianism.

The Rapid Spread of CIs and CCs in Africa

Modelled on the experiences of the Alliance Française (since 1883), the British Council (since 1934), the Goethe-Institute (since 1951) and the Instituto Cervantes (since 1991), CIs were first established in Korea in 2004. They have mainly been set up on university campuses and normally operate as partnerships between Chinese universities and overseas ones. According to the CI Constitution and by-laws, CIs are to meet the demand for learning the Chinese language in other countries or regions and to enhance understanding of Chinese culture (The Hanban, n.d.b.). They are also called upon to strengthen educational and cultural exchange and cooperation between China and the rest of the world, to deepen friendly relationships with other nations, to promote the development of multiculturalism, and to construct a harmonious world (The Hanban, n.d.a).

CCs first emerged in Thailand in 2006 with the same mission of serving Chinese language education and the promotion of Chinese culture, but with a focus on schools. They have adopted the same modality as CIs of educational partnerships between Chinese and overseas schools, offering

Chinese language education and cultural exchange to local schools in a more mass-oriented way. In the African context, some of these universities and schools have listed Chinese language as an elective in their curriculum, thus integrating these programs into their formal curriculum.

Country	CI	CC	Total
Angola	1		1
Benin	1	1	2
Botswana	1		1
Burundi	1		1
Cameroon	1	1	2
Cape Verde	1		1
Comoros		1	1
Congo, The Republic of	1		1
Egypt	2	3	5
Equatorial Guinea, The Republic of	1		1
Eritrea	1		1
Ethiopia	2	4	6
Ghana	2		2
Ivory Coast	1		1
Kenya	4	1	5
Lesotho, Kingdom of		1	1
Liberia	1		1
Madagascar	2		2
Malawi	1		1
Mali		1	1
Morocco	2		2
Mozambique	1		1
Namibia	1		1
Nigeria	2	1	3
Rwanda	1	1	2
Senegal	1		1
Seychelles	1		1
Sierra Leone	1		1
South Africa	5	4	9
Sudan	1		1
Tanzania	2	1	3
Togo	1		1
Tunisia		1	1
Uganda, The Republic of	1		1
Zambia	1	2	3
Zimbabwe	1		1
Total	46	23	69

Note. Data from *Confucius Institute Annual Development Report* by the Hanban (2015). Available from http://www.hanban.edu.cn/report/2015.pdf

Table I. CIs and CCs in African Countries (2015).

As shown in Table I, CIs have been opened in 32 countries and CCs in 14 countries in Africa since 2005, with the first CI established at the University of Nairobi in 2005 and the first CC at China Radio International in Alexandria, Egypt, in 2007. Within a decade, CIs and CCs have reached 36 of the 52 countries in Africa, and they have played a profound role in the China-Africa partnership for educational development.

Dynamic Educational Partnerships

The rapid spread of CIs and CCs has largely relied on educational partnerships between China and African countries over the past decade. The partnerships established might be seen as mechanisms that allow African universities or schools to cooperate with their Chinese counterparts with the support and approval of the Hanban, China's Confucius Institute Headquarters. In general, CIs and CCs have been established in response to the diversified demands from African countries, and their modalities are defined by these demands.

Demands from African Learners and Institutions

CIs and CCs are opened to meet the global demand for learning the Chinese language and culture – a typical *supply-demand* model from which African partners have greatly benefited. Alongside China's economic rise, there has been a widespread interest in expanding trade with China on the part of many countries, including African countries. This has led directly to the practical demand for learning the Chinese language and understanding the culture in African countries. This is clearly observable in Egypt, Kenya, Tanzania and Cameroon – all regarded by the United Nations (UN) as developing countries – and also in South Africa, with its higher level of economic development. It is also consistent with the Chinese government's original intentions in founding CIs and CCs around the globe.

Building educational partnerships with China is another important motivating factor in the spread of CIs and CCs in Africa. Many Chinese and African universities that co-founded CIs have historical partnerships, which are further enhanced through the establishment of CIs. A good example is the CI operated by the University of Cairo and Peking University. Some African universities with no prior ties to China have also launched educational partnerships with Chinese universities through CIs, as seen in the partnership developed between the University of Dodoma in Tanzania and Zhengzhou University of Aeronautics, a specialized institution in Henan Province, North China. These partnerships formed on the basis of CIs have helped universities in Africa establish, expand or strengthen their Chinese language departments or majors. Such partnerships have also enabled Chinese universities to become more internationalized (Li & Tian, 2015).

There can be no doubt that both the Chinese and African partners have benefited from the process of developing CI partnerships.

Many host universities in Africa expect to use their CIs as a platform to deepen the relationship with their Chinese partners and get more closely connected with China. For example, for African students who look for scholarships from the Chinese government, CIs serve as a semi-official channel to provide related information, which is often passed to CIs from China's embassies or consulates in African countries. CIs in Africa have thus tended to expand their roles beyond the official mission of teaching Chinese language and culture.

Implementation Modalities

Based on their Constitution and by-laws, CIs and CCs are mainly partnered for the following functions:

1. Chinese language teaching;
2. Training Chinese language instructors and providing Chinese language teaching resources;
3. Holding the Chinese Proficiency Test (HSK) and tests for the Certification of Chinese Language Teachers;
4. Providing information and consultative services concerning China's education and culture;
5. Conducting language and cultural exchange activities between China and other countries (The Hanban, n.d.b).

Although all CIs and CCs follow these official guidelines, each of them adopts a localized model for the implementation of their particular partnership, and the two main modalities are teaching-centered and community service oriented.

Teaching-centered model: teaching is CIs' core function, and this model is popular in Africa. For example, the CIs at the University of Nairobi in Kenya, the University of Yaoundé II in Cameroon, the University of Cape Town in South Africa and the University of Dar es Salaam in Tanzania focus on teaching Chinese language and culture as their primary mission. Teaching-centered CIs provide extensive course offerings at the host universities. Many are credit-bearing courses for undergraduates, and some CCs provide elective subjects in Chinese language for local schools. In other words, these CIs and CCs have integrated their teaching of Chinese language and culture within the formal systems in various African countries, with their courses and teaching being subject to routine quality monitoring and control by host institutions in Africa.

Community service-oriented model: community service is a popular mission for some CIs in Africa. The CI recently established between Moi University in Eldoret, Kenya, and Donghua University in Shanghai is located in the Moi University Industry-University Cooperative Textile District, serving the district through the industrial development of textiles. Another example is the CI at the University of Stellenbosch in South Africa, which has actively participated in local community activities, such as wine festivals, international food festivals and local Youth Day celebrations. The two CIs have adapted to the local African cultural context, bringing a multicultural element and promoting mutual understanding. Basically they serve as platforms for people-to-people exchanges, offering access to the HSK and scholarships for Chinese studies, alongside other community services.

It is worth mentioning that these two models are not really exclusive to each other. CIs and CCs have been constantly adjusting their missions and approaches to partnership in line with individual circumstances and contexts which vary widely from each other across the African continent.

Operational Models

According to the CI and CC Constitution and by-laws, CIs and CCs are under the leadership of the CI Council, which involves: (a) reviewing and endorsing the development strategies and plans of global CIs and CCs; (b) reviewing and endorsing annual reports and working plans of CI Headquarters; and (c) discussing issues concerning CI and CC development. Under the leadership of the Council, the CI Headquarters carries out its daily operations of overseeing partnerships with overseas institutions (The Hanban, n.d.b). In practice, the operational models of CIs and CCs are highly diverse, rather than uniform, and can be generally grouped into three categories: (a) the Chinese-dominant model; (b) the host-dominant model; and (c) the mutually shared model.

Under the Chinese-dominant model, the Chinese partner takes the lead in the daily operations of CIs and CCs, thanks to the strong and continuous support from the Chinese government. For example, Chinese directors enjoy much more administrative power than their local counterparts, who usually hold a concurrent position as vice-president, dean or department head at the host university. The local directors tend not to be really involved in the day-to-day operations of a CI, though sometimes they are able to provide symbolic support or assistance to their Chinese counterparts. Chinese directors have most responsibility for the course design and offering of Chinese language as well as Chinese cultural activities, in addition to their daily administrative duties. Cases of this operational model can be widely found in such CIs as those at Egerton University (partnered with Nanjing Agricultural University) and Kenyatta University (partnered with Shandong Normal University), both in Kenya; as well as the ones at the University of Yaoundé I in Cameroon (partnered with Zhejiang Normal University) and the University of Addis Ababa in Ethiopia (partnered with Tianjin University of Technology and Education).

The opposite of the Chinese-dominant model, the host-dominant model appears in those host institutions that have a traditionally renowned department of Chinese language or unit of Chinese studies. Local directors have more vision for program development and planning, and are able to play a leading role in various daily operations. For example, the CI at the University of Cairo is dominated by its local director, a professor and department head of Chinese language. In some years the CI at the University of Cairo did not even have a Chinese director for daily management and operation. Another case can be seen in the CI at Stellenbosch University, which was hosted in the Centre for Chinese Studies in its earlier years. Obviously, strong and continuous support from the host institution is a key factor in this model of CI partnerships.

The mutually shared model is somewhere between the two above-mentioned models – that is, both sides enjoy roughly equal leadership and governance in the development of a CI. Chinese and local directors work together for joint decisions, governance and administration. This model is also common in Africa, and good examples can be found in the CI at the University of Cape Town with Sun-Yat-Sen University, and the University of Botswana with Shanghai Normal University.

The Confucian *Zhong-Yong* Model of Educational Partnerships

As shown in the earlier section about the rapid spread of CIs and CCs in Africa since 2005, the dynamism of these educational partnerships has followed a developmental pathway of pragmatism based on a principle of mutual benefit and respect with an approach characterized by responsiveness to demand. The following features are widely observable.

First, the educational partnerships for development through CIs and CCs between Chinese and African institutions are all based on the local demand for learning Chinese language and culture, as well as for the establishment of partnerships with Chinese educational institutions that will support development. Alongside China's rapid rise as a global power, African countries have looked to China as an excellent role model for nation building and socio-economic development (Li & Tian, 2015). Such local demands from Africa have created a huge space for development through partnerships between China and African countries.

Second, the mutual benefit and respect principle of CI and CC partnerships has enabled both Chinese and African institutions to come together and work out practical plans for educational development, including the establishment and operation of CIs and CCs. This principle has served as the rationale and motive on both sides and has been substantiated by ongoing concrete efforts on each side. By and large, the claimed benefit rests on the outcomes envisioned by both partners for development.

Last but not least, as observed in many African CIs and CCs, each partnership has tended to be distinct in terms of implementation modalities and operational models, which are all adapted to local demands and individual contexts. These partnerships have been characterized by feasibility and flexibility, while mutual benefit and respect are maintained as a fundamental principle for all partners.

The three key features of CI and CC partnerships between China and Africa can be summarized as the Confucian *Zhong-Yong* model of educational partnerships, a pragmatic model for educational development centered on Confucianism (Li, 2016a,b), which will be further elaborated later in the chapter.

The UN 2030 Agenda for Sustainable Development Goals (SDGs) from a Confucian Perspective

Partnerships have in fact been viewed by the UN as a crucial means for international development. In September 2015 the global community convened at the United Nations Headquarters to endorse SDGs with a target date of 2030, and since 1 January 2016, the 17 SDGs of the 2030 Agenda have officially come into force. The fourth SDG focuses on ensuring inclusive and quality education for all and promoting lifelong learning, aiming at equitable and quality education around the globe by the year 2030, while the 17th SDG appeals for 'a revitalized Global Partnership' for sustainable development. The 2030 Agenda commits to the following declaration:

> We are determined to mobilize the means required to implement
> this Agenda through a revitalized Global Partnership for
> Sustainable Development, based on a spirit of strengthened global
> solidarity, focused in particular on the needs of the poorest and
> most vulnerable and with the participation of all countries, all
> stakeholders and all people. (UN, 2015, p. 2)

To achieve these 17 SDGs, including SDG4 for educational inclusion, quality and lifelong learning around the globe, the 2030 Agenda highlights the encouragement and promotion of 'effective public, public-private and civil society partnerships, building on the experience and resourcing strategies of partnerships' (UN, 2015, p. 27). In other words, the UN 2030 Agenda demands commitments to, and efforts to create, enduring partnerships which will involve all stakeholders for sustainable development. These commitments and effort are aimed at:

1. achieving effective and inclusive partnerships;
2. improving education policies and the way they work together;
3. ensuring highly equitable, inclusive and quality education systems for all;
4. mobilizing resources for adequate financing for education;
5. ensuring monitoring, follow-up and review of all targets.
(UNESCO, 2015, p. 9)

In addition, it is agreed among all national leaders who endorsed the UN 2030 Agenda that the implementation and success of the 17 SDGs will rely on the following approaches:

> 1. Nationally owned and country-led sustainable development strategies will require resource mobilization and financing strategies.
> 2. All stakeholders: governments, civil society, the private sector, and others, are expected to contribute to the realization of the new agenda.
> 3. A revitalized global partnership at the global level is needed to support national efforts. This is recognized in the 2030 Agenda.
> 4. Multi-stakeholder partnerships have been recognized as an important component of strategies that seek to mobilize all stakeholders around the new agenda.
> (UN, n.d.)

Our puzzle here is as follows: how may the Confucian wisdom of the *Zhong-Yong* model for CI and CC partnerships offer positive policy implications for the UN 2030 Agenda of SDGs? To better implement these SDGs envisioned by the UN 2030 Agenda, it is necessary to have a comprehensive understanding of how Confucianism views education, humanity and development, with particular reference to educational mission, social justice and ways in which these ideal goals may be finally achieved.

Confucianism foregrounds the ethics of individuals or groups in a societal context, offering an East Asian way of life, which is commonly shared in China, Hong Kong, Japan, Macao, Korea, Singapore, Taiwan, Vietnam and beyond. Although Confucianism has evolved into variant forms over 2500 years, its core framework has remained centered on ethics and its tenets can be summed up in the Five Constant Virtues of the humane person – namely, *Ren* (Benevolence), *Yi* (Righteousness), *Li* (Propriety), *Zhi* (Wisdom) and *Xin* (Sincerity), clustered around the core Confucian idea of *Zhong-Yong* or the Middle Way, the core value of Confucian philosophy (Li, 2009).

Education for Love and Peace

For Confucianism, it is impossible to become a humane person without the virtue of *Ren* (benevolence) (Tu, 1979). Literally, *Ren* (仁) means compassion, benevolence or simply love – 'to love your fellow people (仁者愛人 *Ren zhe Ai Ren*)' (*The Analects of Confucius*, n.d., 12.22). The connotations of '*Ren zhe Ai Ren*' can be more accurately understood from their respective etymologies. The Chinese character for the first *Ren* is 仁, composed of (human) in the left and (two) in the right, pictographically carrying the meaning of intimate relationships between two people (Xu, n.d., 8.1). Meanwhile, its pronunciation echoes exactly that of the second *Ren*

(人), which is the most commonly used Chinese character referring to human beings. The word root for *Ai* (愛) means heartfelt and ongoing longing, sympathy and caring for others (Xu, n.d., 5.2), and it is the exact equivalent of the term 'love' in the English language.

Ren (仁) was envisioned by Confucianism as a foundational value, a call to love other people with a sincere heart, through which harmony and peace can be achieved among human beings and among humans, nature and the universe, whether one or many. Human beings are to be freed and cultivated first through morality before excellence can be achieved. In essence, the ultimate mission of Confucian education is for love and peace in China's ancient ideal of the Great Harmony (*The Records of Rites*, 9), and this liberal ideal from Confucianism should be promoted in education around the world today (de Bary, 2007).

Education as Social Justice

With love and peace as the core values for a humanistic education, Confucius extended his mission to include social justice as well. He did not promote *Ren* (仁) alone, but instead always advocated *Yi* (Righteousness) alongside it. The twin values have been so interconnected with each other that a person demonstrating both love and righteousness becomes noble (de Bary, 2004). Additionally, Confucius expected that both *Ren* and *Yi* should be accompanied by *Li* (Propriety), a form of social agreement for proper conduct and behavior in a moral sense.

With these humanistic concepts, Confucius believed that through education and self-cultivation every ordinary individual was equally capable of becoming a sage-king and contributing to society. Based on this idea, Confucius made the point that 'in education there are no classes' [*You Jiao Wu Lei*] (*The Analects of Confucius*, n.d., 15.39) – literally, education should be without discrimination, the first ideal concept of Education for All (EFA) in human history. He further elaborated that the supreme virtue of benevolence involves unreservedly loving everybody and assisting them (*The Analects of Confucius*, n.d., 6.30). More importantly, he was not only a philosopher but was committed to making education available in reality to everybody with a thirst for knowledge. As a pioneer who opened the first private academy two thousand five hundred years ago, he taught more than 3000 disciples over his lifetime.

With a somewhat different connotation, *Ubuntu*, a Zulu word in South Africa, equates social justice with 'the proper relationships between a human person and the universe, between the person and nature, between the person and other persons ... it regulates the relationship of the universe' (Bhengu, 2006, p. 30). *Ubuntu* as social justice is also different from what has been developed in the European context, yet has some parallels. The Genevan philosopher Jean-Jacques Rousseau (1968) articulated the viewpoint that the legitimacy of a society relies on the social contract, an equitable one common to all. Two hundred years later, John Rawls argued that social justice as fairness should be defended with a priority on what is right (Sandel, 1998). Letseka (2014) observes that there actually exists an interconnectedness between Europe and Africa in the notion of *Ubuntu* as fairness.

Education for social justice or EFA is indeed a universal, rich value which promotes learning, teaching and schooling for all in various societal contexts, and it has been advocated differently in diverse civilizations. Regretfully, this value is still far more an ideal than a reality, as is globally evident in the increasing gap between the poor and the rich, the disadvantaged and the advantaged.

Education towards Diversity

Confucianism has given a high value to diversity and tolerance in order to nurture individuality and pluralism in education, rather than a one-size-fits-all conformity. Confucius always focused on heuristic education, enlightening his disciples in accordance with their diverse dispositions and background characteristics, as demonstrated below in the depiction of his actual teaching:

> Zi Lu asked: 'Should I immediately put into action what I have heard?'
> The Master said: 'As your father and elder brothers are still alive (to be consulted), how can you just go ahead to do it?'
> Ran You asked: 'Should I immediately put into action what I have heard?'
> The Master said: 'Yes.'
> Gongxi Hua said: 'When You (Zi Lu) asked whether he should immediately put into action what he had heard, you said No, as his father and elder brothers were still alive. Yet when Qiu (Ran You) asked whether he should immediately put into action what he had heard, you answered Yes. I am puzzled. May I be enlightened?'
> The Master said: 'Qiu always holds back, so I urged him forward; You has more than his own share of energy, I kept him back.'
> (*The Analects of Confucius*, n.d., 11.22)

The Confucian concept of diversity is not limited to teaching and education, but is extendable to an axiological foundation for ethical judgements and life orientation. Confucius called for harmony with diversity and tolerance (*He er Bu Tong*) (*The Analects of Confucius*, n.d., 13.23), and his idea was further developed by his disciples as 'all things being nourished together without hurting one another' and 'all courses being pursued without being conflictual or mutually exclusive' *The Doctrines of the Mean*, n.d., 30.3). It is in this sense that the mission of education should not be narrowed to a simplistic set of technical tools for serving a capitalist world. Rather, a humanist education with diversity should be able to respect, include, encourage and actualize a vast variety of pedagogical and spiritual beliefs and traditions, institutional forms and endeavours, as well as student backgrounds. It should be favourable to the promotion of inter-cultural and cross-national understanding in a global age.

Education in Practicality for Development

As mentioned earlier, the Confucian *Zhong-Yong* model for CI and CC partnerships is centered on Confucianism. Confucianism is not merely a complex and multifaceted philosophy in China, it is a pragmatic orientation which has had a profound impact on Chinese life and social change, historically and in the contemporary period (Li, 2009). Such a practical orientation can be illuminated by *Zhong-Yong*, Confucian wisdom of the Golden Mean (Lin, 1939). Literally, *Zhong* means central, proper, right or just; and *Yong* carries the meaning of ordinary, mediocre, pragmatic or universal (Ku, 1906, p. 7). To secure *Zhong* (the Mean) and *Yong* (the Normality) is not barely to pursue a middle course, but involves a tolerant spirit in which humanity and rationality reach a perfect harmony, without straying to any extreme ends. Fundamental to the two principles are Confucian values based on pragmatism which are balanced in ethical commitments and a collective rationality for development, through which harmony and peace are reached and attuned in ways that overcome the tensions between ideals and realities.

Educational partnerships are viewed in the Confucian *Zhong-Yong* model as a purposive, dynamic and contextualized process which demands that all partners be ethically and practically involved, committed and collaborating. It particularly demands feasible plans that can be agreed on and implemented by participating players in an uncertain, constantly changing environment in a globalizing world. This has been demonstrated in the one-decade experience of CI and CC partnership building between China and African countries. The practicality of this model has multiple policy implications for achieving the UN 2030 Agenda for SDGs through educational partnerships. For example, educational partnerships must be grounded on a solid ethical principle (the Golden Mean) that is commonly recognized and respected by all stakeholders. At the same time, the implementation of partnerships must be tailored individually for enough feasibility to meet local demands of such partnerships.

In fact, in the Confucian *Zhong-Yong* model, international development must be fashioned in ways that can serve to transform unequal societies, restoring freedom through the concerted efforts and commitments of multi-stakeholders, and promoting the social mobility of individuals in all contexts. In this sense, Confucianism has always accommodated a balancing of educational equity and excellence. Furthermore, Confucianism has never been satisfied with a utilitarian mode, but always sought to transcend individual interests for the good of society as a whole. The Confucian practicality of *Zhong-Yong* thus helps balance the extreme swings of the pendulum in educational reform and development, between short-sighted instrumentalism on the one hand, and an overly idealized utopia on the other.

Concluding Remarks: development through educational partnerships for a changing globe that embraces humanistic dialogues

Our age has been perplexed by the dilemma between the ideal and reality in education and development over a long period. When world leaders from all UN member states met at the United Nations Headquarters in New York between 25 and 27 September 2015, they declared a commitment, by the year 2030, to end poverty and hunger, to combat inequalities within and among countries, and to build peaceful, just and inclusive societies by creating conditions for sustainable, inclusive and continuing economic growth, shared prosperity and decent work for all, taking into account different levels of national development and capacities (UN, 2015, p. 3).

Figure 1. Photo by Jun Li, Dar es Salaam, Tanzania, 20 September 2016. The local CI director (standing in the middle) is delivering an intensive training lecture on teaching in Tanzania to his Chinese language teachers in the CI at the University of Dar es Salaam (UDSM) partnered with Zhejiang Normal University, before they can formally assume their teaching job to teach their Tanzanian students. The CI principle of mutual benefit and respect was observable throughout this workshop participated in by all new Chinese teachers freshly arrived from China in UDSM's new fall semester of 2016.

It has never been more urgent than at the current time to critically re-examine the relationship between education and development through educational partnerships for a more inclusive and communicative globe. The philosophy of Confucianism, as well as other philosophies, such as *Ubuntu* in Africa, can enlighten us on how education, development and partnerships should be envisaged in terms of humanity and ethical choices for equity and quality. Their wisdom resonates with values of Christianity, Islam, Buddhism, Hinduism, Shintoism and the philosophy of ancient Greece – all can empower us in alternative ways to more critically examine educational practices for international development around the globe. The Confucian framework of *Zhong-Yong* sheds new light on how education and development can be re-envisioned with partnerships that embrace a humanistic dialogue in the future.

As of 2015, China had opened 500 CIs and 1000 CCs around the globe through educational partnerships, registering over 1.9 million learners in 135 countries (The Hanban, 2015). This new, global form of CI and CC partnerships has networked hundreds of Chinese universities and schools with their overseas counterparts in multi-faceted relationships. The practices of the Confucian *Zhong-Yong* model have enabled 46 CIs and 23 CCs – all through educational partnerships with China – to flourish for mutual benefit and respect in the African continent. These African CIs and CCs have substantially and widely promoted multiple dialogues among civilizations, as advocated by the UN since 2001 (UN, 1998), the same year as the 9/11 tragedy.

Although CIs and CCs in Africa have encountered a range of challenges, including problems related to co-management, infrastructure building, teacher resources and teaching materials (Niu & Gao, 2012), there is no doubt about the profound roles they play in China-Africa partnerships for development. As demonstrated in Africa, the Confucian *Zhong-Yong* model of CI and CC partnerships has the unique potential to re-envision education for international development, and to open up the possibility of a freer and more communicative world in the future, from which international agencies such as the Asian Infrastructure Investment Bank, the World Bank and the UN can all learn!

Acknowledgements

This chapter reflects my lifelong interest in Confucian and East Asian studies and my research project on 'China-Africa University Partnerships in Education and Training: Students, Trainees, Teachers and Researchers' sponsored by the Hong Kong Research Grants Council General Research Fund (RGC/GRF, Ref.: HKU 842912H). Some sections are adapted from my earlier publications – namely, *Quest for World-class Teacher Education? A Multiperspectival Study on the Chinese Model of Policy Implementation* (Singapore, 2016); When Confucianism Meets Ubuntu: rediscovering justice, morality and practicality for education and development, *International Journal of Comparative Education and Development*, 17(1) (2015), 38-45; and China's Humanistic Zhong-Yong Approach of Educational Partnerships for International Development: Confucius Institutes and Classrooms reflected from Ubuntu and Confucian perspectives, *Bandung: Journal of the Global South* (Springer, forthcoming 2018). The author thanks the generous permissions obtained from Springer and Emerald, respectively.

References

Analects of Confucius, The (n.d.) http://www.confucius.org/lunyu/lange.htm (accessed 26 October 2016).

Bhengu, M.J. (2006) *Ubuntu: the global philosophy for humankind*. Cape Town: Lotsha Publications.

de Bary, W.T. (2004) *Nobility and Civility: Asian ideals of leadership and the common good*. Cambridge, MA: Harvard University Press.

de Bary, W.T. (2007) *Confucian Tradition and Global Education*. New York: Columbia University Press.

The Doctrines of the Mean. (n.d.) http://ctext.org/liji/zhong-yong (accessed 6 October 2017).

Hanban, The (2015) Confucius Institute Annual Development Report 2015. Hanban web page: http://www.hanban.edu.cn/report/2015.pdf (accessed 26 October 2016).

Hanban, The (n.d.a) About Confucius Institute/Classroom. http://english.hanban.org/node_10971.htm (accessed 26 October 2016).

Hanban, The (n.d.b) Constitution and By-laws of the Confucius Institutes. http://english.hanban.org/node_7880.htm (accessed 26 October 2016).

Ku, H.M. (1906) *The Conduct of Life, or the Universal Order of Confucius*. London: John Murray.

Letseka, M. (2014) Ubuntu and Justice as Fairness, *Mediterranean Journal of Social Sciences*, 5(9), 544-551.

Li, J. (2009) Confucianism, in D. Pong (Ed.) *Encyclopedia of Modern China*, pp. 347-351. Detroit, MI: Charles Scribner's Sons.

Li, J. (2016a) Chinese University 3.0 in a Global Age: history, modernity and future, in P.C.I. Chou & J. Spangler (Eds) *Chinese Education Models in a Global Age: transforming practice into theory*, pp. 15-35. Singapore: Springer.

Li, J. (2016b) *Quest for World-class Teacher Education? A Multiperspectival Study on the Chinese Model of Policy Implementation*. Singapore: Springer. https://doi.org/10.1007/978-981-10-0837-5

Li, J. & Tian, X.H. (2015) A Global Internationalization Experiment of Chinese Universities: models, experiences, challenges and prospects of Confucius Institutes' first decade, *Zhongguo Gaojiao Yanjiu [China Higher Education Research]*, 260(4), 37-43.

Lin, Y.T. (1939) *My Country and My People*, rev. ed. London: Heinemann.

Niu, C.S. & Gao, H. (2012) The School-running Model of the Cameroon's Confucius Institute and its Cultural Influence, *China's Comparative Education Review*, 6, 29-32 (in Chinese).

Rousseau, J.J. (1968) *The Social Contract*, trans. & intr. M. Cranston. London: Penguin.

Sandel, M.J. (1998) *Liberalism and the Limits of Justice*, 2nd edn. Cambridge: Cambridge University Press. https://doi.org/10.1017/CBO9780511810152

The Records of Rites (n.d.) http://www.confucius.org/lunyu/edcommon.htm (accessed 26 October 2016).

UN (1998) Assembly proclaims 2001 United Nations Year of Dialogue among Civilizations, expressing determination to facilitate international discussion. 4 November. http://www.un.org/press/en/1998/19981104.ga9497.html (accessed 26 October 2016).

UN (2015) Resolution adopted by the General Assembly on 'Transforming Our World: the 2030 Agenda for Sustainable Development'. 25 September. http://www.un.org/sustainabledevelopment/development-agenda (accessed 26 October 2016).

UN (n.d.) The Sustainable Development Agenda. http://www.un.org/sustainabledevelopment/development-agenda (accessed 26 October 2016).

UNESCO (2015) *Education 2030 Framework for Action: towards inclusive and equitable quality education and lifelong learning for all*. Paris: UNESCO. http://www.uis.unesco.org/Education/Documents/incheon-framework-for-action-en.pdf (accessed 26 October 2016).

Xu, S. (n.d.) *Shuo wen jie zi* [*The Analytical Dictionary of Chinese Characters*]. http://www.shuowen.org (accessed 26 October 2016).

CHAPTER 3

The Internationalization of Religious Higher Education: a comparative study of Christian universities in South Korea and Canada

CHRISTINA HWANG

SUMMARY Faith-based higher education institutions (HEIs) are guided by their Christian conviction as declared in their mission statements. In particular, their internationalization policies appear to be driven by the Christian belief in global missions and sharing the gospel of Christianity. This chapter comparatively explores the historical background of Christian higher education in both South Korea and Canada and the role it has played in higher education development. It then considers the theories of globalization, internationalization and Christian world mission. Finally, it presents institutional case studies in each country, which highlight the contributions of evangelical Christian universities to the internationalization of higher education.

Introduction

Christian higher education is a vibrant worldwide movement, yet faith-based higher education has received relatively little attention within the research literature on the internationalization of higher education. Both Korea and Canada have had rich histories in the evolution of their higher education systems. Christian colleges and universities have had a long history in Korea and Canada via Church-related denominations, yet many of these historical Church-founded institutions have now secularized and no longer view their religious identity as the core of their institutional mission. This chapter will therefore distinguish between what might be seen as a university historically founded by the Christian Church, such as McMaster in Canada or Yonsei in

Korea, and a 'faith-based' Christian university. The two case studies that will be presented fall under the latter category. The author thus views them as 'universities or colleges that currently acknowledge and embrace a Christian or denominational confessional identity in their mission statements and also other aspects of their policies, governance, curriculum and ethos' (Glanzer et al, 2011, p. 725).

Although many faith-based institutions of higher learning are guided by their Christian faith as declared in their mission statements, their programs and policy initiatives often mirror the trends and policy imperatives of their secular counterparts. This is particularly notable in processes of internationalization. At the same time, an important element in their international outreach is driven by the Christian belief in world mission, often motivated by biblical imperatives to spread the gospel of Christianity. This chapter presents a comparative overview of the historical background of Christian higher education in both South Korea and Canada and the role it has played in the field of higher education as a whole. This is followed by some discussion of theories of globalization, internationalization and Christian world mission. The final section presents case studies of Christian institutions in Canada and South Korea within the broader context of the internationalization of higher education, pointing out some of the unique features they contribute to the internationalization process.

Historical Overview: Christian higher education

South Korea

The history of education in Korea dates back over 4300 years. In the pre-modern period, formal education was a private matter whereas higher education was meant for the privileged or upper class based on Confucian principles (Lee, 2004; Kang, 2012). The development of modern higher education in Korea can be traced to the turn of the nineteenth century. The shift from a Confucian model to a western or American model was due to the arrival and efforts of western missionaries on the Korean peninsula. The establishment of institutions of higher learning, particularly by western Protestant missionaries, had a great impact on the development of Korean higher education. In 1885, Kwanghoewon (the national hospital), opened by Dr. Horace N. Allen and Dr. O.R. Avison, was the first modern hospital to practice and teach western medicine. With the support of philanthropist L.H. Severance, the hospital added a medical school, Severance Union Medical College, and also a School of Nursing (Lee, 2002a; Lee, 2004). American Methodist missionary Mrs. Mary R. Scranton established Ewha Hakdang in 1886. It was the first college-level school for girls, which evolved into the present-day Ewha Woman's University (Lee, 2004). These mission collegiate schools were modeled after the American colleges of the nineteenth century. Their goal was to help build well-educated Christian citizens rooted in both Christian religious values and liberal attitudes. Courses that were offered reflected this, such as the liberal arts, humanities and natural sciences, along with religious education (Lee, 2002b).

There are many reasons for the success of Christian higher education and its influence, which was parallel to the development of public higher education in Korea, starting from the late nineteenth century. First, American missionaries recognized that education was for all. They believed in helping those who were commoners, working class or of the lower social classes, and also women, who had been traditionally disadvantaged. Confucian norms and the Confucian value system were highly patriarchal and women were discriminated against. They were restricted to activity within the home and they had to be obedient to all male figures in their family, whether it be their father, husband or brother (Kang, 2012). Traditionally the women in this society had very few or no educational opportunities. The establishment of Christian higher education institutions, such as the previously mentioned Ewha Hakdang, pioneered the emancipation of women and their subsequent progress.

Second, the Amercian missionaries introduced the concept of liberal education. This taught the spirit of independence, democracy and self-reliance. Western democratic ideas and values of humanism, individual rights, representative government and primacy of law for the nation were also brought to the forefront of Korean society (Lee, 1989). Christian missionary educators 'emphasized both religious and liberal attitudes, which encouraged an educated citizenry' (Lee, 2002b, p. 56).

Third, the early American missionaries recognized the importance of western practical and scientific knowledge. Consequently, they emphasized new academic studies in western natural sciences in their curriculum and wrote textbooks for biology, chemistry and physics. They also emphasized the importance of manual skills. Educating the Korean people in universities and colleges that trained merchants and industrialists helped greatly in the process of modernization of the Korean nation (Ng & Zhang, 2011).

Fourth, with the establishment of Christian higher education institutions, missionaries utilized the native Korean language, Hangul, for the first time in higher education (Lee, 1989). Before this, all educational texts were written in Chinese characters and were taught and used by men of the noble class. Missionaries translated and published the Bible, textbooks and other Christian materials into Hangul. This was yet another gateway which opened up new opportunities for women and people who were of lower class in Korean society. Literacy dramatically improved because of the missionary endeavors, and social equality eventually spread (Kang, 2012). Park (2007) said that 'it is interesting to note that the advocates of Hangul were not Koreans but foreign missionaries and that Protestant Christianity made a contribution to the creation of a national identity by desinicization or "hangulization" at all levels of social life' (pp. 23-24). Through its higher education institutions, Protestant Christianity 'served as an educational mediator to establish modern higher education in Korea', and counteracted the long-established dominance of the Confucian elite (Lee, 2002b, p. 57).

Finally, Korea was annexed by Japan on 28 August 1910. From this time onward, the policies of Japanization were in full force. Policies such as prohibition of the use of the Korean language in school and changing of Korean names to Japanese were implemented. Education for Koreans was not regarded as urgent, and was different and separate from that for the Japanese. During this tumultuous time, Christian higher education became a promoter of nationalism and helped directly in the process of modernization in the country. Korean citizens who were against the established Japanese higher educational institutions turned to private Christian institutions. These Korean missionary schools were popular because they stood against Japanese imperialism. The Christian ideals they taught supported the national identity of the Korean people, and the people also believed that western values would bring innovation to the nation. Universities such as Chosen Christian College (Yonsei University) and Union Christian College (Soongsil University) were actively integrating Christian faith and nationalism (Ng, 2008). Christian universities opposed Japanese imperialism in Korea, and the connection between Christian education and nationalism in Korea became more obvious when the colonial government of Japan took power. In order to preserve the national identity of the Koreans, Christian higher education institutions were shaping new school curricula; hence they gained popular respect from the people. These schools became safe havens for students who were against the Japanese rule (Ng & Zhang, 2011). There were many political leaders who graduated from the schools and accepted Christianity as a better choice and as a means to promote nationalism and strengthen their national identity. These national leaders were even arrested for their nationalist activities and were involved in the independence movement. As a result, they gained a very good reputation and enjoyed prestige in the country (Ng & Zhang, 2011).

Canada

Historically, the development of higher education in Canada has deep roots in the French and English colonial regimes. Most institutions of higher education were denominationally controlled. Although these higher education institutions (HEIs) were Church controlled, they were not just simply theological seminaries. Catholic (French) institutions were closely aligned with the teachings and intellectual traditions of the Roman Catholic Church. They played a significant role in the establishment of colleges and universities in Quebec before and after the Confederation.

As the British settled in English Canada, they adopted and developed early models of the British universities, which were tied to the Protestant Church. A few of Canada's oldest Protestant denominational colleges were established prior to the Confederation in 1867 through charters granted by the British crown (Jones, 2006; Fernhout, 2014). After the Confederation, more new colleges and universities were established. Some were denominationally affiliated, and the province established others as non-sectarian institutions. A pattern was set when many of the denominational colleges decided to follow a scheme in which they federated themselves within the larger, established public institutions. In the years following confederation, the Church colleges were influenced by considerable change in Protestant thought in Canada. New ideas in science and a more humanist ideal prevailed over more orthodox Christian views where the Bible is regarded as revealed truth, standing above the human intellect. (Masters, 1966; Rawlyk, 1990).

The emergence of evangelical Protestant HEIs began in the late nineteenth century and the first half of the twentieth century. Christians who were outside of the mainline denominations founded many Bible colleges and institutes (Hiebert et al, 2005). A majority of these HEIs were established in Western Canada, yet some were located in other parts of the nation. Evangelicals were frustrated with the trend of secularization that dominated Canada's higher education system. These institutions were specifically created for a more Bible-centered curriculum and to train students for evangelization and missionary service (Stackhouse, 1993). Virginia Brereton (1987) has also suggested that one reason for the establishment of the Bible/theological schools was that the cost of establishing liberal arts colleges was high, while founding Bible schools was a more economical alternative. Another reason was that even though the provincial governments in the twentieth century did not favour giving private Christian colleges degree-granting privileges like their secular counterparts, they were still viewed as a good and 'Godly' alternative for Christians who wanted a Christian post-secondary education for their children (Stackhouse, 1993).

Nonetheless, as public universities embraced a secular ethos, some of the Bible colleges began to increase their own courses in the liberal arts. For example, Ontario Bible College in Toronto became well known by some Ontario universities, gaining a reputation as a kind of religious 'junior college' where students could transfer credits to the public HEIs (Stackhouse, 1993).

This trend changed in the 1960s and new ventures in Christian higher education were launched. In particular, according to Stackhouse (1993), there was a movement where evangelical Christians expanded their idea of vocation being just pastoral/missional to a view that sees all vocations as being in service to God. Thus the development of liberal arts types of colleges and universities began and became an alternative to public universities.[1] Fernhout (2014) identified 'fourteen Protestant/evangelical institutions that fit the profile of "Christian university" at the present time.[2] Six of the fourteen were designed from their inception to offer university-type programs in arts/humanities, sciences, social sciences and/or some professional areas.... the other eight institutions were founded as Bible or theological colleges' (pp. 236-237). As the eight expanded their programs, the respective provincial governments permitted these schools to change their institutional designation to use the term 'university' and seven of the eight were able to transition into 'university' or 'university college' status (Fernhout, 2014). Christian Higher Education Canada (CHEC), a non-profit association of evangelical Christian higher education institutions, services over 17,500 students across Canada. At present there are 34 member campuses in 7 provinces across the country. This includes 11 universities, 16 colleges and 17 seminaries and graduate schools. Of the students, 14,000 are undergraduates and 3500 are at the graduate level (CHEC, 2013).

Even though Canadian faith-based HEIs have a small niche within the bigger national context, there are still cases of some progress and impact in terms of recognition, reputation and legitimacy. Dan Smith's (2013) recent study on faith-based, degree-granting institutions in Manitoba is an example of this. Smith argued that in Manitoba, faith-based institutions were more integrated into the mainstream HEI system as they received legislative approval from the provincial government to have degree-granting authority for more programs (e.g. teacher education certification), 'university' status in their name and formalized government funding. There were also non-legislative actions, such as international students at Christian HEIs being permitted to take part in government employment programs. Affiliation agreements between public HEIs and faith-based institutions, such as that between the University of Manitoba and William and Catherine Booth University College, further validated Christian HEIs' acceptance within the mainstream system.

Since 2002, the *Globe and Mail*, a national Canadian newspaper, has published a report that surveys students who attended member universities in the Association of University Colleges Canada (AUCC), and the evangelical Christian member institutions in this group have consistently ranked at the top in overall student satisfaction, particularly in the last four years (Fernhout, 2014). These AUCC member institutions, as well as other Christian universities that are non-AUCC members, have also ranked well in the national student satisfaction survey conducted by *Maclean's* magazine, another esteemed national news publication. The *Maclean's* survey was based on the results of the National Survey of Student Engagement (NSSE) and the Canadian Undergraduate Survey Consortium (Fernhout, 2014). All this shows that evangelical Christian higher education is alive and well, contributing to Canada's higher education system and having its strengths in terms of quality of teaching and student satisfaction.

Globalization and Internationalization

Globalization in economic terms is a world system that is driven by the global capitalist economy and based on the philosophy of neoliberalism. It emphasizes deregulation, privatization, free markets and international competition. Roger King (King, n.d.) describes it as it consisting of flows of capital, people and information that go across many global highways. Held (1999) describes it as the widening and deepening and speeding up of worldwide interconnectedness. Jane Knight (2008) has a similar view of globalization. She describes it as the flow of people, ideas, values, cultures, knowledge and technology across borders, resulting in a more interconnected and interdependent world. This phenomenon of globalization continues to change the way that people, ideas, cultures and economies interact and is expanding the potential role played by HEIs in the relations between countries. Altbach and Knight (2007) see globalization as the economic, political and societal forces pushing twenty-first-century higher education toward greater international involvement.

The pressure to globalize has also created various formats of higher education that have influenced developmental changes in higher education in many countries (Carnoy & Rhoten, 2002; Altbach & Knight, 2007). Globalization is forcing countries and HEIs in every corner of the world to interact and compete on a global level, or risk becoming irrelevant. Within higher education circles, there has been a constant debate about the differences and similarities between the definitions of 'globalization' and 'internationalization'. Many have seen them as complementary. Others believe that internationalization of higher education is both a reactor to and an agent of the realities of globalization.

The concept of internationalization has been in continual development and there are many different definitions that have been proposed. From the institutional perspective of US higher education, Arum and van de Water (1992) define internationalization as 'the multiple activities, programs and services that fall within international studies, international educational exchange and technical cooperation' (p. 202). Ellingboe (1998) identifies internationalization as 'the process of integrating an international perspective into a college or university system. It is an ongoing, future-oriented, multidimensional, interdisciplinary, leadership-driven vision that involves many participants working to change the internal dynamics of an institution to respond and adapt appropriately to an increasingly diverse, globally focused, ever-changing external environment' (p. 199).

Knight (2008) holds that internationalization at the national, sectoral and institutional levels can be defined as 'the process of integrating an international, intercultural or global dimension into the purpose, functions or delivery of post-secondary education' (p. 21). Knight uses the term 'process' deliberately to convey the point that internationalization is an ongoing and continuing effort (Knight & de Wit, 1999).

The European Parliament Directorate-General for Internal Policies on Culture and Education (2015) most recently proposed a new definition of internationalization, which is 'the intentional process of integrating an international, intercultural or global dimension into the purpose, functions and delivery of post-secondary education, in order to enhance the quality of education and research for all students and staff, and to make a meaningful contribution to society' (p. 29).

The fundamental principles guiding internationalization have been traditionally considered to be a process based on values of cooperation, partnership, exchange, mutual benefit and capacity building among nations and their institutions (de Wit, 2002; Knight, 2012). Thus the relationships between nations and how they collaborate and share with one another are key to the notion of internationalization in higher education.

Understanding Evangelicalism

To appreciate more clearly the beliefs of individuals and institutions that profess the evangelical Christian faith and values, one must define the meaning of 'evangelical'. There are two senses in which the term 'evangelical' is used today in the early twenty-first century. The first is to view Christians who affirm key doctrines as 'evangelical.' David Bebbington (1989) approaches evangelicalism from this direction and notes four tenets of the evangelical Christian faith: 'conversionism', the belief that lives need to be changed; 'activism', the expression of the gospel in effort; 'biblicism', a particular regard for the Bible; and 'crucicentrism', a stress on the sacrifice of Christ on the cross. 'Bebbington's Quadrilateral' has become most accepted definition by the majority of scholars. Second, Stackhouse (2007) further defines 'evangelicals' as people or a group belonging to a movement known as 'evangelicalism'. It is based on the historical phenomenon that arose from revivals of the eighteenth century. It is as much a style as it is a set of beliefs.

Christian World Mission

What is the theology of mission? First, one must understand the term 'mission'. Mission is the overarching term describing God's mission in the world – 'missio Dei'. In other words, it is the 'mission of God to bring about redemption to the world, or human participation in this mission' (Sunquist, 2013, p. 7). Missiologists Ott, Strauss and Tennent (Ott et al, 2010) consider the task of missions in four motifs: (a) proclamation and conversion; (b) church planting and growth; (c) civilization and moral improvement; (d) philanthropy, humanization and liberation. Within these theological mission motifs, one can see that there are two major themes – evangelism and social action.

David Bosch (1991) places the Christian mission endeavor within the realm of several paradigmatic shifts within the history of Christianity and examines its contextual nature. More specifically, Bosch's paradigm theory of mission employs the historico-theological subdivisions of the history of Christianity used by the prominent theologian Hans Küng (1988). Küng puts forward an understanding of the Christian faith according to six periods.[3] Bosch (1991) then develops this idea by conceiving a unique interpretation of Christian mission according to these same periods. Bosch also uses Thomas Kuhn's (1970) scientific paradigm theory framework. Taking together Küng's six subdivisions along with Kuhn's paradigm theory, Bosch (1991) conceptualizes the broader mission process as fundamentally changing from one era to the next and having an 'effect on our understanding of how Christians perceived the church's mission in the various epochs of the history of Christianity' (p. 183). Bosch's thesis is that the events of the twentieth century, including the end of colonialism, the rise of nationalism, the destruction resulting from two world wars, the advancement of technology, the increasing environmental threat and the growth of Christianity in the global South, all mean that a new paradigm of mission is necessary, and in fact is emerging. Furthermore, one of Bosch's main emphases is that mission will be practiced in partnership. In essence, mission can no longer be thought of as the one-way street of 'from the West to the rest of the world', but rather as being a two-way journey that is from 'everywhere to everywhere' (Ott et al, 2010).

Within the emerging postmodern-ecumenical paradigm falls another mission theory paradigm – holistic/integral mission. In the late 1960s, the evangelical Church and its members began a movement called the Lausanne movement. The movement particularly embraced this theory and made it a part of its covenant. In order to understand integral mission theory, we must first examine the previously mentioned theological-historical contexts from which the shifts in paradigms occurred. For the purpose of this chapter, we will focus on the period beginning from the Enlightenment or modern paradigm up to the emerging Ecumenical or postmodern paradigm of the present time.

Protestant missions evolved in the midst of the Enlightenment, colonialism and Evangelical awakenings (Bosch, 1991). All three make up the context of the rise of the Protestant mission and have shaped the modern understanding of mission. The earliest Protestant mission efforts were motivated by the Puritan and Pietist traditions of the seventeenth and eighteenth centuries. This theology 'emphasized the need for personal conversion and discipleship in the life of the individual Christian' (Ott et al, 2010, p. 107). Thus the foundational understanding of mission was that every person needed to hear the gospel because humanity was sinful, and proclaiming that news for individuals and later on planting churches was the most important task. Therefore evangelism was at the heart of Protestant missions until the late nineteenth century (Ott et al, 2010). Evangelicalism as a branch of Protestantism also drew upon those ideals. In the late nineteenth century/early twentieth century, a more ultra-conservative movement within the evangelical community was fundamentalism. Those who were a part of this movement had a much more narrow view of the Bible and signed up to a dispensationalist theology. The focus of mission was exclusively on saving souls. This was also the time in which many Bible schools and institutes were founded (Sunquist, 2013).

On the other side of the spectrum was the social gospel movement. The belief held by theologians such as Walter Rauschenbush (1861-1918) and Emerson Fosdick (1878-1970) was one of 'God on earth through social action and change, a Christianization of the social order' (Ott et al, 2010, p. 128). It was a theology of liberation and transformation through social processes. The priority was to meet the social needs of people rather than proselytizing. Missionaries and missionary organizations went across the world to bring social improvement by building modern schools and hospitals, educating women and spreading the ideals of democratic governance (Ott et al, 2010; Sunquist, 2013).

The founding of the first Protestant missionary societies in the late eighteenth century brought cooperation and unity to the Christian mission. The first major Ecumenical Missionary Conference in Edinburgh, in 1910, highlighted and defined this idea. It marked the beginning of the modern ecumenical movement (Sunquist, 2013). The second meeting in Jerusalem in 1928 led to the founding of the International Missionary Council. In 1948 the World Council of Churches (WCC) was formed to organize all the national Churches from different regions around the world (Sunquist, 2013). Although mission was still at the core of the member Churches, alternative understandings of salvation and theology were being discussed. The Ecumenical or Conciliar movement in the twentieth century became much more distinct after the Uppsala Assembly of the WCC in 1968. The divide between evangelicals and ecumenicals escalated when the conference resonated with a horizontal aspect of mission, with more emphasis on humanization than on salvation, as theologian Hoekendijk had argued. His viewpoint of the world setting the agenda for the Church rather than the kingdom of God and his Word was controversial (Bevans & Schroeder, 2004; Ott et al, 2010).

Evangelical and conservative Churches and their mission bodies then turned against the progressive, ecumenical environment of Christian mission represented by the WCC. They were not pleased with the idea that the evangelical core of mission (evangelism) was being ignored. They held two major conferences in 1966. The Berlin Congress on Evangelism had the theme of 'One Race, One Gospel, One Task' and emphasized 'the gospel for all nations (one race) and the responsibility of all Christians (one task)' (Sunquist, 2013, p. 161). The Wheaton Congress on Christian World Mission followed. Both were created in order 'to give wider visibility to the Evangelical movement' (Bevens & Schroeder, 2004, p. 260) and to offer a more biblically based alternative to ecumenism.

In 1974, Reverend Billy Graham sponsored another meeting, the International Congress on World Evangelization, in Lausanne. Led by John Stott, a highly regarded evangelical voice within the WCC, evangelicals then endorsed the Lausanne Covenant, which affirmed the authority of the Bible and the uniqueness and universality of Christ (Stott, 1996). Despite the fact that the Lausanne Covenant strongly advocated the priority of evangelism as outlined by the Great Commission of Matthew 28:16-20 [4], it also acknowledged the importance of social justice. Together they were two vital components of the Christian mission. The social justice component of mission was already being practiced in the non-western world, particularly in Latin America. During the Lausanne conference, the idea of 'mission integral' was championed by Latin American theologians Rene Padilla, Orlando Costas and Samuel Escobar (Bevens & Schroeder, 2004). This theology of mission was then translated into what has become known as 'holistic' or 'integral mission'. 'Holistic transformation is the proclamation and demonstration of the gospel. It is not simply that evangelism and social involvement are to be done alongside each other. Rather, in integral mission our proclamation has social consequences as we call people to love and repentance in all areas of life. And our social involvement has evangelistic consequences as we bear witness to the transforming grace of Jesus Christ' (Micah Declaration on Integral Mission, 2014). In other words, integral mission is not just proselytizing, nor is it just social action, rather it is looking at the person as a whole – mind, body and spirit – on the principle that 'faith without works is dead' (Stott, 1996, p. 24).

Context: internationalization in Christian higher education

Before we briefly explore each institutional case study, let us first examine the internationalization policies and strategies within the larger national contexts of each country. Canada has never really had an official national internationalization policy strategy for higher education until most recently, when in 2011, the federal government rolled out a report that focused on international education as an economic and trade benefit. Among the policies, it emphasized student mobility and mainly the recruitment of international students, with the objective of doubling the number attracted to Canada by 2022. This constituted a shift in tone on the part of the Canadian government, given that previous to this Canada's internationalization strategy was generally viewed as 'soft power', through the foreign policy lens of international development aid (Trilokekar, 2010).

South Korea's national strategy was somewhat similar. Since the early 1990s the government quite aggressively implemented internationalization policies that would allow its HEIs to compete in the global higher educational market. Investing in research and development through HEIs in order for them to compete globally was a priority (Lee et al, 2012). More pointedly, their goal was for at least one of their HEIs to be ranked among the top 10 'world-class' universities. Policy initiatives such as the 'BK21', 'World Class University' and 'Study Korea' projects were fairly successful. However, the quest for cultivating 'world-class' universities is still a work in progress and the government continues the push towards knowledge production and international competitiveness in fields such as communication and technology. It is thus within this context that the two case-study universities presented in the next part of this chapter are operating.

Case Studies of Christian Universities

Tyndale University College and Seminary located in Ontario, Canada was founded as a Bible college in the late nineteenth century. It remained as a college until it was granted university status by the Ontario legislature in 2003. There are currently over 1600 students at both the University College and the Seminary and 12,000 alumni worldwide. Tyndale University College offers degrees in the humanities, the social sciences and business. It was approved by the Ontario legislature to open a Faculty of Education and grant BEd degrees in 2007. Its graduate school was developed in the 1970s as a theological seminary. Tyndale's mission states that it is dedicated to the pursuit of truth, excellence in teaching, learning and research, and enrichment of character all to serve the Church and world for the glory of God. Following Knight's (2012) framework for internationalization 'at home' and 'cross-border education', analysis shows that a majority of Tyndale University College's internationalization strategies and programs mainly fall within the 'at home' framework; however, there are a few 'cross-border education' strategies at present.

When looking at the types of academic programs and curricula at Tyndale University College, there has been a shift in majors offered that have a global and comparative dimension, such as the BA in History and Global Studies as well as the Business Administration and International Development program. An integral part of the latter requires the student to take part in an internship with an international development agency in the field. This gives real-world experience to help effect change not only in the classroom but in the world. Foreign language courses in French and an Intercultural Studies minor are also offered. Tyndale also has a degree program in theology where Mandarin is the language of instruction. It is a joint partnership with a Canadian Chinese Theological Seminary. In the Office of Student Life they have appointed a coordinator of Global and Community Engagement. This person oversees the support of international students on campus, and acts as a liaison for the intercultural ministry partnerships around the city and the student service mission trips. There are many extracurricular activities that contribute to the 'at home internationalization', such as a club for Third Culture Kids [5] and cultural programs in the city that are organized specifically for international students to help them learn more about their new environment and meet new friends. 'Cross-border' internationalization happens through study abroad programs to countries such as the UK or China. Finally, as previously mentioned, students participate in yearly service learning mission trips in countries such as Japan, Israel and Guatemala.

Handong Global University (HGU) is an example of a newer Christian university, and is located 200 kilometers south of Seoul, South Korea. It opened its doors 21 years ago as a private, co-educational faith-based university. Its mission is to educate honest and competent global leaders through whole-person education based on the Christian faith, for the technology-driven marketplace of the twenty-first century. Handong currently has an enrolment of approximately 4000 students, a curriculum with 20 undergraduate majors, 8 graduate programs and 130 faculty members, with 20% of the faculty being international. Following Knight's (2012) framework for internationalization 'at home' and 'cross-border education', the majority of HGU's internationalization strategies and programs also fall within the 'at home' framework. However, there are a few 'cross-border education' strategies that are observable.

Beginning with curriculum and academic programs, Handong offers majors that focus on global leadership skills, such as degrees in Global Management in Business, US and International Law and Global Development and Entrepreneurship. The Law School is Asia's first international law school. These programs are offered fully in English and 46% of the lectures in other programs are also taught in English, which is quite unique for universities in Korea since the language of instruction is predominantly Korean. HGU has many partnerships not only with international organizations but also with 130 universities in 43 countries. Partnerships make possible internship opportunities for the students with such international organizations as the United Nations (UN) and the Organisation for Economic Co-operation and Development (OECD). In addition, there are many extracurricular activities that contribute to the internationalization on campus. There is an 'International Buddy System' that is hosted by the student government to provide better opportunities for international students and Korean students to get to know one another and learn about different cultures. Another support for international students is the Korean Culture Experience program through the Office of International Community Advancement (OICA). The OICA hosts a variety of cultural programs for international students which allow them to familiarize themselves with local culture. Co-curricular programs include a 'Global Entrepreneurship Program' (GEP). The program teaches students to develop entrepreneurial skill sets and to work with students from other countries in an overseas setting. For 'cross-border' strategies, HGU has opportunities for students to go on exchange visits with one of its partner institutions. Likewise, many scholarships are available for students from developing countries and for children of missionary families, and these are used as one of their international recruitment strategies. Lastly, twice a year, over 400 students and faculty participate in service learning mission trips to various locations around the world. These opportunities are done on a volunteer basis, and many are focused on academic capacity building projects in largely under-served nations.

Conclusion

The higher education systems of both South Korea and Canada have been through many changes and growth over the past hundred years. During this period, the relationship between religion and education cannot be separated. This was manifested through the world mission endeavors of western missionaries to South Korea, who brought not only the Christian gospel but also a new social order that 'liberated' its people through education. In Canada, it was the zeal of the evangelical Churches and their members who wanted to keep the core of that same biblical message which practically created a new sector of private higher education and pushed the provincial governments to change policies in order to support them, despite the overarching trends of secularization. For Tyndale, part of its internationalization strategy has been utilizing its location in Toronto, Canada's most multicultural city, to its advantage in reaching the global community through partnerships with local churches and Christian organizations. Handong, on the other hand, focuses on its partnerships with international organizations (e.g. UN) and its partner HEIs, many of which are also Christian and located in Asia. Equally in both contexts, the international orientation is shown through a dedication to world mission, and within this, through an emphasis on the Christian commitment to social justice and helping those in need. A similar emphasis can be seen in Chapter 11 in this volume, on faith-based schools in Kenya and Haiti. It is the Christian HEIs' connection to the spiritual faith dimension that has played a valuable role in transforming to some degree both the Korean and the Canadian higher education systems.

The internationalization of higher education continues to be largely focused on the secular public university and college sectors. However, the two case studies in this chapter demonstrate that internationalization takes a somewhat different form within the smaller, private context of Christian higher education. This is something that needs to be further studied, and it may be interpreted within the frame of holistic or integral mission presented above. These universities are emerging in ways that bring some alternatives in terms of curriculum, pedagogy and program approaches as the concept of internationalization is applied through a mission-minded, faith-based lens.

Notes

[1] Trinity Western College (later Trinity Western University) in British Columbia, The King's College (later The King's University College) in Alberta and Redeemer College (later Redeemer University College) are examples of this (see Stackhouse, 1993; Li & Jones, 2015).

[2] This is based on the definition of 'Christian' university/college as described in the introduction (see Glanzer et al, 2011).

[3] The six periods described are: 1. the Apocalyptic paradigm of early Christianity; 2. the Hellenistic paradigm of the patristic epoch; 3. the Roman Catholic paradigm of the Middle Ages; 4. the Protestant Reformation paradigm; 5. the Enlightenment (modern) paradigm; 6. the developing Ecumenical (postmodern) paradigm.

[4] Matthew 28:16-20: Then the eleven disciples went to Galilee, to the mountain where Jesus had told them to go. When they saw him, they worshiped him; but some doubted. Then Jesus came to them and said, 'All authority in heaven and on earth has been given to me. Therefore go and make disciples of all nations, baptizing them in the name of the Father and of the Son and of the Holy Spirit, and teaching them to obey everything I have commanded you. And surely I am with you always, to the very end of the age' (NIV).

[5] 'Third Culture Kid' is a term referring to children who were raised in a culture outside of their parents' culture for a significant part of their development years. The 'third culture' is an amalgamation of the country from which the parents originated and the culture in which the family resides.

References

Altbach, P.G. & Knight, J. (2007) The Internationalization of Higher Education: motivations and realities, *Journal of Studies in International Education*, 11(3-4), 290-305. https://doi.org/10.1177/1028315307303542

Arum, S. & van de Water, J. (1992) The Need for a Definition of International Education in U.S. Universities, in C.B. Klasek (Ed.) *Bridges to the Future: strategies for internationalizing higher education*, pp. 191-203. Carbondale, IL: Association of International Education Administrators.

Bebbington, D. (1989) *Evangelicalism in Modern Britain: a history from the 1730s to the 1980s*. London: Routledge. https://doi.org/10.4324/9780203359907

Bevans, S.B. & Schroeder, R. (2004) *Constants in Context: a theology of mission for today*. American Society of Missiology Series. Maryknoll, NY: Orbis.

Bosch, D.J. (1991) *Transforming Mission: paradigm shifts in theology of mission*. Maryknoll, NY: Orbis.

Brereton, V.L. (1987) The Bible Schools and Conservative Evangelical Higher Education, 1880-1940, in J.A. Carpenter & K.W. Shipps (Eds) *Making Higher Education Christian*, pp. 110-136. Grand Rapids, MI: Eerdmans.

Carnoy, M. & Rhoten, D. (2002) What Does Globalization Mean for Educational Change? A Comparative Approach, *Comparative Education Review*, 46(1), 1-9. https://doi.org/10.1086/324053

Christian Higher Education Canada (CHEC) (2013) CHEC: the facts. http://www.checanada.ca/about-us/

de Wit, H. (2002) *Internationalization of Higher Education in the United States of America and Europe: a historical, comparative, and conceptual analysis*. Westport, CN: Greenwood Press.

Ellingboe, B.J. (1998) Divisional Strategies to Internationalize a Campus Portrait, in J.A. Mestenhauser & B.J. Ellingboe (Eds) *Reforming the Higher Education Curriculum: internationalizing the campus*, pp. 198-228. Washington, DC: American Council on Education.

European Parliament Directorate-General for Internal Policies on Culture and Education (2015) *Internationalisation of Higher Education*. http://www.europarl.europa.eu/RegData/etudes/STUD/2015/540370/IPOL_STU (2015)540370_EN.pdf

Fernhout, H. (2014) Quest for Identity and Place: Christian university education in Canada, in J.A. Carpenter, P.L. Glanzer & N.S. Lantinga (Eds) *Christian Higher Education: a global reconnaissance*, pp. 230-256. Grand Rapids, MI: Wm. B. Eerdmans.

Glanzer, P.L., Carpenter, J.A. & Lantinga, N. (2011) Looking for God in the University: examining trends in Christian higher education, *Higher Education*, 61(6), 721-755. https://doi.org/10.1007/s10734-010-9359-x

Held, D. (1999) *Global Transformations: politics, economics and culture*. Stanford, CA: Stanford University Press.

Hiebert, A., Bates, C. & Magnus, P.E. (2005) *Character with Competence Education: the Bible college movement in Canada*. Steinbach, MB: Association of Canadian Bible Colleges.

Jones, G. (2006) Canada, in J.J.F. Forest & P.G. Altbach (Eds) *International Handbook of Higher Education*, pp. 627-645. Dordrecht: Springer.

Kang, S.J. (2012) Protestant Influence on Korean Education Development, in W. Jeynes & D.W. Robinson (Eds) *International Handbook of Protestant Education*, pp. 537-551. Dordrecht: Springer.

King, R. (n.d.) *Globalization and Higher Education*. www.acu.ac.uk/yearbook/may2003/kingfull.pdf

Knight, J. (2008) *Higher Education in Turmoil: the changing world of internationalization*. New York: Sense Publishers.

Knight, J. (2012) Concepts, Rationales and Interpretive Frameworks in the Internationalization of Higher Education, in D. Deardorff, H. Wit, J. Heyl & T. Adams (Eds) *The SAGE Handbook of International Higher Education*, pp.27-41. Thousand Oaks, CA: SAGE.

Knight, J. & de Wit, H. (Eds) (1999) *Quality and Internationalization in Higher Education*. Paris: Organisation for Economic Co-operation and Development.

Kuhn, T.S. (1970) *The Structure of Scientific Revolutions*. Chicago: University of Chicago Press.

Küng, H. (1988) *Theology for the Third Millennium: an ecumenical view*. New York: Doubleday.

Lee, C.J., Kim, Y. & Byun, S.Y. (2012) The Rise of Korean Education from the Ashes of the Korean War, *Prospects*, 42(3), 303-318. https://doi.org/10.1007/s11125-012-9239-5

Lee, J.-K. (2002a) *Korean Higher Education: a Confucian perspective*. Seoul: Jimoondang Publishing Company.

Lee, J.-K. (2002b) The Role of Religion in Korean Higher Education, *Religion and Education*, 29(1), 49-65. https://doi.org/10.1080/15507394.2002.10012295

Lee, S. (1989) The Emergence of the Modern University in Korea, *Higher Education*, 18(1), 87-116. https://doi.org/10.1007/BF00138962

Lee, S. (2004) Korean Higher Education: history and future challenges, in P.G. Altbach & T. Umakoshi (Eds) *Asian Universities: historical perspectives and contemporary challenges*. Baltimore, MD: Johns Hopkins University Press.

Li, S.X. & Jones, G.A. (2015) The 'Invisible' Sector: private higher education in Canada, in K.M. Joshi & S. Paivandi (Eds) *Private Higher Education: a global perspective*, pp. 1-33. Delhi: B.R. Publishing.

Masters, D.C. (1966) *Protestant Church Colleges in Canada*. Toronto: University of Toronto Press.

Micah Declaration on Integral Mission (2014) http://www.micahnetwork.org/projects/review-micah-declaration-integral-mission

Ng, P.T. (2008) Globalization, Nationalism, and Christian Higher Education in Northeast Asia, *Christian Higher Education*, 8(1), 54-67. https://doi.org/10.1080/15363750802319110

Ng, P. & Zhang, Y. (2011) Nationalism, Modernization, and Christian Education in 20th Century East Asia: a comparison of the situations in China, Japan, and Korea, in J.A.B. Jongeneel, J. Liu, P.T.M. Ng, P.C. Ku, S.W. Sunquiest & Y. Watanabe (Eds) *Christian Presence and Progress in North-East Asia: historical and comparative studies*, pp. 57-86. Frankfurt am Main: Internationaler Verlag der Wissenschaften.

Ott, C., Strauss, S. & Tennent, C. (2010) *Encountering Theology of Mission: biblical foundations, historical developments, and contemporary issues*. Grand Rapids, MI: Baker Academic.

Park, Y.S. (2007) The Church as a Public Space: resources, practices, and communicative culture in Korea, *International Journal of Korean History*, 11, 17-37.

Rawlyk, G.A. (1990) *The Canadian Protestant Experience, 1760 to 1990*. Burlington, ON: Welch.

Smith, D. (2013) Differentiation and Diversification in Higher Education: the case of private, faith-based higher education in Manitoba, *Canadian Journal of Higher Education*, 43(1), 23.

Stackhouse, J.G. (1993) *Canadian Evangelicalism in the Twentieth Century: an introduction to its character*. Toronto: University of Toronto Press.

Stackhouse, J.G. (2007) Defining Evangelical, *Church and Faith Trends*, 1(1), 1-5.

Stott, J.R.W. (1996) *Making Christ Known: historic mission documents from the Lausanne Movement, 1974-1989*. Grand Rapids, MI: Wm. B. Eerdmans.

Sunquist, S. (2013) *Understanding Christian Mission: participation in suffering and glory*. Grand Rapids, MI: Baker Academic.

Trilokekar, R. (2010) International Education as Soft Power? The Contributions and Challenges of Canadian Foreign Policy to the Internationalization of Higher Education, *Higher Education*, 59(2), 131-147. https://doi.org/10.1007/s10734-009-9240-y

CHAPTER 4

Islamic Education in Post-Soviet Tajikistan: a tool in creating and sustaining a nation-state

SARFAROZ NIYOZOV

SUMMARY Central Asia has become a site not only of Islamic revival, but also of a heated contestation between diverse local and international interpretations and versions of Islam and Islamic education. Islam, and subsequently Islamic education, are key highlights of post-Soviet development all across Central Asia. This chapter takes Tajikistan as a case study, because it is in this country that Islamic education became most prominent in the initial post-Soviet landscape. The chapter takes the reader on a brief journey into the continuity and changes in Islamic education over the last 30 years since Perestroika (1985), when a window for religious education in Central Asia opened up as the country emerged from the Soviet Union's collapse, survived five years of civil war, began its market-oriented development trajectory and internal political and social consolidation as an independent state, as well as carved a space for itself in the global geo-politics. The chapter speaks to the purpose, forms, pedagogy, content and challenges of Islamic education in post-Soviet Tajikistan.

Introduction

In this chapter I present the nature, processes, purpose and forms of Islamic education in post-Soviet Tajikistan, the kind of challenges this form of education faces, and how they are addressed. I make a number of arguments: first, Islamic education and Islamization in Tajikistan are taking place in a time of desecularization, globalization, and nation-state building. The interaction of these factors creates multiple contestations and opportunities for societal exposure to and engagement with Islamic education. Second, Islamic education in Tajikistan, as elsewhere, is a social construct, created and organized by various circles with vested interests. As such, it exists in multiple formal and informal expressions that feed into each other in direct

85

and indirect ways. Islamic education therefore serves not only the common Muslim aspirations, but also its organizers' and promoters' economic and political interests. Third, Islamic education in Tajikistan is not a single, objective and immutable programme; it has changed in its goals and forms and represents a continuum of continuities and changes across historical time and space. A key challenge faced by the Tajik people and authorities involves how to create proactive polices within the education sector to ensure that Islamic education serves the purposes of harmony, social justice and national development.

To that end, Islam and its education need to be engaged in their variety of forms, purposes and expressions in order to be better understood, managed and employed for constructive purposes. Islamic education is not fixed and monolithic. It cannot be described in simple dichotomous and binary terms. Islamic education is a journey of continuity and change, adaptation and stability, contradicting and complementing approaches, positions, attitudes, contents, pedagogies and outcomes a mixture of contextualized and universal principles messages, and developments. It can be purposeful, organized, formal and ambiguous, as well as ad hoc and informal; accommodating and oppositional; affected by the political establishments and ruling elites, who often tailor Islam to their political and economic needs. It, however, also survives various political establishments and forms of marginalization. Islamic education is also affected by students', teachers' and parents' class, gender, ethnic identities, and resources, and by teachers' skills, resource availability and cultural factors. Islamic education could be submissive and passive, but it can also be subversive, transformative and even disregarding.

It has many forms, goals, methods and contents. It can survive without structure or create alternative structures. Islamic education could be a social construct of a particular people, time and place, as long as the above factors do not contradict the 'true', never-changing, decontextualized and not socially constructed (given/divine) messages of Islam. Islamic education can provide a totalizing ethical framework for life, proposing an opposing socio-political alternative to the secular and nationalist ideology or provide a supportive framework for this ideology. Such complexity allows us to understand the dimensions of state–society–Islam relations and the role of Islamic education in these relationships. . While I find the current active engagement of the Tajik policy makers, educators and religious authorities to be valuable, I argue that their engagement *approach*es and *methods* could be more critical, creative, and constructive. To enable Muslim children of Tajikistan to live in the twenty-first century, Islamic education should go beyond uncritical socialization and indoctrination of the youth and develop their capacities to use critical textual and discursive analyses of the local and external religious discourses that are through formal and informal media.

Data Sources and Analysis Approach

The data for this analysis come from my long engagement with Islamic education generally (e.g. Niyozov & Memon, 2011) and in Tajikistan (Niyozov et al, 2017). I have also examined journalistic articles from websites (such as that of the Dushanbe Islamic Institute, the newspaper *Najot, Kumita oid ba Korhoi Din* (Committee of Religious Affairs)[1] and secular school textbooks (e.g. Boronov, 2003). My data analysis includes distilling issues and themes, situating them within the context of place and history, and drawing their implications for policy and practice in engaging Islamic education in Tajikistan. The key research areas are comprised of (i) the nature, purposes and types of Islamic education in Tajikistan; (ii) how Islamic education has become a battlefield between government and non-governmental, global and local, traditional and modern, passive and revivalist stakeholders; and (iii) how the interplay of nationalism, globalization and de-secularization provides possibilities and hindrances to Islamic education in post-atheist Tajikistan. I start this chapter with a brief conceptual summary of Islamic education in order to guide the reader into the rest of the chapter. I skip pre-Soviet and Soviet-era Islamic education (for more on this, see Niyozov et al, 2017). I detail the reemergence and proliferation of the Islamic discourses in the post-Soviet time resulting from the collapse of the anti-religious state and the arrival of the globalized Islamic discourses, their impact on societal secularization, and how all these have affected Islamic education's various forms. I conclude with implications for policy and practice in the future of Islamic education in Tajikistan.

Islam in Tajikistan: a contextual brief

A brief summary of Islam in Tajikistan is critical for understanding the context of the continuities, changes, developments and challenges in post-Soviet Islamic education. Tajikistan currently comprises over 8 million people, living on 143 thousand square kilometers of land. Of this land, 93% is comprised of medium-and high-altitude mountains, hard for living on and farming. Of Tajikistan's diverse populations, 98% are Muslims. Out of this, 95% are Sunni and around 4-5% Ismaili Shi'a Historically, the current Tajikistan has been a part of the Persian, Greek, Arabo-Islamic, Mongol, Tsarist Russian and Soviet empires and various kingdoms (Samanids, Ghaznawids, Seljuks, Timurids, Safavids, Shaibanids and Bukhara Manghits). By the end of the eleventh century most of the Zoroastrian, Greek, Arian and Buddhist socio-political, economic and cultural norms and terminologies had disappeared under the Arabization and Islamization policies (Bertels, 1959). Persian and smaller local languages barely survived, embracing between 40 to 60% of Arabic words and constructs; the intra-Islamic diversity (Twelver and Ismaili Shi'as and Sunnis) were absorbed by the Hanafi *madhab* of the Sunni Islam. Local Turkic dynasties, as guardians of Sunni Hanafi Islam, zealously defended and spread it into the lowlands, mountains and steppes of Central Asia, China and India. Shi'a Islam spread in much smaller ways, mainly through the work of the *dai's*, Sufi orders and other clandestine practices (Stern, 1960).

With the Russian annexation of Central Asia (1860-1895), the Muslims of Tajikistan became involved in the Great Game, the subsequent socialist-capitalist rivalry (1917-1992), and the Cold War (1945-present). While the Tsarist Russians kept the political status quo unchanged and largely intervened in the economic, cultural and education realms (to develop pro-Russian loyalty among the Muslims), the Soviet Bolsheviks insinuated radical reforms between 1917 and 1936. Ideologically, the Soviets executed a comprehensive strategy: First, they eliminated the *shari'a* courts and religious schools and closed almost all the mosques. Next, they marginalized, imprisoned, exiled and eliminated many local religious teachers and preachers. Simultaneously, they defeated the anti-Soviet *jihad* of the *Basmachis* (local Islamic nationalist rebels) and closed the borders with the rest of the Muslim world. In the late 1920s, the Soviets changed the Arabic/Persian alphabet to Latin and then in the 1930s to Russian, depriving the majority from accessing their rich but Islamicaly-infused legacy in Persian and Arabic scripts.

As alternatives, the Bolsheviks successfully created pro-Communist structures to replace Islamic and traditional institutions. These structures ranged from kindergartens (for 3 to 5 years of age), to unions of Oktyabrist (aged 6-8), to Pioneer (9-14 years), and Komsomol (aged 14-18), ending with units of the Communist party (18 years old and above), as well as All-Union Societies of Militant Goddesses, which were later turned into more moderate Knowledge Societies. In other words, the Soviets tried to create a completely new, comprehensive (alternative to both religious and capitalist) world view, based on their Socialist-Communist principles of equity and justice. Many active creators of the Soviet system were Central Asian Muslims, at times from religious families, including the former Jadids, who sincerely identified with the anti-colonial, anti-imperialist and pro-Islamic tenets of the early Soviet Marxist rhetoric (Khalid, 1998; McGlinchey, 2011).

Teachers were in the vanguard of this new Socialist system and its antireligious movement and creators of the Soviet citizens and society. Like the revivalist Islamic perspective, this new socialist society was supposed to be the best and final stage of human progress in justice, equity and freedom, a true democratic ideal. The difference was in the change in the source of truth: the message of God was replaced with the message of natural science and the scientific communist paradigm. Almost like "true Muslims", the Soviet citizens were to be above class, race, sectarian, linguistic and cultural prejudices. The intellectual and political elites of the Soviet republics were assigned to critically examine their religiously oriented legacy, take from it what served the purpose of new system and ignore and hide what they saw as harmful and as superstitious. This crystallization led to a bizarre reconceptualization of such deeply Islamic scholars as al-Farabi, Ibn Sina, Rudaki, Nasir Khusraw and Hafiz. Often they were presented as non-religious or anti-religious, as rationalists or proto-Marxists, and as defenders of the poor peasants, and working classes. Such reconceptualization was grounded in these thinkers' intellectual and artistic opposition to the official ritualistic and legalistic Islamic discourses and the corrupt and unjust political establishments of their times.

Overall, the Soviets' relationship with Islam and Muslims was not simple, linear and one-dimensional. Contradictory and paradoxical, it was punctuated with continuity and change, submission and subversion, adoption and adaptation, modification and mutual exploitation. During the early Soviet revolution, Muslims and Soviets aligned against the Tsarist establishment, which represented capitalism, tyranny, colonialism and Orientalism. The1930s witnessed massive purges of Muslims, especially intellectuals such as the Jadidis (modernists), Muslim nationalists and even Muslim communists (Keller, 2001; Kemper et al, 2009). Religious education rescinded to the traditional religious families and their close confidants. The concept of clandestine teaching cell (*hujra*) emerged (Poliakov, 1992). The 1940s saw a warming of Soviet-Muslim relationships, which helped mobilize Central Asian Muslims to fight the Nazis during the Great Patriotic War.

Gradually, the Soviets realized the impossibility of 'finishing' Islam in a rapid way, and saw a potential for using it to socialism's ends. The tactic shifted to 'tailoring' Islam and Muslims and using them for the state's goals, emphasizing the similarities between Islam and socialism, and acknowledging that militant atheism might be too far a stretch to apply to Central Asia in the foreseeable future. During the 1940s to the 1950s, the Soviets created regulatory-controlling structures such as the Spiritual Administration of the Muslims of Central Asia and Kazakhstan (*Sredne-Aziatskoe Duchovnoe Upravlenie Musul'man*, or SADUM). The state also reopened the madrasa of *Mir-i Arab* in Bukhara in 1946, an Islamic institute named after theologian al-Bukhari in 1971 in Tashkent (Ro'i, 2000; Kemper et al, 2009). Studying Islam and the languages spoken by the Muslim population (Arabic, Persian, Turkish and Urdu) was also promoted at this period in the newly established departments of Oriental studies in the capital cities in Baku, Tashkent and Dushanbe (Kemper & Connermann, 2011).

Parallel to the state's tailoring, private and clandestine schools also spread, promoting oppositional instruction against both state-atheist schools and state-controlled Islamic institutions. An example of such two-way work could be Muhammadjon Rustamov (aka Domullo Hindustoni, 1892-1989), who simultaneously worked as an expert of Islamic manuscripts at the state department of Oriental Studies of the Academy of Sciences and also ran his own underground teaching circles in the very capital city of Dushanbe, which functioned from mid-1960s until the late 1980s (Rahnamo, 2009).

Two global events further reinforced Islamic revival: (i) the Islamic revolution in Iran; and (ii) the Soviet invasion of Afghanistan. These events galvanized Muslims, revived their belief in themselves, and connected Muslims to the outside world. Anti-Soviet rhetoric, launched by the western and Islamic media aimed at internal disruptions. Political groups emerged such as the Youth Islamic Revival, which was transformed into a political party, *Hizbi Nahzati Islom* (Party of Revival of Islam)[2] in Tajikistan. The emerging clandestine literature challenged both the Soviet system and traditional Islamic practices from within. Central Asian communist leaders started to openly play a double game: to their fellow countrymen, they blamed the Russians for not letting their countries grow and use their languages and cultural traditions, many of which were Islamic anyway to their Moscow bosses, they blamed their compatriots for being too backward and anti-modern, at times too fanatical and dangerous and who needed to be tamed and controlled. Achieving the double legitimacy, these political and intellectual elites more openly participated in religious ceremonies, turned a blind eye to religious practices, and in fact sought religious counsel from the local *eshon*s (Poliakov, 1992).

The 1980s saw Perestroika and Glasnost and the surfacing of the Soviet failures; the terrible acts of the Communist party and Soviet state's security apparatuses and the defeat during the Afghan war; the nascent identity and language politics and spread of religious literature; the breaking of the iron walls and cages; and the emergence of Islamist movements at home and around the globe. All these gave further impetus to the revival of Islamic education. The existing socialist-communist model of development, recently branded as a success, was now vanishing rapidly. Communism was projected as alien, antihuman and anti-Islamic. Western-supported and radically construed Jihad was declared not just against the Soviet troops in Afghanistan, but against the Soviet Union as a whole. The West and Islamic states saw Islam and Muslims as the best tool to finish the Soviet Union, spread capitalist hegemony, and subdue Russia. Perestroika led to the collapse of the Soviet Union; Glasnost to the demise of Communism as ideology and discourse. The vacuum was quickly filled with the Islamic groups that were very recently operating underground and struggling to survive. Speaking Islamic languages, attending religious classes and seeking the blessing of religious scholars/clergy were the new fashion. The newly emerged Islamic clergy represented a mixed bag: well-known scholars such as Turajonzoada's family members, the above-mentioned Hindustani, graduates of the Oriental and philological departments, as well as traders and former prisoners jailed for theft and corruption.

Islamic Education in Post-Soviet Times

In September 1991, Tajikistan declared independence, underwent a multi-part election process, and descended into a five-year civil war (1992-1997). Islam, and Islamically inspired groups such as *Hizbi Nahzati Islom* (Islamic Revivalist Party, IRP) played a central role in the internal conflict. Slogans about Islamic society, showed on the religiously-filled Iranian TV, open public prayers, the demolishing of Soviet statues and the shaming of local scholars and communists became the routines in 1990-1992. Confronted by the pro-Communist and secularist forces, who openly spoke against Islam and fought Islamic 'fundamentalism', a five year civil war ensued, which led to the defeat of Islamo-nationalist-democratic forces and, in the process, to major destruction of the Tajik society, economy and education. In 1997 a national reconciliation treaty was signed by which Islam and the IRP were legally acknowledged as parts of Tajik societal fabric. Since 1997, Tajikistan has been undergoing steady development, asserting itself as a rapidly developing economy, reviving culture and actively participating in regional and international alliances. Throughout this history, Islam has held a critical space, creating opportunities and challenges for unity, cohesion and national development. The key Islamic challenge of Central Asia, including the Tajik state, is aptly expressed by Peyrose:

> How is it possible to maintain a secular framework, erase the memory of militant atheism, and also promote religion in its many denominations? How can a key place be granted to Islam while maintaining the principles of secularism, and controlling the movements that the authorities consider, rightly or wrongly, as 'dangerous', 'extremist' or terrorist'? (Peyrose, 2007, p. 246)

Since independence in 1991, Islamic education, like Islam as a whole, has been a field of contestation between the various groups and parties. The initial anti-Islamic discourse led by the government shifted to tolerating Islam, to acknowledging it as part of the Tajik cultural-social fabric, to identifying local, Tajik, non-Arabic and non-Turkic, non-Salafi and non-Wahhabi Islam, to witnessing the inflow of the global radical and moderate discourses through globalization, development projects, immigration, media, petrodollar investments and the return of madrasa graduates from the Middle East and South Asia. This also led to increasing dissociation from Iran and movement towards Arabic – that is, towards, Sunni Islam.

Formal Islamic Education

Formal Islamic education at school level, like the private Islamic schools of the western type (Douglass & Shaikh, 2004), almost does not exist in Tajikistan. There was an Islamic high school (Islamic gymnasium) for boys and girls in Dushanbe catering for around 1400 enrolled students from Grade 1 to 11 [3] with an integrated secular and religious curriculum. In addition to learning subjects from the national curriculum, the school also allowed studying the Quran, Arabic grammar (s*arf wa nahw*), recitation (*tajwid*), exegesis *(tafsir)*, *ethics (adab, akhloq)* and history of religions. Most of the classes were co-educational, but girls and boys sat in different rows of the classrooms. The secular subjects were taught by teachers who had graduated from the secular universities, while the religious subjects were taught by the graduates of the Islamic Institute or those who had studied Islam abroad. This gymnasium prepared graduates for further higher religious education at a madrasa or Islamic Institute in Dushanbe and for joining the workforce in the market. In 2015, the school was closed due multiple reasons, including lack of teachers and materials, and oversight.

Higher Islamic education, however, continues. There is an Islamic institute (*Donishkadai Islomi*) that was initially formed as the education unit of the *Qaziate* in Tajikistan in 1992 and was named an Islamic institute after Imam Tirmizi (824-892 CE). In 1997, it was transformed into an independent higher academic institution. Since 2008, the institute has taken the name of Imam Abu Hanifa (d.767 CE), a Persian Sunni scholar and the founder of the Hanafi discourse. By 2013 the institute had around 1500 students. Its students include both males and females, who attend undergraduate and graduate studies. The curriculum, textbooks and methods of teaching are all aligned with the modern education system. The Islamic education (both in the gymnasium and the institute) is integrated and assessed by the Ministry of Education for quality assurance. They use modern textbooks for teaching and learning of Arabic and other Islamic sciences. Lectures, seminars, discussions, practicum, examinations and degree conferral all follow the secular system.

The actual extent to which the teaching is interactive or transmissive depends on the particular teacher's skills and knowledge and dispositions. But the expectations from the Islamic education system are aligned with those of the public system (interview, June 2013). At present, the institute has two departments: (i) Islamic sciences; and (ii) Oriental Studies. The institute's curriculum includes both religious and secular sciences. The courses include Quranic studies, *hadith*, *shari'a*, Arabic, history and philosophy of Islam, languages, and IT. In addition, history of Tajik people, English, Russian and Tajik are taught. Those who specialize in Arabic philology also take courses in economics, geography, political sciences and international relations. The institute publishes a scholarly cultural journal, *Ma'rifati Islomi*, in Tajik and Arabic. In 2010, the institute established a section on the analysis of societal relations and issues, and a center for research and scholarly activities. Since 2011, the institute has had its own publishing house and operating website, islam.tj.

The institute produces Islamic Studies teachers, *imam-khatib*s, and specialists in areas of Quranic Sciences, Arabic philology, history of Islam, history of religions, *fiqh* and Islamic philosophy. The Department of Oriental Studies produces translators and diplomats. In addition to the university there are currently 19 registered madrasas throughout the country which seem to follow the traditional forms of religious curriculum mentioned above. Formal education promotes the Hanafi Islam, which was established by Imam Abu Hanifa, a Muslim theologian of Khurasani Persian origin. The Hanafi Islam is presented as tolerant of local customs, other religions, and the ruling powers, and as supporting civilizational dialogue. Given the proliferation of old and new Islamic discourses, the state's reductionist approach renders other approaches as un-Islamic, wrong or extremist.

The 'curriculum' of these formal instructional spaces includes basic and advanced texts. Content- or text-based instruction predominates. For example, the basic texts such as *Chahor Kitob* and *Haftyak* teach Persian and Arabic languages, Quranic verses, recitation, *hadith* and Islamic manners (*odob*) at the same time. The *Domullo*s (male teachers) and *Bibikhalifa*s (female teachers) code-switch between Arabic and Persian (Tajik) as they teach the letters, words, meanings, pronunciation of the Quran, its memorization and the pillars of religion (*arkoni din*). As the students move from the family *hujra*s to the extended ones, the texts and expectations become more advanced: The *shogird*s (students, *murid*s) studied intermediate Arabic grammar books *Qo'idai Baghdodi*, *Qofiya*, *Sharhi Mullo*, as well as learning the lines from the poetry of Bedil, Hofiz, Saadi and so on. At a more advanced level, students are exposed to *shari'a* and *fiqh* (i.e. the whys of Islamic behaviour and thought). With the advent of global discourse, these texts include readings from local and foreign Islamic and other sources (Aksakolov, 2014).

Within the family *hujra* co-education is possible, while the extended *hujra*s are multigrade, but gender-separate. Students sit on the ground in rows or circles. The *Domullo* would ask them about the previous homework and questions, and correct them and move forward to new texts. Depending on the teacher, the students may ask different kinds of questions: some teachers allow critical questions, while others reprimand students who ask such questions. The relationship between student and teacher and the whole system is religiously defined and hierarchical: there is a top-down hierarchy of knowledge, with religious knowledge, especially of the Quran, at the top, and the teacher as the central authority; subordination and respect, as well confidentiality and devotion to teacher are a must; there are strict roles, rules and defined spaces. Informal and flexible in nature, the *Domullo* could promote a Hanafi perspective, a Salafi or even a Wahhabi perspective or provide a comparative mixture of all these; or he may tell the students about the Shi'a-Sunni differences, if needed. In sum, formal Islamic education is limited, highly controlled, and tailored to the state's interest and legitimacy, and it promotes a localized ethno-religious identity. Informal education falls short of presenting the whole spectrum of Islamic education in the country.

Informal Islamic Education and Socialization

Due to the limited scope of formal Islamic education and the proliferation of various Islamic discourses, informal Islamic education has continued its existence. The 25 years of independence witnessed both the rapid expansion of informal Islamic education, as well as its contraction, especially in the last five years. Debates between the so-called Wahhabis – with strict Islamic rules coming from the south, the Persian Gulf and the followers of the traditional Central Asian Hanafi interpretation, which also includes Sufi groups – have raged about the Islamicity of every aspect of people's lives, starting with traditional marriage, and including dress code, head cover (e.g. green cap vs. white cap; black, fully covering vs. colourful, not fully covering headscarves) and rites of passage, as well as local customs and traditions (e.g. *pir*s, *sayyid*s and *eshon*s as intercessors between the followers and Allah; taking amulets and blessings from them; visiting shrines, revering trees, stones and other items) that had already flourished during the last years of the Soviet Union, but that have become further contested.

Private religious instruction spaces such as the *hujrai khonawodagi* (family private classroom) and the extended *hujra* (an informal school at the level of few villages, districts, and even an entire province) have quickly surfaced. These classes (*sabaq*) were led by persons (male or female), often the descendants of religious clerics, and occasionally graduates of the eastern philology departments, who had managed to travel to Muslim countries. In the post-Soviet era, hundreds of Tajik youth left for South Asia, the Middle East and North Africa and studied at their universities and madrasas. Upon return, many of them became religious teachers and mosque leaders. These brought different, activist and subversive notions of Islam, which challenged the existing religious, cultural and political status quo. Concerned about possible frictions in society, Tajik authorities have sent many of them back home (Abramson, 2010).

The rise of informal Islamic education is also reflected in the increase in the number of mosques with attached *hujra*s in the country. Mosques grew in number from 17 to over 2500 in the post-Soviet period, out of which there were 262 Friday Mosques (*masjidi jome'*). Mosques constitute the backbone of Islamic education and promote a comprehensive approach to Islamic socialization of their attendants/members. In addition to prayers, mosques serve as key socialization and mobilization spaces for the community. They try to present a space that offers a different milieu. The sermons (*amri ma'ruf*) in the mosque call the faithful to know, learn and follow their perceived Islamic canons and principles. Until 2010, the preachers used to be relatively free in delivering their sermons. At times, exclusivist sermons against women, Shi'as, the secular state, the West and/or the status quo would be heard in these mosques. These led to the state authorities checking on and taking control of the mosques and attesting mullahs' and *imamkhatib*s' knowledge and perspectives. The process led to the closure of many mosques, the rationalizing of others, and the laying off a great number of mosque clerics. Predominantly, however, the mosques and community leaders have been cautious in their teaching, preaching and other tasks. Their lessons and sermons serve the purposes of instilling the importance of good morals and manners, respect, modest dress, halal food and family values, and providing opportunities for negotiating one's identity, realizing ambitions, and achieving socialization into the morally infused social order and traditions, which were perceived to be lacking in the secular society and schools (Stephan, 2010).

Globalization and the Internet have been playing an unprecedented role in informally educating and Islamizing Tajik society. First, they have opened venues for the various local and global perspectives. The government has its own websites.[4] The oppositional Hizbi Nahzat (banned in Tajikistan since 2015) operates from its bases abroad. Independent preachers such as Hoji Mirzo, Eshon Nuruddin and others have recorded multiple CDs, DVDs and other media tools. Tajiks also listen to the media outlets from Iran, Afghanistan and Russia. The Saudi Arabian news outlet Al-Arabia also operates in Persian. Radical groups, such as *Salafia*, *Ansar ul-Allah*, *Hizbi Tahrir*, *Jamaat ul-Tabligh*, Islamic State and al-Qaeda, have also started preaching in Persian for the Persian-speaking populations around the world. Given that millions of Tajiks live and work in Russia, they are exposed to a variety of Islamic discourses within Russia itself, and some of them differ from the Tajik official Islamic discourses.

As a result of this proliferation and diversification, Tajik Muslims have been overwhelmed not only with information/knowledge about various concepts, tenets and rules of Islam, but with the contradictions and confusions that these various perspectives have created. Given any possible accusations, the majority of Tajik Muslims today, as in the Soviet time, are once again learning to be careful and are sifting through the multiple viewpoints on every Islamic item, learning when and where to utter which perspective and view point. The key question is whether Islamic and secular education are preparing them for engaging with this competing diversity and for making informed decisions that critically engage their minds, feelings and souls. A key concern in official circles has been the fact that many Tajik youth are attracted to the radical Islamic discourse of ISIS and the Islamic Movement of Uzbekistan.

Overall, the state and society in Tajikistan are facing an overwhelming tide of Islamization of the society. Openly standing against Islam is not just out of fashion, but also too costly socially and physically. Unlike the Soviet and early post-Soviet times, for today's Tajik leaders, scholars and laymen, the key question is not about whether Islam should be there, but what kind of Islam it should be, what dose of Islamization is enough for society to remain secular, democratic and pluralistic and a Tajik national state? Can a new Tajik society maintain the rich pre-Islamic, the Soviet, the post-Soviet ideas, practices and value systems? Can it be secular and nationalistic and Islamic at the same time? The Tajik state is increasingly realizing the existential challenges that Islamization may create for this syncretic endeavour and has developed a multi-pronged strategy to contain the level and pace of Islamization.

Reflecting on the role of informal Islamic education in the civil conflict of the early 1990s, as well as on the current global events around Islam and Muslims, Tajik authorities and society understand that Islam and Islamic education cannot be taken for granted, but needs to be watched and, if possible, to be controlled. This awareness is similar to that in the West and in the Arab Islamic world and even in Russia (see chapter 15, by Elena Lisovskaya, in this volume).

The Tajik state apparatus is actively regulating and tailoring Islamic education to ensure social cohesion, stability and transformative reproduction. Regulatory policies and laws have been adopted to reduce the role of Islam in cultural and political senses. These include a law on the freedom of conscience and religious organizations (adopted in 2009); a law of 2011 regulating traditions, festivals and rituals; a law on parents' responsibility over the education and upbringing of their children (2011); and a law on education (2004). These regulations have led to the careful selection, appointment and attestation of Muslim clerics, including mosque imams, to ensure conformity with the state's secular ethos. More than 1500 unregistered mosques and many unregistered schools were closed or transformed into cultural centres, social centres or fitness clubs between years 2010 and 2015. The state has been vigorously promoting Hanafi Islam as the true face of Islam and guards it from Salafi, Wahhabi Sunni as well as possible Shi'a and Turkic influences. Gülen's schools in Tajikistan were transformed long before the recent controversy around them elsewhere. Contrary to the current Turkish state accusations of Gülen, the Tajik authorities had suspected these schools to be promoting Turkic Islam – that is, an Islam that promoted Turkic nationalism and Ottomanism.

Two schools of thoughts (*mazhab*s) are officially allowed in Tajikistan: Hanafi Sunni and Ismaili Shi'a. These are considered indigenous and representing tolerant and peaceful Islam. To connect Hanafi Sunnism with Tajik nationalism, the Tajik-Persian origin of its founder Abu Hanifa and of other early Muslim thinkers (e.g. Bukhari, Tirmizi, Ghazali, Ibn Sina, Farabi) is highlighted. In October 2009, the Tajik government organized an international symposium on *The Heritage of Abu Hanifa* and its importance in the dialogue of civilizations in Dushanbe. Over 300 Islamic scholars from around the world visited the Tajik capital to generate dialogue among the cultures and civilizations which are grounded in Islamic tradition. Numerous publications by well-known scholars in Tajikistan such as Turajonzoda (2007), Himmatzoda (2009), and Muhaqqiq (2015) highlight the strengths of the Hanafi Islam and the need to promote and defend it. In 2010 Tajikistan hosted the Organisation of the Islamic Conference sessions. The country's president, Emomali Rahmon, spoke against the misuse of Islam toward political ends, claiming that terrorists have no nation, no country and no religion and that using the name 'Islamic terrorism' only discredits the pure and harmless religion of Islam.

Students who have been studying Islam at universities in foreign countries have been called back. According to Abramson (2010), in 2009 there were 500-1000 Tajik students studying Islam in Egypt, 350-700 in Saudi Arabia, 200+ in Iran and 300 in Pakistan. Audio and video cassettes produced by those preaching religious intolerance, gender inequity and antigovernment sentiment are confiscated and penalties imposed. Parties such as Hizb al-Tahrir and various movements such as al-Qaeda and ISIS are viewed as extremist and banned. In secular schools, teachers are not allowed to preach about Islam or grow long untrimmed beards; girls are not allowed to wear hijab and niqab. Tajik authorities, supported by the Mufti, *Shuroi Ulamo* (Council of Ulama), *Kumitai Din* (Religious Committee) and other state-led organizations, have created alternative Islamic national dress code, beard style and headscarf. School-age children are not allowed to attend mosques so as to not fall under the influence of radical Islamic messages. State employees are forbidden to attend mosques during work time, including Friday congregational prayers. Mosque imams have been tested for knowledge of basics of Islam. In-service courses are offered to the *imam-khatib*s on various topics, not only theological but also religious-political, such as fundamentalism, extremism, caliphate, secularism and religious values, local traditions and Islam (e.g. Nawruz and Islam, Islam and nation state). In addition to their daily duties, Tajik *imam-khatib*s are expected to defend Nawruz, the nation-state and other festivals as compatible with Islamic values.

There is surveillance of social media and mosques for signs of Islamic extremism. Imams and religious teachers are trained in identifying and fighting against Islamic extremism. Tajik authorities are learning from their experiences (such as that of 1992) and borrowing from global practices (e.g. banning school-age children has long been practiced in China and Turkey; radical Islamic parties and organizations are banned almost everywhere; hijab is banned in schools in France and parts of Canada; niqab is being banned more and more across the world, including in Islamic countries; 'illegal' mosques and schools are closed in Pakistan, Egypt and elsewhere) (Doumato & Starrett, 2006). With the recent ban and removal of the Islamic Renaissance Party (IRTP) of Tajikistan from the political and religious scene, the Council for Religious Affairs (*Kumita oid ba Korhoi Din*), the Council of Ulama (*Shuroi Ulamo*) and other state-based think tanks such as the Islamic Center under the President's Office have assumed full control of the religious situation.

The fact that the state and society are actively engaged with Islam and Islamic education implies that Islamic education cannot be taken for granted. Whether such engagements and state actions mentioned above are productive and sustainable is currently under debate, especially in international scholarship on Central Asia. Some claim that such heavyhanded measures may lead to the revival of clandestine religious education and religious radicalism (Saroyan, 1997; Zelkina, 1999; Sodiqov, 2011). A few anthropological studies have challenged the linking of Islam to the security problems that the nation-states face in Central Asia (Turajonzoda, 2007; Himmatzoda, 2009).

Islam in Higher Education

Two interlinked forms Islamic tertiary-level education are worthy of consideration: (i) Islamic higher education; and (ii) Islam as a subject of study at secular higher education institutions.

Islamic Higher Education

The early post-Soviet period saw a steady outflow of Tajik youth attending higher Islamic education (such as Sunni madrasas and Shi'a hawziyas) abroad. Inside, Islamic higher education was still obtained at the madrasas in Samarqand and Bukhara. As Tajik-Uzbek relations became strained and the returning youth brought in an anti-establishment Islamic discourse, Tajik authorities established local higher education institutions across the country. In 2007, an official state Islamic Institute was established in Dushanbe, which replaced the Imam Tirmizi Islamic University, founded in 1991 but officially inaugurated in 1997. It works in close collaboration with the Religious Affairs Committee and the President's Islamic Center. Until 2007, the institute had two departments: *Usuli Din* (Religious Foundations), and *Shari'at*. Since 2008, the institute has been offering new specialties, such as Quranic Sciences; Arabic Philology, History of Islam, *Fiqh* and Islamic Philosophy, Islamic Studies, and Translation. In addition, the students are exposed to studying Tajik history, Tajik, Russian and English languages. Those studying, philology and translation also take courses in history, economy, geography, politics and international relations of Arabic and Muslim countries. The institute produces a journal of *Ma'rifati Islom* (Islamic Enlightenment) in Tajik and Arabic. To promote the policy and research capacity and impact, the Institute has also opened an analytical section of societal analysis and relationships and a Center for Scientific and Research Activities. The Institute reports to the Government's Committee on Religious Affairs (not to the Education Ministry). In 2008, the institute was renamed after Imam Abu Hanifa. The institute currently has around 1500 students and offers bachelor's degree courses (four years), master's (two years) and PhD (three years).

A typical class at the Islamic institute is teacher centered, but has strong question and answer as well as discussion elements: A teacher of the course on *Tahorat* (Cleanliness) at the Department of *Fiqh* and *Shari'a*, teaching the topic of *ghusl* (washing one's body before the prayer or on other occasions), would start with a Quranic verse or a hadith sentence on the item. Next the verse/sentence would be translated and sentenced word by word, with each word explained. Following this, the whole verse/sentence's essence, importance and context are explained. After this, the students are asked to read and repeat the sentence, and explain its meaning and value. A question and-answer session would come next, in order to remove any misconceptions. Lastly, students are asked by the instructor to make sure they understood the concept of *ghusl* and its application in various contexts.

Similarly, in the course on hadith, hadiths are divided according to categories and themes, according to the curriculum that is approved by the Center of Islamic Studies, the Committee of Religious Affairs and the Ministry of Education. Similar to the above, a *hadith* will be recited by the instructor (let's say *Innama al-a'malu bin-niyat* [Indeed, actions are defined by their intentions]. The teacher reads and then asks students to read the sentence. Then the instructor explains the meaning, word by word and of the whole sentence; explains whether the hadith is strong or weak, is of a Makah or Medina origin, the *isnad* (chain) of the hadith, and the collector of the hadiths. Then the hadith is expected to be memorized. Once done, the instructor moves to the next hadith. Overall, the students are expected to have up to 10 hadiths on every topic memorized and understood for further teaching and explanations.[5]

An Islamic gymnasium (secondary school) was opened under the institute in 2009. There the enrolled students studied both secular and Islamic subjects such as an overview of the Quran, prophetic hadith, history of Islam and Arabic language. Since June 2016, however, the gymnasium has been temporarily semi-closed due to lack of quality teachers and material – and also a lack of classrooms and students' dormitories. The Islamic Institute also shares these challenges. While most of the students are financially sustained by the state, there is an increasing number who pay for their study at these institutions. Overall, four key aspects of the Islamic institute and gymnasium differ from the secular higher education institutions: (i) strict observance of *shari'a* norms and Islamic ethos; (ii) promotion of Sunni-Hanafi Islam; (iii) gender separation; and (iv) curriculum that has both Islamic subjects and secular ones.

Islamic Studies in Secular Higher Education

As a continuation from the Soviet era, Islam is visibly present at the higher education level. More than 80% of scholarly studies in the social science departments at Tajik universities explore historical and contemporary Islamic issues (interview, June 2013). Studies in ethno-pedagogy such as those by Hafizova, Lutfulloev and Sulaimoni and curricular materials in humanities produced by the Aga Khan Humanities Project (Sulaimoni, 2008; Lutfulloev & Sulaimoni, 2009; Aga Khan Humanities Project [6]) make many references to the pedagogical-humanistic-ethical ideas and practices that have existed in Tajik history, which need critical appropriation for twenty-first century Tajikistan. Academic discussions of Islam are characterized by more or less open and critical approaches to Islam and Islamic education. Historical-comparative methods of analyses with eclectic theoretical frameworks are employed to guide the local studies. Atheistic or openly critical approaches to the study of Islam are not in favour in Tajik academia and society today.[7]

Many scholars have abandoned the Marxist-Leninist approaches in favour of classical positivist or critical humanist approaches.[8] For example, the 2016 social sciences, humanities and education issue of the journal of the Tajik National University (*Vestnik*)[9] has 12 out of its 73 articles directly referring to Islamic subjects and themes. During the 2013 Sociology of Education course in Dushanbe, I noticed a critical approach to discussing Islam and Islamic education by its participants, the majority of whom came from university settings. Thirty participants' passionate discussions revealed sophisticated knowledge and concern about the need to defend Hanafi-tolerant Islam, de-link Islam from terrorism, see the state and Islam as partners, and highlight the humanist dimensions of central Asian Islam. The participants spoke about how Islam has been used by the global powers for utilitarian purposes; some considered the conflicts in the Muslim world as a global conspiracy; some warned against the instigation of Sunni-Shi'a conflict in Tajikistan; some separated Ismaili Shi'as (as an indigenous form of Islam) from the Twelver Shi'as (which they considered an Iranian import); some critiqued some local preachers (via their CDs and DVDs) as misogynist, sectarian and unhelpful and considered black female clothes as non-Tajik Muslim dress. While many supported the government's strict regulations on Islam, a few carefully examined it, doubting the efficacy of the state's approach, as they referred to the failure of the Soviet system. High-level conferences are held on Islam in Tajikistan, while Tajik scholars, whenever affordable, take fellowships and attend conferences on Islam and Islamic education globally.

Islamic Education in the School System

Post-Soviet Islamic education also permeated the secular school system. As part of local culture, identity and tradition, Islamic literature is brought to schools; specific subjects such as *Ma'rfati Islom* (Understanding Islam, Grade 9) and *Ta'rikhi Din* (History of Religion, Grade 10) have been brought in and out of the school system. *Ta'rikhi Din*, a new subject, has emerged a result of the argument that religious illiteracy causes extremism, including the Tajik youth joining groups such as al-Qaeda and Daish (ISIS) (Muhaqqiq, 2015) *Ma'rfati Islom* focuses on Islam, while *Ta'rikhi Din* takes a comparative approach similar to the western textbooks on religion.[10] These textbooks also take what is called an academic, neutral position toward religions, emphasizing the good nature of all religions, delinking religion from terrorism. In addition to these directly connected subjects, books on history and literature and the Book of Manners (*Odobnoma*) are filled with religious, especially Islamic, content. For example *Odobnoma*, a textbook for grades 3-4, explains that *adab* (ethics) is like a crown from God's light that, if you put on, will save you anywhere you go (p. 3); it also relates the story of the prophet Yusuf (Joseph; p. 15); tells of the the perils of soul (*nafs*) and Satan (*Shaitan*) (p. 69); describes how Ibn Sina learnt the Quran at the age of 10

(p. 111); narrates how Sultan Mahmud Ghaznawid changed his intention to punish his teacher into rewarding him (p. 118); tells how Sadruddin Aini studied at the old pre-Soviet madrasa (p. 119); and recounts the sayings of the Prophet Muhammad on the need to care for animals and manage one's anger (p. 132).

Overall, social science subjects such as literature, language, history and geography quote events, names, verses, stories, proverbs and other items related to Islam. Notably, the post-Soviet teachers' initial active use of Islam in their teaching and moralizing has been tempered by state intervention: teachers are primarily creators of a nation-state that is secular. Teachers stress nationalism, and refer to Islamic themes to promote tolerance, good behaviour, patriotism and the Tajik language. This contrasts with the early post-Soviet era, when many secular teachers became mullahs and imams of the mosques and their villages.

Islamic Education among the Ismailis of Tajikistan

In the Post-Soviet era, the Shi'a Ismaili interpretation is considered as legitimate indigenous *mazhab* by state policies (Rahmonzoda et al, 2016). As a result, Tajik Ismailis, similar to the way they did in the Soviet time, enjoy a certain degree of freedom and safety. Notably, however, the Ismailis have been an integral part of Tajikistan's history across the ages. Many Tajik prominent luminaries such as Abu Abdullah Rudaki (858-943), Ibn Sina (980-1037) and Nasir Khusraw (1004-1077) had a close affinity with the Ismaili view of Islam. After the fall of the Samanid dynasty (819-999 CE), the Turkic dynasties fervently persecuted the Shi'as and diminished the Ismaili influence. With the Mongols' destruction of the Ismaili strongholds in Iran, and the post sixteenth-century Sunni–Shi'a conflicts, the Ismailis went into survival mode, taking refuge in the mountains of Pamir and Karakoram, using *taqiya* and other forms of coping to maintain their identity. The Russian takeover of Eastern Bukhara (current Tajikistan) saved the Ismailis from the centuries-long conditions of survival and near-disappearance created by the Afghan Pushtun and Bukhara Manghit emirs. The Russo-British delimitation, however, also cut the Ismaili population of the Pamir and Karakoram into four countries (Tajikistan, Afghanistan, Pakistan and China).

During the Russo-British rivalry over Central Asia, Ismailis were divided into rusophiles and anglophiles. (Kharyukov, 1995) The majority of the Tajik Ismailis, including its religious leadership, joined and worked for the Tsarist Empire (1887-1917), the socialist Soviet Union (1917-1992) and the independent Tajik State (1992-present).

Currently, the Tajik Ismailis constitute around 4-5% of the country's rapidly growing population, and are concentrated in Badakhshan, Dushanbe, the southern districts of Jilikul and Qumsangir, and the northern cities of Chkalovsk and Khujand. Since 1992, the Tajik Ismailis have also migrated to

Russia, Canada, the United Kingdom and the USA, maintaining a close relationship with Tajikistan as their ancestral homeland. Today, Tajik Ismailis are connected to the strong Ismaili global community, whose contribution exceeds its small size.

Prior to 1992, the religious education of the Ismaili children at the primary level was similar to that of the rest of Tajikistan's Sunni population. The Ismaili child studied at home, from a *Pir, Khalifa* or *Okhon* (i.e. a religious teacher). The curriculum included the above-mentioned *Haftyak, Chor Kitob,* learning Arabic, *sarf wa nahw* (morphology and syntax), Persian, the Quran, *Hafiz, Bedil, Adab* and calligraphy in an integrated, co-educated and multi-graded manner. At secondary age (from 13-14 onward), however, the Ismaili curriculum would change into studying and emphasizing the Ismaili and general Shi'a texts, such as legal interpretation through *Wajhi Din* and the poetry of Nasir Khusraw, *Hafiz,* and other texts such as *Haft Bob* of Hasan Mahmud Katib (thirteenth century CE), the Rumi's *mathnawi* and Sanai's poetry (Elnazarov & Aksakolov, 2011). Gradually the Ismaili children would also be exposed to comparative theology, learning the differences between the Sunni and Shi'a approaches, such as the *zahir* (external, literal meaning) and *batin* (internal, allegoric meaning) of the Islamic tenets (e.g. prayer, fasting, *hajj, zakat*), as well as concepts of Imamah, Ahl-al Bait and the sayings of the imams, especially the 48th Imam Sultan Muhammad Shah, who resided in Bombay, British India. Texts and verses that praised the Prophet's immediate family, Imam Ali, subsequent Shi'a imams (including Twelver Shi'a imams) and heroes would be delineated to promote the differences, uniqueness, pride and also the legitimacy of the Shias and their imams' rule. Stories about the fights of Imam Ali and his uncle Hamza, and of Imam Hussain's martyrdom (*shahodat*) would be recited during various religious ceremonies.

As in the Sunni circles, formal education was accessible only to the Ismaili elite. It is the informal Ismaili education that played a critical role in the community socialization into the Shi'i (Panjtani) faith and its survival in the pre-Soviet time and during the Soviet time: *Charogh-rawshan* (Luminous Light), *maddoh-khoni* (devotional singing accompanied by musical instruments), visitations of the *oston*s and *mazor*s (shrines and sacred places), rites of passage (marriage, circumcision, burial), Nawruz (New Year) and other ceremonies helped the faith transmit from one generation to the next. Similar to their fellow Sunnis, Ismaili religious leaders also underwent repression, co-optation, negation and resistance during the Soviet years of continuity and change.

Since 1992, a key event in the life of the Ismailis of Tajikistan was the personal connection with the Imam of the Time, Shah Karim al-Hussaini, Aga Khan IV, and his vast global network. The Aga Khan Development Network, one of the most powerful development agencies in the world, provided a seven-year relief program (1993-2000) that saved not only the Ismailis, but also their Sunni neighbours in the Badakhshan and Rasht regions from hunger, cold and other calamities. From 1995, the network shifted to development activities. One of the network affiliates, the Londonbased Institute of Ismaili Studies (IIS), established offices of the Ismaili Tariqa and Religious Education Committee (ITREC), which took charge of reforming and establishing modern Ismaili education called *Ta'lim*.[11] *Ta'lim* is based on modern education principles as well as on civilizational and inclusive approaches, situating Islam in the context of history and society, and emphasizing the inevitable theological diversity. The institute's approach was in strong contrast to the existing traditional religious education, in both Ismaili and Sunni circles, as described above. *Ta'lim* adopted the best western thoughts and practices to learning and teaching (e.g. child-centered pedagogy) in the preparation of the curriculum and teacher training. The London-based institute has also produced centralized curricular materials for primary years (Grade 1 to 6) and is in the process of developing secondary *Ta'lim* textbooks, which include illustrated high-quality texts, activity books and teacher guides about the basics of Islam. These materials are translated into Tajik, followed by teacher training on their use by the ITREB (since 2014 the ITREC has been transformed into the Ismaili Tariqa and Religious Education Board [ITREB]). Ismaili Tajik teachers from the secular schools are involved in the teaching of the children on a voluntary basis.

In Badakhshan, the teaching of religious education is called *Akhloq wa Ma'rifat* (Ethics and Knowledge).[12] It has been held in the secular schools as an extra-curricular hour. Outside Badakhshan, the courses are offered at community centers (such as the Noor Cultural Center in Moscow), and the recently opened Ismaili Center in Dushanbe. The IIS has realized that quality teaching needs high-quality teachers. To that end, teacher education has been pursuing a professionalization path, offering a one-year professional course to primary teachers and a two-year double master's degree to secondary teachers. These programmes are centralized and offered by the Institute of Ismaili Studies, involving Ismaili and non-Ismaili scholars and educators. The initial preparation is followed by various follow-up workshops and seminars on Islam and education to equip teachers with updated knowledge and best practices. More recently, the Institute has established early childhood religious education centers which embrace the whole spectrum of K-12 religious education of the community. The education of the children, particularly at the early childhood education and development (ECED) and primary level, involves parents and volunteers, while secondary education has since 2010 moved toward recruiting professionally prepared and paid teachers.

The primary curriculum provides basic knowledge about the history of Islam, the history of the Prophets, the Prophet Muhammad, his family (*Ahl al-Bait*) and the Shi'a imams, and an introduction to Muslim countries and societies. The emphasis is on the ethical principles of Islam and how they reveal themselves in the life of the prophet and his progeny. Islam is presented not just through a theological lens, but as a civilization which contains more than religious precepts. The contributions of Islamic intellectuals and Islamic architecture, arts, science and music to the development of human knowledge are given primary attention in the educational materials. Political dimensions of Islam, as well as controversial topics, are either avoided or addressed in a soft, non-confrontational way. Thus, the Ismaili religious education is different from the general Islamic education in Tajikistan in terms of its content, focus and the employment of various teaching and learning methods. The designing of the *Akhloq* and *Ma'rifat* employs innovative methods of teaching which seem to inform the teaching methods of the secular school teachers.

The ITREC (since 2014, the ITREB) looks after both formal and informal religious education. In addition to the above *Ta'lim* curriculum, these institutes also work with youth and adults of the community. They regulate religious practices, making modifications to *maddo, Charogh-i rawshan*, prayers and so on. Unlike the Sunni faithful's contestation of Nawruz, the Ismaili community has incorporated it as part of religious history. Similarly, *Charogh-i rawshan*, disputed elsewhere as pre-Islamic [13], is now considered as an Islamic practice (Khan, 2013).

Some of the changes brought in during the encounter between traditional and modern and local and global approaches to Ismaili practices have resulted in tensions in the Tajik community, but ultimately the unity of the community and its modernization have prevailed. The ITREB office also reads the *farman*s and guidance that come from the Imam and his office in Aiglemont, France; it also organizes group readings, recitation competitions, youth camps, Olympic games and other activities to ensure the transmission of the standardized Ismaili practices within the Tajik community. The Ismaili community is viewed as a moderate cooperating community by the Tajik authorities, as well as by traditional Hanafi scholars, and their religious education has not been as strictly monitored as that of the Sunni community. More recently the state has, however, attested the local *khalifa*s in their knowledge and the ITREB is required to coordinate their activities with the state offices across the country.

Conclusions: implications for policy and practice of Islamic education in twenty-first-century Tajikistan

Integral to Tajik society and history, Islam and Islamic education constitute key elements of ethnic and cultural identity. They promote an alternative discourse and approach to the societal issues and development in what is still a secular and nationalism-driven society. In the Post-Soviet era, Islamic education is occurring in its formal and informal, academic and popular forms. In all its forms, the education of Muslims, whether secular or religious, has remained a contested practice, fought over between various approaches to Islam and various groups: the 'secular' state, traditional Hanafi *mazhab*, the Ismaili interpretation, the *Hizbi Nahzat*, *Hizb-al-Tahrir* [14], and other Salafi and Wahhabi groups which bring in Islamization discourses. Notably, the central locus of Islamic education has been the informal type, for it caters to the majority, occurs in numerous forms, is flexible, affordable, tacit and elusive and serves as an alternative/oppositional discourse that is difficult to control. The state, via learning from its own and international experiences, tries to tailor Islam and Islamic education toward the Hanafi version, which is presented as tolerant, dialogue-oriented and status-quo friendly. Islamization and Tajikization (which, in addition to the Hanafi-Islam also includes pre-Islamic and Soviet-Russian cultural traditions) are two key inter-connected trends in the Tajikistan ideological landscape. The relationship is contradictory and confusing, as it is affected by local secularist and nationalist sentiments as well as by global pressures around human rights and financial incentives from the Middle East and the West. Time will show whether Tajikization (nationalist) or Islamization will take over or whether the two will harmoniously synthesize into a new model. With the growing population, the search for identity, and the shortcomings of the state-led approaches, the demand for Islamic education will increase. At the same time, the civil war of 1992-1997 and current international events suggest that Islam is vulnerable to misuse: Islamic education is a social construct that can contribute to social cohesion, tolerance and development; but it can also be used to promote discontent, destruction and intolerance (Kadi, 2006; Hefner & Zaman, 2007).

To avoid Islam is not possible and to repress it is not workable, as the experience of the Soviet Union, Turkey and the Iranian monarchy have revealed. Questions arise as to whether one-sided uncritical romanticization of the Hanafi Islamic discourse and one-sided demonization of the other Islamic discourses is helpful. Is it possible to sustain this approach at a time of a digitized and globalized cultural economy?

I believe that a blind romanticization of Islam may lead to the stifling of freedom and creativity, while demonizing it creates discontent and blowback (Sodiqov, 2011; Swerdlow, 2016). A more appropriate approach is to engage Islam via open and constructive critical dialogue and pluralistic pedagogy (Aydin, 2001; Kassam, 2003; Abramson, 2010; Niyozov et al, 2017). The constructive-critical approach proposes the following: first, Islamic education needs to enable the Muslims of Tajikistan to recognize the diversity of perspectives within and outside of Islam, the globality of today's reality, the need to accept and engage conflicting perspectives and difficult knowledges through critical appreciation; second, it should enable Tajik Muslim clerics, students, leaders and laymen to appreciate Tajikistan's ancient history, its pre-Islamic and Soviet-era achievements and identity features that can be incorporated into its curriculum and pedagogy. Third, the constructive critical pedagogy of Islamic education should make the nuanced and critical understanding of Islam and society accessible to ordinary Muslims. The recent move to re-introduce comparative religious education in Tajik public schools, along with the pluralist pedagogy of the Ismaili *Ta'lim*, already in place, constitutes a hopeful direction forward. A similar constructive critical engagement should be about other forms of Islamic education, both informal and academic, and the university-based. It suggests that no Islamic subjects, including Islamic education, should be outside critical analysis. Furthermore, tailoring Islam needs to be related to caring for the economic and material concerns of people's lives in Tajikistan. Such a multi-dimensional constructive critical approach, I believe, will undoubtedly contribute to the Sustainable Development Goals (SDGs) in Tajikistan and Central Asia, providing cohesion, including diversity, and ensuring quality and access.

Notes

[1] http://islamnews.tj/taj/tajikistan.html

[2] Throughout this text, we will be using both the commonly accepted transliteration of the Islamic terms as well as their Tajik version, such as *Islom, mullo, imom, zakot* etc.

[3] In June 2015, the gymnasium was announced to be closed. Even until now (i.e. 2017), it is temporarily closed. According to the official explanation, this happened because of unresolved issues around the land and its hostel. There is a plan to build a new building for the gymnasium with a hostel (see Asia Plus 15/06/2015: Islamic Institute rector denies information about the closure of Islamic high school as 'baseless'. Available at: http://www.news.tj/en/news).

[4] http://www.islamnews.tj; http://www.mit.tj/; and http://shuroiulamo.tj/tj

[5] Interview, June 2013.

[6] http://www.akdn.org/uca_humanities.asp

[7] One such study, presumably carried out by a group of scholars led by the philosopher Komil Bekzoda, has quickly disappeared from the shelves.

[8] This is obvious if one compares leading philosopher Khayolbek Dodikhudoev's Soviet tome *Philosophy of Peasants' Rebellion* (1984) with his *Philosophical Ismailism* (2014, both in Russian).

[9] http://vestnik-g.tnu.tj/vestnik/2016/vestnik2016_3_7.pdf

[10] These textbooks are authored by social science and humanities scholars from the Academy of Sciences. Turajonzoda (2007) reacted, suggesting that textbooks on Islam should be written by Islamic scholars, not philosophers and secular academics.

[11] While *Ta'lim* implies teaching, in the Ismaili interpretation this teaching is initiated, conceptualized, endorsed and supported by the Imam of the Time. 'Imam of the Time' is a Shi'a theological concept suggesting the eternal necessity of the guide and intercessor for the faithful after the death of the Prophet Muhammad, who is also considered as God's last prophet (see Madelung, 2014).

[12] *Ma'rifat* is considered a more inclusive, higher-level and nobler form of knowledge than a subject-based form.

[13] For debates on the origin, meaning and context of the practice, see Niyozov & Nazariev (2005), pp. 605-611, 656-670.

[14] *Hizbi Nazhzati Islom* (Party of the Revival of Islam) is an indigenous religio-political organization which received the status of a legally functioning party as a result of the inter-Tajik peace and reconciliation treaty in 1997. It participated in the work of parliament, and has its written media. The party has had a serious influence on the development of Islamic education in the post-Soviet period. *Hizb al-Tahrir*, on the other hand, is a global Islamist party/discourse that proposes global Islamic solidarity and *khilafat* (Islamic empire). This party is forbidden in Tajikistan and other Central Asian countries. Its impact on education is restricted to clandestine lessons.

References

Abramson, D. (2010) *Foreign Religious Education and the Central Asian Islamic Revival: impact and prospects for stability.* Washington, DC: Central Asia-Caucasus Institute & Silk Road Studies Program. http://www.silkroadstudies.org/resources/pdf/SilkRoadPapers/2010_03_SRP_Abr amson_Central-Asia-Islam.pdf\

Aga Khan Humanities Project. http://www.akdn.org/uca_humanities.asp (in Tajik).

Aksakolov, S. (2014) Islam in Soviet Tajikistan: state policy, religious figures and the practice of religion (1950-1985), PhD thesis, SOAS, University of London.

Aydin, M. (2001) Religious Pluralism and Islam: a challenge for Muslim – a theological evaluation, *Journal of Ecumenical Studies*, 38(2-3), 330-352.

Bertels, A. (1959) *Nasir Khusraw and Ismailism.* Moscow: Prosveshenie (in Russian).

Boronov, B. (2003) *Book of Ethics: a textbook for grades 3-4.* Dushanbe: Sarparast Publishing.

Dodikhudoev, K. (1984) *Philosophy of Peasants' Rebellion.* Dushanbe: Maorif Publsihing House.

Dodikhudoev, K. (2014) *Philosophical Ismailism.* Dushanbe: Irfon Publishing House (in Russian).

Douglass, S. & Shaikh, M. (2004) Islamic Education: differentiation and application, *Current Issues in Comparative Education*, 7(1), 5-18.

Doumato, E.A. & Starrett, G. (Eds.) (2006) *Teaching Islam: textbooks and religion in the Middle East*, pp. 103-124. Boulder, CO: Lynn Rienner Publishers.

Elnazarov, H. & Aksakolov, S. (2011) The Nizari Ismailis of Central Asia in Modern Time, in F. Daftary & G. Miskinzod (Eds) *A Modern History of the Ismailis: continuity and change in a Muslim community*, pp. 45-76. Ismaili Heritage Series. London: I.B. Tauris.

Hefner, R. & Zaman, M. (2007) *Schooling Islam: the culture and politics of modern Muslim education.* Princeton, NJ: Princeton University Press.

Himmatzoda, M. (2009) *Life and Legacy of Imam Abu Hanifa.* Dushanbe: Dewashtij Publishing (in Tajik).

Kadi, W. (2006) Education in Islam – Myths and Truths, *Comparative Education Review*, 50(3), 311-324.

Kassam, T. (2003) Teaching Religion in the Twenty-first Century, in B. Wheeler (Ed.) *Teaching Islam*, pp. 191-215. New York: Oxford University Press.

Keller, S. (2001) *To Moscow, Not Mecca: the Soviet campaign against Islam in Central Asia, 1917-1941*. Westport, CT: Praeger.

Kemper, M., Motika, R. & Reichmuth, S. (2009) *Islamic Education in the Soviet Union and its Successor States*. London: Routledge.

Kemper, M. & Cornemann, S. (2011) (Eds) *The Heritage of Soviet Oriental Studies*. London: Routledge.

Khalid, A. (1998) *The Politics of Muslim Cultural Reform: Jadidism in Central Asia*. Berkeley, CA: University of California Press.

Khan, M. (2013) *Chiragh-i Roshan*: prophetic light in the Ismaili tradition, *Islamic Studies*, 52(3-4), 327-356.

Lutfulloev, M. & Sulaimoni, S. (2009) *Anthology of Pedagogical Thoughts of Tajik People*. Dushanbe: Matbu'ot Publishing House (in Russian).

Madelung, W. (2014) Introduction: theology, in F. Daftary & G. Miskinzod (Eds) *The study of Shi'i Islam: history, theology and law*, pp. 455-464. London: I.B. Tauris.

McGlinchey, E. (2011) *Chaos, Violence, and Dynasty: politics of Islam in Central Asia*. Pittsburgh, PA: University of Pittsburgh Press. https://doi.org/10.2307/j.ctt5vkhbq

Muhaqqiq, A. (2015) Banning Islamic Education and Mosque Attendance Have Helped Salafism to Grow, *IslamNews, Tj*, June. http://www.islamnews.tj/taj/interview/472-abdullo1203imu1203a11791179i1179-mani-talimi-islom-va-raftan-ba-mas1207id-bois-barushdi-salafiya-shud.html (in Tajik).

Niyozov, S., Elnazarov, H. & Aksakolov, S. (2017) Islamic Education in Post-SovietTajikistan: a field of contestations, in D. Ashraf, M. Tajik & S. Niyozov (Eds) *Educational Policies in Pakistan, Afghanistan and Tajikistan: contested terrain in the twenty-first century*, pp. 63-80. Lanham: Lexington Books.

Niyozov, S. & Mcmon, N. (2011) Islamic Education and Islamization: evolution of themes, continuities and new directions, *Journal of Muslim Minority Affairs*, 31(1), 5-30. https://doi.org/10.1080/13602004.2011.556886

Niyozov. S. & Nazariev, R. (Eds) (2005) *Nasir Khusraw: yesterday, today, tomorrow*. Khujand: Noshir.

Peyrose, S. (2007) Islam in Central Asia: national specificities and post-Soviet globalization, *Religion, State & Society*, 35(3), 245-260. https://doi.org/10.1080/09637490701458676

Poliakov, S. (1992) *Everyday Islam: religion and tradition in rural Central Asia*, trans. A. Olcott. New York: Sharpe.

Rahmonzoda, A., Barotzoda, F., Walizoda, O., Azizi, P. & Marambekov, M. (Eds) (2016) *The Place and Role of Islam in the Republic of Tajikistan*. Dushanbe: Irfon Publishing House (inTajik).

Rahnamo, A. (2009) *Islamic Ulama in Tajikistan*, Book 1. Dushanbe: Irfon Publishing House. (in Tajik).

Ro'i, Y. (2000) *Islam in the Soviet Union: from World War II to Perestroika*. London: C. Hurst.

Saroyan, M. (1997) *Minorities, Mullahs, and Modernity: reshaping community in the former Soviet Union*, ed. E.W. Walker. Berkeley, CA: California University Press.

Sodiqov, A. (2011) Tajik Authorities Impose Heavier Restrictions on Islamic Education, *Tajikistan Monitor*, 7 June. http://tjmonitor.wordpress.com/2011/07/18restrictions/

Stephan, M. (2010) Education, Youth and Islam: the growing popularity of private religious lessons in Dushanbe, Tajikistan, *Central Asian Survey*, 29, 454-473. https://doi.org/10.1080/02634937.2010.538283

Stern, S. (1960) The Early Ismaili Missionaries in North West Persia and in Khurasan and in Transoxiana, *Bulletin of the School of Oriental and African Studies*, 23, 56-90. https://doi.org/10.1017/S0041977X00148992

Sulaimoni, S. (2008) *Islamic Pedagogy: the system of education in Islamic Republic of Iran*. Dushanbe: Irfon.

Swerdlow, S. (2016) Tajikistan's Fight against Political Islam: how fears of terrorism stifle free speech. https://www.hrw.org/news/2016/03/15/tajikistans-fight-against political-islam

Turajonzoda, A. (2007) *Shari'a and Society*, 2nd edn. Dushanbe: Nodir Publishing House (in Tajik).

Zelkina, A. (1999) Islam and Security in the New States of Central Asia: how genuine is the Islamic threat? *Religion, State and Society*, 3-4, 355-372. https://doi.org/10.1080/096374999106548

CHAPTER 5

The Role of the Church and Religious Learning of Young Women Migrant Workers in Western China

VILMA SEEBERG, SHUJUAN LUO & YA NA

SUMMARY This chapter documents the vital role of incidental informal religious learning for young Catholic rural women seeking a new life in the city as migrant workers in Western China. The participants in this study came from the same remote village lying in the Qinling Mountains, where all residents had 'always' been Catholic for as long as anyone knew. The authors found that being surrounded with others of the same religious upbringing, participating regularly in church activities, and accepting religious moral values served to shield these young women from typical urban hazards. Thus protected from the harshest dangers faced by female migrant workers, these young women were able to cultivate and exercise agency, experience well-being and form aspirations for a better future. The authors propose that a dialogue regarding the role of religion in promoting a harmonious society be considered in China and reintegrated into mainstream development discourses in the Sustainable Development Goals (SDGs).

Introduction

In China the question of religious practice in society is not settled [1] and communities of faith feel themselves under a cloud of political suppression, subject to the whims of recurring political campaigns.[2] The families in one village in the midst of the Qinling mountain range in Western China have 'always' been Catholic, as long as anyone can remember, despite persecution and the demolition of their two-steeple church in the Cultural Revolution, and continual government crackdowns to this day.[3] The daughters of this village were raised in the Catholic faith, regularly attended church, studied in

111

the local lower schools, and around age 16 to 17 moved to a city nearby, a few to attend senior secondary school and then go on to college or, the majority, to make money and a new life in the migrant labor economy.

Despite the controversial nature of the issue, it seemed reasonable to assume that the religious upbringing experienced in the village would play a role in people's lives and, in the case of our migrant young women, in their adjustment to the uncertain urban surroundings and migrant labor jobs. In this chapter we explore their informal, incidental religious-moral learning, sometimes called socialization in the faith, and the role it played in contributing to the young migrant women's well-being. In particular, we are looking at the religious context and moral education and its interaction with identity formation, personal security, socio-economic opportunity, formal schooling, formation of agency and aspirations, and the young women's well-being as rural migrants in the fast-paced world of China's cities.

In this research, we are not concerned with the formal structures of religious education but rather with the way that religion is lived. Given the taboo on talking about the 'indoctrination' that a religious organization like the church might carry out, this research did not seek to ascertain where and how formal religious education took place. No mention was made by the Xiangcun Sisters of participating in organized catechism sessions in the church in the village nor in the city. We focus instead on the informal and incidental learning and its expression in the lives of the young migrant women challenged by the social adjustment to an urban modern life.

It is our observation after 16 years of field work that the religion in their lives, doings and being held for these villagers both intrinsic and instrumental value (field notes, 2004-16). Though the Chinese Constitution provides for religious freedom, it is limited by a vague boundary described as 'normal religious activity' (Constitution of PRC, ch. 2, article 36).[4] In practice, after the excesses of the Cultural Revolution in destroying all forms of religious practice and material facilities, the organization of religion has been questioned on the principle of loyalty to the Party and practitioners have been under duress. Hence expression of religious beliefs and practices still often remains covert (see endnotes 1-4).

To respect the position of our participants vis-à-vis religion, we needed a sensitive and secure way to allow the young women to convey their views of the importance of their religiosity in their values and practice. The participatory method often used in conjunction with the capability approach to human development (Sen, 2001) opens up this kind of inquiry. The capability approach is centered on the person and what is ultimately important to her to lead the kind of life she values (Sen, 2001). The participatory method explores how a person feels about something and judges it to be of importance (White & Pettit, 2004). The capability approach is based on the normative principle that the enhancement of freedom is the objective both of a better life that she values and of collective human development (Robeyns, 2016). Religion is one of the civic freedoms that she may be able to realize in her daily living and, hence, also an element of collective human development (Sen, 2001; Robeyns, 2016, p. 403). Though a substantial and diverse literature exists on religious forces in civil society and human development (e.g. the Global Civil Society Report 2004/5 and other works reviewed by Alkire, 2006), little has been written on its role in China and in China's migrant labor economy.

The framework of the capability approach stipulates that individual freedom, in this case to practice religion, occurs in the context of opportunities, constraints, liberties, social arrangements and facilities that meet basic survival needs. In the terminology of the capability approach, a person may have an intrinsic capability to be religious, but may be able to practice it only within contextual arrangements which may be conducive or oppressive. Sen (2001) argues that the interconnections between different capabilities, such as religion and education and how they are practiced by persons, create social change (several dimensions). Sen (2001) concludes that 'free and sustainable agency emerges as a major engine of [human] development' (p. 4). Accordingly, based on a subjective or objective aspiration, a person exercises agency that converts her intrinsic and instrumental resources into enhanced capabilities and achieved freedom – a changed state of being. Because the capability approach presupposes that constraints and opportunities are embedded in capabilities, the person identifies whether an action is taken on the basis of an imposed structural context, and whether the change constitutes enhanced freedoms or worsening deprivation. The participatory methodology attempts to capture exactly that – how a person feels about and judges a changed state. Thus, enhanced freedoms, individual and collective, describe and evaluate social justice.

In this chapter, we explore the interconnection between the young migrant women's religiosity, other capabilities, agency, aspirations and their well-being.

Methodology

The study discussed in this chapter is part of a long-term ethnographic investigation of the lives of the daughters of one set of villages in the remote Qinling mountains in Shaanxi Province. The current sample of 23 rural young women was drawn from a study population of 31 rural girls/young women known as the 'Xiangcun (village) Sisters', whose ages ranged from 16 to 24 and who were interviewed by us in 2010, 2014 and 2015. Of the 23 Xiangcun Sisters, by 2015, 22 had become migrant laborers and one was still attending an urban senior secondary school.

The interviews held all three years addressed questions regarding the Xiangcun Sisters' well-being in school and at work. We did not focus in our field research over the years on the role of religion nor in the interviews ask any single direct question about religion. We respected the request by our local contact Pang to avoid delving into the subject due to the precariousness of the political environment around organized, particularly 'western', religion, including the Catholic Church in China. What we know about religious practices of the villagers is based on stories villagers volunteered or mentioned in passing during interviews and from sixteen years of ethnographic field work in the village and surrounding area.

For this current research, we set out to focus on the role of their religion in the Xiangcun Sisters' lives. Twenty-three of the 31 Xiangcun Sisters used words related to religion, such as 'church', 'faith', 'Bible', in a range of answers to the interview questions. We then categorized their responses in themes based on a fuzzy frame of intrinsic and instrumental capabilities and their context. The themes derive from theorizing the human development and capabilities approach (Sen, 2001) in the local context (Seeberg & Luo 2012; Seeberg, 2014), where what the Xiangcun Sisters 'do' and 'are' is analyzed in terms of domains of freedom to practice intrinsic and instrumental capabilities.

Limitations

We want to point out that of the 31 Xiangcun Sisters in the research population, only 23 volunteered information about their religion, its role in their lives and how they felt about it. Among these 23, the minority who worked in Xi'an showed less regularity in their church attendance; however, they were perhaps more adventurous than the Xiangcun Sisters in the smaller country city S, and participated in the more intensive mission trips. We could not detect in their stories any differences in how they evaluated the importance of religion in their lives; their expressions were personal to their lives but shared many similarities. These commonalities we chose and categorized into themes. There were no stories of falling away from the church or the faith among the 23 Xiangcun Sisters who mentioned religion in their interviews. We cannot draw any inferences about the remaining eight sisters in the study population who did not use any of the terms related to religion. We cannot assume anything about how they felt about the incidental learning of faith that imbued the ethos of their village surroundings during their upbringing. Due to the delimitation of the study design, variability in strength or religiosity was not necessarily determinable.

The Physical Setting, Religious Setting and Time of Life

The home of the Xiangcun Sisters was a remote mountain village lying at an altitude of 2000 meters (6000 feet) along the slopes of the massive Qinling mountain range in Shaanxi Province, Western China. Their county and surrounding counties were designated by the People's Republic of China (PRC) central government as official 'poverty counties'. In the second decade of the twentieth century subsistence farming had been supplemented, and by 2015 finally abandoned, by the parents of the Xiangcun Sisters. A Confucian world view persisted, emphasizing a close kinship network enforced through role obligations (Seeberg & Luo, 2012). Yet these villagers had long considered themselves Catholic.

We include photos here that we took in 2016 to show how the villagers expressed their religion and its interaction with Chinese folk ways and Confucian traditions. The type of objects are completely normal aspects of life rather than formal religious practice, which we interpret to show that the religion had become part of the ethos of the village, absorbed seamlessly into everyday culture. Figure 1 shows the Confucian home altar, which honors the family's ancestors as well as Catholic icons.

Figure 1. Family home altar.
Photograph by V. Seeberg in 2016.

We see a similar symbiosis of beliefs in Figure 2, which shows the family tomb constructed in local Chinese tradition, carrying graphic symbols such as the character for good fortune, dominated by a large Christian cross.

Figure 2. Family tomb.
Photograph by V. Seeberg in 2016.

The Catholic Diocese in Xi'an was re-established after the end of the Cultural Revolution (1979), and it had sent a priest and later a nun to the village to rebuild the church and revive the religious practices in the village. Oral history had not preserved the early history of when and how this village became Catholic. It was known only that there had always been a two-steeple church building, and that the village head had served as the priest in the church. All the villagers had called themselves Catholic and life had 'always' revolved loosely around the Catholic and the Chinese traditional calendar. The question of the church's allegiance to the Vatican or the Chinese Catholic Church was left unspoken, but the diocese in Xi'an was public and therefore associated with the official Chinese Catholic Church (personal communication, 2003).

Village families had been attending church a few times a week, often walking long distances down precarious mountain goat paths. The Xiangcun Sisters, after they had gone away to board at the middle school in the market town, a four-hour walk away from the village, continued to come home to attend church on weekends. Those Xiangcun Sisters who had managed to pass their senior secondary qualifying exams had to board at schools in either city S. or metropolitan Xi'an. Here they had little free time due to extremely heavy study loads, and attended church on a much less regular basis.[5] The village priest, however, took it upon himself to keep updated on their well-being through his connections with the priests and nuns of the diocese (personal communication, 2016).

Figure 3. Church compound at the entrance to the village center.
Photograph by V. Seeberg in 2016.

When the families or young girls migrated to work in various cities, they attended Catholic churches there. By 2015, hardly any working-age members of families remained living in the villages; most of the able-bodied young women and men had migrated for work outside. The Xiangcun Sisters who migrated to the prefecture-level city S. attended its Catholic church once or several times a week, depending on time availability. They built strong bonds with fellow villagers who had migrated before them which helped secure their well-being in the unfamiliar urban environment.

The Xiangcun Sisters who migrated all the way to the capital city Xi'an or beyond to major metropolitan areas faced a more dispersed setting. Though having a choice of several churches, they would face a long bus ride from their urban village. Due to the long distances, traffic and their busy work schedule, the Xiangcun Sisters in Xi'an attended church less frequently than their fellow sisters in city S. – every two to three weeks. They had fewer encounters with their Catholic relatives and friends from their home village either in the city churches or in their daily lives, hence there was less helpful bonding available to them. Some of the Xiangcun Sisters didn't get to know the priest or any members of the church. They lived a more anonymous life in Xi'an, though they stayed in close phone contact with their peers and relatives from the village.

Urban Villages in the City

The migration to an urban area presented many challenges requiring adjustment, even acculturation, by the Xiangcun Sisters. Their lives in the city largely took place in so-called urban villages, which held a connotation of 'inner-city ghettos', and consisted of temporary transitional-housing neighborhoods densely populated by rural migrant workers. Serious safety concerns in their living quarters were commonplace, and theft, sexual harassment and even rape were reported frequently in public media. The pace of life was hectic where it had been slow-moving in the village. Migrants from peripheral villages or suburbs continued to flood into these urban villages, adding to overcrowding and a palpable sense of unrest, a sense of a frontier town.

Age at Migration

The age of the Xiangcun Sisters is part of the setting of their lives in the village or the city. Around the age of 16 to 19, in the days of village life, they would enter the phase of marriage negotiation and move on to become a member of another family. In the early twenty-first century, this life phase began with the end of schooling, whether before or at the end of the compulsory nine years. Deep traditions associated with our human biology may change in specifics but not quickly in importance. Hence, we consider the Xiangcun Sisters' age at migration part of their life setting, a significant context structuring their lives. The prospect of marriage was a given, it would occur either sooner or later, as an inevitable next step. Their parents assumed they would marry in the faith, and many among the Xiangcun Sisters preferred to marry into a Catholic family; it signified a favored and familiar moral standard. Pang Ranran said, 'It would be best to find a Catholic man; if not, he needs to become Catholic before we get married. In that case, he can understand why I go to church and we will share more common understanding in life.' Though it was more likely they would find eligible Catholic men in the cities, the parents of the Xiangcun Sisters favored Catholic men from their own village or neighboring villages with whose families they were familiar. Parents expected to, and did, make use of their connections and resources to arrange such a marriage – but most of their daughters told us they still had some choice in the matter. Some Xiangcun Sisters resisted for years by not visiting their parents' home (Seeberg & Luo, 2012), while others consented without problems. We did hear two stories of forced arrangements that ended in bitterness, and one of them in the death of the husband (field notes, 2015), but both Xiangcun Sisters regained their independence.

Next, we will describe how the sisters saw the role that religion played in their lives, using the dimensions of the theorized capability approach that apply to this specific setting.

Religion and Moral Education as Identity Formation

Identity formation is a fundamental goal of adolescence (Erickson, 1968). In order to construct a strong, positive and stable self-identity, an intrinsic capability, an adolescent must be able to incorporate a positively valued social identity as well. Vermeer (2010) claimed that religious education in schools has often served to promote the simultaneous development of both a positive personal identity and a social identity such as people need in modern society. We will explore how the informal and incidental religious education the Xiangcun Sisters received promoted their personal and social identity development as they grew up in the village and then migrated to the cities. Changing their setting that drastically, from a sleepy impoverished rural village to a fast-paced, unstable urban village, added a greater difficulty and urgency to achieving a stable positive personal and social identity for the Xiangcun Sisters.

Personal Identity Formation

Many of the Xiangcun Sisters spoke about how during years of Bible study and going to church they absorbed their personal identity and values from the teachings of the Bible such as the importance of being 'kind and nice' and 'tolerant and considerate', and the need to 'have a big heart' and 'forget bad things'. Luo Mengmeng took a practical lesson from these Bible teachings:

> If somebody's words hurt me, I used to feel bad, even hated the person. After reading the Bible, I think it's meaningless to feel that way. Even if I complain that I got hurt and became unhappy, the other person may not feel anything. Sometimes it's good to forget something. I need to learn to be tolerant and understanding. (2015 interview)

For the Xiangcun Sisters, the religious teachings and doctrine set the moral standards for their behavior. 'I connect the Bible with real life and I've learned to be a good person' (Pang Ranting, 2015 interview). Vermeer (2010) described religious education as informal and incidental learning of moral values. The Xiangcun Sisters demonstrated this process. They learned from their religious studies how to manage their sense of self, how to enhance their personal identity to be more consistent with the norms of their community, and how to experience greater well-being. Thus we agree with Huang's (2014) elaboration on Beijing Christian migrants – that 'their familiar faith ... meant ... ways of understanding, approaching, and experiencing God, and of course new understandings of self and the world' (p. 246).

Social Identity Formation in the City

Social identity 'entails the transmission and internalization of core values of the dominant cultural and social system ... It is necessary in order to create ... a minimum level of cultural-normative integration' (Vermeer, 2010, p. 110). When the Xiangcun Sisters migrated to a city, they were either encapsulated in the school grounds or shunted into a segregated migrant-worker labor market ('Most of my colleagues are migrants from other rural regions' was shared by most of them) and urban village neighborhoods [*chengzhong cun*] shared with other rural migrants [*waidi ren*]. Migrants were residentially, economically and socially marginalized by the urban middle class. Church, however, was one of the few physical spaces where they could mingle with urban residents. 'You know I go to church. If I go there a few more times, I may get to know more people there and make friends with them' (Duan Yanting, 2015 interview).

Since all of the Xiangcun Sisters attended urban churches regularly, they were exposed to some core values of the urban cultural and social system in the safety of the church and in the process of socializing with urbanites within church, which contributed to the formation of social identity, as Vermeer had posited.[6] Their religious agency achieved for them a minimum level of cultural-normative integration into modern city life.

Personal Security

A large body of literature (Li et al, 2004; Feng et al, 2005; Shi et al, 2012) documents that premarital sexual relations, sexual reproductive health risks and HIV-STD risk were encountered frequently by young rural-to-urban migrants in China. Massage centers or beauty parlors, especially in urban villages, secretly and illegally operated prostitution on the side (Liu, 2007; Xu, 2011; Cunguan, 2014). Many of the Xiangcun Sisters claimed that they disagreed with premarital sexual relations or prostitution because of their religious belief.

> My family also asked me to protect myself, which means I
> shouldn't live with my boyfriend before marriage. They are strict
> on this with me. You know, I am a Catholic, I believe in the
> tradition that a woman should not have sex with man before
> marriage. (Pang Jin, 2015 interview)

> I worked as a cashier in a massage parlor. Later ... I got to know
> ... they switched me to be a receptionist and told me to solicit the
> sexual services to customers. It's not appropriate for me as a

Catholic to do this, so I quit the job. (Pang Linsha, 2015 interview)

The Xiangcun Sisters were clear about what they had been taught in the church, that it was a sin to have sexual relationships before marriage. This helped them to protect themselves against such possibilities or threats in city-scapes.

Managing Intimate Relationships

Young migrant women worldwide are often the most vulnerable groups in the city due to their age, gender and isolation from families (Kristof & WuDunn, 2010; He et al, 2012; Guo et al, 2015). The Xiangcun Sisters learned how to handle healthy relationships with young men in church-related activities. Lu Xiaofen learned from the priest, 'Our Father in the church always teaches us to get along with guys in the proper way.' She illustrated, 'I know one lady in the church who had a "sugar daddy".... I have been Catholic since childhood; my mom is a Catholic too. I knew definitely that I shouldn't get involved in such kind of relationships' (Lu Xiaofen, 2014 interview).

Pang Jin learned how to manage relationships from a dating event for single Catholics:

Last year my mom asked me to join an event for single people in a church in Xi'an. The event taught us how to get prepared for a relationship and how to manage it. I learned that when two people are in a relationship, one shouldn't be very demanding but give the other enough personal space. One should be considerate while requesting the other to do something. (Pang Jin, 2015 interview)

The Xiangcun Sisters were often without the proper guidance on managing intimate relationships since many were on their own and isolated from their families. They learned how to handle healthy relationships with young men in the church, which took on an *in loco parentis* role for the young.

Religion and Socio-economic Facilities

Moreover, church, as a social gathering place, also served as an informal source for social and job opportunities. Huang (2014) found that churches provide essential social connections for migrant workers to the city since members of the church share information about job opportunities and other information about how to manage city life. Some of the Xiangcun Sisters benefited from social networking in the church:

My second internship was recommended by a friend in the church. My uncle is a priest in the Eastern Catholic Church in Xi'an. He knew one 'auntie' whose husband worked in an architecture firm.... I went to the church a lot and met the auntie frequently. She liked me and always asked me what I was doing. I told her I wanted to find an internship and then she asked her husband to find me an intern position; and he did. (Pang Junjun, 2015 interview)

Others had difficulties connecting with other people and with the priests in the urban churches, perhaps due to their newness, relative infrequency of attendance or communication style. 'I am not familiar with people who go to my church. I chatted with a few of them, maybe four or five people, but none of them can recall my name' (Luo Mengmeng, 2015 interview).

Some of the Xiangcun Sisters recalled that they socialized with people in a variety of activities sponsored by churches, such as summer Bible camp and pilgrimage trips, which provided the Xiangcun Sisters with opportunities to interact with Catholics from different social and economic backgrounds who also potentially opened up new occupational opportunities for them. 'All Catholics from different places came to Xi'an L. district to join in the camp. There were college students, high school students and middle school students' (Lu Xiaofen, 2014 interview).

Pan Ranran had gone on pilgrimages organized by the church to places as far away as Hong Kong, Macao and Inner Mongolia. On the way she learned about the tourism industry, which stimulated her interest in becoming a tour guide in the future. She gained some social capital as well when one of the drivers was willing to introduce her to the tourism company where he worked.

Pang Ranfei went on a pilgrimage trip to Songcheng, where, she said, 'people wore delicate make-up' which motivated her to work to become involved in the cosmetics industry in a bigger city.

The pilgrimage trips exposed the Xiangcun Sisters to multiple ways of living and inspired them to seek alternative career paths they valued. In this way, the activities sponsored by churches not only provide essential social connections for migrant workers so that they can have better lives in the city, but also inspired them to pursue possible lifestyles.

Church and Formal Schooling

We have seen above how the Church sometimes served as a community and informal learning center where the Xiangcun Sisters were able to learn and consolidate religious values and find out how to apply them in their lives. We have no record of any of the Xiangcun Sisters having taken organized catechism instruction in the church either in the village or in the city. Though it may seem obvious, religious content was not taught in formal schooling, the curriculum of which is under strict central government control.

However, interactions between the Church and the schools did occur, usually through the offices of individuals with connections in both spheres.

Two of the Xiangcun Sisters, Dang Yanfei and Pang Junjun, received financial aid from the Church in city S. and Xi'an, respectively, for their secondary [7] and tertiary schooling respectively. Pang Junjun (2015 interview) explained:

> I went to a tertiary school in Xi'an. A non-profit foundation and the Catholic Church in Xi'an supported me with the tuition and partial living expenses. I covered the rest expense myself, which was not a big burden for me.

In her case our local contact Pang got her the scholarship support through his association with the Xi'an diocese. He was employed by Catholic Relief Services, his sister was a nun in the diocese, and his elder brother, as former head of the village, often collaborated closely with the village priest.

For Dang Yanfen, the church in city S. provided accommodation in its buildings for Catholic students going to secondary schools in the city. Dang Yanfen was one of the students. She shared: '[Living in the dormitory of] the church is better than living in my home [housing conditions are better]. I live and eat for free in the church. The fathers and sisters take care of us very well' (2010 interview). Her uncle was an elder in the Church administration of city S. and had made this arrangement for her.

The churches in Xi'an were helpful in another way, by looking after the well-being of the children in the village. Every summer the village priest contacted Xi'an clergy to recruit some of their parishioners who were college students to volunteer in the village. Those volunteers conducted arts, music and dance summer camps in the village for the younger 'left-behind' children. The contact with the college students broadened the horizons of the village children and directly enhanced their well-being. Most importantly, their visits opened up new vistas of possibilities and aspirations for advanced education for the remote village children.

Although we could not identify any connection between church attendance or expressions of religious faith and educational attainment level, it is clear that some of the Xiangcun Sisters did benefit educationally from having relatives in the Church hierarchy.

Religion and Agency and Aspirations

Kabeer (2000) elevated agency to a place of significant importance in women's empowerment similar to Sen (2001; see above). Agency to her is composed of resources, be they human, social or material, which are used in ways deemed desirable by the individual. It is more complex than observable actions and encompasses the meaning, motivation and purpose individuals bring to their actions, including intangible cognitive processes such as reflection and analysis, as well as instrumental observable actions, to attempt to achieve something they have reason to value. When these values belong to the future, they are aspirations. Likewise, Appadurai (2004) argued that ideas of the future are embedded in culture as norms and that 'aspiration is a "navigational capacity" that provides a map of norms that leads to future success' (p. 69). It is therefore difficult to separate agency from aspirations, because without aspirations, agency would be meaningless, lacking motivation, purpose and action. From the narratives of the Xiangcun Sisters, it was evident how religiosity, agency and aspirations were inextricably connected.

Pang Ranting connected the teachings of the Bible with real life and aspired to be 'a good person' (2015 interview). Duan Yanting intended to attend the urban church more frequently because she aspired to 'get to know more people there and make friends with them' (2015 interview). Pang Linsha deemed a task she was assigned at work as inappropriate 'for me as a Catholic (prostitution is immoral and illegal), so I quit the job' (2015 interview). Pang Jin 'learned' about how to handle intimate relationships at a church workshop in preparation for marriage (2015 interview). Pang Junjun wanted to get an internship when she was still in school and pursued a relationship with a well-connected 'auntie' in church (2015). She and Dang Yanfen exerted agency to acquire and make good use of the financial support of their churches to achieve their educational aspirations.

We also found that active participation in church increased aspirations to be deeply religious and to act on that faith. Lu Xiaofen (2014 interview) reflected that 'after that summer's camp, I am more determined about my faith. I want to strengthen others' faith and organize charitable activities, such as helping elders who don't have children, chat with them so they will not feel lonely.'

Religion and Enhanced Well-being

In this section, we discuss how the sense of being religious, their religiosity, served as one of the dimensions directly interconnected with the well-being that the Xiangcun Sisters experienced.

Sabine Alkire (2006) argued that the intrinsic value of religion 'may contribute directly to a person's flourishing or contentedness, and comprise a dimension of human well-being' (p. 502). The Xiangcun Sisters spoke about the value of religion to them in a similar manner, feeling 'happy', 'peaceful', 'relaxed' in church, and 'feeling good to read the Bible in church quietly', or, when Pang Xuxu, for example, felt 'upset, burdensome, or irritated', she wanted to go to church to clear her mind. Pang Ranran shared, 'I like going to church from the bottom of my heart. I like the environment, like the truth of the Bible.' They genuinely enjoyed going to church and internalized the sense of the church, the sermons and the Bible such that it constituted well-being per se. The religious doctrine served as a moral standard that guided them as strangers, living their Catholic faith in the often perilous urban environment. To the Xiangcun Sisters their religion was an intrinsic, very personal faith. Our findings confirmed Jianbo Huang's (2014) claim that

Protestant rural migrants had an emotional connection with church gatherings, prayer and personal experiences. The Xiangcun Sisters attended church regularly, regardless of inconvenience, and had such an emotional connection.

Discussion and Conclusion

In this chapter, we have explored the role of informal, incidental religious-moral learning in the Chinese Catholic Church in contributing to the young migrant women's well-being as they broke into the urban migrant labor market. We found that religious education and capability development interconnected to contribute positively to their adjustment to city life. The informal and incidental religious education of the Xiangcun Sisters included learning from sermons, church teachings and Bible lessons, and other church-related activities, which promoted their personal and social identity formation and enhanced their well-being. They had internalized the Catholic doctrine on virginity and chastity, which kept most of them out of trouble and protected them from sexually risky behavior, inappropriate intimate relationships or involvement in prostitution. Attendance at urban Catholic churches afforded them social connections which helped expand their occupational opportunities and contact with urban life. Two of the Xiangcun Sisters even had their secondary schooling financed by the Church through the intercession of well-connected relatives.

Both the religious context of their village of origin and the informal, incidental religious education contributed to the Xiangcun Sisters' formation of agency and aspirations, and their achievement of relative well-being. In the stories of migration told by the Xiangcun Sisters, we see evidence of Sen's (2001) point that 'free and sustainable agency emerges as a major engine of [human] development' (p. 4).

Having the social and economic support and internalizing moral imperatives of the Church community served as a resource and enhanced their capabilities in a spiral that was interconnected with a sense of agency, or being able to act on their aspirations, advancing further capablilities. Sen's evaluative paradigm that interconnected capabilities engage agency helped us to view the Xiangcun Sisters as powerful agents who pursue, achieve and accumulate capabilities as they convert intrinsic and instrumental resources. In the process, the Xiangcun Sisters achieved well-being, demonstrating the process of empowerment as strangers in the city.

The experience of the Xiangcun Sisters is consistent with Huang's (2014) findings that for 'rural migrants who find themselves in a strange city, a support group becomes even more significant and attractive' (p. 244).

Despite recent government suppression of religious practices, using a participatory capability approach, the Xiangcun Sisters' and other participants' stories, along with field work observations, revealed the workings of faith and religious practices in the lives of young women migrants. We are curious to see whether using participatory approaches focused on capabilities and context rather than policy and structural barriers can reveal the strength and direction of religion in social change. It is entirely plausible that the agency promoting elements of religion and the practices of religious communities enhances a vector of change turned further toward social justice. That is, if Sen is right, and we agree that he is – that the enhancement of freedom is the objective of a better life and of collective human development (Robeyns, 2016) – then our conclusion, that the Xiangcun Sisters have exercised agency based on their religious values and converted this resource into enhanced capabilities and achieved freedoms they value, points to the creation of social change in the direction of greater social justice.

Though this is but a small case study, we believe it indicates that religious belief can contribute to a more harmonious society, an aim of the Chinese government. For the discourse of international development, drawing attention to the role of religion exercised as 'free and sustainable agency' can 'emerge as a major engine of [human] development' (Sen, 2001, p. 4) and promote lifelong learning, goal 4 of the Sustainable Development Goals (SDGs).

Notes

[1] The Catholic Church in China is formally recognized as the Catholic Patriotic Association of China (CPA) and regulated by the State Administration for Religious Affairs, Regulations on Religious Affairs [*Zongjiao shiwu tiaoli*], issued 30 November 2004, effective 1 March 2005, articles 6, 12. Freedom of religion is stipulated in the PRC Constitution, issued 4 December 1982, amended 12 April 1988, 29 March 1983, 15 March 1999, 14 March 2004, article 36. It 'limits protection of religious activities to "normal religious activities"' (CECC, 2015, p. 1). Excluded are the recognition of the Roman Catholic Pope and the Holy See, the central governing body of the Catholic Church.

[2] On 20 May 2015, President and Party General Secretary Xi Jinping at the CCP Party Central United Front Work Conference reiterated that members must 'handle religious affairs ... [on the] principle of independence, and actively guide religions to adapt to socialist society' (Xinhua Net, 2015), warning that foreign influences were attempting to turn Chinese domestic religious groups against the party and state. This signaled an ongoing clampdown on religious expression, including the removal of crosses from churches (*Guardian*, 20 May 2015; Johnson, 2016b), a three-year campaign including the demolition of hundreds of churches (CECC, 2015, p. 8), arrests of priests and pastors (Wong, 2016), and suppression of non-state-licensed religions, such as 'house-churches' (Johnson, 2016a).

[3] New rules about to be enacted threaten 'those who provide conditions for illegal religious activities' with fines and confiscation of property; they also

'restrict contact with religious institutions overseas', and warn such people that they 'must not harm national security' (Johnson, 2016a, A4, A9).

[4] The government protects what it calls 'normal religious activity', but warns 'not to use religion to engage in activities that ... interfere with the educational system of the state ... within government-sanctioned religious organizations and registered places of worship' (Constitution of China, n.d.), but this does not extend to informal moral education. That space is covered by required courses in moral education in public schools, called 'thought and moral' [*sixiang pinde*] in primary education, 'government' [*zhengzhi ke*] in secondary school education, and Marxism Studies [*Makesi zhuyi zhexue*] in higher education.

[5] The exception was that two Xiangcun Sisters were housed in the church or otherwise supported by relatives in the church.

[6] Huang (2014) found that in Beijing many house-churches were often formed on the basis of regional affiliation [*laoxiang*]. We think the difference is explained by the big difference between the number of Protestant migrant workers and house-churches in the yet larger city of Beijing and the much smaller number of Catholic migrants in Xi'an and the small number of churches there.

[7] Senior secondary schooling is not compulsory and not supported by the state. Tuition is often as high as for higher education.

References

Alkire, S. (2006) Religion and Development, in D.A. Clark (Ed.) *The Elgar Companion to Development Studies*, pp. 502-510. Cheltenham: Edward Elgar.

Appadurai, A. (2004) The Capacity to Aspire: culture and the terms of recognition, in V. Rao & M. Walton (Eds) *Culture and Public Action.* Stanford, CA: Stanford University Press. http://www-wds.worldbank.org/external/default/WDSContentServer/IW3P/IB/2004/08/19/000160016_20040819153703/Rendered/PDF/298160018047141re0and0Public0Action.pdf

Congressional Executive Commission on China, US Government (CECC) (2015) AR Religion. https://www.cecc.gov/sites/chinacommission.house.gov/files/documents/2015%20AR%20Religion.pdf

Constitution of PRC (n.d.) Chapter 2, article 36. English translation of the Constitution of the People's Republic of China of 1982. http://en.people.cn/constitution/constitution.html

Cunguan (2014) Xi'an xi yu chang suo an cang se qing fu wu, gong zuo ren yuan cheng gao ding pai chu suo [Hidden sex service in public baths]. 29 October. http://www.shanxicunguan.com/xianxinwen/20141029/3515.html

Erikson, E.H. (1968) *Identity: youth and crisis*. New York: Norton.

Feng, W., Ren, P., Shaokang, Z. & Anan, S. (2005) Reproductive Health Status, Knowledge, and Access to Healthcare Among Female Migrants in Shanghai,

China, *Journal of biosocial Science*, 37, 603-622. https://doi.org/10.1017/S0021932004006844

Guo, C., Pang, L., Zhang, G. & Zheng, X.Y. (2015) Migrant Health: reproductive health awareness and access, in M. Lim & Y.F. Wu (Eds) *Urbanization and Public Health in China*, pp. 213-229. London: Imperial College Press.

He, D., Zhou, Y., Ji, N., Wu, S., Wang, Z., Decat, P. & Cheng, Y. (2012) Study on Sexual and Reproductive Health Behaviors of Unmarried Female Migrants in China, *Journal of Obstetrics and Gynecology Research*, 38, 632-638. https://doi.org/10.1111/j.1447-0756.2011.01753.x

Huang, J. (2014) Being Christians in Urbanizing China, *Current Anthropology*, 55(10), 238-247. https://doi.org/10.1086/677882

Johnson, I. (2016a) China Seeks Tighter Grip in Wake of a Religious Revival, *New York Times*, 7 October. http://www.nytimes.com/2016/10/08/world/asia/china-religion-regulations.html

Johnson, I. (2016b) Decapitated Churches in China's Christian Heartland, *New York Times*, 21 May. http://www.nytimes.com/2016/05/22/world/asia/china-christians-zhejiang.html?action=click&contentCollection=Asia%20Pacific&module=Relate dCoverage&region=Marginalia&pgtype=article

Kabeer, N. (2000) Reflections on the Measurement of Women's Empowerment, in A. Sisask (Ed.) *Discussing Women's Empowerment: theory and practice*, pp. 17-57. www.sida.se

Kristof, N.D. & WuDunn, S. (2010) *Half the Sky*. New York: Penguin Random House.

Li, X., Fang, X., Lin, D., et al (2004) HIV/STD Risk Behaviors and Perceptions Among Rural-to-Urban Migrants in China, *AIDS Education and Prevention*, 16(6), 538-556. https://doi.org/10.1521/aeap.16.6.538.53787

Liu, Y. (2007) Cheng Zhong Cun Zhao Dai Suo Bian Shen Se Qing Chang Suo, Fa Lang Xiao Jie Sui Jiao Sui Dao [Prostitutions in the motels of urban villages]. *Shan'xi News*, 12 July. http://shaanxi.cnwest.com/content/2007-07/12/content_596010.htm

Robeyns, I. (2016) Capabilitarianism, *Journal of Human Development and Capabilities*, 17(3), 397-414. https://doi.org/10.1080/19452829.2016.1145631

Seeberg, V. (2014) Girls' Schooling Empowerment: enhanced capabilities and social change in the village, *Comparative Education Review*, 48(4) (November), 678-707. https://doi.org/10.1086/677774

Seeberg, V. & Luo, S. (2012) Do Village Girls Gain Empowering Capabilities through Schooling and What Functionings Do They Value? *Frontiers of Education in China*, 7(3), 347-375.

Sen, A. (2001) *Development as Freedom*. Oxford: Oxford University Press.

Shi, Y., Ji, Y., Sun, J., Wang, Y., Sun, X., Li, C. Wang, D. & Chang, C. (2012) Lack of Health Risk Awareness in Low-income Chinese Youth Migrants: assessment and associated factors, *Environmental Health and Preventive Medicine*, 17, 385-393. https://doi.org/10.1007/s12199-012-0264-z

Vermeer, P. (2010) Religious Education and Socialization, *Religious Education*, 105(1), 103-116. https://doi.org/10.1080/00344080903472774

White, S. & Pettit, J. (2004) Participatory Approaches and the Measurement of Human Well-being. WeD Working Paper 08. Bath: Economic & Social Research Council, University of Bath.

Wong, E. (2016) Pastor in China Who Resisted Cross Removal Gets 14 Years in Prison, *New York Times*, 26 February. http://www.nytimes.com/2016/02/27/world/asia/china-zhejiang-christians-pastor-crosses.html?action=click&contentCollection=Asia%20Pacific&module=Related Coverage&region=Marginalia&pgtype=article

Xinhua Net (2015) Xi Jinping: Gong Gu Fa Zhan Zui Guang Fan De Ai Guo Tong Yi Zhan Xian [Xi Jinping: speech on consolidating and developing the broadest possible patriotic united front]. 20 May. http://news.chinaso.com/detail/20150520/1000200032808661432111432306678 420_1.html

Xu, J. (2011) Xi'an Se Qing Fu Wu Ye Yu Ai ZI Bing Chuan Bo Chu Tan, [Sex industry and dissemination of AIDS in Xi'an], *Sex Science of China*, 19 August. http://www.zgxkx.org/sexjk/xx/201108/1028.html

CHAPTER 6

Inter-religious Dialogue and Education: three historical encounters between Christianity, Buddhism and Confucianism

RUTH HAYHOE

SUMMARY This chapter adopts a historical approach to consider three encounters between China and Europe, when core educational and religious values from each civilization had a profound and transformative experience of interaction. In each encounter the author notes how Christianity was enriched and enhanced through respectful dialogue with Buddhist, Daoist and Confucian adherents. The chapter seeks to draw lessons from history on how respectful dialogue among religions can enrich education even under circumstances of geo-political imbalance and imperialist threat or domination.

Most chapters in this book deal with current issues of religion and schooling or higher education, while this chapter seeks to provide a broad historical frame for reflection on ways in which dialogue across religions and civilizations has resulted in educational enrichment. The twentieth century was dominated by competing macro theories of modernization and socialist construction, which predicted increasing secularism and the gradual dying out of religion. Yet with the end of the Cold War in 1991, it became evident that persisting and deep-rooted values of religion that have shaped education since the earliest times were essential to human well-being in the new global age.

The decade of the 1990s was characterized by both the clash of civilizations, depicted in Samuel Huntington's much-quoted article (1993), and a dialogue among civilizations, encouraged by the United Nations (Hayhoe & Pan, 2001).

An important task for education in the twenty-first century is thus the re-integration of religious and spiritual understanding into forms of education that nurture the whole person, including spiritual, psychological, aesthetic and cognitive dimensions, a core concern of this volume. It is also a time for rebalancing the influences of the European heritage with those of other civilizations whose historical contributions to education around the world were submerged as a result of the triumph of European science and the successive influences of a series of European trading empires – the Portuguese, Dutch and British – and then the competing influences of the United States and the Soviet Union over the twentieth century. Given my personal engagement with educational values and patterns from China over several decades, in this chapter I seek to illustrate the kinds of reciprocal learning that could create a renewed holism through interaction between East Asia and the West, though I acknowledge also the rich religious heritage of other regions, which are dealt with in other chapters of this book.

The chapter begins by considering two influential academics of the twentieth century whose scholarship kept alive the spiritual heritage of Christianity and Confucianism through decades in which secularism and ever-increasing academic specialization dominated the research literature. Author of *The Company of Strangers* (1981), *To Know as We are Known* (1983) and *The Courage to Teach* (1998), Parker Palmer developed an influential literature on the necessity of the spiritual element in the work of teachers at all levels of education. His recent book, *The Heart of Higher Education* (with scientist Arthur Zajonc; Palmer & Zajonc, 2010), elaborates a vision for holistic education which only spiritual renewal can bring. On the Confucian side, William Theodore de Bary, former Provost of Columbia University, devoted a lifetime to researching and teaching the classical civilizations of East Asia, and communicating the spiritual vitality of the Confucian tradition. This was over a period when it was violently attacked in Maoist China as the cause of China's backwardness and identified as responsible for the economic success of the East Asian tigers by sociologists who paid little attention to its spiritual dimension (Vogel, 1991). De Bary highlighted its rich spiritual content, with titles such as *Approaches to the Oriental Classics* (1958), *The Buddhist Tradition* (1969), *Neo-Confucian Orthodoxy and the Learning of the Mind and Heart* (1981) and *East Asian Civilization: a dialogue in five stages* (1987). From his most recent book, *The Great Civilized Conversation: education for a world community* (2013), emerges a vision for the spiritual revitalization of education in the twenty-first century that draws on this East Asian heritage in ways that may be seen as complementary to the Christian heritage.

The intention of this chapter is to show the possibilities of reciprocal learning between these two spiritual heritages by looking at three historical encounters between Christianity, Confucianism and Buddhism in the Chinese context. The focus will be on the process of dialogue and reciprocal learning in each encounter, in order to discern both the attitudes and the actions that made possible a mutually enriching holism in the resulting experiences of education. The chapter thus foregrounds the emphasis on dialogue and on religious education as encounter that is found in Ghosh and Chan's chapter (Chapter 16) of this book.

The first encounter took place in 635 CE, when a group of Syrian monks from the Church of the East travelled across the Silk Road and were welcomed by leading scholar officials of China's Tang Dynasty. They translated Christian texts into Chinese, developed an indigenous Christian literature and became integrated within local Chinese life of the seventh and eighth centuries. Only in the mid-ninth century were they were suppressed, alongside Buddhists (Palmer, 2001, p. 233), leaving behind a stone stele and written texts, which were rediscovered in the seventeenth and early twentieth centuries. These provide insights into the ways in which this remarkable encounter broadened and deepened the spiritual understanding of this Christian community in the context of an emerging economic relationship between Europe and China through the movement of traders across the Silk Road from Mesopotamia to the Chinese empire.

The second encounter took place seven centuries later, in the late sixteenth century, a time when Portuguese traders had established sea routes to East Asia. Unlike the seventh century, this was a time when China was alert to the threat of emerging European economic encroachments and far less open than it had been under the great Tang dynasty. Thus Matteo Ricci, an Italian Jesuit who felt called to establish a Christian mission in China, moved very gradually from Macau through southern China to Beijing, gaining the trust of local scholar officials at each stage along the way. As he established connections through scholarly discussion, the introduction of scientific knowledge, religious teaching and publications, his work had remarkable influence, both in China and in Europe, enriching higher education on both sides of the world.

The third encounter took place 300 years later, when China's last dynasty, the Qing, was facing collapse as the Opium Wars of 1840 and 1852, and the unequal treaties imposed, created conditions of openness to western merchants and missionaries that were deeply resented. Under these circumstances Welsh Baptist missionary Timothy Richard fostered interactions with both Buddhist and Confucian officials that would contribute to China's self-strengthening. The university he helped to establish in Shanxi Province with British Boxer indemnity funding was handed over to full Chinese control less than a decade after its founding and achieved a remarkable balance between Chinese and western knowledge, both religious and secular, in its curriculum.

Keepers of the Spiritual in Twentieth-century Education

Before elaborating on the three historical encounters that are the main focus of this chapter, I will consider the work of Parker Palmer and William

Theodore de Bary, in order to create a frame for reflecting on the process of inter-religious dialogue. In *The Heart of Higher Education* (Palmer & Zajonc, 2010), Palmer provides the following dynamic depiction of a truly integrative education:

> Human knowing, rightly understood, has paradoxical roots –
> mind and heart, hard data and soft intuition, individual thought
> and communal sifting and winnowing… Integrative education
> aims to 'think the world together' rather than 'think it apart', to
> know the world in a way that empowers educated people to act on
> behalf of wholeness rather than fragmentation. (p. 22)

In suggesting an integrative pedagogy, Palmer makes the case that 'ours is an approach to teaching and learning faithful to new understandings of how the cosmos is constituted' (Palmer & Zajonc, 2010, p. 29). Given the atomistic and competitive nature of the hidden curriculum in most higher institutions, he calls for an examination of the very foundations of education and the creation of learning spaces that facilitate a pedagogy shaped by 'relational principles and practices' (Palmer & Zajonc, 2010, p. 29). In terms of the moral dimensions of learning, he notes that 'an integrative pedagogy is more likely to lead to moral engagement because it engages more of the learner's self and teaches by means of engagement: the curriculum and the "hidden curriculum" in such a pedagogy support a way of knowing that involves much if not all of the whole self in learning about the world' (Palmer & Zajonc, 2010, p. 32).

In a subsequent chapter dealing with the practice of integrative education, Palmer notes that 'integrative education … will always be an adventurous, exploratory and discovery-oriented form of learning that will never accommodate itself to the foregone conclusions and predictable outcomes on which standardized tests are built' (Palmer & Zajonc, 2010, p. 39). He further insists there must be 'capacity to hold a paradox' and a clear 'heart-mind connection' (Palmer & Zajonc, 2010, pp. 41, 42). He also notes that 'the great spiritual traditions … were centuries ahead of science in positing the interconnectedness of reality that physicists and others now proclaim', and thus 'an integrative higher education can play a role in that process of illumination' (Palmer & Zajonc, 2010, p. 48).

From here Palmer hands over the volume to his co-author, Arthur Zajonc, Professor of Physics at Amherst College, who points to the way in which post-relativity physics has challenged the positivism, objectivism and orientation towards increasing specialization that marked the sciences of the eighteenth and nineteenth centuries. By contrast, 'the new physics encourages an epistemology that knits together the observer and the creative world in an indissoluble manner' (Palmer & Zajonc, 2010, p. 67). There is a fascinating discussion of light as particle and wave and the development of quantum theory that challenged the understanding of wholes as 'merely parts juxtaposed and bound together by forces' (Palmer & Zajonc, 2010, p. 79).

The lesson learned from this is fundamental to integrative education: 'The universe was and is a whole, but the method by which we chose to observe the universe fragmented it, and we mistakenly assumed our method gave us a true reflection of reality' (Palmer & Zajonc, 2010, p. 79).

Zajonc goes on to depict the practice of contemplative inquiry as an expression of the *epistemology of love* and by definition a practice that must be carried out collectively or in community. The seven stages that he proposes for this practice might be viewed as a set of guideposts or principles that can be seen to some degree in the inter-religious encounters considered in detail later in the chapter. Here are Zajonc's phases: *respect*, or a positive ethical orientation to our object of study; *gentleness*, in contrast to the Baconian notion of 'extracting' nature's secrets; *intimacy*, that retains clarity and balanced judgement while close up to the subject of study; *vulnerability*, or an openness to the other that involves learning to be comfortable with ambiguity and uncertainty; *participation* in the unfolding phenomena – a living out of ourselves into the other; *transformation* by experience in accord with the object of contemplation; and finally, *imaginative insight* – born of an intimate participation in the course of things (Palmer & Zajonc, 2010, pp. 94-96).

Let me turn now to William Theodore de Bary, who promoted the spiritual in education based on his in-depth understanding of the East Asian classics. His efforts began in the 1950s, when he was developing a core curriculum at Columbia University through the selection of classical texts 'that had proven themselves capable of speaking to generations of humankind in terms that could still be meaningful to their own life and times, reaching into their hearts and touching them personally' (de Bary, 2013, p. 27). He noted how distinguished European writers and thinkers had engaged with the Chinese classics in the seventeenth and eighteenth centuries yet this was not 'a substantial engagement with Chinese culture and civilization in its mature forms'. It was thus important to 'extend the conversation to 21st century education in ways that do justice to the Asian classics not just as museum pieces but as part of the historical process to be factored into an emerging world civilization' (de Bary, 2013, p. 36).

De Bary goes on to write about discussions around ideas for a core curriculum that were being widely adopted. 'A core program should make the repossession (both sympathetic and critical) of a given society's main cultural traditions the first priority and then move on, in a second stage, to a similar treatment of other major world cultures.' For purposes of cross-cultural discussion, he suggests, we should be looking for centers of gravity, points of convergence, common denominators (de Bary, 2013, pp. 51-52).

In describing how he had read the Confucian *Analects* with students over a period of sixty years, de Bary made the following comment: 'If this is what is meant by "general" education, then the Analects speak to the generality of human beings – to their common, perennial, "core" concerns more than to the farthest outreaches of abstract thought' (de Bary, 2013, p. 65). In the opening lines, de Bary points out the moral and spiritual lesson at the heart of the *Analects*: 'To be unembittered even if one is not recognized, is that not to be a truly noble person?' 'Here the *junzi* refers to the traditional leadership elite, an aristocratic class born to privileged status of would-be rulers. But Confucius emphasizes the learning process for what it takes to be worthy of a leadership role or become an exemplary person; in other words, that it means to command respect as a person, whether or not one finds oneself in a position to lead or rule. Thus he reconceives the traditional concept of *junzi* from that of nobleman to one that emphasizes the noble person as one whose personal character, not status, establishes him as a model to be followed' (de Bary, 2013, p. 64).

In a recent review of *Education for a World Community*, I pointed out ways in which the Confucian classics could bring a spiritual dimension into North American classrooms. If primary school teachers in North America could read Zhu Xi's compilation of the *xiaoxue*, they could learn how to initiate children into 'a religious attitude of reverence toward all life, one that links the self to others and to the whole life process, ... bridging the active and contemplative sides of human life' (Hayhoe, 2014, p. 77). While teachers in the western world know all about how to foster student-centered pedagogy through activity, possibilities for nurturing the innerliness of the child are far less well understood.

For secondary school teachers, the distinction between individualism and personhood in Confucian thought might help to nurture a sense of responsibility for the self such that each student can 'find the Way in themselves', while at the same time building healthy connections to the community. Zhu Xi's *Reflections on Things at Hand* might enable them to guide teenagers not only to master the foundational knowledge areas needed for their future professional lives but also to adopt the Confucian approach of 'studying extensively, inquiring carefully, pondering thoughtfully, sifting clearly and practicing earnestly' (Hayhoe, 2014, pp. 77-78) so as to become morally responsible citizens at local, national and global levels.

For higher education, Zhu Xi's *Articles for the White Deer Academy* could contribute to a re-thinking of both pedagogy and curriculum in higher education in North America, such that personal dialogue, based on mutual respect, is the primary mode of interaction between students and professors, as well as among students. Practical lessons could be learned from the organizational patterns and curricular structure of the *shuyuan* or local academies, including the commitment to a kind of voluntarism that 'respects the essential autonomy of the self in weighing and sifting whatever is to be learned ... in a creative interaction with others' (Hayhoe, 2014, p. 78).

Bringing together the perspectives from Parker and Zajonc on the American side and de Bary on the East Asian side, we can see a vision for a more holistic approach to education in the twenty-first century which could be fostered through a revival of the spiritual dimension of education, from the classroom level to that of inter-civilizational understanding.

The next three sections of this chapter look at three encounters between Christianity and the religions of China at very different historical periods with a particular focus on understanding how Christian spiritual practices and educational thought were enriched by inter-religious dialogue.

The First Encounter: Orthodox
Christianity meets Buddhism and Daoism

This first encounter took place in 635 CE just two years after the death of Mohammed at a time when the Syrian-based Church of the East was reaching out to India, Afghanistan, Persia and various parts of the Sassanian empire (Palmer, 2001). The journey of 21 monks across the Silk Road to Chang'An, China's capital during the Great Tang Dynasty, culminated in the formation of numerous Christian communities. The earliest was located very close to Lou Guan Tai, the most sacred centre of Daoism, where Lao Zi was thought to have left his *Classic of the Way* (Dao De Jing) to his followers as he went off into the Far West. The fact that the Tang emperor assigned this location to the Religion of Light from the Far West showed China's openness and confidence in this period.

What actually happened in this encounter is shrouded in mist and could have been forgotten by history had not the Chinese Christians carved a stone stele with a detailed account of the life of these Christian communities between 635 and 781 CE. All were suppressed in 845, along with Buddhist institutions, through an edict by an emperor concerned by the extent of Buddhist power. The burial of the stele meant little was known until it was unearthed in 1623, more than six hundred years later.

The other source materials that reveal various facets of this encounter are a series of Jesus Sutras, buried in 1005 CE, along with a large quantity of Buddhist scrolls, in a cave in Dun Huang in northwest China, and rediscovered in 1907. Of the ten sutras, several are translations from the Syriac, the earliest being dated 641 CE, while others are original Chinese texts. A careful reading of these texts reveals a great deal about these early Christian communities and the influence of Buddhism and Daoism on their thought and language. One of the buildings, erected in 635 CE as a library for the monastery, is still standing and has recently been turned into a major tourist site, with statuary, a cultural centre and other facilities opened to the public in 2014 to celebrate this historical encounter.

In terms of actions, what we can learn about these early Syrian and Chinese Christians is that they adopted vegetarianism, in line with Buddhist practice, they refused to own slaves, though it was common among the Buddhist majority of the time, they insisted on equality for women and they were committed to living together in mutual learning and respect. Their stele was written in both the Chinese and Syriac languages and the earlier texts were translations from Syriac, while later ones were expressions of indigenous belief and worship.

In terms of thought and conceptualization, we can see a Christian faith that was enriched and enlarged by exposure to and interaction with Buddhism and Daoism. The language of the stele expresses this beautifully in its opening lines:

> In the beginning was the natural constant, the true stillness of the
> Origin and the primordial void of the Most High. Then, the spirit
> of the voice emerged as the Most High Lord, moving in
> mysterious ways to enlighten the Holy Ones. He is Joshua, my
> True Lord of the Void, who embodies the three subtle and
> wondrous bodies, and who was condemned to the cross, so that
> the people of the four directions can be saved.
> (Palmer, 2001, p. 225)

The text goes on to outline the main teachings of Christianity, while stating that the truth 'cannot be named', but if forced to give it a name, it can be called 'The Religion of Light'. Images are drawn from both Buddhist and Daoist thought: 'abstinence to subdue thoughts of desire' (Palmer, 2001, p. 226), 'a Way that does not have a common name ... a message mysterious and wonderful beyond our understanding' (Palmer, 2001, p. 227). In summary, the Christians are called 'to penetrate the mysteries, to bless with a good conscience, to be great and yet empty, to return to stillness and be forgiving, to be compassionate and to deliver all people, to do good deeds and help people to reach the other shore' (Palmer, 2001, p. 229).

Of the eight sutras that were recovered from the Dun Huang Caves, the first set of four were written in Chang'An between 640 and 660 CE, one translated from Syriac, another possibly from Greek and the third and fourth being compilations from various sources. While containing an accurate description of the core events of the life and teaching of Christ and the Christian Gospel, these texts are expressed in Daoist and Buddhist language. There is also a fascinating excerpt in one of them about the women who witnessed the resurrection of Christ:

> As the first woman [Eve] caused the lies of humanity, so it was
> women who first told the truth about what happened, to show all
> that the Messiah forgave women and wished them to be treated
> properly in future, for he appeared and confirmed all they had
> said. (Palmer, 2001, p. 59)

In the first text the Daoist term 'qi' for breath or spirit is used, and given credit for enabling Jesus to escape from the hold of death (Palmer, 2001, p. 66). Buddhist influence is evident in the way Jesus is presented as a bodhisattva who helps others find the way by shining a light on reality, so that truth could prevail (Palmer, 2001, p. 66). In the second sutra, the five skandas are discussed (form, sensation, perception, mental formations and consciousness), and Jesus is depicted as God clothed in human flesh so as to liberate human beings by taking on these five fetters. However, in this

Christian version, human bodies, thoughts and behaviours are not only seen as fetters, but if used appropriately, 'the five Skandas ... all become strong and worship the one Sacred Spirit for their creation and for the image they have been made in' (Palmer, 2001, p. 144).

The second set of four sutras were written later, mainly by Chinese monks, and have been described as liturgical sutras or a kind of prayer book. All four deal with original nature, seeing all human life as innately good, but having become corrupt and lost its way through the compromise of life and existence, as distinct from the Augustinian doctrine of original sin (Palmer, 2001, p. 176). The first of the four, written in 720 CE, is called 'Taking Refuge in the Trinity'. Palmer notes the remarkable achievement of the Church of the East in developing a truly indigenous theology and terminology, with the use of phrases such as 'the Jade-faced One', with jade being highly prized in the Chinese context, a supreme metaphor for purity and eternity (Palmer, 2001, p. 179).

The other three sutras are almost certainly written by the Chinese monk Jing Jing, who composed the stele, and they can be dated to about 780 CE. The opening lines of 'The Christian Liturgy in Praise of the Three Sacred Powers', the third of Jing Jing's creations, probably best illustrates the reciprocal learning that had taken place – the enlargement of Christian thought and expression through its indigenization in local Daoist and Buddhist language:

> The highest skies are in love with you, the great earth opens its
> palms in peace.
> Our truest being is anchored in your purity, you are Allaha,
> Compassionate Father of the three,
> Everything praises you, sounding its true note, All the enlightened
> chant praises,
> Every being takes refuge in you and the light of your Holy
> Compassion frees us all,
> Beyond knowing, beyond words, You are the truth, steadfast for
> all time
> Compassionate Father, Radiant Son, Pure Wind King – three in
> one. (Palmer, 2001, p. 203)

Allaha seems to be adapted from Elohim in the Old Testament, fitting with the Buddhist term for Arhat, a perfected being, while the Holy Spirit is called the Pure Wind King, bringing the Spirit close to Chinese sensitivity. Jesus, the Light of the World in John's Gospel, is the Radiant Son. What we see is both an adaptation that makes Christianity understandable in a Chinese world and an enhancement of Christianity as its truths are expressed in Chinese cultural terms.

What can this tell us about holistic education and reciprocal learning? I guess the first point is that the spiritual was an integral foundation for all knowledge in this period of history, and that reciprocal learning made possible deep understanding between two very different educational traditions that resulted in enlargement. The processes identified by Zajonc – respect, gentleness, intimacy, vulnerability, participation and transformation – can all be seen to some degree in the texts left by these Syrian and Chinese Christians. The fact that they were invited to participate in official ceremonies alongside Buddhists and Daoists and were permitted to establish their own distinctive communities is a remarkable testimony to the tolerance and openness of the rulers of the Tang Dynasty.

The Second Encounter: Roman Catholic Christianity meets Confucianism

It was a very different China in the late Ming dynasty, when Matteo Ricci responded to a call to establish a mission in China, just a few decades after Francis Xavier had established a mission in southern Japan in 1549. Under the Wanli emperor (1572-1620), China was suffering decline and facing encroachments from the Manchus to the North, which culminated in the collapse of the dynasty in 1642. There was also considerable awareness of the rising power of Europe, particularly through the Portuguese trading ships plying their way via Goa to Macau, a trading port rented from the Chinese empire from 1557 and made into a colony in the nineteenth century. The Portuguese had first arrived in Japan in 1543, and the port of Nagasaki was opened up in 1671. Their ships took luxury goods from China, only much later bringing products from Europe. Meanwhile the Spanish were establishing their influence in the Philippines. The Chinese emperor was aware of the threat posed by these European powers and determined to protect China's territory and keep the foreigners from entering.

Matteo Ricci arrived in Macau in 1582, after spending a couple of years in Goa on India's west coast to prepare for his great venture. Along with Michele Ruggieri, he felt the call to establish a Jesuit mission in China and dedicated himself to mastering spoken and written Chinese, while also preparing scientific books and gifts such as the astrolabe, clock, clavichord and other scientific instruments that he believed would be welcomed. The first entry to China from Macau was in March of 1583, when Ricci and Ruggieri attended a trade fair in Guangzhou along with some Portuguese merchants. Rather than returning to Macau they then proceeded to the nearby city of Zhaoqing, where they had petitioned a local official for permission to establish a residence. There they settled for several years, establishing relationships with local officials, receiving people in their home and focusing on developing a catechism in Chinese as well as introducing valued knowledge from Europe, such as map making, clock making and geometry. Given that Buddhism was undergoing a revival at the time, they were first viewed by the Confucian literati as Buddhist monks, and they dressed accordingly, while seeking to introduce Christianity. By 1586, they had twelve converts, all of whom came from a lay Buddhist background and viewed Ricci and Ruggieri as monks who had come from India (Hsia, 2010).

When the Confucian official who had sponsored them moved away, Ricci and his colleagues were driven out of Zhaoqing but found a way to move north to Shaoguan through the network of officials and literati they had come to know. Their home had become a magnate for those interested in the books, maps and instruments they had brought. With this move they also decided to identify with the Confucian literati, changing from the robes associated with Buddhist monks to the scholarly apparel of Confucian literati (Hsia, 2010, p. 135). While living in Shaoguan, Ricci translated three of the four books of Confucius into Latin and came to view early Confucian teaching as a set of moral teachings together with a belief in Heaven as a deity that aligned closely with Christianity. This approach led to a deepening of relations with powerful Confucian literati and in 1592 to a move on to Nanchang, the capital of Jiangxi province.

In Nanchang, Ricci's career took off as he 'entered the inner corridors and chambers of Ming society' (Hsia, 2010, p. 141). The city was a centre of scholarship in a province that had a vibrant intellectual life and more academies than any other province; among these academies was Zhu Xi's famous White Deer Academy. Here he wrote and published two books in Chinese. The first, entitled *On Friendship* (*Jiaoyoulun*), became a best seller, while the second, *A Treatise on Memnomic Arts* (*Xiguo jifa*), was of great interest in a society where successful examination preparation was the key to advancement (Spence, 1984). Here his network of connections with high-level officials grew exponentially, since scholars came from all over to meet and converse with the 'Man of the Mountain from the Great Western Region', as he signed himself in his publications (Spence, 1984, p. 156).

In 1598 he moved on to Nanjing, the early southern capital of the Ming dynasty, after a first visit to Beijing, where he had stayed two months. This invitation north had come through his network of contacts, and through the widespread admiration for his map of the world. Nanjing proved a good location over a four-year period for solidifying his achievements and preparing for the culminating move to Beijing in 1602. There he would live out his final years and be laid to rest in the celestial capital that had become his adopted home. Crowning achievements were his *True Meaning of the Lord of Heaven* (*Tianzhu shiyi*), which introduced Christianity within a Confucian frame, and the conversion of a number of influential officials, including Paul Xu Guangqi, who rose to the status of prime minister.

In the content of his writing, Ricci took a position alongside of those Confucian scholars who were critical of Buddhist and Daoist influences and wished to strengthen social governance and moral rectitude through the inculcation of knowledge from the earliest Confucian classics in all levels of society. Within Confucianism, Ricci distinguished between the rationalized version of Confucian thought that had emerged as Song neo-Confucianism (*lixue*) and the early Confucianism of the Han dynasty (202 BCE to 220

CE), where he detected a more explicit theology in the presentation of Heaven and Heaven's purposes. On the basis of these early Confucian texts, Ricci felt he could introduce Christian teachings as a fulfillment in the Chinese context that was parallel to the ways in which Aquinas had presented Christian theology as a fulfillment of Greek classical understanding.

If we think in terms of action, Ricci's slow and careful progress from the periphery to China's heart of power, building friendship, gaining trust and introducing advanced scientific knowledge, alongside Christian teaching, demonstrated respect, a growing intimacy and considerable vulnerability – including the loss to illness of several close Jesuit colleagues. One can also see an ever-deepening participation that resulted in his personal transformation, not in terms of any diminution of his Christian commitment, but rather in its enlargement and a vision of what Confucianism had to say to Europe. Although it was to be 1687, decades after Ricci's death in 1610, before *Confucius Sinarum Philosophus* was published in Europe, Ricci is credited with laying the foundations of Western Sinology (Mungello, 1989), and also for the fact that China was seen for a time as a model for Europe both in terms of its patterns of governance, based on meritocracy, and on the basis of elements of its traditional science in the areas of agriculture and engineering (Maverick, 1946). Finally, the fact that Ricci never thought of returning to Europe, but died and was buried in the land he had adopted showed the depth of the connections he had built through friendships, collaborative scholarship and mastery of the language.

Only some decades after his death, when the Chinese rites crisis broke out, did it become evident how remarkable this reciprocity was in a time of rising European global dominance. From the 1640s, Dominican missionaries associated with the Spanish influence in the Philippines began to accuse the Jesuits of an unacceptable accommodation to Confucian rites and ceremonies. Much has been written on the details of this controversy, but all that needs to be said here is that the Chinese emperor issued a decree in 1706 that only missionaries who followed the 'Ricci practice of allowing Christians to observe the rites' (Noll, 1992, p. 27) could remain in China. The Vatican, for its part, condemned the Chinese rites, a decision only reversed centuries later in 1939! Catholic missionaries were driven out of China and the Society of Jesus was also suppressed in Europe between 1767 and 1824. Without going into detail on these controversies, one can easily see how remarkable Ricci's vision and openness to genuine reciprocity was, given the times in which he lived!

As for holistic education, the famous Ratio Studiorum, which had been adopted by the Jesuits in 1599, a little too late for Ricci's own education, was intended to support 'the balanced development of intellect and will, of mind and spirit' (Jiang, 2014, p. 61). A foundation was laid in the Latin and Greek classics, and on this basis the humanities, poetry, history, moral philosophy, mathematics and science were studied, with theology as the culminating field. The Jesuit order distinguished itself as an order committed to education around the world, and this curriculum was adapted to many different geographical and civilizational contexts in the hundreds of colleges subsequently developed. In the case of China, the Jesuits returned in 1840, less than two decades after the society was rehabilitated in 1824, founding the Xuhui Gongxue (College St Ignace) in Xu Jia Hui, a district of Shanghai associated with the family of Paul Xu Guangqi, the most influential of the scholar officials who had become Catholic under the influence of Matteo Ricci.

Probably the educator of modern China who made the most consistent effort to develop a holistic education in the nineteenth and twentieth centuries was Ma Xiangbo. He came to the Xuhui Gongxue as a student at the age of 12 in 1852, rose to be principal of the college and a member of the Jesuit order, and developed a vision for a higher curriculum that would have a foundation in both the Chinese and the European classics, and that would build upon them knowledge of mathematics, sciences, geography, history and modern languages. Frustrated by the imperialistic attitudes of French Jesuits at the time, he left the order to serve in major national self-strengthening projects for several decades. He returned in 1903 to get help in establishing a modern university and donated his considerable family property to this end. The struggle for space to create a holistic curriculum that integrated the best from the European and Chinese heritages in a period of China's external humiliation and internal political disarray led him to establish l'Université Aurore (Zhendan) in 1903, Fudan (a revived Aurore) in 1905, and finally Furen University in 1927 (Hayhoe, 1988).

Furen's curriculum paralleled the features of the Ratio Studiorum, though American Benedictines took over in 1927, then the German order of the Divine Word in 1933, a connection which enabled the university to remain open in Beijing right through the devastating period of Japanese occupation and subsequent civil war. Ma Xiangbo felt the Benedictines could bring in modern scientific understanding from an American context while also valuing the European scholastic tradition and embracing China's Confucian heritage. He was confident that Furen would not be 'just another foreign enclave on Chinese soil' (Hayhoe, 1988, p. 56).

Although Furen moved to Taiwan in the late 1940s, and its Beijing campus was given to Beijing Normal University in 1952, its spirit of a holistic education that embraces both the European and the Chinese classics is now being revived, with the establishment of liberal arts programs in some of China's top universities. A recent study of these programs in three Shanghai universities by Jesuit scholar Youguo Jiang (2014) contains interesting insights into how reciprocal learning across civilizations is making possible an education that connects the cognitive, aesthetic, moral and religious dimensions of learning. That volume also gives some insight into the remarkable track record in Jesuit education for the ideas around learning from religion that are presented in Chapter 16 of this book as a third approach to religious education.

The Third Encounter: Protestant Christianity
meets Buddhism and Confucianism

If the context of Matteo Ricci's encounter with China was shaped by an emerging sense of threat in the face of burgeoning Portuguese and Spanish trading interests, by the mid-nineteenth century the threat had exploded into deep resentment at the unequal treaties imposed by western powers after the Opium Wars of 1840 and 1852. It was no wonder that the Protestant missionaries in China over this century were viewed by Chinese officials as cultural imperialists, using education and religious teaching to further the interests of foreign powers. It was also understandable that in the Boxer Rebellion of 1899, when members of a secret Chinese organization who believed themselves invincible attacked all westerners they could find, missionaries constituted the majority of those who lost their lives. It was over the difficult years leading up to the Boxer Rebellion and the collapse of the Qing Empire in 1911 that Welsh Baptist missionary Timothy Richard lived and worked in China, from 1871 to 1916.

Richard was born in a small farming community in Wales. Welsh was his mother tongue and education in a local theological college prepared him for ordination in the Baptist Church. As a student he protested against the emphasis on classical Greek and Latin texts coming from the university, favoring a more practical, science-oriented curriculum. This was an early indication that he would not be oriented toward promoting a British university model in China!

Richard moved to China as a Baptist missionary at the age of 27 and began his career with village evangelism. Within a short time, however, he felt called to interact with 'those who are worthy', following Matthew 10:11: 'Whatever town or village you enter, find out who in it is worthy, and stay there until you leave.' This led him to build close connections with officials, scholars and religious leaders, including Confucian, Buddhist and Islamic thinkers. Like Matteo Ricci, he committed himself to mastering the Chinese language and reached a level where he could translate scientific texts into Chinese as well as classical texts from Chinese into English.

In terms of action, Richard was deeply concerned by the poverty and backwardness he saw all around him, and realized early on that only serious reform efforts by Chinese officialdom could bring about change. In the later 1870s he took up famine relief for a number of years and then made tremendous efforts to get support for the development of modern higher education, envisioning one college in each of China's provinces. When he failed to get support for this from the Baptist mission, he turned his efforts to the promotion of scientific literature, serving as General Director of the Society for the Diffusion of Christian and General Knowledge for 24 years, from 1891 to 1915.

Finally the opportunity to create a modern institution of higher education arose in the wake of the Boxer Rebellion of 1899 and the imposition of an indemnity by the western powers as a recompense for the lives of diplomats and missionaries that had been lost. Due to his extensive connections to Chinese officialdom, Richard was selected to negotiate on behalf of the British, and so became the co-founder of the Imperial University of Shanxi in Taiyuan in 1902, with an arrangement that channeled substantive funding from the province to the new institution as its contribution to the indemnity payment. The negotiations for the founding of this new institution, with separate colleges of Chinese and western learning, were complex. Perhaps the most remarkable feature lay in the fact that it was handed over to full Chinese jurisdiction in 1909 and was never seen as a British university in China. Richard handpicked missionaries from England, Germany and Sweden for teaching and leadership in the College of Western Studies, and arranged for translation of textbooks in all the major subject areas into Chinese. All students were first enrolled in the College of Chinese Learning in order to have a foundation in Chinese culture, and then took up advanced studies in the College of Western Learning, which enabled them to get degrees at the master's and doctoral level.

Clearly, Richard had no wish to serve the interests of British cultural imperialism by establishing a British university model. Rather, he thought in terms of introducing advanced scientific knowledge that would nurture future leaders who would make China strong. Main subjects in the curriculum of the College of Western Learning included mathematics, physics, chemistry, zoology, geography, law, history and gymnastics, while all students were expected to take a core course in comparative morals and religions, which included the teaching of Christianity as well as other religions.

In spite of China's perceived and evident weakness over this period, Richard acted in a spirit of reciprocity, clearly seeing the importance and value of introducing Chinese moral and religious teachings to the West. He was particularly struck by parallels he saw between the core concepts of Mahayanan Buddhism and the Christian Gospel, and he thus made the effort to translate elements of the famous Lotus Sutra into English in a text that was published in 1910 under the title 'The New Testament of Higher Buddhism'. In his introduction to this text, Richard wrote the following lines:

> In China we possess the lofty Ethics of Confucius, advocating Benevolence, Righteousness, Propriety, Knowledge and Mutual Confidence, in as strong and eloquent language as that of any of the Hebrew prophets. With regard to the doctrine of Immortality taught in the New Testament to Western nations – we find that in the Far East there is what might be called a Fifth Gospel or the 'Lotus Gospel', which for fifteen centuries has shone throughout the Buddhist world in China, Korea and Japan with such brilliancy that countless millions trust to its light alone for their hope of Immortal Life ... [T]he wonderful truths taught therein have precisely the same ring as those taught in the fourth Gospel about the *Life*, the *Light* and the *Love*. The bearing of the Cross, by patient endurance of wrong and undeserved insults, is also

inculcated over and over again, in the same gentle language as that of the Apostle of Love himself. (Richard, 1910, p. 134)

It has often been said that there will never be peace in the world until there is peace among the religions, and Richard's strenuous efforts for peace showed how strongly he believed this. In 1896 he put forward a proposal for a 'League of Peace for Princes', and he was tireless in his efforts to facilitate dialogue among leaders in China, Japan, Korea, England and the United States. While visiting Boston and Paris in 1900, he proposed an 'international parliament of man' to create and apply international law (Johnson, 2014, p. 123). In 1903 and 1904 he discussed with leaders in Tokyo and Peking (Beijing) the idea of a federation of ten powers with a joint army and navy to keep each other in check and police the world. With the outbreak of the Russo-Japanese War his mediation and relief efforts as Shanghai's Red Cross Secretary won him great appreciation. In 1905, he served as a delegate to the Lucerne Peace Conference, 'which he addressed with his proposal to create a federation to ensure universal peace' (Johnson, 2014, p. 124), a proposal that was to be taken to the next conference at the Hague. In 1906 he visited American President Theodore Roosevelt shortly after the latter was awarded the Nobel Peace Prize for his efforts to resolve the Russo-Japanese War.

Richard died in London in 1919, the year in which the League of Nations was founded. Unusually for a Baptist missionary, he requested cremation and his ashes were laid to rest in London's earliest crematorium in Golders Green. The simple plaque identifying his cubicle in one of the columbaria is inscribed as follows: 'In Most Happy Memory of Timothy Richard, Li T'i Mo-T'ai. Blessed are the Peacemakers, for they shall be called the children of God' (Johnson, 2014, p. 150).

Conclusion: inter-religious understanding and education

Unlike other chapters in this volume, which deal with current issues of religion and schooling in different parts of the world, this chapter has highlighted three historical encounters between different forms of Christianity and the religions of China. Each has illustrated the possibility of learning across religions and civilizations at a deep level, even under conditions of geo-political threat and imbalance. Matteo Ricci has left an enduring example of the seven phases of Zajonc's epistemology of love, which continues to inspire respect more than five hundred years after his death in Peking in 1610. Timothy Richard is a lesser-known figure, but his 45 years in China demonstrated a commitment to education and inter-religious understanding that won him the conferral of the Double Dragon from China's imperial government in 1907 and overflowed into proposals and actions for world peace that have been seen as anticipating the mission of UNESCO after World War II. In each of the three encounters there was an evident enlargement and expansion of understanding on both sides as distinctive religious and spiritual traditions interacted at a deep level.

Hopefully this chapter can provide a backdrop to later chapters in this volume, especially those in Part Three, that deal with religion and conflict resolution. It has become increasingly clear that the secularization of modern society anticipated in both structural functionalist and Marxist theories of social change has not taken place. Religion remains vitally important for many in the modern world, and the ability of educational institutions to deal with it appropriately is a key concern. Chapter 15, on the desecularization of Russian schools after the collapse of the Soviet Union, illustrates the importance of balance and breadth in bringing religion back into the school curriculum, while Chapter 13 shows how the teaching of Christianity can contribute to peace building and conflict resolution in the complex historical context of Northern Ireland. Chapter 16 outlines approaches to religious education that may serve to counter violent extremism, and its emphasis on encouraging dialogue and learning from religion resonates with the encounters depicted in this chapter.

References

de Bary, W.T. (1958) *Approaches to the Oriental Classics.* New York: Columbia University Press.

de Bary, W.T. (1969) *The Buddhist Tradition.* New York: Random House.

de Bary, W.T. (1981) *Neo-Confucian Orthodoxy and the Learning of the Mind and Heart.* New York: Columbia University Press.

de Bary, W.T. (1987) *East Asian Civilizations: a dialogue in five stages.* Cambridge, MA: Harvard University Press.

de Bary, W.T. (2013) *The Great Civilized Conversation: education for a world community.* New York: Columbia University Press.

Hayhoe, R. (1988) A Chinese Catholic Philosophy of Higher Education of Republican China, *Tripod*, 28, 49-60.

Hayhoe, R. (2014) Essay Review of William Theodore de Bary, *The Great Civilized Conversation: education for a world community*, New York: Columbia University Press, 2013, in *Sino-Western Cultural Relations Journal*, XXXVI, 74-79.

Hayhoe, R. & Pan, J. (2001) Introduction: a contribution to dialogue among civilizations, in R. Hayhoe & J. Pan (Eds) *Knowledge across Cultures: a contribution to dialogue among civilizations.* Hong Kong: Comparative Education Research Centre, University of Hong Kong.

Hsia, R.P. (2010) *A Jesuit in the Forbidden City: Matteo Ricci 1552-1610.* Oxford: Oxford University Press. https://doi.org/10.1093/acprof:oso/9780199592258.001.0001

Huntington, S. (1993) The Clash of Civilizations?, *Foreign Affairs*, 72(3), 22-49. https://doi.org/10.2307/20045621

Jiang, Y., S.J. (2014) *Liberal Arts Education in a Changing Society: a new perspective on Chinese higher education.* Leiden: Brill.

Johnson, E. (2014) *Timothy Richard's Vision: education and reform in China 1880-1910.* Eugene, OR: Pickwick Publications.

Maverick, L.A. (1946) *China: a model for Europe.* San Antonio, TX: Paul Anderson.

Mungello, D.E. (1989) *Curious Land: Jesuit accommodation and the origins of sinology.* Honolulu: University of Hawaii Press.

Noll, R. (Ed.) (1992) *100 Roman Documents Concerning the Chinese Rites Controversy (1645-1941).* San Francisco: Ricci Institute for Chinese-Western Cultural History.

Palmer, M. (2001) *The Jesus Sutras: rediscovering the lost scrolls of Taoist Christianity.* New York: Ballantine Wellspring.

Palmer, P. (1981) *The Company of Strangers.* New York: Crossroads.

Palmer, P. (1983) *To Know as We are Known: a spirituality of education.* San Francisco: HarperCollins.

Palmer, P. (1998) *The Courage to Teach.* San Francisco: Jossey-Bass.

Palmer, P. & Zajonc, A. (2010) *The Heart of Higher Education.* San Francisco: Jossey-Bass.

Richard, T. (1910) *The New Testament of Higher Buddhism.* Edinburgh: T. & T. Clark.

Spence, J. (1984) *The Memory Palace of Matteo Ricci.* New York: Viking Penguin.

Vogel, E. (1991) *The Four Little Dragons: the spread of industrialization in East Asia.* Cambridge, MA: Harvard University Press.

SECTION TWO
Curriculum, Pedagogy and School Leadership

CHAPTER 7

Religious Education in a Multi-religious Context: an examination of four religious schools in Hong Kong

MEI-YEE WONG

SUMMARY Numerous recent studies have discussed religious education in a multi-religious context. However, few have explored single religion-based curricula in a multi-religious setting. With reference to Hong Kong, this chapter aims to fill this research gap by providing empirical evidence regarding religious education for all students with religious or secular backgrounds in four government-subsidised religious schools. The chapter first examines the social and educational contexts of religious education in Hong Kong. Religious schools have autonomy in implementing religious curricula, whereby both religious and secular teachers and students work together. Second, it introduces the specific settings of the schools, investigating religious education from a single-religion perspective with educational contents concerning moral and values education. Finally, the chapter explores the practices implemented in the schools, emphasising the special position of the sponsoring bodies of religious schools and their autonomy in curriculum development regarding religious education.

Introduction

As societies become increasingly multi-cultural and multi-religious, they strive to maintain societal peace and foster dialogue among the various religions, often through religious education (see Hull, 2002; Jackson, 2004; Copley, 2008; Knauth, 2009; Weisse, 2009). Western studies on religious education (e.g. Copley, 2008; Teece, 2008, 2010; Baumfield, 2009; Hella & Wright, 2009; Kalloniemi, 2010) have focused on teaching approaches in religious education in multi-religious contexts where religious education is a complex matter; students could be secular or from one of several religions. These studies have revealed that religious educational curricula in multi-religious contexts have a potential requirement to be generally educational (i.e. focusing on personal development more generally) rather than simply religious (i.e. focusing on religious beliefs). Regardless, few empirical studies have explored how religious education curricula are implemented in multi-religious contexts. Therefore, this chapter aims to explore this practice by providing a case study of Hong Kong, which is a multi-religious city where eastern and western religions as well as practices of various cultural and historical backgrounds coexist.

A Multi-religious Context for School Religious Education: the case of Hong Kong

This section examines the current multi-religious context of Hong Kong society to convey the historical development of religious education in Hong Kong.

The Sociocultural, Religious, and Educational Contexts of Hong Kong Society

The Hong Kong Special Administrative Region (HKSAR) of the People's Republic of China (PRC) had a population of 7.32 million at the end of 2015 (CSD, 2016). Its largest ethnic group is Chinese, comprising approximately 94% of the population (CSD, 2012).

There are various religions in Hong Kong, including Buddhism, Taoism, Confucianism, Protestant Christianity, Catholicism, Islam, Hinduism, Sikhism and Judaism. The most popular religions are Buddhism and Taoism, with over 1 million followers each; the second-largest religions are Protestantism and Catholicism, with 480,000 and 379,000 followers, respectively (HKSAR Government, 2014). Numerous western and eastern religious organisations have provided education as well as medical and social welfare services for Hong Kong residents during the past years, including the Hong Kong Baptist Convention, the Hong Kong Buddhist Association, the Catholic Diocese of Hong Kong, Sik Sik Yuen (a religious charitable organisation affiliated with Taoism, Buddhism and Confucianism), and the Hong Kong Taoist Association.

Regarding education, most schools in Hong Kong have religious affiliations. In the academic year 2015-16, approximately 61.52% of Hong Kong primary schools were funded and managed by religious organisations (CHSC, 2015) (Table I).

	Government	Government subsidised	Direct subsidised	Private	Total
Religious primary schools	0 (0%)	275 (53.71%)	10 (1.95%)	30 (5.86%)	315 (61.52%)
Buddhism	0	16	0	0	16 (3.13%)
Catholicism	0	95	1	13	109 (21.29%)
Protestantism	0	148	9	17	174 (33.98%)
Taoism	0	8	0	0	8 (1.56%)
Others[b]	0	8	0	0	8 (1.56%)
Non-religious primary schools	34 (6.64%)	146 (28.52%)	11 (2.15%)	6 (1.17%)	197 (38.48%)
Total	34 (6.64%)	421 (82.23%)	21 (4.10%)	36 (7.03%)	512 (100%)

Notes:
[a]According to the funding type, the schools in Hong Kong are categorised as government schools, government-subsidised schools, direct-subsidised schools, or private schools. Direct-subsidised schools are free to select students and design their own curricula under a special arrangement with government.
[b]The data shown in *Primary School Profiles 2015* was self-reported by the schools. The original categories, including 'Confucian', 'Muslim', and 'other religion (not specified)' were grouped as 'others' in this table.

Table I. Number and percentages of primary schools in Hong Kong (by school religion and funding type).[a]
(*Source*: CHSC 2015).

Historical Development of School Education and Religious Education in Hong Kong

In Hong Kong, numerous schools were established by religious organisations, which greatly affected the historical development of the formal schooling system in Hong Kong. During the colonial period following 1841, schools in Hong Kong were largely established by missionaries who were either Protestants or Roman Catholics of various denominations (Sweeting, 1990). During the post-war period, church school attendance significantly increased. In the aftermath of the Japanese occupation of Hong Kong, the rapid population growth among Chinese migrants led to an urgent need for schools. As a result, with cooperation between the Hong Kong government and local Church leaders, there was a substantial growth of Church schooling in Hong Kong from 1953 (Leung, 2005).

The development of non-Christian education (such as Taoist and Buddhist education) in Hong Kong was initiated by a number of Taoist and

Buddhist associations that dated from the early 1900s. For instance, the Hong Kong Buddhist Association was founded in 1945 with the objective of propagating Buddhism (HKBA, 2016). A few informal free schools were organised by various Buddhist parties and temple personnel before the establishment of the association, which later became formally funded Buddhist schools after the implementation of the nine-year compulsory education system (i.e. primary Grade 1 to secondary Grade 3) in 1978 (Gao, 2000). Regarding Taoist schools, Sik Sik Yuen and the Hong Kong Taoist Association were the two major forces in developing Taoist education in Hong Kong, founded in 1921 and 1957, respectively. Both associations established their first school in 1969. Since then, an increasing number of funded schools were founded to serve the community and promote Taoism (HKTA, 2016; SSY, 2016).

On the basis of this historical development, the implementation of religious education in Hong Kong schools mainly relies on the contributions of religious schools and their school-sponsoring bodies. The implementation of religious education in Hong Kong primary schools is based on each school's or school-sponsoring body's decisions regarding curricula. No government-suggested religious curriculum is provided, and religious education is not a subject for public primary school student examinations. In other words, Hong Kong school religious education is only carried out in religious schools that were established by religious organisations and are subsidised by the Hong Kong government. Table I presents the distributions of religious schools by funding type. Each individual school and its sponsoring body have autonomy in deciding the development of religious education in the corresponding schools. However, public schools do not have a religious background and seldom implement religious education as a formal subject. This general situation forms a specific context for the provision of religious education in Hong Kong schools, which is distinct from the educational contexts of certain other countries, such as New Zealand and Norway. Christian religious education classes (under an opt-out programme known as Bible in Schools) are conducted in 42% of government primary schools in New Zealand (CEC, 2014; Bradstock, 2015), whereas Norway's public school children aged 6-16 years (accounting for approximately 98% of all Norwegian public school students, excluding those in private schools and home schooling) are enrolled in a compulsory religious education curriculum on the subject of Religion, Philosophies of Life, and Ethics (NMER, 2010; Hovdelien, 2015).

Implementation of Religious Education in Four Religious Primary Schools

In this study, four religious primary schools were selected to illustrate how religious schools implement religious education in the multi-religious Hong Kong society. As indicated previously, Protestant, Catholic, Buddhist and

Taoist schools are the most common religious schools, respectively accounting for 33.98%, 21.29%, 3.13% and 1.56% of Hong Kong primary schools (Table I). Therefore, one religious primary school in Hong Kong was randomly selected to represent each type of school religion.

For the fieldwork, data were collected through multiple methods at the schools. Individual interviews and document reviews were the major methods, which were supplemented with lesson observations. In total, 11 school personnel participated as interviewees, comprising four religious education teachers (including one religious education subject panel head and one school pastoral assistant), one school curriculum leader (i.e. the teacher in charge of school curriculum development), two vice principals and four principals. Some school documents were collected, such as school calendars, annual development plans, curriculum plans, religious education work schemes and textbooks. Furthermore, six religious education lessons were observed.[1]

Multi-religious School Contexts in the Four Schools

Like all other Hong Kong religious schools, the four religious schools in this study were established and managed by their respective religious organisations and financially subsidised by the HKSAR government (Table II). Schools C and P were respectively founded by branches of international Catholic and Protestant Churches, whereas Schools B and T were respectively established by Hong Kong Buddhist and Taoist associations. Each school was government subsidised; therefore, they acquired the same approximate level of government support for curriculum and instruction, school management, teacher recruitment and student intake.

Regarding the school teachers' religious background, there was no requirement for the teachers to follow the religion affiliated with their school. The government-subsidised religious schools had autonomy in recruiting teachers to promote the school's mission and implement religious education. The teachers sharing religious affiliations with their respective schools accounted only for 6%, 17%, 25% and 7% of the total number of teachers in Schools B, C, P and T (Table II), respectively. According to the school principal interviews, none of the four schools had strict requirements for their teachers' religious affiliation and none insisted on hiring only followers of their schools' affiliated religion. However, the principals from Schools B and P believed that it was beneficial to have teachers who were followers and who would have similar values and beliefs to those promoted by the school (B/Interview–Principal; P/Interview–Principal).

Furthermore, student religion was not the major selection criterion for student enrolment in the four government-subsidised religious schools. In Schools B, C and P, only approximately 10%, 1% and 15% of students respectively adhered to the religion affiliated with the school (Table II) (unknown for School T). According to the policy of Primary One Admission

(EDB, 2016), government-subsidised schools provide free school education for Hong Kong student residents, regardless of whether the students have a religious or secular background; students are eligible to apply to religion-affiliated schools as they wish. Therefore, the students in religious schools may not necessarily adhere to the religion affiliated with the schools, even though students of the same religion could receive an additional five points when considered for enrolment.[2]

	School B	School C	School P	School T
School religion	Buddhism	Catholicism	Protestantism	Taoism
Management body	A local Hong Kong Buddhist association	A branch of the international Catholic church	A branch of an international Protestant denomination	A local Hong Kong Taoist organisation
Funding type	Government-subsidised	Government-subsidised	Government-subsidised	Government-subsidised
Percentage of religious followers who have same religion with the school				
Teachers	6%	17%	25%	7%
Students	10%	1%	15%	N.A.[a]

[a]No relevant data for the number of Taoist students was provided by School T.

Table II. Backgrounds of the four religious primary schools.

In other words, each religious school was a multi-religious learning environment; religious and secular students worked together in the schools. This situation could potentially facilitate the development of religious education as well as the general personal development for all religious and secular students, rather than solely nurturing the religious development of religious students with a shared religious affiliation.

Formal and Informal Religious Education Curricula Inside and Outside Class

To serve all students who had different religious and secular backgrounds, all four schools generally employed two major curriculum strategies in organising and implementing religious education, including formal and informal curricula.

Informal curriculum. The two Christian schools (Schools C and P) had a stronger religious emphasis through the development of informal curriculum. According to the fieldwork observations of their daily school life, the students

156

in Schools C and P prayed up to three times daily: at the morning assembly, before lunch and before leaving school (C/FieldJotting01, p. 1; P/FieldJotting08, p. 2). In addition, School P held a 'religious morning assembly' every Friday, often had students sing Christian songs during daily assembly, and held worship services during Easter (P/Document36–AssemblySchedule, pp. 1-3). Furthermore, some Christian prayers and songs in the assemblies were led by Christian students (P/FieldJotting01, p. 8). At the Buddhist school (School B), although students were not asked to pray every day, they used the Indian greeting and valediction, Namaste, before and after class lessons as well as to greet teachers and guests when meeting in the hallway. School B also occasionally organised Buddhist activities for students, such as a '*Juegong Shangren* memorial activity' (B/Document02–SchoolNewsletter, pp. 2-3) and 'the ritual of bathing the Buddha on Buddha's birthday' (B/Interview–PanelHeadTeacher). Similar to School B, the Taoist school (School T) did not have any regular daily religious rituals. Instead, it relied on occasional Taoism-related activities to implement Taoist education in the school, such as by promoting Taoist culture and knowledge through 'Taoist education talk' (T/FieldJotting04, pp. 3-7) and a 'Taoist Festival' (T/Interview–VicePrincipal). In summary, the two Christian schools (Schools C and P) organised more regular religious activities outside of class to promote religious practices and education than did the other two schools (Schools B and T).

Formal curriculum. The formal religious education curricula in the schools played a substantial role in developing religious education. Each school taught their respective religious practices through subject lessons; however, the organisation of the curricula in each school varied slightly (Table III). This reflects the relationship between religious education and moral education. Schools B, C and P had independent religious education subjects (called Buddhist Studies for School B and Religious Studies for Schools C and P); moreover, they also implemented formal moral- and values-education-related school subjects (called Moral Education, Moral and Civic Education, and Personal Growth Education). Unlike the other three schools, School T delivered Taoist Education solely through its Moral Education curriculum; no formal school subject of Religious Studies was implemented in School T.

Religious education teachers. Religious Studies curricula were taught by teachers who were Catholic and Protestant at Schools C and P – for example, the pastoral assistant (at School C). In School B, the subject of Buddhist Studies was mainly taught by Buddhist teachers; if there were not enough Buddhist teachers, the secular teachers were assigned for this purpose; teachers who had other religious beliefs did not teach this subject (B/Interview–PanelHeadTeacher). In School T, the Taoist Education curriculum was merged with the Moral Education curriculum and was taught by class teachers who were Taoist or secular, or who adhered to any other religion.

	School B	School C	School P	School T
Religious education related subjects				
Subject name	Buddhist Studies	Religious Studies	Religious Studies	Nil.
Taught by	Buddhist or secular teachers	Catholic teachers	Protestant teachers	N.A.
Moral and values education related subjects				
Subject name	Moral Education	Moral and Civic Education	Personal Growth Education	Moral Education (including Taoist Education)
Taught by	Class teachers	Class teachers	Class teachers	Class teachers (who are secular or from any religion)

Table III. Religious moral and values education curricula in the four schools.

Multi-religious identities among teachers and students. According to the aforementioned curriculum and teacher arrangements, the learning environment in the religious education classes was complicated. Teachers and students partaking in the religious education lessons might not share religious identities with one other or with their own school. Three critical situations of religious identity could be observed in the schools' religious education classes. The first general situation was that the students in the four schools were mainly secular, with few of them sharing the religious affiliations of their schools or teachers. Regarding student religious identity, School T's principal mentioned that this situation could affect the student motivation and engagement in religious education (T/Interview–Principal), whereas School C's principal saw this situation involving multiple identities as an excellent opportunity for 'missionary preaching' (C/Interview–Principal). Second, particularly in Schools B and T, there could be a situation whereby the students were Buddhist or Taoist whereas the teacher was secular but teaching Buddhist Studies or Taoist Education. School T's Taoist Education lesson (T/Lesson1) on the topic of *Daode Jing*, the fundamental text for Taoism, was taught by a secular teacher; she prepared her lesson by herself with the school-provided teaching materials and information she found on the Internet (T/Interview–Teacher). Third, more notably, School T's religious education teachers could belong to other religions, whereas their students could be Taoist followers, although this was a relatively uncommon situation. In the second and third situations, the teachers' religious identity could act as a barrier in teaching the religious subjects: the teachers taught Buddhist Studies or Taoist Education from a non-follower's perspective.

Taken together, multiple religious identities were found in the classrooms at the schools at various learning levels, showing the complexity and dynamics of implementing religious education in religious schools in Hong Kong.

A Single-religion Perspective for Teaching
Single-religion Content in Religious Education

Despite the multiple religious identities of the schools, this study determined that the four schools planned and taught religious education mainly from a single-religion perspective in their formal independent religious subjects, rather than employing various religions as learning contexts and curriculum content to teach religious lessons.

Overall, single-religion learning content was clearly evident in the schools' religious education curricula. Schools B, C and P had their respective religious textbooks published by their own sponsoring bodies (including the local Buddhist organisation and branches of international Catholic and Protestant Churches), clearly favouring their own affiliated religion. For example, School B's Buddhist Studies curriculum aimed 'to nurture students' positive and correct life values and living attitude, and encourage them to contribute to society and serve others in order to achieve the goal of a happy life' (B/Document06–TeacherHandbook1A, preface). The curriculum contents ranged from basic knowledge of Buddhist Studies (e.g. the background of Buddha, for Grade 1) to the concept of the immeasurable greatness of Buddhism (*Fufa Wubian*, for Grade 6) (B/Interview–PanelHeadTeacher). In School C, Religious Studies 'was a religious curriculum specifically designed for Catholic schools in Hong Kong' that aimed 'to match the students' growth and nurture their correct life values and attitude' (C/Document03–TeacherHandbook4B, preface). In an interview, School C's principal stated that the major content of Religious Studies involved learning about Christ as a role model, stating: 'While teaching Religious Studies, the Bible's guideline is very important; we need to follow it. We teach our students to follow the Christ and learn his behaviour.' She even saw the Christian perspective as 'the only reference' in religious teaching (C/Interview–Principal). School C's school curriculum leader also offered a similar remark, stating that the teaching of religious education in the school 'was started from the basic knowledge of the Bible', viewing Christianity-based content as the foundation of the subjects in their Religious Studies curriculum (C/Interview–SchoolCurriculumLeader). In another interview, School P's principal explained that the school's education and curriculum should be 'religion-related', emphasising a strong commitment to promoting Christian love through school education. She stated:

> When talking about our school's education, it must be related to
> religion, since our school is a Protestant school. Similar to other
> Christian schools, we run the school based on Christ's love; we
> love our students, and the beloved students then know how to
> love others. (P/Interview–Principal)

School P's Religious Studies curriculum was Christianity-oriented. The
school's religious educational aims included 'connecting religion with the
daily life experience of the students' and 'enhancing their participation in
praying' (P/Document63–PrayingHandbook, afterword). As the school's
religious teacher further explained, 'I think our school has a set of clear
beliefs [for our religious curriculum] that fundamentally comes from the
Christ' (P/Interview–Teacher). When teaching Religious Studies, Christian
teachers in both Schools C and P also used 'a particular set of references
from the Bible to teach' (P/Interview–Teacher) and 'refer[red] to the Bible
and the Church's guideline' (C/Interview–Teacher). The Religious Studies
lessons in Schools C and P also exhibited a strong religious atmosphere and
Christian teaching content during the lessons – for example, using the Bible
verse 'I came not to call the righteous, but sinners to repentance' (Luke 5:32)
during lessons (C/Lesson02), and praying together with the words 'Dear
father, we humbly ask of you. Amen!' (P/Lesson01).

Similar to the two Christian schools, but with a slightly different
application of single-religion orientation, School B stressed its Buddhist
perspective as the major focus of its religious education. School B's panel
head teacher of Buddhist Studies shared his teaching experience, stating:
'While teaching Buddhist Studies, we will not involve others' religions ... and
do not preach other religions, and are not involved in other religious rituals'
(B/Interview–PanelHeadTeacher). However, the school allowed some time
for other religious cultural activities. School B's principal explained her views
on the role of the subject of Buddhist Studies in the school, believing that
'Buddhist Studies as philosophy' could help students 'to learn to be good'
and that this 'benefited their spiritual development' (B/Interview–Principal).
Moreover, as a Buddhist, she did not perceive Buddhism as the sole religious
tradition that the students should learn. Therefore, she did not discourage
other religious cultural education; using Christmas as an example, she stated:

> My colleagues had asked me whether they could teach the written
> text for greetings in Christmas card format and teach students to
> sing Christian songs. I said 'why not?' It is a festival... That's fine,
> but not the promotion of other religions and organising other
> religious rituals in the school, like receiving baptism.
> (B/Interview–Principal)

Regarding School T's religious curriculum, it did not use religious textbooks
published by the school-sponsoring body as the other three schools did.
School T's teaching materials were prepared by the school's vice principal
with assistance from the teachers who were members of the school's Taoist

Education curriculum team. The vice principal explained that their teaching contents were matched with the school's Taoist activities. She stated: 'In Taoist Education lessons, we read the text of the *Laozi*... Students started learning to read it during Grade 1, and learn how to perform a series of three low bows to Laozi' (T/Interview–VicePrincipal). In another interview, the principal of School T emphasised the aim of their Taoist Education, stating: 'Our Taoism is concerned much about the values of harmony and inclusion. In the school, the important thing is that teachers do not preach other religions and follow our school mission. That's the real aim of the school's education' (T/Interview–Principal). Therefore, the aim and content of School T's Taoist Education are still mainly Taoism oriented; no learning content taught from other religious perspectives could be found in the school's religious curriculum, although they included Christmas and Easter holidays on their school calendar, as do most secular and Christian schools in Hong Kong.

In summary, all four schools generally taught formal religious curricula from the single perspective of their own school's affiliated religion, strictly disallowing the preaching of other religions in their schools. Although School B had a relatively liberal policy that allowed other religious cultural activities and provided students with opportunities to learn more about different religions, there was no content on other religions in the school's formal Buddhist Studies lessons. School B's panel head teacher of Buddhist Studies emphasised: 'As a Buddhist school, to employ Buddhist beliefs in teaching religious education is the basic principle' (B/Interview–PanelHeadTeacher). In other words, the aim of its religious education excludes the promotion of multiple religions.

Moral and Values Education in Religious Education Curricula

While investigating the curriculum planning of the four religious schools and school personnel perceptions towards religious education, moral values were determined to be crucial.

Almost all interviewees believed that religious education fundamentally had a moral function, although they interpreted this function from the various perspectives of their school's religion. For example, School C's religious education was guided by Christian values and Christ's good deeds; the principal stated that 'besides teaching religion from the knowledge perspective, the teaching also embeds Catholic values... From the moral education perspective, the teaching should also have the Christ's good behaviour demonstrated within it' (C/Interview–Principal). A similar view was offered by a teacher from School C, who explained that 'in teaching, we taught students what the Christ had done and set him as well as various patron saints as role models' (C/Interview–Teacher). In School P, the Protestant teacher also held a similar idea concerning his Religious Studies curriculum. He emphasised that 'morality is always to be associated while talking about religion' (C/Interview–Teacher), believing that Christian education and moral education were interrelated. However, preaching Christianity was not his aim in teaching; rather, his aim was applying a lower-level goal to allow his beginner students to 'know what religion is ... what praying is and how we pray' (P/ Interview–Teacher).

School B's panel head teacher taught Buddhist Studies by incorporating certain moral values; teachers of these lessons aimed 'to teach school children to understand Buddhist knowledge that further develops their values' (B/Interview–PanelHeadTeacher). The panel head teacher viewed this practice as easily justifiable, claiming that 'there are many moral-related values, such as filial piety, love, and honesty ... in fact, which have been mentioned in Buddhism already'. Unlike School B, which taught Buddhist Studies with moral-values-related contents, School T simply used values teaching as a means of promoting its Taoist Education. School T's principal stated: 'The Taoist Education teaching materials are highly relevant to those traditional Confucian values of filial piety, faithfulness, honesty and honour ... they are interrelated' (T/Interview–Principal). The vice principal, as the Taoist Education curriculum team head, further explained: 'In our Taoist Education curriculum, we teach students frugality, humbleness and caring, as well as how to align with nature in order to achieve a state of inaction' (T/Interview–VicePrincipal). Teaching Taoist Education with applied moral values was the principal goal of curriculum planning and teaching in School T.

In summary, teaching students moral values in addition to preaching the beliefs of the affiliated religion was one of the major aims of religious education subjects for the four schools.

Conclusion

Hong Kong is a multi-religious international city. However, the data of this study present a contrasting phenomenon: religious education in religious schools is taught from single-religion perspectives. In the four investigated religious schools, the schools did not focus on multi-religious learning when curriculum planning and teaching religious subjects, but strictly adhered to the schools' respective religious affiliations. Moreover, the schools included moral education in their religious education curricula; the teaching of religious education had both religious and moral purposes. This practice suggests that the major aim of religious education in Hong Kong is somewhat different from that of some international religious education curricula that aim to provide multi-religious education for the benefit of students holding various cultural and religious values.

The practice of implementing single-religion curricula is, in the case of Hong Kong, mainly attributable to factors such as the significant effects of religious organisations on the Hong Kong schooling system, the autonomy of religious curriculum development in the schools, and the lack of government-suggested religious curricula for primary schools.

First, religious organisations were placed in a special position in the Hong Kong educational sector. As shown previously, these organisations have provided substantial contributions to schools with the support and collaboration of the Hong Kong government since the 1800s. This traditional role has had a deep-rooted influence on the development of school religious education in Hong Kong. Despite the transfer of sovereignty from the United Kingdom to the PRC in 1997, the religious organisations in Hong Kong still maintained substantial authority and continued to influence religious education in schools after the handover; the political transfer did not decrease religious organisational power in managing the religious education in the affiliated schools. Furthermore, their right to manage the affiliated schools' religious matters is guaranteed by the Basic Law of HKSAR: 'the Government of the Hong Kong Special Administrative Region shall not restrict the freedom of religious belief' (CMAB, 2015, Article 141); '[s]chools run by religious organisations may continue to provide religious education, including courses in religion' (Article 137). This reinforced the crucial role and influence of religious organisations in formal religious education.

Second, each religious school's sponsoring body has autonomy in developing religious education curricula. Each affiliated school strictly followed its respective organisation's mission by promoting a certain religion, forming task groups for curriculum development, and designing its own religious education curricula. Accordingly, single-religion curricula were used in the investigated religious primary schools.

Third, there are no government-suggested religious curricula and no corresponding official examinations in Hong Kong primary schools. However, for religious secondary schools in Hong Kong, there are two optional government-suggested religious curricula: Religious Studies (CDC, 1999), which was designed for lower secondary schools; and Ethics and Religious Studies (CDC & HKEAA, 2007), which was developed for upper secondary schools and is a formal public school subject requiring examination. The curriculum content includes various religious traditions. All religious or secular secondary schools are eligible to offer these religious curricula. Unlike public secondary schools, the sponsoring bodies of religious primary schools can develop their own religious curricula and teaching materials, without any restrictions; it is unnecessary for these organisations to consider multiple religions as compulsory elements in developing their curricula. This further evidences school-sponsoring-body autonomy in developing religious education curricula.

In conclusion, the special position and autonomy of religious organisations in managing religious matters and religious curricula in religious primary schools in Hong Kong are the major factors in explaining why the schools in this study designed and taught single-religion contents and excluded multi-religious elements, which might otherwise seem surprising. This chapter shows that the implementation of religious education curricula in Hong Kong schools does not always entail multi-religious activities; religious primary schools in Hong Kong evidently do not include elements of multiple religions in curriculum planning and teaching because of the deep-rooted influence and role of their founding organisations. This chapter provides empirical evidence regarding the unique character of the development of religious education in the particular multi-religious society of Hong Kong.

Notes

[1] No lessons were observed in School B because of a limited arrangement.

[2] According to the points system for the Primary One Admission policy, student applicants who have the 'same religious affiliation as the sponsoring body which operates the primary school' will receive an additional five points (EDB, 2016, n.p.).

References

Baumfield, V. (2009) Learning about and from Religion Education, *British Journal of Religious Education*, 31(1), 1-2. https://doi.org/10.1080/01416200802560294

Bradstock, H. (2015) Religion in New Zealand's State Primary Schools, *Journal of Intercultural Studies*, 36(3), 338-361.
https://doi.org/10.1080/07256868.2015.1029885

Census and Statistics Department (CSD) (2012) *2011 Population Census: summary result*. Hong Kong: Census and Statistics Department, HKSAR.
Document42http://www.statistics.gov.hk/pub/B11200552011XXXXB0100.pdf (accessed 22 February 2016).

Census and Statistics Department (CSD) (2016) Population (end–2015), in *Hong Kong Statistics*. Hong Kong: Census and Statistics Department, HKSAR.
http://www.censtatd.gov.hk/hkstat/sub/bbs.jsp (accessed 19 February 2016).

Churches Education Commission (CEC) (2014) Religious Instruction: recommended procedure guidelines for boards of trustees in New Zealand schools. Auckland: CEC.
http://cec.org.nz/Portals/0/Documents/Recommended%20policy%20guidelines%20for%20BoTs.pdf (accessed 11 May 2016).

Committee on Home-School Co-operation (CHSC) (2015) Primary School Profiles 2015. http://www.chsc.hk/psp2015/eng/index.php (accessed 19 February 2016).

Constitutional and Mainland Affairs Bureau (CMAB) (2015) Chapter VI: Education, Science, Culture, Sports, Religion, Labour and Social Services, in *The Basic Law of the Hong Kong Special Administrative Region of the People's Republic of China*. Hong Kong: HKSAR.
http://www.basiclaw.gov.hk/en/basiclawtext/chapter_6.html (accessed 19 February 2016).

Copley, T. (2008) Non-indoctrinatory Religious Education in Secular Cultures, *Religious Education*, 103(1), 22-31. https://doi.org/10.1080/00344080701807411

Curriculum Development Council (CDC) (1999) Syllabuses for Secondary Schools Religious Education (Secondary 1-3). Hong Kong: Hong Kong Education Department. http://www.edb.gov.hk/attachment/en/curriculum-development/kla/pshe/CSS13REE.pdf (accessed 12 March 2016).

Curriculum Development Council (CDC) and Hong Kong Examinations and Assessment Authority (HKEAA) (2007) Personal, Social and Humanities Education Key Learning Area: ethics and religious studies curriculum and assessment guide (Secondary 4-6) (with updates in November 2015). Hong Kong: Education Bureau. http://www.edb.gov.hk/attachment/en/curriculum-development/kla/pshe/8.ERS_CA_Guide_updated_e__2015.10.pdf (accessed 12 March 2016).

Education Bureau (EDB) (2016) Primary One Admission for September 2016. Hong Kong: Education Bureau. ttp://www.edb.gov.hk/attachment/en/edu-system/primary-secondary/spa-systems/primary-1-admission/poa2016_leaflet_en.pdf (accessed 22 March 2016).

Gao, Y. (2000) *Tan xianggang fojiao yixue de shizhong* [Historical development of free Buddhism education in Hong Kong], *Buddhist in Hong Kong*, 476. http://www.hkbuddhist.org/magazine/476/476_11.html (in Chinese) (accessed 26 February 2016).

Hella, E. & Wright, A. (2009) Learning 'about' and 'from' Religion: phenomenography, the variation theory of learning and religious education in Finland and the UK, *British Journal of Religious Education*, 31(1), 53-64. https://doi.org/10.1080/01416200802560047

HKSAR Government (2014) Religion and Custom, in *Hong Kong: the facts*. Hong Kong: Information Services Department. http://www.gov.hk/en/about/abouthk/factsheets/docs/religion.pdf (accessed 22 February 2016).

Hong Kong Buddhist Association (HKBA) (2016) History [of Hong Kong Buddhist Association]. http://www.hkbuddhist.org/ (accessed 26 February 2016).

Hong Kong Taoist Association (HKTA) (2016) List of Schools Founded by Hong Kong Taoist Association. http://www.hktaoist.org.hk/index.php?id=101 (accessed 9 March 2016).

Hovdelien, O. (2015) Education and Common Values in a Multicultural Society: the Norwegian case, *Journal of Intercultural Studies*, 36(3), 306-319. https://doi.org/10.1080/07256868.2015.1029887

Hull, J.M. (2002) The Contribution of Religious Education to Religious Freedom: a global perspective, in *Religious Education in Schools: school education in relation with freedom of religion and belief, tolerance, and non-discrimination*, pp. 4-11. Essex Hall, UK: International Association for Religious Freedom (IARF).

Jackson, R. (2004) *Rethinking Religious Education and Plurality: issues in diversity and pedagogy*. London: RoutledgeFalmer. https://doi.org/10.4324/9780203465165

Kalloniemi, A. (2010) Religious Education Curricula of Finnish Minority Religious Groups: an example of different approaches to religious education in a diverse world, *Religious Education Journal Australia*, 26(2), 9-15.

Knauth, T. (2009) Incidents Analysis: a key category of REDCo classroom analysis: theoretical background and conceptual remarks, in I. Avest, D.P. Jozsa, T. Knauth, J. Rosón & G. Skeie (Eds) *Dialogue and Conflict on Religion: studies of classroom interaction in European countries*, pp. 17-27. Münster: Waxmann Verlag.

Leung, K.F.B. (2005) Church, State and Education, in B. Bray & R. Koo (Eds) *Education and Society in Hong Kong and Macau: comparative perspectives on continuity and change*, pp. 99-108. Hong Kong: Comparative Education Research Centre, University of Hong Kong.

Norwegian Ministry of Education and Research (NMER) (2010) Act of 17 July 1998 no. 61 Relating to Primary and Secondary Education and Training (the Education Act). https://www.regjeringen.no/en/dokumenter/education-act/id213315/ (accessed 11 May 2016).

Sik Sik Yuen (SSY) (2016) Overview. http://www1.siksikyuen.org.hk/en/communityservices/educationservices/overview (accessed 24 February 2016).

Sweeting, A. (1990) Chapter Three: Variation on a Missionary Theme 1841-65, in *Education in Hong Kong, pre-1841 to 1941: fact and opinion*, pp. 139-153. Hong Kong: Hong Kong University Press.

Teece, G. (2008) Learning from Religions as 'Skilful Means': a contribution to the debate about the identity of religious education, *British Journal of Religious Education*, 30(3), 187-198. https://doi.org/10.1080/01416200802170037

Teece, G. (2010) Is it Learning about and from Religions, Religion or Religious Education? And is it Any Wonder Some Teachers Don't Get It?, *British Journal of Religious Education*, 32(2), 93-103. https://doi.org/10.1080/01416200903537399

Weisse, W. (2009) Classroom Interaction: a foreword, in I. Avest, D.P. Jozsa, T. Knauth, J. Rosón, & G. Skeie (Eds) *Dialogue and Conflict on Religion: studies of classroom interaction in European countries*, pp. 17-27. Münster: Waxmann Verlag.

CHAPTER 8

State Schooling and Religious Education for Muslim Hui Students in Northwestern China: changing perceptions and new developments

XINYI WU

SUMMARY This chapter uses rural Muslim Hui students from the Ningxia Hui Autonomous Region as a case study to examine the trajectories of state schooling and religious education in China. By looking at individuals' dilemmas of *Nianshu* (attending state schooling) and *Nianjing* (participating in religious education), it focuses on how state schooling is perceived and understood as it comes into contact with the local religious education and how this relationship generates complementary rather than contradictory life possibilities. It concludes that religious education, as a tradition of cultural inheritance, offers Muslim Hui children and youth an opportunity to learn how to share secular life with their belief system and the virtue it fosters.

Introduction

Education for ethnic minority groups has always been a challenge for the Chinese government, especially the issue of quality. Because of the complexity and multiplicity of geopolitical, historical, cultural and economic conditions of each ethnic group, a single national solution to improving quality is far from sufficient. For Muslim Hui, the challenges often lie at the intersection of state schooling and religious education. It is a difficult decision that Muslim Hui parents struggle to make, as they are required by law to have their children attend state schooling, particularly to complete nine years of compulsory education. While state schooling aims to provide Muslim Hui students with knowledge and skills that enable them to pursue material prosperity, particularly in the case of underdeveloped rural Muslim Hui people, religious education is considered indispensable in that it is an essential component of Muslim Hui people's daily life. It provides moral guidance, transmits Islamic knowledge and practices, passes on family traditions to younger generations, and helps maintain an ethnoreligious Hui identity. Therefore, the educational challenges Muslim Hui face are not only about quality but also about how quality education is intertwined with their perceptions and expectations of education. As Tan and Ding (2014) stressed, for Muslim Hui, education is seen as more than formal schooling and it includes 'continuous and often spontaneous teaching and learning that takes place at home and in the community' (p. 57). Therefore, understanding education for Muslim Hui requires attention to its broader concept, no matter where education takes place, whether it is home based, community based or state provided. It is important to note that religious education is often carried out at home and in the community, whereas secular education is usually provided by the state. The relationship between state schooling and religious education thus reflects the roles of home, community and state schooling in defining quality.

Previously, discussions of the relationship between state schooling and religious education have centered on how state schooling, as a site of cultural reproduction and cultural exclusion, modernizes, civilizes and assimilates Muslim Hui into a unified multiethnic nation state (Qian, 2007; Zhu, 2007; Wang, 2013). However, the tensions between state schooling and religious education are much more complex, and their interactions have created a unique Muslim Hui education with both 'Chinese and Muslim characteristics'. This chapter will uncover these complexities by demonstrating how state schooling and religious education interact and maintain a distinctively harmonious relationship through negotiating a common ground which preserves Hui culture and prepares the next generation of Muslim Hui. It will start with an overview of the Muslim Hui population and introduce the dual education system currently available for Muslim Hui, both the state schooling and religious education. Then, it will discuss the dilemmas between *Nianshu* (attending state schooling) and *Nianjing* (participating in religious education). Finally, it will use rural Muslim youth from the Ningxia Hui Autonomous Region as a case study to show how state schooling is perceived and what is expected of it, as it comes into contact with the local religious education.

Muslim Hui in China

China is a politically unified but culturally diverse nation. Within 56 ethnic groups, one ethnic group, the majority Han, constitutes 92 percent of the Chinese population, and the other 55 ethnic groups, recognized and classified as ethnic minorities, represent the remaining 8 percent. The majority of ethnic minorities reside in the five designated ethnic autonomous or self-administered regions, with the rest scattered around China (Wang, 2004). Among the 55 ethnic minority groups, the Muslim Hui is the second-largest ethnic group, with over 10 million people either concentrated or dispersed throughout China at provincial, prefectural, county, township and village levels (National Bureau of Statistics of China, 2010). According to Yang (2006), the majority of the Hui Muslims (60.75%) live in Western China, and the Ningxia Hui Autonomous Region located in the northwest is the designated provincial-level administrative region, with approximately 35% of the Hui population (Ningxia Statistics Bureau, 2011).

Although *Hui* is currently used as an ethnic marker to denote a group of Chinese Muslims or a Hui nationality (Mackerras, 1999), the term itself is indefinite. It also refers to other ethnic groups, including *Baoan*, *Dongxiang* and *Sala*, who identify themselves as *Hui* people but who are politically categorized by the Chinese government as other ethnic groups (Jian, 2004). It additionally includes Tibetan and Mongolian Muslims who do not speak Chinese (Gladney, 2003). *Hui*, therefore, has both ethnic and religious connotations, with the ethnic classification defined by the government and the religious affiliation often expressed by the people themselves. Muslim Hui, in this chapter, are defined in a narrow sense, referring to the Hui ethnic group who can be viewed as both cultural and religious minorities (Tan & Ding, 2014). By using 'Muslim' Hui, it emphasizes their belief in Islam that is embedded in their ethnic consciousness and religious identity (Bai, 2001).

In order to better understand Muslim Hui in China, it is important to know how Islamic religion was first introduced and then interpreted, eventually becoming an integral part of Muslim Hui culture. Historically, Islam was introduced to China during the Tang Dynasty, when large numbers of Arabic and Persian traders started their import-export business with Chinese people. For hundreds of years, many of them had settled down and become more or less permanent residents, living within their own communities with freedom to engage in such Islamic practices as praying and eating *Halal* food. At that time, intermarriages were common, as few Arabic and Persian women followed the foreign merchants to China. A majority of the merchants had to marry Chinese women who converted to Islam and taught their China-born children to speak local dialects of Chinese. After a few generations, permanent Sino-Muslim communities started to form in China. During the Yuan Dynasty, which was governed by a Mongol minority, the process of integration was driven by the fear of political instability. Muslims were given local government positions and higher political status, which forced them to have more interactions with Chinese. As a result, intermarriages became more common, which ensured a 'constant exposure to Chinese culture in intimate family circles and through genetic incorporation into civilized China' (Lipman, 1997).

In addition, large numbers of Muslims in the Mongol military arrived in northwestern regions when the Mongol empire conquered vast territories in that area. These Muslim troops settled in rural places and grew crops to make a living. This shift deepened the process of integration such that Muslims became familiar with the feudal system and traditional Chinese culture. Since then, Muslims in China found themselves less connected with Central Asia and more tied to China itself (Lipman, 1997). They lived communally around mosques and bonded by sharing a Muslim identity across different communities, though surrounded by non-Muslim communities. Their language was a combination of local dialects with Arabic and Persian phrases inserted. They didn't eat with non-Muslims and made sure their children married within their own groups. The integration process continued, but Muslims' religious practices remained strong and were given new interpretations, which laid a foundation for the Muslim Hui culture.

The new interpretations of Islam were initiated by Chinese Muslim scholars who felt intellectually associated with both Islamic culture and Confucianism. These scholars wrote various genres of literature in Chinese, Arabic and Persian, the majority being in Chinese, and this collection of literature was called *Han Kitab*. Because the *Han Kitab* contains texts related to Islamic knowledge and practices, it became the basic curriculum of Muslim Hui students' religious education (Ben-Dor Benite, 2005).

During the Ming Dynasty, the process of integration was expanded, and Chinese Muslims were further assimilated into Chinese society in many ways. They spoke mainly Chinese, wore Chinese clothes and adopted Chinese surnames, which meant fewer of them were able to read and understand Arabic and Persian though they maintained their own lifestyle and religious belief, and considered Islamic culture as the core of their everyday interactions. Therefore, they needed someone who understood Arabic and Persian to lead the conduct of religious activities. In addition, with increasing numbers of Hui people living in China, the traditional method of passing Islamic knowledge from father to son and from teacher to student was no longer able to meet the religious needs. A new form of education, *Jingtang Jiaoyu*, or Spiritual Hall Education, was established for the purpose of teaching the masses basic Islamic knowledge and training prospective religious leaders. Until now, *Jingtang Jiaoyu* is still the most influential form of religious education and is widely practiced within Muslim Hui communities. More details about *Jingtang Jiaoyu* will be provided in the following section.

Education for Muslim Hui

Since religious education has a long tradition and has played a dominant role in transmitting, maintaining and preserving Islamic knowledge and practices historically, it is regarded by many Muslim Hui as more vital and essential than modern state schooling, especially in the areas with a concentrated Hui population. Typical Muslim Hui parents often educate their children to understand that they are not only Chinese but also Chinese Muslims. They teach children to recite the Muslim creed, to refrain from drinking alcohol and eating pork or other food from non-Muslims, and to celebrate religious festivals. It is also a common practice that they send children to mosques to receive religious education or *Jingtang Jiaoyu* taught by *Ahong* (imam). Although, these informal forms of education, home based or community oriented, are popular among Muslim Hui parents, they are not intended to teach knowledge and skills that could aid them in pursuing a better material life.

Compared with religious education, state schooling is seen as a modern form of education, with attendance required by law. It is also regarded by some Muslim Hui parents as a second choice to religious education. Correspondingly, a dual educational system is allowed in Muslim Hui concentrated regions to satisfy different needs of Muslim Hui, such as Ningxia Hui Autonomous Region, consisting of both relatively independent state schooling and religious education that includes state-sponsored Islamic Institutes, mosque-based *Jingtang Jiaoyu* and private Chinese-Arabic schools.

State Schooling

State schooling is a form of education provided by the Chinese government with a major aim of teaching school-aged children universal knowledge and skills for living as well as socialist ideology. All school-aged children are required by law to attend compulsory education, a nine-year state schooling, regardless of their ethnic affiliations. According to the 'Compulsory Education Law', formulated in 1986 and amended in June of 2006 by the National People's Congress, the purpose of compulsory education is:

> to provide quality-oriented education, to improve the quality of instruction, with a view to enabling school-aged children and adolescents to achieve well-rounded development – morally, intellectually, and physically, so as to lay the foundation for bringing up well-educated and self-disciplined builders and successors of socialism imbued with lofty ideals and moral integrity. (National People's Congress, 2006, Article 3)

In short, state-funded compulsory education is not only a knowledge-based education, it is also an ideology-oriented system that teaches children morality, self-discipline and socialist values. In this vein, state schooling for ethnic minority students, such as Muslim Hui, also has additional implications. Besides providing these students with quality education through specific policies and regulations, it also intends to help the nation achieve a homogeneous culture by orienting its ethnic population towards the goals of modernity and common prosperity, as it is believed that ethnic minority groups are generally more backward than the majority Han and it is anticipated that they will remain in a transitional period for a longer time (Dreyer, 1976).

For this dual purpose, a national standardized curriculum is upheld, characterized by universal knowledge and skills and socialist values and ideology, which is not culturally targeted at any specific ethnic groups.

However, schools in ethnic regions are allowed a certain amount of flexibility in implementing policies, and there are special educational programs designed to meet the needs of ethnic minorities, such as using bilingual curricula and textbooks, implementing preferential treatment for minorities, designating special funds to ethnic education, and prioritizing allocation of educational resources to poverty-stricken ethnic regions. Therefore, state schooling plays a key role in reproducing a politically unified, socially integrated and ethnically assimilated nation while also trying to maintain a certain level of cultural diversity (Chen, 2008; Wu & Han, 2011).

Religious Education

While state schooling is a major modern form of education for Muslim Hui and contributes to the development of their knowledge, skills and national identity, religious education is also believed to be fundamental in shaping and maintaining the distinctiveness of the Muslim Hui identity. In rural Ningxia, although the majority of Muslim children attend state schooling and go to mosques to obtain religious education when they have free time, some who want to be employed in Islam-related jobs, such as working as *Ahongs* (mosque clergy members), do choose religious education as the only pathway to receive education. Currently, there are three types of religious education: state-sponsored Islamic Institutes; *Jingtang Jiaoyu* (Scripture Hall Education); and private Chinese-Arabic schools. Each has its own target students and missions.

State-sponsored Islamic Institutes are specialized four-year higher institutes with primary missions of preparing students to work in religious professions and ensuring their patriotism by improving their cultural and religious knowledge. They are affiliated with the China Islamic Association, a state-recognized Islamic organization, and are located in ten provinces and autonomous regions with the most concentrated Muslim populations. Since these institutes only accept high school graduates with basic knowledge of Islam and aim to train prospective religious leaders and personnel, they are limited in offering Islamic teaching for the larger Muslim population.

Jingtang Jiaoyu therefore becomes the dominant form of religious education for the masses with an aim to teach children and youth basic knowledge of Islam. *Jingtang Jiaoyu* was first introduced by Hu Dengzhou, an *Ahong* or imam, in the middle years of the Ming Dynasty (Wang, 2012). For hundreds of years, *Jingtang Jiaoyu* was considered by the Muslim Hui as a way to gain knowledge of Islam and satisfy the needs of preserving religious and cultural practices (Ma, 2002). It was also seen as a professional education that cultivates future religious leaders and personnel (Ma, 2014). Since many Hui people believe that they can't identify themselves as Muslim Hui if they don't have basic knowledge of Islam, the teachings covered by *Jingtang Jiaoyu* are critical to connecting Muslim communities, facilitating religious activities and, even more importantly, ensuring the preservation of Islamic knowledge and practices for the next Muslim generation.

As a mosque-based and community-supported form of education, *Jiangtang Jiaoyu* is usually free. The cost of teaching and training as well as attending is covered by communities and donations from local Muslim families. *Jingtang* language is also created uniquely for this type of education as a response to the need for accurately teaching and explaining the classical texts in Arabic and Persian. It uses Chinese characters to imitate the moods, syntax, and structure of Arabic (Ma, 2014), which makes it easier for Muslim children to read and take notes.

There are two levels of *Jingtang Jiaoyu*, the primary level and the advanced level. The primary level of *Jingtang Jiaoyu* focuses on teaching basic knowledge and practices of Islam, such as reading Arabic texts and learning how to cleanse oneself, how to fast and how to recite Quranic verses in prayers. This level is intended for Muslim children at age 6-7, and it usually lasts for three years. The advanced level of *Jingtang Jiaoyu* is targeted at teenagers and adults who want to further their learning of the language and grammar of the Quran. Muslims who want to pursue religious professions, such as becoming an Imam, will be further taught 'philosophical and juridical works and scriptural exegeses' (Alles et al, 2003). The years spent in *Jingtang Jiaoyu* overlap the time that children are required to attend state-sponsored compulsory education. Therefore, it is a tough decision for both Muslim parents and children whether to keep *Jingtang Jiaoyu* as an addition to or sacrifice it for state schooling.

Unlike *Jingtang Jiaoyu*, Chinese-Arabic schools are usually private, and they prioritize Arabic language learning over theological knowledge teaching. They are also considered more suitable for Muslim girls, who are not supposed to attend religious education in the mosques after nine years of age in many parts of Ningxia, though some *Nusi* (female mosques) admit younger girls (Hong, 2013). Many Chinese-Arabic schools are vocational and technical schools, and they provide alternatives for Muslim youth who choose not to, or who are not able to, enter regular state-sponsored high schools. Their curricula are also more systematic than that of *Jingtang Jiaoyu*, which tends to be loosely structured (Tan & Ding, 2014). For example, students enrolled in a Chinese-Arabic school in Ningxia learn about translation techniques, computer skills, international trade, and etiquette in relation to the Arabic language or Arab countries.

Dilemmas between *Nianshu* and *Nianjing*

Since state schooling and religious education coexist, with the former being mandatory and the latter being indispensable, the dilemma arises when both forms of education require commitment from Muslim Hui students to attend. We have discussed the point that Muslim Hui students have always had dual goals of education. First, through mainstream state schooling, they gain knowledge and skills to adapt to the modern state and the mainstream Han ideology. Second, through religious education, they learn basic knowledge and practices of Islam to acquire Hui identity and fulfill their responsibilities to inherit and transmit Hui culture. However, whether to choose one over another or both isn't easy because their expectations and perceptions of both forms of education are divergent, and they often encounter dilemmas between *Nianshu* and *Nianjing*. The phrase *Nianshu* (literally translated as 'read books') refers to attending state schooling and is used in comparison with *Nianjing* (literally translated as 'read Quranic scriptures') or receiving religious education.

Traditionally, Muslim Hui students' education is usually carried out via three channels. The first one is the family, through which Hui children develop their ethnic consciousness by inheriting Islamic knowledge from their parents while developing some work skills. The second one is the community, where *Jingtang Jiaoyu* was conducted. Hui also participate in activities centered on the mosques to practice Islamic culture and traditions. The third channel is the region, in which Hui people gradually become familiar with Chinese traditional culture through attending state schools and interacting with other ethnic groups in daily life (Wang, 2012). Maintaining a Hui identity is so important, as the majority of Muslim Hui families believe that all children need to have *Nianjing* and that *Nianshu* cannot replace *Nianjing*.

In the current time, these three channels of education seem limited in meeting the needs of Hui society. *Nianshu* has gradually become acceptable as a way of promoting the economic and spiritual development of the Hui, and an overemphasis on home-based and community-based religious education is sometimes seen as holding the Muslim Hui back in terms of development. In addition, the concept of *Nianjing* is expanded beyond solely referring to religious education to include Hui ethnic culture, as the Hui are also an ethnic group (Li & Wang, 2003). Having settled in China for a long time, the Hui are not only a religious minority, they are also an ethnic minority that has its own traditions and customs, such as its music, clothing and dance.

Education for Muslim Hui is now encountering new challenges, and integrating *Nianjing* with *Nianshu* is one of them. According to Li and Wang (2003), new education theories were established to explain and elaborate the complex relationship between *Nianshu* and *Nianjing*. *Nianshu* is newly interpreted as being fundamental to preserving religion because intellectual knowledge gained through *Nianshu* could better serve the development of religion. Furthermore, popularization of *Nianshu* is the key to a nation's growth. If Hui people want to survive and become stronger, they have to choose *Nianshu* as the pathway to material prosperity. *Nianshu* is also perceived as being essential in fostering Muslim Hui talents that are the critical components of the Hui society. The Hui society needs not only religious leaders and personnel, but also talented people in all occupations, such as teachers, engineers, doctors and business people.

However, as people strive to seek the 'ideal' integration of the two, conflicts still exist between *Nianshu and Nianjing*. On the one hand, the Chinese government has formulated specific educational policies, allocated specialized resources and provided more teachers in an attempt to develop ethnic Hui education that incorporates the content of Hui culture into *Nianshu*; on the other, *Nianjing* has blossomed with increasing financial resources from domestic and overseas donations in the form of *Jingtang Jiaoyu* and Chinese-Arabic schools. A large number of Muslim parents and students still believe *Nianjing* is the only channel to fulfill educational needs, while overlooking the value of state schooling.

The complex relationship between state schooling and religious education, or *Nianshu* and *Nianjing*, continues to influence Muslim Hui as an ethnic and religious minority. Although the choice is personal, the collective impact could be significant. In the following section of the chapter, I will use rural Muslim Hui in the Ningxia Hui Autonomous Region to examine this complex relationship and demonstrate how state schooling is perceived and what is expected of it, as it comes into contact with the local religious education.

Negotiating State Schooling and Religious Education:the case of Ningxia

The Ningxia Hui Autonomous Region is the designated provincial-level administrative region for Muslim Hui, and many of them reside in impoverished mountainous regions of the rural south. In comparison with Muslim Hui in other parts of China, rural Muslim Hui in Ningxia express strong Hui identity by practicing their Islamic beliefs and participating in rituals (Gladney, 1991).

The southern mountainous part of Ningxia borders on Gansu province on the southwest and is located on the Huangtu Plateau or Loess Plateau. Historically, it was an important hub for import and export trade on the Silk Road, where many Muslim traders finally settled and became integrated into Chinese society. Because of its unique geographical location, the culture of pastoralism from the north interacted with and became integrated within the culture of farming in the central plain. The isolation of the region by mountains and by the cultures of sedentary pastoralism and farming has led to slow development of the area and caused large-scale poverty. Islamic practices are maintained relatively well as the core of local Muslim Hui life. However, Ningxia is one of the areas with the lowest completion rate of state schooling. According to Xu and Luo (2012), the primary school graduation rate was 66.3% and the completion rate of compulsory education was 61.3% between 2003 and 2006 in Ningxia.

Situated in a context where religious education is prevalent and state schooling is controversial, quality education defined by the Chinese government cannot be justified in any simple way. What is believed to be quality education may be perceived as ineffective; what seems to be essential and indispensable might actually hinder the overall development of Muslim Hui in poverty-stricken regions; and what could be a solution to accommodate both forms of education may be found insufficient to satisfy a variety of needs. In the following sections, three pairs of relationships are examined to demonstrate how *Nianjing* and *Nianshu* are perceived and the dilemmas that emerge from these perceptions.

Backwardness and Modernity

White (1998) argues that the Chinese government conducts economic, political and educational activities for ethnic minorities based on three principles: social modernity, social evolutionism and a 'civilization project'. In his argument, modernity can be achieved through science and technology education, and in this way ethnic minorities can evolve from primitive societies to communism in a unilineal mode. In other words, state schooling is perceived as helping ethnic minorities eventually achieve modernity and leave backwardness behind. On this trajectory of achieving economic development and social modernity, the uncivilized barbaric ethnic culture will also be civilized by Han ideology towards the goal of common prosperity (Harrell, 1996). Therefore, quality state schooling is expected to carry a dual mission of modernizing and civilizing ethnic minorities.

In rural Ningxia, the binary relationship between backwardness and modernity is reflected in the outcomes of education activities and the imagined results from both state schooling and religious education. The perceptions of these two forms of schooling are different for the majority Han and the Muslim Hui, and also for different generations of Muslim Hui.

For the majority Han and some state-educated Muslim Hui, state schooling is perceived to be a pathway to meet modern needs and achieve prosperity; whereas religious education is seen as backward and its teachings are seen as possibly hindering Muslims from developing and living a modern life. *Wenhua luohou*, or cultural backwardness, is a commonly used phrase to describe Muslim Hui people's collective lack of intellectual knowledge as well as their lack of quality (*suzhi*), or of specific individual characteristics, and also a collective manifestation of a lack of overall development (Kipnis, 2006). It is often associated with lacking good-quality state schooling that is oriented to improving intellectual knowledge.

For the younger generation of Muslim Hui, religious education is seen as related to backward practices because it has kept people from attending state schooling and has reinforced Islamic values and practices that led to the older generation being ideologically backward. For example, Muslim girls often criticize early marriage and oppose their parents' decision to marry them off at 15 or 16 years old. Their attendance of state schooling, to a certain extent, is a way of avoiding early marriage and of fighting for their own destiny. The Muslim youth also disagree with the practice of not being allowed to talk with the opposite sex and think that this practice reflects a backward feudalistic mentality. State schooling, however, is modern because it provides them space for intergender communication.

Therefore, this backwardness–modernity relationship often leads to difficult decisions, because Muslim Hui parents deem religious education to be traditional and something that cannot be abandoned; whereas modernity perpetuated by state schooling could threaten tradition, and the civilization project may eventually result in assimilation. However, more and more parents start to perceive that acquiring cultural knowledge and accumulating *Suzhi* through state schooling could bring material prosperity to families and to provide opportunities for the younger generation to pursue various employment opportunities.

Morality and Survivability

The second relationship between state schooling and religious education reflects the purpose of each form of education. State schooling is viewed as providing secular knowledge that could equip children and youth with survival skills to live in the mainstream society through employment. Religious education, on the other hand, uses a holistic method that teaches not only Islamic doctrines but also virtue (Ma, 2014).

According to Jaschok and Chan (2009), 'The Qur'an, Islamic doctrines and Muslim practices, reflecting the strong identification with a spiritual "home" (the birthplace of Islam) that ultimately overrides the home of their birth, are the pillars of education in Muslim contexts' (p. 490). Receiving religious education at home and in the mosques serves Muslims' desire to be closer to the spiritual home and their wish to continue the traditions. The moral component of religious education is closely related to religious doctrines. Respecting parents and elders, loving children, helping people in need and in poverty, showing courtesy and empathy, and maintaining diligence are some of the virtues a typical local Muslim family wants their children to learn, along with learning Islamic doctrines.

Muslim parents also try to set up a good example for their children by strictly practicing these virtues. For example, the Quran (17:23) says, 'Thy Lord hath decreed that ye worship none but Him, and that ye be kind to parents. Whether one or both of them attain old age in thy life, say not to them a word of contempt, nor repel them, but address them in terms of honour.' The Quran (4:36) also states, 'Serve Allah, and join not any partners with Him; and do good – to parents, kinsfolk, orphans, those in need, neighbors who are near, neighbors who are strangers, the companion by your side, the wayfarer (ye meet), and what your right hands possess: For Allah loveth not the arrogant, the vainglorious.' These teachings of how to treat superiors, parents, relatives, orphans, those in need, neighbors and strangers reflect the interconnectedness of doctrines and virtue. During childhood, these teachings are particularly important, because early childhood education is essentially moral development, and learning about virtues will be beneficial for children's development in the future. Therefore, the majority of Muslim parents want their children to participate in religious education, not only to learn how to read the Quran but also to learn how to be good Muslims.

While religious education is regarded as invaluable, state schooling has recently become more acceptable to some Muslim parents because they start to see the value of state schooling in preparing their children to survive and earn a living. Very few Muslim parents completely oppose state schooling, though some may consider state schooling unnecessary and useless and others are ignorant and indifferent about state schooling. Very few students refuse to attend state schools, though some may prefer a less discipline-oriented learning environment in the mosques and others are struggling with finding a balance between *Nianshu* and *Nianjing*. Fear of lasting poverty has persuaded Muslim families to believe that if they reject state schooling, prosperity will never arrive. It is not contradictory but rather complementary to acquire cultural knowledge (*wenhua zhishi*) through state schooling and religious knowledge (*zongjiao zhishi*) from mosques.

However, allocating time for learning at school and in the mosques is where the conflict emerges because state schooling requires the full-day commitment of students and learning itself is tiring and time-consuming. Muslim Hui students find it impossible to have free time to go to the mosque for prayers during weekdays, and they have to try to find time on weekends to participate in some religious activities. Even during winter and summer vacations, only a small group of students are able to participate in religious education, and many others are forced by parents, or choose themselves, to get additional coursework in Chinese, math and English in cram schools to improve their academic performance. Nowadays, only *manla*, or students of *Ahongs*, are the regulars in the mosques, and they are among the few choosing not to attend state schooling. As a result, they no longer share the common language with those students who go to state schools. The shifting perception of state schooling has changed the landscape of religious education. More emphasis has been placed on state schooling, as it is believed to be fundamental to improving survivability. Many more Muslim Hui students choose state schooling to be their first choice of learning, and they see religious education as an alternative if their academic endeavors are unsuccessful. Also, with cultural knowledge (*wenhua zhishi*) obtained from state schooling, some Muslim students believe that they could better understand and interpret Quranic texts and be better prepared to pursue professional training in religion. After all, without religious education, students are not morally educated; without state schooling, students will have to endure hardship to earn a living.

Identity and Adaptability

The third relationship between state schooling and religious education is manifested in what Ma (2008) observed to be 'distinctive but harmonious' coexistence. The 'distinctiveness' speaks of Muslim Hui students' strong belief in maintaining Hui identity through religious education; and the 'harmony' refers to Muslim Hui students' acquisition of secular knowledge and learning in order to be adaptable in different environments, whether dominated by Han or surrounded by Hui.

In order to maintain a distinctive Hui identity, religious education needs to include unique aspects of Hui culture that are different from the culture of the majority Han. *Nianjing* is one of the tasks Muslim Hui students in their childhood must undertake because they are told that *Nianjing* would ensure them a better life after death, even though it might be difficult and painful in the beginning. Being able to read some Quranic scripts is expected, and reciting chapters and verses is needed for special occasions, such as festival celebrations. Second, a strict observance of consuming *Halal* food is also emphasized in religious education. Muslims Hui students often distinguish themselves from Han by referring to Han as those eating pork and non-*Halal* food. They are also taught to prepare their own food with their own utensils if no *Halal* food is available. Similarly, Muslim Hui parents also enforce the practice by telling their children not to eat non-*Halal* food in any circumstances, even when the children go to college in other cities. Third, celebrating Islamic holidays is also considered important in that such rituals could enhance students' connections with their 'spiritual' home. For example, *Kaizhaijie*, or Eid al-Fitr (Festival of Breaking the Fast), is one of the most celebrated Islamic festivals in the local area. The majority of Muslim families observe fasting for the month of Ramadan, and children learn to reconnect with Allah by reading the Quran, praying and practicing virtuous actions with their parents. Religious education plays a crucial role in constructing Muslim Hui identity, and makes it possible for Hui to maintain Islamic traditions and lifestyles even when they are in a region that does not have a concentration of Muslims. For example, with urbanization and the transformation of rural villages, many Muslim youth choose to become migrant workers after completing compulsory education, and many of them do not want to sacrifice their beliefs for economic benefit. It is the religious education they acquire in childhood that connects them and distinguishes them from non-Muslims.

Although maintaining Muslim Hui identity is central, being adaptable to different environments and living harmoniously with other ethnic groups is also vital. Therefore, state schooling is perceived necessary to empower Muslim Hui and as something that ultimately benefits them as individuals and the Hui as a collective ethnic group. Students find that they are more adaptable after attending state schools because they acquire common knowledge and skills needed for living. One student commented that if they can go to college and secure positions in society, then they would have the power to influence others and bring more benefits to the Muslim Hui ethnic group.

However, succeeding in state schooling isn't always easy for rural Muslim students, because religiously educated students are less exposed to subjects such as math, English, physics and chemistry taught in state schooling. Lack of a solid foundation in these subjects makes it difficult for them to perform well in school and test well to get into good high schools and colleges. Only a small number of Muslim Hui students can successfully enter college and find employment afterwards. Thus, many others regard state schooling as a possible channel to prepare them for uncertainty and to be open to opportunities.

In the past, Muslim youth were mainly engaged in hard labor jobs because they lacked *the necessary cultural knowledge* to work in other professions. Many were illiterate or semi-literate and were often found on the farm, in small businesses or at construction sites. Although one could pursue *Jingtang Jiaoyu* to the advanced level and eventually become a respected *Ahong* in the local area, the competition was high and the chance was slim. Now, with state schooling, Muslim youth have more opportunities to get high-paying jobs in different professions. In the meantime, they also learn how to interact with people from the majority Han and other ethnic groups, which further helps them adapt to different working environments.

Conclusion

What is quality education for Muslim Hui students? Is the quality education defined by the Chinese government the same as what the Muslim Hui see as quality? This chapter has discussed the complex relationship between state schooling and religious education and demonstrated how these two types of education interact and construct a unique system of education for Muslim Hui in the Ningxia Hui Autonomous Region. *Nianjing* and *Nianshu* are no longer contradictory possibilities, but rather complementary in creating an integrative education experience for Muslim Hui. State schools, as a site of cultural production, provide Muslim students with a space to interpret and reflect on their Islamic faith and choices in life. Religious education, as a tradition of cultural inheritance, offers Muslim children and youth an opportunity to learn how to share secular life with their belief system and the virtue it fosters.

References

Alles, E., Che´rif-Chebbi, L. & Halfon, C. (2003) Chinese Islam: unity and fragmentation, *Religion, State and Society*, 31(1), 7-35. https://doi.org/10.1080/0963749032000045837

Bai, S. (2001) *Memoir on Ethnicity and Religion*. Shijiazhuang: Hebei Education Publishing House.

Ben-Dor Benite, Z. (2005) *The Dao of Muhammad: a cultural history of Muslims in late imperial China.* Cambridge, MA: Harvard University Asia Center. https://doi.org/10.2307/j.ctt1tfj9f0

Chen, Y. (2008) *Muslim Uyghur Students in a Chinese Boarding School: social recapitalization as a response to ethnic integration.* Lanham, MD: Lexington Books.

Compulsory Education Law of the People's Republic of China (2006) Article 3, 29 June. http://english.gov.cn/archive/laws_regulations/2014/08/23/content_28147498304 2154.htm

Dreyer, J.T. (1976) *China's Forty Millions: minority nationalities and national integration in the People's Republic of China.* Cambridge, MA: Harvard University Press.

Gladney, D. (1991) *Muslim Chinese: ethnic nationalism in the People's Republic.* Cambridge, MA: Harvard University Press. https://doi.org/10.2307/j.ctt1tg5gkz

Gladney, D. (2003) Islam in China: accommodation or separatism? *China Quarterly,* 174, 451-467. https://doi.org/10.1017/S0009443903000275

Harrell, S. (1996) *Cultural Encounters on China's Ethnic Frontiers.* Hong Kong: Hong Kong University Press.

Hong, Y. (2013) *Between Sacred and Secular Knowledge: rationalities in education of a Muslim village in northwest China.* Retrieved from the HKU Scholars Hub. https://doi.org/10.5353/th_b5053380

Jaschok, M. & Chan, H.V. (2009) Education, Gender and Islam in China: the place of religious education in challenging and sustaining 'undisputed traditions' among Chinese Muslim women, *International Journal of Education Development,* 29, 487-494. https://doi.org/10.1016/j.ijedudev.2009.04.004

Jian, Z. (2004) The Change of Ethnic Identity in Nation Building, *Journal of Guangxi University for Nationalities,* 26(5), 85-91.

Kipnis, A. (2006) Suzhi: a keyword approach, *The China Quarterly,* 186, 295-313. https://doi.org/10.1017/S0305741006000166

Li, S. & Wang, Y. (2003) The Choice Made when Faced with the Dilemma in the Hui Nationalities' Education at Present, *Researches on the Hui,* 50, 100-106.

Lipman, J. (1997) *Familiar Strangers: a history of Muslims in northwest China.* Seattle, WA: University of Washington Press.

Ma, X. (2014) From *Jingtang* Education to Arabic School: Muslim education in Yunnan, in S. Buang & P.G. Chew (Eds) *Muslim Education in the 21st Century: Asian perspectives,* pp. 70-89. New York: Routledge.

Ma, Z. (2002) Duo yuan yi ti ge ju zhong de hui han min zu guan xi [Hui-Han relations in the unified multinational China], Ningxia, China: Ningxia People's Press.

Ma, Z. (2008) *Research on the Living Villages of the Hui Ethnic Group.* Ningxia, China: Ningxia People's Press.

Mackerras, C. (1999) Religion and the Education of China's Minorities, in G. Postiglione (Ed.) *China's National Minority Education: culture, schooling, and development,* pp. 23-54. New York: Falmer Press.

National Bureau of Statistics of China (2010) National Population Census. http://www.stats.gov.cn/tjsj/pcsj/rkpc/6rp/indexch.htm

National People's Congress (2006) *Zhong hua ren min gong he guo yi wu jiao yu fa* [Compulsory education law of the People's Republic of China]. http://www.gov.cn/ziliao/flfg/2006-06/30/content_323302.htm

Ningxia Statistics Bureau (2011) Report of Ningxia 6th census. http://party.cei.gov.cn/index/dqbg/showdoc.asp?blockcode=DQBGNXGB&filena me=201105110266

Qian, M. (2007) Discontinuity and Reconstruction: the hidden curriculum in schoolroom instruction in minority-nationality areas, *Chinese Education and Society*, 40(2), 60-76. https://doi.org/10.2753/CED1061-1932400204

Tan, C. & Ding, K. (2014) The Role, Developments and Challenges of Islamic Education in China, in S. Buang & P.G. Chew (Eds) *Muslim Education in the 21st Century: Asian perspectives*, pp. 55-69. New York: Routledge.

Wang, S. (2004) The People's Republic of China's Policy on Minorities and International Approaches to Ethnic Groups: a comparative study, *International Journal on Minority and Group Rights*, 11, 159-185. https://doi.org/10.1163/1571811041631272

Wang, Y. (2012) *Research on Society Development Mechanism of Hui People in the Northwest of China*. Ningxia: Ningxia People's Press.

Wang, Y. (2013) *Language, Culture, and Identity among Minority Students in China: the case of the Hui*. New York: Routledge.

White, S. (1998) State Discourses, Minority Policies, and the Politics of Identity in the Lijiang Naxi People's Autonomous County, *Nationalism and Ethnic Politics*, 4(1-2), 9-27.

Wu, Z. & Han, C. (2011) Cultural Transformation of Educational Discourse in China: perspectives of multiculturalism/interculturalism, in C.A. Grant & A. Portera (Eds) *Intercultural and Multicultural Education: enhancing global interconnectedness*, pp. 225-244. New York: Routledge.

Xu, M. & Luo, J. (2012) *Wo guo yi wu jiao yu qu yu fei jun hen fa zhan de jing ji xue fen xi* [Economic analysis of regional disequilibrium in the development of compulsory education], *Economic Forum*, 12, 28-31.

Yang, J. (2006) *Xian zhuang yu dui ce: xi bei shao shu min zu ji chu jiao yu jun hen fa zhan yan jiu* [Reality and Countermeasures: a study of balanced development in northwest minority elementary education], *Northwestern Normal University Journal*, 5.

Zhu, Z. (2007) Ethnic Identity Construction in the Schooling Context: a case study of a Tibetan Neidi boarding school in China, *Chinese Education and Society*, 40(2), 38-59. https://doi.org/10.2753/CED1061-1932400203

CHAPTER 9

The Buddhist Approach to a School-based Curriculum: the effective learning innovation that promotes human values to learners for sustainable living in Thailand

PRAPAPAT NIYOM,
ART-ONG JUMSAI NA AYUDHAYA,
WITIT RACHATATANUN
& BENJAMIN VOKES

SUMMARY This chapter will examine the development of religion in education in Thailand. It will present three case studies: Sathya Sai School, Roong Aroon School (RAS) and Panyaprateep School. Each focuses on integrating religious principles into the school-based curriculum and on the contemplative practice and learning process of their classroom management. Through scientific analysis of the human learning process, the integration of core religious teachings and encompassing the complete environment, these three cases provide examples of how Buddhist and other religious mindfulness practices are integrated into the curriculum, along with sustainable living, learning principles and values which serve to holistically transform learners in the Thai school system.

Historical Background: religious-based education in Thailand

More than one hundred years ago, prior to the establishment of the Ministry of Education, the first Thai schools were started in Buddhist temples, with monks as teachers teaching only Thai boys to read, write and solve mathematical problems, along with Buddhist principles. Subsequently, a few conventional private schools with a western standard curriculum were established by Christian missionaries. Later, the Ministry of Dhamma-karn (the management of holistic teaching and learning) was established to launch a conventional school system that combined Buddhist principles in its curriculum (Chaiyaphon, 2011). In 1941, the name of the ministry was changed to the Ministry of Education. Thai schools, public and private alike, are required to teach morality and ethics as one of the main subjects in their curricula (Chaiyaphon, 2011). Buddhism has been the foundation of Thai education.

The Current Situation of Religion in the Education System in Thailand

The Thai Constitution states that Thai people are free to believe in any religion of their choice (Office of National Human Rights Commission of Thailand, 2011). However, the Buddhist religion has been strongly rooted in the Thai nation. Consequently, more than 94.6% of the Thai population are Buddhist, while 4.2% are Islamic, 1.1% are Christian, and others 0.1% (National Statistical Office, 2015). However, every Thai person has the liberty to choose his/her religion, as well as the school type in which he or she wants to study. Actually no matter which religion the students' families are, it is not uncommon that Buddhist students as well as those of other religious backgrounds also attend the same Christian Church-supported schools as well as public government-supported schools. Nevertheless, morality and ethics are still required as subjects in the compulsory curriculum of the Thai basic education system provided in every school in the country (Bureau of Academic Affairs and Educational Standards, 2002).

Schools in Thailand can be grouped into six major types of school offering different religious-based education in their curriculum:

1. The government conventional public schools include 30,816 schools which accommodate over 6,856,272 students (Ministry of Social Development and Human Security, 2016). These schools follow the basic standard curriculum which requires eight major subjects in terms of content. Social Studies include morality and ethics, which can be individually arranged to offer the specific study of either Buddhism or other religions at every level.

2. Within the above numbers of government public schools, 79 schools were admitted into the Buddhist Approach School Project, launched by the Bureau of Educational Innovation Development in Education, under the Ministry of Education, in 2003. At present, 22,736 schools are in this project incorporating traditional practices and additional activities in addition to the regular curriculum (Bureau of Educational Innovation Development, n.d.).

3. Twenty-eight private schools under the support of Christian Churches provide and maintain separate religious teaching, either Christian or Buddhist practices of three periods of 50 minutes a week. However, the different practices in the above three types of religious-study in

these schools do not generate any conflict (Office of the Private Education Commission, 2015).

4. A total of 2548 schools with 247,471 students are privately owned Islamic schools called Tadeega or Pornou schools, mostly situated in the southern part of Thailand, that teach the Muslim students religious subject matter in the evening after conventional school hours (Office of the Private Education Commission, 2015).

5. In order to support poor families in the remote villages, there are 409 schools with 47,089 Students (National Office of Buddhism, 2017). Phrapariyatidham, or government-supported boarding schools, have been developed from the Buddhist temples which offer dual systems of conventional education together with Buddhist teaching for the novice monks.

6. Nearly 20 privately owned Buddhist/religious approach schools have been applying the Buddhist principles with mindful meditation and similar practices fused with learning. The curriculum design, pedagogy, evaluation process and learning environment, including school culture, are created in order to nurture in students the characteristics of self-learners and sustainable living. One of the differences between these schools and those in the previous categories is that Buddhist or other religious practices are not limited or confined within either the traditional practice or the conventional learning (Chuencharoensok, 2013).

The three case studies in this chapter are part of this last group of 20 schools. They are known as alternative and innovative schools because they integrate inner life learning into the modern schooling system. This current movement of integrating contemplative and inner development into the existing schooling system is gradually being experimented with in Thailand. Although these schools are different in their learning process they share a common ultimate goal of human development. Moreover, the leaders of these three schools are not educators by field of study. They are an engineer, an architect and an economist by training but they all have direct experiences in Buddhist/universal religious-based practices. They share the common vision of wanting to transcend the limitations of formal religion and they strive to interpret the true essence of human living which could be learnt through daily school activities.

Methodology

To understand education and the learning process, scholars developing the transformation of 'Buddhist Schools' contemplate the true meaning of education and its ultimate goals. The learner's environment and how it is interacted with and interpreted can lead to self-knowledge and wisdom.

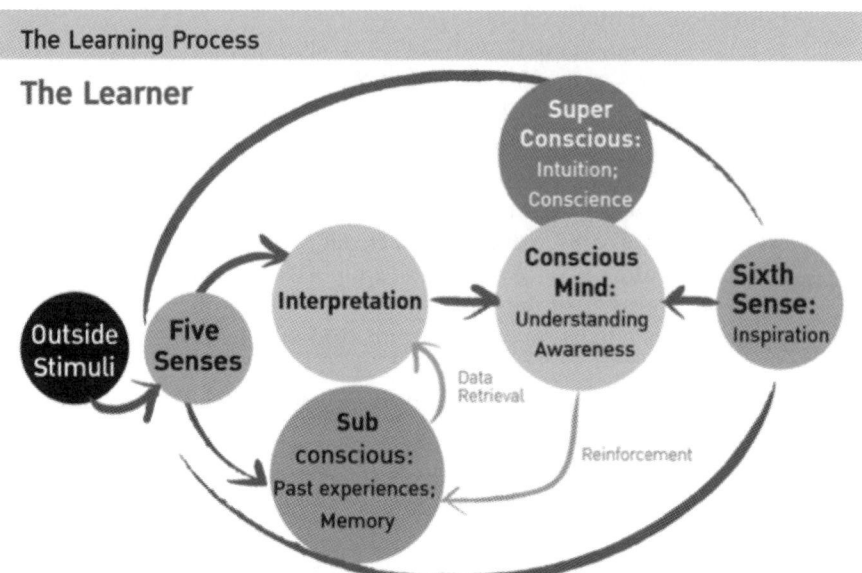

Figure 1. The learning process of Sathya Sai School from Dr Art-ong Jumsai Na Ayudhya.

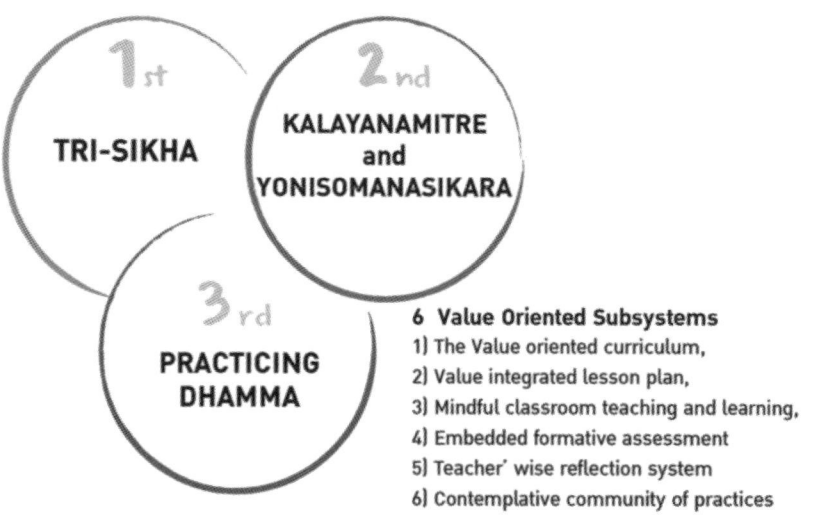

Figure 2. The three major Buddhist principles and six subsystems for the conceptual framework of Roong Aroon School.

The roles of love and compassion are noted as critical factors to the framework for developing right thoughts and actions and conduct with others. The development of these schools was founded on this principle of integrating this deep learning process for the development of the whole human in ways not limited to an individual child, but affecting the potential of the entire learning community. It is essential to develop the learner's capacity to interpret the information from the environment and develop self-knowledge and wisdom in order to expand love and compassion. This process of reflection is deeply rooted in Buddhist core principles and practices (Jumsai Na Ayudhya, 2003).

The Buddhist Approach to a School-based Curriculum is based on the three major Buddhist principles – Tri-Sikha, Kalayanamitre and Yonisomanasikara – and on the four principles of Satipatthana on the Noble Eightfold Path (Niyom, 2001).

1. Tri-Sikha

Tri-Sikha is comprised of 'Sila' (right speech, right action and right livelihood), 'Samadhi' (right effort, right mindfulness and right concentration) and 'Panna' (right view and right intention), which are learned to enlarge and deepen the capacity of detachment from the causes of grievances and uncontrolled likes and dislikes, and to nurture truth and the most possible harmony in living (Payutto, 2004).

Our subconscious mind stores all our past experiences as 'memory' by interpreting information from our environment. What we saw, heard, received through our sensory organs, or emotionally felt, experienced, thought or acted on, as well as our environment, are stored in our subconscious mind, as shown in Figure 1. The school leaders understand that aggressive behavior can be programmed into children's subconscious minds through a variety of stimuli. It is now becoming clear that in order to promote good character in children, the desired human values must become an integral part of all subjects taught in schools to be infused as part of the data stored in children's subconscious minds. The school's atmosphere or climate should be charged with love and peace. All teachers should be a model of the values and desired characteristics in children (Jumsai Na Ayudhya, 2003).

In these Buddhist Approach Schools, the physical environment is carefully considered to include open natural spaces to allow the students to experience and learn from nature.

2. Kalayanamitre and Yonisomanasikara

Kalayanamitre means wise spiritual guides or trainers, which includes teachers and parents who have a direct impact on the learners. In the specific meaning identified by Venerable Somdet Phra Buddhakosajarn (Prayudh

Payutto) in *The Dawn of Education* (Payutto 2002) there are seven characteristics, as follows: being lovable; being worthy of esteem; able to be emulated; being a counsellor; being a patient listener; able to deliver deep discourses; and not leading to a useless end.

Yonisomanasikara means wise reflection, or the 10 deliberate thinking systems. Phra Buddhakosajarn (Prayudh Payutto), the venerable Buddhist scholar, also mentions these in his book (Payutto, 2013), and puts forward Yonisomanasikara as a thinking framework which contains the following 10 elements:

1. Applying good inner values
2. Awareness of true state
3. Focus on present situation
4. Problem solving according to Four Noble Truths
5. Explaining based on facts
6. Element stratification
7. Finding cause-effect
8. Connecting concept-objective
9. Judging true-artificial values
10. Comparing advantages-disadvantages

Another viewpoint, according to the explanation from Steve Weissman (2011), is that 'Yonisomanasikara', as 'wise reflection', helps us integrate the concentration and mindfulness developed during formal meditation into everyday life. In every facet of interaction these two concepts are nurtured and developed in the school communities. These schools have analyzed the learning outcomes and organized their inputs and outputs in a process to intrinsically develop these core states of learning.

3. Satipatthana: the key principles of mindfulness practices

According to the Buddhist belief, truth can be found in the search within. This is the beginning of the search for self-knowledge or knowledge about self or self-realization. When it is found that the conscious mind becomes calm and peaceful and does not react emotionally to various stimuli as before, the ability to concentrate is improved and memory is enhanced. As a result, there is an improvement in the learning process. The conscious mind needs to be stilled and completely calm for intuition to occur.

The Buddhist Approach Schools interpret and apply these principles of the exterior and interior to support the process and encourage deeper learning holistically and build a contemplative community by adding more input of learning opportunities and practices for the spiritual development of their teachers and students, including parents. They also change the learning process to facilitate more time and space for learning by doing through the real situation and problem-based learning, whereas the formative assessments are more concentrated. Certainly, the output and outcome of the students cover more dimensions of moral and ethical character building as well as cognitive achievement. This brings out inner strength and wisdom in children (Panich, 2014).

Three Case Studies

The three case studies are Sathya Sai School, Panyaprateep School and Roong Aroon School. Table I provides basic information about each school.

Name of schools	Sathaya Sai School	Panyaprateep School	Roong- Aroon School
Founder	Dr. Art-ong Jumsai Na Ayudhya	Dr Witit Rachatatanun	Assoc. Prof. Prapapat Niyom
Organization and Funding	Sathaya Sai Foundation Private School	Panyaprateep Foundation Private School	Roong- Aroon School Foundation Private School
Honoured Adviser-	Sai baba	Venerable Phra Acharn Jayasaro	Venerable Somdet Phra Buddhakosajarn, (Prayudh Payutto)
Established	1992	2008	1997
Location	Lop Buri, Thailand	Pak Chong, Nakorn Rachasima, Thailand	Bangkok, Thailand
Setting	Rural/119 acres	Rural/32.4 acres	Urban/20 acres
Type of a	Boarding	Boarding	Day school
School Level	K1-K3,G1 – G12	G7-G12	K1-K3, G1 – G12
Selection process	Interview and essay both parents and students	Parent workshop, selection based on parent's attitude	Parent workshop, selection based on parent's attitude
Fees	Full scholarship	Tuition based	Tuition based
Number of Students first year/current	14/356	10/100	96/1200
Number of teachers	59	40	140

Note : More than 85% of students are Buddhist.

Table I. Basic information of the three schools.

First Case Study: Sathya Sai School

Sathya Sai School is a privately owned school situated in the Lopburi province, in the north of Bangkok. Dr Art-ong Jumsai Na Ayudhya, a former NASA engineer, established this school through funding by the Sai-ba-ba, a renowned leading spiritual master from India. It was the second Sathya Sai School to be established outside of India. Today there are many Sathya Sai Schools around the world – for example, in Australia, Nepal, Indonesia and Canada. Sathya Sai Schools follow the national curriculum of Thailand but it is imperative that the essence of human values is blended into the academic subjects.

The school provides full grants to every child, from grade 1, especially to those from poor families in the remote areas. The emphasis on knowledge becomes the second stage after the need to develop how the learner interprets his or her environment. This process is 'mindfulness' as described in Buddhism. In the educational environment, these principles of practice are organized to promote a learning environment that carefully cultivates a curriculum to guide teachers and parents along this path.

With the goal to provide life-skills training and self-sufficiency, Sathya Sai School has organic farms located near the campus to support their meals as well as a solar farm which generates electricity and additional income for the school.

Second Case Study: Roong Aroon School (RAS)

Roong Aroon School (RAS) was established with support from the Plan group of companies and their partners as a private school in Bangkok. Associate Professor Prapapat Niyom, from the Faculty of Architecture of Chulalongkorn University, was the leading pioneer for laying out the concept of the school according to the Buddhist principles. Its expansion to a higher education institution, Arsom Silp Institute of the Arts, in 2007 was supported by the Roong Aroon School Foundation, with a similar conceptual direction to the school. The institute offers three major programs of study: Holistic Education; Architecture for Community and Environmental Development; and Social Entrepreneurship. Both RAS and Arsom Silp Institute apply the Buddhist concept in their teaching/learning direction, academics, curriculum, pedagogy and school culture.

The heart of all of Buddha's teachings is the concept of learning at RAS. The meaning of education has been interpreted in Roong Aroon School according to the Buddhist principles which view the most powerful human value as the learning capacity cultivated through proper practices. The school's core belief is that 'life is learning or learning is life' (Payutto, 2004).

RAS has rearranged and redesigned the basic standard curriculum into the school-based curriculum to enlarge and deepen its goal of learning achievement to go beyond merely content- or subject-based learning. The school's core philosophy is that child development, particularly spiritual wisdom, needs the holistic learning system and process that can be obtained by special spaces, practices and key factors for learning corresponding to the Buddhist principles. The ultimate goal of education should be to enlarge and deepen the students' accomplishments while also attending to human development (Chantrasook, 2006).

Third Case Study: Panyaprateep School

Panyaprateep School, located in Nakorn Rachasima province, was established with a view to serve as a prototype of Buddhist wisdom education – a holistic form of learning, covering both aspects of body and mind development and the essential academic and life skills and occupational development, infused with training of moral values. The vision of the school is to enable the community of students, teachers and parents to develop their own self-reliance and to constantly train to become wise persons. The school's founder, Dr Witit Rachatatanun, notes the tendency of authorities to see Buddhism as a belief system and therefore overlook the unrivalled system of human education that lies at its heart.

The school is a co-educational secondary boarding school under the guidance of British-born Buddhist monk and Chief Spiritual Advisor of the School, Venerable Ajahn Jayasaro. Panyaprateep's vision is to enhance the depth of the education it offers by providing a warm and supportive environment, or 'a second home', in which students may navigate their way into adulthood guided by the Buddhist principles of all-round flourishing. Panyaprateep's aim is to create an atmosphere, environment and curriculum that are in harmony with the Buddhist path to enlightenment, but adapted appropriately to the needs and capacity of the school students.

Whole School Revolutions:
value-oriented curricula and pedagogy

At Satthya Sai it is observed that in order to promote good character in children, the desired human values must become an integral part of all subjects taught in the school. This way, human values will become an integral part of the data stored in children's subconscious minds. The school's atmosphere or climate should be filled with love and peace. Teachers should be a model of the desired characteristics in children. Values and desired characteristics should also be an integral part of all sports and extra-curricular activities. The long-term memory is activated when there is an association or connection with real-life situations and experiences. Thus, instead of teaching values as a separate subject, there should be an integration of values in all subjects. Both intra-disciplinary and inter-disciplinary integration are necessary. The children are brought up in an atmosphere of love, reverence, mutual respect, cooperation and spiritual discipline.

The children begin their day at 5.45 a.m. in the prayer hall along with teachers and the other staff of the school. They respect all religions. They start with a Buddhist prayer, 'Buddha Sharanam Gachami', and chant a few

Buddhist verses. This is followed by three Aums and Gayathri mantra which leads to Light Meditation. The prayer session ends with an Education on Human Values (EHV) teacher narrating a value-based story. This is the healthy start to induce in the child right thinking, right behavior and right living throughout the day. Sattyha Sai employs a variety of teaching techniques to ensure the students are engaged in the learning process. The school has a unique way of teaching these values. For instance, Peace could be the theme for one of the weeks. During that week all subjects taught will carry the significance of Peace and its sub-values such as concentration, honesty, patience and self-confidence.

The three major components in the Roong Aroon School (RAS) learning process are head, hands and heart. According to this holistic process of learning, the major learning units in RAS from kindergarten to primary and secondary are designed with the aim of integrating the real-life situations into whatever subject matter the students should have. The main themes of each year or three semesters are to be agreed by the teacher team of each level. According to the selected theme, the teacher team will design the lesson plan into a project/problem-based unit which is derived from three objectives: Knowledge, including subject matter; Skills, covering the essential twenty-first-century learning skills; and Values, the most important part of learning outcomes. Then the learning process, space, media and activities are arranged according to those achievement targets. Modifying the conventional system to achieve a value-oriented curriculum, RAS has included the 'Value Integrated Learning Curriculum', based on the three major learning mindsets of heart-hand-head, as the framework as well as the process of development.

The teacher teams work with the principals regularly through the year. The standard curriculum is studied and analyzed to understand the whole structure in terms of the O-L-E (Objective-Learning process-Evaluation), and the requirements of each course, including the indicators. The teachers are able to identify and integrate any special requirements in addition to the core value aspects into that O-L-E system. With this adaptation of the standard Thai curriculum, RAS has developed its own system where the 'roadmap' of key-stage implementation for the year and the term is designed and prepared in advance.

The principals provide guidance based on the Yonisomanasikara thinking system, to help teachers understand the correlation of dynamic cycles. The increased understanding of the complete learning cycle corresponds to the outcome-based curriculum. The more the value outcomes of the students are expected, the more 'learning by doing' or 'active learning' through project/problem-based learning units is required. The learning process also requires a thematic approach to lesson plan design, which normally integrates the critical issues of Thai society, such as conservation and management of natural resources – forests, rain water systems, soil, energy and so on – which requires a longer field study period. When the teachers understand this thinking system of cause and effect, they are able to integrate these value aspects into most steps.

The aim of Panyaprateep School is to integrate developmental principles across all school activities, both in and out of class (Ratchatatanun, 2006). To implement this, each year has an integrated study theme, which includes a theme-based subject and field trips, and culminates in an end-of-term exhibition and performance for the school community. Each theme addresses the challenges we face in the world today and aims to equip the students with the appropriate skills, tools and knowledge to address these issues. Thus, the first area of education is devoted to the physical world in which we live and to developing a wise and balanced relationship towards it, including obesity, its causes and associated health risks, consumerism and media and its influence on our relationship to possessions and the use of technology and consumption habits and their detrimental impact on the environment. Although the core curriculum (including such subjects as Thai language, mathematics, science, and social and cultural studies) is stipulated by the Ministry of Education, the guidelines are flexible enough to accommodate the unique concerns of a Buddhist developmental model. In the holistic system of this model, education is conceived of as being fourfold – namely, an education of:

1. the child's relationship with the material world;
2. the child's relationship with the social world;
3. the child's ability to deal wisely with toxic mental states and cultivate uplifting mental states; and
4. the child's ability to think well and to reflect on experience.

This model not only prepares children to make a good livelihood, but also allows them to see that life is deeper and richer than working in order to consume.

Panyaprateep School identifies the critical component of the curriculum as being to develop the child's ability to think well and to reflect on experience. The 'gem' of the Buddhist tradition includes training the ability to think with reason and without bias, to think creatively and innovatively, to think constructively about one's thinking, and to be able to reflect on experience and learn from it. This skill can be used to evaluate, solve problems and make decisions, and ultimately raise student achievement. A tool of the school is to use the Buddhist approach of the Four Noble Truths in order to develop perspective and understand what causes things to happen. First, the students identify the problem, then they evaluate the causes of the problem, before deciding the solution. Finally, they decide the path of action that will lead to and achieve the solution.

Examples of Integrating Buddhist
Principles into the School Systems

The ultimate goal of the three case studies is human development through the holistic learning system which aims to encourage the highest achievement of each learner, not only in their knowledge and learning skills but also in their spiritual development. These three schools have been applying the Buddhist principles into the school system in various ways. One example from RAS shown in Figure 2 illustrates how these three principles are applied and organized in school practices.

Applying major Buddhist principles to the school system through the core value-oriented operating systems, the Buddhist School's mission is designed to create the right activities and platforms according to the purpose of students, teachers and parents. Academic and pedagogy subsystems in the school are thoughtfully designed to apply the true meaning of learning content embedded with suitable values in the contexts which are rarely found in traditional institutions.

First Tri-Sikha

Most Buddhist approach schools usually apply this principle as their school's core value. Tri-Sikha is more likely interpreted as the right way of human learning and living (Prayutto, 2004). From these three example schools, these principles are integrated into the classroom and the greater community as explained below.

Meaningful Teaching and Learning

The more meaningful the teaching and learning in the classrooms, the higher the engagement and learning ownership that the students have. In this 'integrated or holistic learning process', learning spaces are provided for the students to experiment, which includes observing, trial-and-error practicing, problem solving, sharing and learning, managing information and communication, etc. The most efficient learning context is based on real-life situations and work-based, problem-based platforms that the learners can participate and engage in.

In addition to the basic knowledge and the twenty-first-century learning skills, the students' experience should be enhanced and nurtured through either the regular mindful classroom learning or the meaningful routine activities, both at school and at home, to achieve well-rounded capacities developed from self-awareness, self-actualization, wise reflection and being fully directed learners with values.

Moral and Ethical-based Routine Activities

This process includes extra-curricular teachers who inspire and impact the students who also need regular development of self-awareness and actualization in extra-curricular classes (i.e. arts, sports and music classes). Once these teachers realize the value and their impacts on the teachers and learners, they become more inspiring teachers or change agents rather than teachers who transfer content or knowledge to students that are mere transmitting messengers.

The teachers are able to tap into the students' inner power of learning from inside, through regular contemplative dialogues, sharing knowledge alongside their students or challenging the students with more difficult or complicated exercises than they can imagine.

Developing the Child's Emotional Development

Emotional development includes strengthening the ability to restrain negative impulses, promotion of the wholesome desire for truth and goodness, patient endurance, resilience and good humor, meditation practices to enhance mindfulness, inner peace and clarity of mind, and the promotion of loving kindness and compassion.

In addition to the morning activities at Satthya Sai school, students are led in mindfulness activities before each and every lesson to prepare them to go deeply into the area discussed.

In another approach, Panyaprateep School uses the 'Four Right Efforts' as a tool for self-development. The first is to 'stop' negative actions that are causing problems. The second is to 'prevent' negative actions from arising. The third is to bring about and 'generate' positive actions that have not yet arisen. The fourth is to 'sustain' and develop further the positive things.

An integral part of school life at Panyaprateep involves daily as well as weekly 'awake and aware' practices that are geared to stimulating self-awareness and self-reflection. Students and teachers gather for a period of morning and evening chanting and mindfulness activities such as sitting meditation, walking meditation or Qi Gong. On a weekly basis, the Chief Spiritual Advisor, Venerable Ajahn Jayasaro, comes to the school to receive alms, meet with students in small groups, and give school-wide teachings. This is a special opportunity to consult with the teacher on any important matters.

Value-oriented Lesson Plan Design

In preparation for teaching, RAS teachers prepare each lesson plan with the recognition of the values behind that subject content and of the value of building character through specific learning activities. The teachers consider the issues and systematically identify the objectives in every lesson plan. Although teachers plan individually, they also have the opportunity to practice Kalayanamitre through teamwork as often as possible with the school principal and other teachers. This collaboration is essential in order for them to share and learn from each other and practice mindfulness in their planning (Niyom, 2008; Mohjhaw et al, 2013).

The Mindful Classroom Teaching and Learning System

The teacher is able to facilitate all students in this type of classroom and lead each student to the learning attainment targets, and ultimately to the targeted values. Through this type of classroom, the students are able to learn to cultivate their self-actualization and characteristics of right intention. Skillful teachers can provide different larger spaces, and learning activities in which students can share their creativity. This is the crucial opportunity which brings mindfulness practice into real-life situations and helps to cultivate the students' character.

The Embedded Formative Assessment System

With this systematic thinking process, the teachers will learn to be aware of relative cause and effect through the use of skills by applying wise reflection. This platform was selected to obtain the embedded formative assessment suggested by Professor Vijarn Panich in his 2014 book (Panich, 2014), and the constructive way of learning evaluation corresponding to the mindful classroom teaching and learning.

Whenever the learning objectives focus on the students' outcomes and the required standard, the teachers' observation of their students will be more accurate. It is easier for the RAS teachers to follow the more attentive assessment introduced by Professor Panich than the previously used guidelines, which followed only the learning objectives stated in the lesson plan. Through the properly pre-planned learning activities, the teachers are able to anticipate the outputs and the outcomes to achieve better results. As the teachers have already prepared the 'value'-integrated learning objectives in their lesson plan in advance, they can easily focus their observation on 'students' ability to learn', as well as exercise more constructive reflection.

At the last part of those plans, teachers need to prepare the evaluating system to apply the embedded formative assessment in order to help each student develop through his or her performance. In doing so, the teachers are trained to have a mindful, thoughtful and compassionate relationship with their students as if they are their learning partners in the classrooms.

The Teachers' Wise Reflection System

Teachers prepare the evaluation system to apply the embedded formative assessment in order to help develop and guide each student through his or her performance. The most important facet of the teacher's teamwork is the group reflection/dialogue which is organized as the BAR (Before Action Review) and AAR (After Action Review) activity.

The AAR-BAR platform guided by Kalayanamitre principles provides an open and secure space for sharing and learning from the results obtained from the classroom teaching and learning. Both success and failure are candidly reflected upon and respected as the teachers' learning experiences. This practice helps support the more effective development of both teachers and students.

Through these regular dialogues in weekly meetings, RAS finds that the teachers develop wise reflection and the ability to share better than being given evaluation notes. Similarly, the teachers prefer in-class observation by their team to enhance sharing their experiences in the AAR-BAR meetings. Mindful speaking and deep listening are also essential.

Contemplative Community of Practices

In the three case studies, social awareness and interpersonal skills are fundamental to achieving both school and life success and play a key role in both the curriculum and life in school. The aim is for students to develop a wise and balanced relationship with others by developing self-awareness and communication skills and contributing to the well-being of the school and society. It includes teaching the foundations of Buddhist morality as a scheme for living together wisely with trust and integrity, as well as learning about sociology and history forged with life skills.

As a tool towards developing good relationships and harmony among community members, Panyaprateep School uses a so-called circle of friendship. The school uses the circle meeting as a weekly open forum to express gratitude and appreciation for all the good things one sees in other people, and to offer apologies and forgiveness for unskillful actions one has done to others. This regular heart-opening exercise, in a sincere manner, proves to be a powerful tool to strengthen positive and constructive relationships among all community members and helps resolve a lot of conflicts that have arisen.

The Community and Learning Partners: families-community-social groups

Another unique aspect of the Buddhist Approach School is the community that is comprised of Family-Temple-School. The interconnected relationship of sharing and learning among students, teachers, parents and monks and other contemplative wise spiritual teachers or trainers has been encouraged in a variety of different platforms and activities, such as formal mindfulness meditation training, daily praying and morning assembly, Kalayanamitre classroom contemplative practices and Buddhist traditional activities.

The schools also stress the need for continuous practice in order to get used to mindful behavior, knowledge and investigation. This practice guides students out of attachment to desire, as taught by the Buddha. Students are taught mindfulness even through their body's every movement (i.e. every time we breathe, swallow or chew). At RAS, students are introduced to the formal practice of four or more continuous days of these mindfulness practices to help sharpen the basic skills of awareness in addition to informal practices for applying self-awareness in daily life.

In order to provide a convenient place for regular contemplative practices, RAS has built a retreat center named 'Guru Sati Sathan', which can accommodate 60 trainees at a time, with full facilities. It has well-arranged meditation areas for individuals and groups, with monthly scheduled activities for their staff or other interested people. Many experienced teachers and monks willingly help teach participants at the retreat center.

In addition, the development of the 'Mindful Parents Classroom' at RAS is composed of a prerequisite 30 hours of training workshops of sharing and learning activities combined with mindfulness practice for parents of new students held over nine continuous weekends before the beginning of the first academic year. During the training the school designs simple activities to challenge the parents' self-awareness and to build the basic relationship of trust between parents and children. For example, when parents and children have lunch together, the teachers observe how parents behave towards their children. Are they over-directing or under-disciplining their children? In another example, when playing sports in the field with teamwork regulations, could parents recognize themselves if they are blocking their child's motivation by either over-deciding or stealing the child's opportunity to do it by him/herself?

The mindful reflection discussion in AAR helps remind them of their mind's behavior, such as how they feel when they see their children fail to manage their lunch according to their expectation, and how they react to that feeling. These reflective questions are necessary to help parents practice mindfulness in their parenting. For example, if they could revisit the actions, what would they rather do or not do?

Many kinds of activities can be exercised as long as the AAR session is integrated as an important element for everyone to be able to share and delve deeper into the value of self-awareness or actualization to be more ready to be Kalayanamitre to their children. Currently, the parents' self-organized group of Buddhist training and studying activities has regularly arranged special events in the school. They invite renowned guests or monks to present the essence of Buddha's teaching or lead the contemplative practices in daily life, in addition to organizing religious excursions. These activities help inspire and encourage strong attentiveness to one's development of self-awareness, which results in the improvement of the parents' behavior and of their relationship to their family.

Teachers' and Parents' Mindful Dialogue

At Panyaprateep, parents in the school system are regarded as the 'second-tiered students' who have to be trained continually to be skillful parents. They are invited to be closely involved in the school activities, in the learning process of the students and for their own training and development. Parents are strongly encouraged to participate in parents' retreat programs organized fourteen times per year as a half-day event. They are also invited to join school trips.

At RAS, a platform is scheduled for teachers and parents to make their relationship more mature and develop communication with the right view and trust. The teachers are guided and trained to apply dialogue skills. During face-to-face conversation, mindful listening and speaking in accordance with the guidelines of Kalayanamitre and Yonisomanasikara are encouraged.

In addition to teachers and school personnel, others in the broader school community are able to network and establish this culture of a Buddhist-approach community as a focal point of contemplative development and as a foundation to support a strong civic society. As families become more involved in the children's activities, the children will be happy and will develop their own good habits. In this regard, the dynamic system of interconnection will help sustain the sense of community and create a more harmonious society.

In Conclusion

When compared with the past and the conventional approach of Christian schools or the Buddhist temple schools, including the novice monk schools in Thailand during the previous century, this chapter has shown a new direction of religious application in the schooling system in Thailand. The discussion of the concept of learning and teaching in the three case-study schools represents the different ways of applying the essences of religious principles as guidelines for practice in schools. These case studies have clearly demonstrated how the deep interpretation from the heart of any religion as well as the integration of this into the whole process of the schooling system can leverage the modern education system. Not only students, but teachers and parents also are able to be trained in the holistic mode of learning and contemplative practice, in order to develop both body and mind as well as academic and life skills infused with moral values.

The key to achieving a holistic learning process is the interpretation of a value development system derived from religious principles. While each of these schools are different from each other they still share the ultimate goal of a state of wisdom in human development. These schools demonstrate how the interfaith dialogue between the different religions could be shared and learned. Furthermore, we realize from these schools' experiences that the power of knowing oneself and of the moment of here and now is always found existing in each individual, no matter what the spiritual practice. These practices can be strengthened to develop personal understanding, love and compassion and to transform learners within a revolutionized system with religion integrated into education.

References

Bureau of Academic Affairs and Educational Standards (2002) *Basic Standard Curriculum 2001*. Bangkok: Bureau of Academic Affairs and Educational Standards.

Bureau of Educational Innovation Development (n.d.) *The School of Buddhism: education for a complete human being*. Bangkok: Bureau of Education Innovation Development. http://www.vitheebuddha.com (accessed 1 March 2016).

Chaiyaphon, Chatchaphon (2011) *A Vision towards Education of the Chakri Monarch; His Majesty the King Rama 1-9*. Bangkok: Education Council of Thailand.

Chantrasook, A. (2006) *Instilling Moral Childhood through the Creative Process of Leaders' Buddhist School*. Bangkok: The Moral Center.

Chuencharoensok, S. (2013) *Development of Educational Standards and Indicators for the External Quality Assessment of Alternative Schools and Specific Curriculum Schools*. Bangkok: National Education Standards and Quality Assessment(ONESQA).

Jumsai Na Ayudhya, A. (2003) A Development of the Human Values Integrated Instructional Model Based on Intuitive Learning Concept. Doctoral thesis, Department of Secondary Education, Faculty of Curriculum and Instruction, Chulalongkorn University.

Ministry of Social Development and Human Security (2016) *The Number of Schools, Students and Classrooms, Educational Year 2012-2016*. Office of the Basic Education Commission. https://www.m-society.go.th/article_attach/18126/20173.pdf (accessed 7 March 2017).

Mohjhaw, A., Tubsree, C. & Chomdokmai, M. (2013) *Integration of the Buddhist Yonisomanasikara Thinking Framework with the Problem Solving Cycle: phenomenological research at Roong Aroon School*. Chonburi: Burapa University.

National Office of Buddhism (2017) Phrapariyatidham Schools. http://www1.onab.go.th/index.php?option=com_content&view=article&id=5380: 2012-01-06-16-14-42&catid=77:2009-07-14-14-27-10&Itemid=389 (accessed 7 March 2017).

National Statistical Office (2015) Statistical Yearbook Thailand 2015. http://service.nso.go.th/nso/nsopublish/pubs/e-book/esyb58/files/assets/basic-html/index.html#1 (accessed 7 March 2017).

Niyom, P. (2001) *Roong Aroon School's Conceptual Framework for Holistic Learning Application 1*. Bangkok: Roong Aroon School Foundation.

Niyom, P. (2008) *Kalyanamitta = Spiritual Friend*. Bangkok: Roong Aroon School Foundation.

Office of National Human Rights Commission of Thailand (2011) *The Thai Constitution of 2007*. Bangkok: Office of National Human Rights Commission of Thailand.

Office of the Private Education Commission (2015) Private Education Statistics Year 2015. http://www.opec.go.th/content.php?page=content&group=statistic (accessed 7 March 2017).

Panich, V. (2014) *The Evaluation for Restoring of Learning Power: embedded formative assessment*. Bangkok: Saanaksorn.

Payutto, P. (2002) *The Dawn of Education*. Bangkok: Sahathammik.

Payutto, P. (2004) *Educational Principle in Buddhism*. Bangkok: Four Element Group.

Payutto, P. (2013) *Yonisomanasikara: thinking in ways of buddhadhamma*. Nakhon pathom: Wat Nyanavesakavan.

Ratchatatanun, W. (2006) *12 Morality for Success in Buddhist Education*. Bangkok: Thawsri School.

Weissman, S. (2011) *Wise Reflection: the importance of wise reflection in meditation*. Sri Lanka: BPS Transcription Project.

CHAPTER 10

Modernizing Islamic Education: Bangladesh and Senegal

LAUREN HERZOG & NATHANIEL ADAMS

SUMMARY Islamic religious bodies or individuals operate significant parts of education systems in various countries. In some (quite rare) cases, these schools are recognized and integrated as part of the public education system. Elsewhere, they are informal, with varying links to other parts of the system. Their roles are actively debated at national and international levels. This chapter describes Islamic school systems in Bangladesh and Senegal, highlights the contemporary challenges they face, and outlines efforts to modernize and integrate the systems, led by both religious and secular actors.

Introduction

Islamic education systems represent a critical, if often neglected, aspect of education policy, sparking lively debates. While security concerns (about radical Islam spreading through these institutions) dominate much discourse, Islamic education institutions can and do play important roles in meeting the basic global goal of education for all. They reflect a common and growing demand for attention to values and culturally appropriate curricula in schools. In many countries (Bangladesh and Senegal among them), Islamic school systems are major education providers, filling gaps in state-run education systems, for example, in reaching marginalized populations. In both countries, demand for religious education is significant, as are challenges in assessing quality. Exploring how Islamic education fits within broader national education strategies is thus an important priority. The chapter draws on a teaching case study prepared by the Georgetown University Berkley Center for Religion, Peace and World Affairs and the World Faiths Development Dialogue (see Adams et al, 2017).

Islamic Education and Reform: a disputed topic

Access to quality education undergirds all other development efforts. Education is critical to sustained development because of its role in building the skilled workforce necessary for economic transformation. It is also fundamental to cultivating the informed citizenry necessary for an engaged democracy and the plural societies that characterize much of the world.

Education is likewise a central preoccupation for major faith traditions. Islamic teachings highlight learning the revealed word of God (the Quran) as a central part of religious worship. The first Islamic schools, which began in the seventh century, taught Arabic literacy and were aimed mainly at memorizing the Quran (Hefner, 2009). In the ensuing centuries, the body of knowledge associated with Islam grew. The words and deeds of the Prophet Mohammed were compiled into what is now known as the hadith; scholarship associated with Islamic legal schools (*madhab*) developed, and Islamic law (*fiqh*) was standardized. The expanding Islamic corpus necessitated a deeper and more rigorous approach to study. Schools for advanced Islamic learning and scholarship appeared in the tenth century, first in what is now Iran, then spreading rapidly. Islamic schools, or madrasas, began to develop a standardized physical format with a mosque and ablution house, dormitories and classrooms. The madrasa curriculum also assumed a familiar form around this time, teaching Quranic recitation (*qira'a*), hadith, Arabic grammar (*nahw*), Quranic interpretation (*tafsir*), jurisprudence (*fiqh*), religious principles (*usul ad-din*), legal sources (*usul al-fiqh*) and Islamic theology (*kalam*) (Hefner, 2009). Many madrasas began to incorporate subjects such as mathematics, medicine, astronomy, philosophy and poetry based on classical texts. From the eleventh until the fourteenth centuries, there were important Muslim scholars in all these disciplines. Islamic schools cultivated some of the most influential thinkers of the medieval era, including Al Ghazali, Al Farabi, Ibn Rushd, Ibn Sina, Ibn Al Haytham and Al Qurtubi.

After the so-called Islamic golden age, this cosmopolitan tradition in Islamic education slowly faded. Madrasas became increasingly interested in the preservation of tradition, notably in the face of European colonialism. Both externally and internally driven madrasa reform projects were launched. In many contexts, including in Bangladesh and Senegal, colonial authorities took a keen interest in madrasa education, believing that changing or eliminating these traditional religious education systems could contribute to the modernization and secularization of societies and lessen the social influence of antagonistic religious authorities. Madrasas also trained local civil servants, particularly those that dealt with Islamic law.

Externally driven madrasa reforms of the colonial era were often contemporaneous with internal Islamic reforms, many linked to emerging movements, which aimed at returning Muslim communities to fundamentals that would protect and perpetuate a 'pure' Islamic knowledge and practice in the face of modernization. Movements across the Muslim world varied in approach, with many involved in articulating anti-colonial resistance. In some cases, distrust of the West extended to include ambivalence toward or outright rejection of what was considered to be 'western knowledge'. Islamic education today is something of an ideological battlefield, with debates around the roles that religious institutions and beliefs play in society and who is seen as speaking for the 'true' Islam.

The term 'madrasa' refers to various and quite different Islamic educational institutions, and the term is often used imprecisely. Madrasa can refer to a range of Islamic schools, from primary schools or 'kindergartens' – known in Bangladesh as *maktabs* and in Senegal as *daaras*, which focus primarily on rote memorization of the Quran – to Islamic universities, some of which teach predominantly secular subject matter, including engineering or medicine. Most policy discussions of madrasa reform focus on Islamic schools at the primary and secondary levels.

Traditionally, most Islamic education institutions functioned to train religious clergy and to teach the Quran to children, especially boys. Although important education providers in parts of the Muslim world, perceived deficiencies in curriculum and pedagogical approaches have led education policymakers to fear that madrasa education can marginalize impoverished youth by providing a poor-quality education that imparts few skills necessary for employment. In the aftermath of 9/11 and the ongoing 'war on terror', international security and development agendas have focused on madrasas because of a widespread perception that Islamic schools are breeding grounds for extremist and militant ideology, though many specialists argue that this narrative rests on limited and patchy evidence.

Motivations for different reform efforts vary. Some essentially aim to convert these traditional institutions into 'secularized' schools that can meet the demands of students and a modern economy. Others encourage more open and cosmopolitan intellectual traditions within Islam by engaging with a wider range of theological and secular scholarship. The most common reform approach has been to secularize madrasas or to integrate them into a national education system, offering cash and material incentives to those schools which integrate secular subject matter into curricula and submit to government regulation. Reform efforts have seen some success at least in terms of expanding curriculum and increasing oversight. Bangladesh and Senegal present two different yet illustrative examples of the broader debates and reform experience at country level.

Islamic Education in Bangladesh and Senegal

Bangladesh: the context

A small and densely populated country (population 160 million in 2015), Bangladesh faces many development challenges. At independence in 1971, Bangladesh faced what seemed intractable problems of poverty, but it has seen robust economic growth in recent years and has achieved better results on various health indicators than many countries at comparable income levels. Much credit for this progress goes to an active civil society.

Education is a leading development priority for Bangladesh. In 2015, some 96% of the labor force did not have a secondary school certificate, and two-thirds had not completed primary schooling (World Bank, 2013). However, innovative education programs have driven major growth in enrollment: primary school enrollment increased from 60% in 1990 to 92% in 2012 (World Bank, 2016h). Gender parity in enrollment, long a major challenge in South Asia, has been achieved at the primary and secondary level (World Bank, 2013). These gains have been driven primarily by gender-focused public interventions, including stipend programs for girls, improved access (girls often have stronger mobility restrictions) and changing social norms (UNICEF, 2009).

Bangladesh is renowned for development innovations. This is true in the education sector. Novel public-private partnerships have included active government collaboration with non-governmental organizations (NGOs) and with madrasas. These partnerships have extended access to school for millions of children, but also resulted in a large and complex system with 13 types of providers, 10 examination boards, over 150,000 institutions, 40 million students and one million teachers (World Bank, 2013).

Deficiencies in education are nonetheless a major hindrance to social and economic development. These center on widespread quality issues, low student retention and pockets of poor access in some rural areas. Only a third of primary school students in Bangladesh achieve expected numeracy and literacy skills for their grade (World Bank, 2013). Student-teacher contact time is one of the lowest in the world, averaging only 2.5 hours per day (Falkowska, 2013). Completion rates for the five-year primary school cycle are only 50.7%, and the average number of years to complete the cycle is 8.6 years (UNICEF, 2009). Approximately five million children are not enrolled in school, having either never attended or dropped out prematurely (UNICEF, 2009).

Poor children and those living in rural areas are far more likely to face significant barriers to school attendance and worse educational outcomes when they do attend. Enrollment inequity between poor and non-poor children has been nearly eliminated at the primary level, but the secondary gross enrollment ratio for poor children is only 45%, versus 76% for non-poor children (World Bank, 2013). Petty corruption presents barriers to education, especially for the poor. Despite nominally free education in public schools, informal payments are common, and government cash stipends may not be paid out properly. Bribes can influence exam pass rates (van Nuland & Khandlewal, 2006).

Islamic Education

Roughly 89% of the Bangladeshi population is Muslim, with a regional Islamic tradition dating back to the twelfth century. Bangladeshi Muslim beliefs and institutions reflect diverse influences, including Sufi mysticism (Sufis were among the first to spread Islam in Bengal), as well as orthodox Islamic reform traditions dating from the nineteenth century.

Madrasas today are larger and perhaps more influential than at any time in Bangladeshi history. The number of madrasas has grown dramatically since Bangladesh gained independence from Pakistan, increasing from fewer than 2000 in 1971 to roughly 15,000 registered madrasas by 2014, with at least as many unregistered, though likely many more (Bano, 2014). Madrasas contribute to the expansion of access to education and, less appreciated, to Bangladesh's success in achieving gender parity in enrollment. Bangladesh stands out worldwide in terms of the contribution madrasas make to education provision. Madrasas account for roughly 2% of enrollment in Pakistan and 4% in India, while in Bangladesh, approximately 13.8% of students enrolled at the primary level and 21% at secondary level attend madrasas (Asadullah et al, 2009). Thus, these 'traditional' institutions are increasingly popular in rapidly modernizing Bangladesh.

In Bangladesh, madrasas are divided between Alia, or 'reformed' madrasas, and Quomi. Alia institutions, as a condition for financial support, submit to government regulation and oversight by the Madrasa Education Board. They have adopted and follow the national curriculum, retaining elements of the traditional religious subjects. Alia degrees are recognized by the government, whereas Quomi degrees are not. As of 2014, the Alia system consisted of 9341 institutions with 3.6 million students (Thornton & Thornton, 2012). Much less is known about the independent and unregistered madrasas collectively termed Quomi; estimates range between 15,000 and 64,000 schools (Bano, 2014). The government has put increasing pressure on Quomi institutions to register and join the reform efforts, with limited success.

Madrasa Reform in Bangladesh

The quasi-public Alia system in Bangladesh has purposefully sought to bridge different approaches to education while building on traditional Islamic approaches. Alia madrasas trace their history to colonial-era madrasa reforms undertaken by the British authorities in Bengal. In 1782, Governor General William Hasting sponsored the creation of the Alia Madrasa in Calcutta. Combining western pedagogical and administrative approaches for traditional subjects, including Arabic, Persian and Islamic Law (*fiqh*), it trained Muslims to occupy lower posts in government offices and to act as interpreters of the Muslim civil code. Over the years, further secular subjects were added, including English, math and science. While British madrasa reforms in this era were fairly limited, the tradition of the secularized, state-supported madrasa endured, retaining the moniker Alia.

The Alia system now includes any madrasa that has adopted the national curriculum of Bangladesh and is subject to state regulation. Alia madrasas are in many ways comparable in quality and outcomes to government schools. As state-supported and regulated Islamic schools, Alia madrasas are somewhat unique entities in the Muslim world.

The reform approach for Alia madrasas involves government provision of financial incentives to madrasas; in exchange, the schools adopt secular subject matter and submit to government oversight and regulation. Incentives take the form of bolstered teacher salaries and material support, including textbooks and computers. Alia schools are thus state supported, but not state owned. The government pays 90% of salary costs for teachers, who cover both religious and secular subjects, while the local community maintains the school facilities. Roughly 72% of the budget of an Alia madrasa is borne by the government. Alia madrasas offer comparable education to government schools, or in some cases better quality. Given the reorientation in curriculum, adding secular subjects while substantially abbreviating traditional religious coursework, Alia madrasas aim to equip students with the practical skills necessary to join the workforce upon graduation.

The central strategies and character of Alia madrasas have thus shifted toward more worldly concerns, with largely positive results in expanding access to quality education, particularly in rural areas. Alia madrasas have, however, largely ceded their position within the hierarchy of Islamic education in Bangladesh. The Quomi institutions are now seen as the seat of Islamic authority and the home of true Islamic scholarship in Bangladesh. Alia madrasas no longer train Islamic clergy, the traditional function of the madrasa in Islam. Nearly all ulama (Islamic scholars) and imams in Bangladesh are products of the Quomi system, and it is these institutions that are seen to speak for Islam and define what it means to be a 'good Muslim' (Bano, 2014). Thus, if a goal of madrasa reform is to contribute to a more enlightened Islamic discourse that engages with the full breadth of the Islamic and western intellectual traditions and responds to contemporary challenges, Alia madrasas fall short.

The female secondary school stipend program introduced in 1993 involved Alia madrasas. The goal was to increase girls' enrollment and attendance. Tuition was waived for girls, and additional funding went to schools that enrolled girls. With madrasas included in the program, traditionally all-male institutions opened to girls. The number of female students in madrasas jumped from 7.7% in 1990 to 52% in 2008. Madrasas accounted for 35% of the expansion of enrollment for girls in that era, thus contributing significantly to achieving gender parity in education nationally (Asadullah & Chaudhury, 2013). This was also true at the secondary level. The opening of Alia madrasas to girls pushed many Quomi institutions to open girls' madrasas in order to compete with Alia schools in this new market.

Growing access to religious education for women, despite concerns about perpetuation of regressive gender norms, has allowed women to become somewhat better integrated into religious structures, long the exclusive domain of men. Increased presence in these conservative institutions has expanded women's influence in the public sphere in new ways, though these are very little studied and understood currently. At present, most women Quomi students and graduates do not appear to be motivated by a desire to challenge male dominance in these institutions or in Islamic communities and practice, but the long-term effects remain to be seen (Begum & Kabir, 2012).

Quomi madrasas are heirs to a very different madrasa tradition, part of the orthodox Deobandi tradition that stretches across the Indian sub-continent. This educational movement still shapes the insular and protective approach many institutions take toward Islamic scholarship. Founded in the immediate aftermath of the Sepoy Rebellion against the British in the mid-nineteenth century, the Deobandi movement was an anti-colonial Islamic revival movement. The central aim of the founders of the Darul Uloom Deoband madrasa was to establish Islamic schools that could serve as a critical bulwark against western cultural imperialism. They envisioned madrasas as sites where Islam would be curated in a 'pure' form, free from outside influence, to provide an intellectual counterweight to western knowledge. The approach was predicated on the quest to uncover a singular 'true Islam', at the expense of engaging in dialogue with more pluralist perspectives within the Islamic tradition. Most Quomi madrasas in Bangladesh still operate on this Deobandi model and look to Darul Uloom Deoband in India as the standard bearer in Islamic education.

Many Quomi institutions retain a strongly protective, independent orientation and have been reluctant to adopt government reforms and introduce 'western' subject matter into curricula. Quomi schools utilize the Dars-i-Nizami curriculum developed by Mulla Nizam Uddin at Firangi Mahal in Lucknow in the eighteenth century. Actual curriculum content can vary depending on the competencies of instructors. While Quomi madrasas are not registered with or regulated by the government, many operate under one of five independent education boards which have some influence over curriculum and teaching methods: Bangladesh Quomi Madrasa Education Board (Befaq) in Dhaka; Befaqul Madarisil Arabia in Gopalganj; Azadbini Edaraye Tamil Madarisil in Sylhet; Ettehadul Madarisil Arabia in Chittagong; and Tanjimul Madarisil in Bogra. Darul Uloom Moniul Islam Hathazari, founded in Chittagong in 1901 by a group of Deoband-trained scholars, is considered the most prestigious of Bangladesh's Quomi madrasas and has considerable influence throughout the Quomi network.

Quomi institutions focus on developing skills required to fulfill the duties of a religious leader. Those include the writing of *khutbas* or sermons delivered during Friday prayer, the articulation of *fatwah* or Islamic legal rulings, and skills associated with the art of religious debate and discussion. Ulama from leading Quomi madrasas tend to emphasize the authority of orthodox canonical teachings, which can be at odds with today's lived experience of Muslims. This tension can undermine consensus on vital ethical questions posed by social change and transformation. Ulama from leading Quomi madrasas tend to emphasize the intensive study of scripture and privilege literal interpretations.

Quomi institutions produce the majority of Bangladeshi religious leaders. Graduates of Quomi madrasas analyze and comment on social issues from a theological perspective and purport to speak for the 'true' Islam. Many Bangladeshi citizens turn to them for guidance on domestic and community matters.

Most Quomi madrasas are boarding schools. Alia madrasas, in comparison, follow a standard school schedule of 9 a.m. to 2 p.m. Quomi madrasas stress an austere and pious life, so facilities can often be quite basic. Likewise, as these schools often depend entirely on local donations for their operating costs, educational materials and other supplies can be scarce. Quomi madrasas have a restrictive schedule and can be fairly closed environments for students, with limited opportunities to interact with the wider community. In the current climate of anxiety and suspicion around radicalism, this can undermine social trust on both sides.

Employability of Quomi graduates is an ongoing concern. The number of graduates of these schools far outpaces the availability of religious jobs in Bangladesh, and degrees from Quomi madrasas are not recognized by the government, curtailing access to higher education and to many jobs. Quomi madrasas often impart few pragmatic skills traditionally associated with modern life. Many graduates struggle to find mainstream employment. Quomi madrasa students experience economic marginalization and social alienation.

Many Quomi madrasas have diversified their curriculum to compete with Alia madrasas and other public and private education providers, slowly introducing non-religious subjects into Quomi curricula. This has been a sporadic and uneven process that is not widely known and appreciated. A recent survey showed that roughly 73% of rural Quomi madrasas teach some English, 70% teach some science, 59% teach the Bengali language, and 44% teach some math (up to grade 8 or equivalent) (Asadullah et al, 2009). Changes have not been systematic, in part due to the fractured nature and limited authority of Quomi madrasa boards. While recent changes within Quomi madrasas can be seen as an indirect response to the educational approaches of other providers, they are also linked to the major social and economic shifts in Bangladeshi society, suggesting a natural evolution. Indeed, younger madrasa teachers with technological savvy are more connected with the wider world, and thus more likely to see value in 'secular' knowledge. Empirical studies within Quomi madrasas are limited, so there is little information about these changes.

The Bangladeshi government has moved with increasing urgency to bring Quomi madrasas under government oversight and regulation, in large measure responding to the growing threat of Islamic militancy and fears about the spread of radical ideology. Because Quomi institutions value their independence, reform efforts are highly sensitive, and the government has moved cautiously, seeking support from key Quomi figures. In April 2015, the government engaged several high-ranking members of Hefazat-e-Islam.[1] Chief Shah Ahmad Shafi was appointed head of a 17-member panel to explore reforms. Internal divisions among Quomi institutions ultimately doomed this effort. Shafi eventually unilaterally released an eight-point charter that agreed to reforms as long as they did not require government aid to madrasas and did not necessitate a change in teaching methods. Thus, Quomi reform efforts have stalled. Further progress may depend on the level of trust that can be built between the government and Quomi madrasa leaders, as well as on resolving divisions among Quomi leaders. Diversifying curriculum in madrasas to include a wider, richer and more diverse collection of Islamic theological scholarship seems the best approach.

Senegal: the context

Senegal (population 14 million) has a long-standing reputation for interreligious harmony. Senegalese Islam (some 94% of Senegalese are Muslim) is heavily influenced by Sufism, and most Muslims identify with one of four Sufi orders (Tijaniyya, Muridiyya, Qadiriyya and Layeniyya). Christians (4% – largely Catholic) are a respected religious minority. Though aspiring to middle-income status, Senegal remains a poor country in a region with some of the world's highest incidences of poverty.

Improving education quality and equity are central to Senegal's development agenda and education strategies (Ministère de l'Education Nationale, 2014; Government of Senegal, 2015). Senegal has made important gains in gross enrollment (56% in 1994 to 81% in 2014) and gender parity at the primary level (0.75 ratio of girls to boys in 1994 to 1.09 in 2014), but significant challenges remain (World Bank, 2016c,g). Girls attend primary schools at higher rates than boys, but drop out in high numbers at each successive education level. An estimated nearly 600,000 primary school-age children are out of school, although school attendance to age 16 is mandatory by law and public education is free for students aged 6 to 16 (World Bank, 2016f; Government of Senegal, 2005). Costs of school materials are prohibitive for some families, and weak government oversight means that quality and curriculum are inconsistent. Just 51% of females aged 15 to 24 were literate in 2013, compared with 61% of males of the same age (World Bank, 2016d, e).

Senegal's educational offerings are quite diverse, with various formal and informal options. The formal sector includes public preschool, primary school, secondary school and higher education, plus a variety of technical and professional training institutions. Teaching is primarily in French. Formal private schools adhere to government regulations and, at times, receive government funding. The informal sector is subject to little regulation. This complexity and duality is reflected in significant limitations on data.

The public education sector faces challenges, exacerbated by rapid expansion to accommodate growing numbers of students and the goal of universal primary education. Insufficient facilities, materials, and even teacher training are issues (Ministère de l'Education Nationale, 2015). There are stark regional differences. Many teachers teach double shifts (6.6% of classes in 2013) or multi-grade classes (28% of classes in 2013) to increase education access (Ministère de l'Education Nationale, 2013). The government works closely with many partners, such as UNESCO, the World Bank, USAID and private institutions and foundations, toward sustainable solutions.

The private education sector includes many religious schools (both formal and informal), notably Islamic schools. The small Catholic education system has a strong reputation. Other private schools include non-religious schools, either entrepreneurial or associated with non-profit efforts. Private schools can be recognized and regulated by the government; those that are follow the national curriculum.

Islamic Schools in Senegal Today

Islamic education in Senegal dates back to the early introduction of Islam during the eleventh century (Ware, 2009). Quranic schools were the principal form of schooling and education, reaching both elites and wider communities. Islamic schools were the main education providers in Senegal for centuries, with few other options. Islamic education centered largely on *daaras*, Quranic schools grounded in the Sufi tradition. A Quranic instructor (referred to locally as a *marabout* or *serigne daara*) heads each school and teaches students, or *talibés*, the Quran. *Talibés* typically memorize the Quran over the course of a few years and are to internalize and display the comportment expected of a good Muslim. Teaching is in Arabic (a foreign language in Senegal). *Daaras* were seen as instilling important values in children, such as humility, submission and perseverance.

Senegal's diverse and complex Islamic education system has changed significantly since independence. Reasons include the rapid increase in modern state education, the growth of a variety of private schools, social and cultural changes across the society (including rapid urbanization) and pressures on the traditional *daara* system. Protracted drought in the 1970s transformed the rural landscape. Many *daaras* moved to the cities (along with many rural families), changing the pattern of relationships between students and Quranic instructors. *Daaras* had relied on agricultural labor from the students – seen as fostering a strong work ethic, developing useful skills and helping them to cope with hardship – to support the *daara* and provide food. Options for Islamic education became more diverse, and new school types emerged, resulting in several different models of Islamic education.

Most *daaras* are informal schools operated by a Quranic instructor (typically affiliated with a Sufi order). In the traditional model, students (mostly boys) lived in the *daaras*. Today, there are different models of *daaras*; many remain boarding-style, but in some, students attend during evenings, weekends or school holidays. *Daara* education is often viewed as complementary, as students attend another school as their primary source of education. Girls often attend, and, at least at very young ages, classes consist of both girls and boys. Although there are organized groups of Quranic instructors, the system is very decentralized, with very little government regulation.

The *Franco-Arabic school* is an important emerging model. First established in the 1970s as private schools, they are an alternative, somewhere between a French-style school and an Islamic school, offering a hybrid style of education, where students study Arabic and Islamic studies in addition to the normal public curriculum that includes French. Many private Franco-Arabic schools are operated individually; others belong to a network of schools. Some are affiliated with a specific Sufi order, but others are unaffiliated; many schools claim to accept students regardless of order affiliation. The private Franco-Arabic schools established in the 1970s served as a model for education reforms, and public Franco-Arabic schools are now officially part of the national education system. The education reforms of 2002 saw the Senegalese government adopt this model as a potentially integral part of the public school system, but it has expanded slowly. As of 2013, 27.7% of private schools were Franco-Arabic, compared with only 3.4% of public schools. Numbers are growing: Shortly after the reforms were launched, there were only nine public Franco-Arabic schools (2003), but the number had increased to 266 in 2013 (Ministère de l'Education Nationale, 2013).

Referred to as 'modern' *daaras*, an increasing number of Islamic schools are operated privately, but regulated by the government with the objective of integrating them into the official education system (Villalón & Bodian, 2012). The government can now recognize the modern *daaras* as private schools, and some receive government support. The number of modern *daaras* is still small, but expanding the 'modern' *daara* program is a government priority. Modern *daaras*, much like Franco-Arabic schools, offer a hybrid-style education. They typically offer trilingual instruction, with Arabic, French and national languages (Villalón & Bodian, 2012).

Senegal has never developed an Islamic education system extending to higher learning (though options are currently under study). Those who sought to further pursue religious subjects studied with a Sufi teacher; some studied abroad, in Mauritania, Morocco or the Middle East.

A widely discussed debate in Senegal is whether traditional forms of Islamic education, like that offered in many Senegalese *daaras*, are stagnant and antiquated in their curriculum and practices, failing to prepare students for today's realities. Various Islamic schools and communities are innovating and introducing new approaches to Islamic education, and the importance of addressing what amounts to a bifurcated educational system is recognized. However, reform is a complex topic with intensely political, as well as cultural and religious, dimensions; overall progress has been slow, with many issues to resolve.

Today's debates about Islamic education reflect a complex history dating back to French colonial administration policies (nineteenth and early twentieth centuries). Policies that favor the French system and language date from that period, when cultural assimilation was the goal, at least for a small elite. Reform efforts included measures designed to limit Quranic schooling and drive Senegalese children to French schools. Senegalese French speakers had opportunities in the colonial administration (Duke Bryant, 2015). However, many parents and Quranic instructors resisted the colonial mandates; some Quranic instructors gave an air of compliance, but resisted subtly (Gellar, 2005; Duke Bryant, 2015). Facing tensions, colonial authorities attempted to make public schools more attractive by integrating Islamic education and Arabic into the curriculum (Bouche, 1974). Some Senegalese religious leaders advised followers not to attend French schools. At the same time, demand for Quranic schools rose, and rural populations preferred *daaras* (and in any event, there were few government schools in these areas).

At Senegal's independence in 1960, it inherited both the formal education system introduced by the French colonial administration – a very classic French system with a curriculum modeled on the metropole – and the Islamic education system that had existed for centuries. Senegal's new leaders had largely emerged from the French system and valued it; French was designated as Senegal's official language and continued as the official language of instruction in the public education system. The government chose to continue the French-style secular education model. There were lively debates, though, about religious education in public schools and the *daara* system.

In 1981, the nature of Senegalese education was the central focus of the *Etats Généraux de l'Education et de la Formation*, a national dialogue process. Religious communities called on the government to integrate religious curriculum into public schools and provide government support to religious schools. Debates about religious education intensified after Abdoulaye Wade became president in 2000, with tensions between those concerned that the public education system was not responding to the public's needs and those advocating for secular values. The reforms, which became law in 2004, altered the secular nature of public education in Senegal. Successive measures have focused on introducing public Franco-Arabic schools, modernizing the *daaras* and introducing religious education into public schools. Some *daaras* have undertaken reforms, both independently and as an official part of government programs. The government's *daara* modernization program began in 2002, but some *daaras* began independent reforms long before, often with outside funding (Anti-Slavery International, 2011).

The integration of four hours of voluntary religious education per week into public primary schools was significant; before 2004, religious education was entirely absent. Parents can choose between an Islamic or a Christian curriculum for their children. Debates around this reform reflect the long-standing debates about whether the public education system is well adapted both to Senegal's culture and the population's economic and social needs. There are questions as to whether four hours of voluntary religious education in public primary schools is sufficient in a country where religious education is seen as a central element of raising good citizens grounded in Senegalese culture and values (personal communication, May 2016).

Until 2013, students in Senegal educated in Arabic rather than French had few options; the state-administered *Baccalauréat* [2] examination was available only in French, and the limited French language skills of students receiving a primarily Islamic education were rarely sufficient to pass it. An Arabic *Baccalauréat* was offered, but it was not organized by the government. However, the Senegalese government now offers an Arabic *Baccalauréat* exam, and there is some space in the Arabic Department at the university in Dakar for students who excel.

Issues for Madrasa Education in Bangladesh and Senegal

Demand for madrasa education in Bangladesh has clearly increased, but the reasons are not fully understood. Better understanding of how and why parents value madrasa education is needed. A common narrative is that because many madrasas fully subsidize expenses for students, they can be the only educational options available to the very poor. Others believe that the expansion of madrasas is driven by increased religiosity and a demand for religious subjects to be more emphasized in school curricula, part of a growing 'Islamization' of Bangladeshi society as new Salafi interpretations of Islam are imported from the Middle East.

Backlash against perceived westernization that has accompanied rapid economic growth and development is another factor. But no single factor fully explains why madrasa education is so attractive. Educational decisions of Bangladeshi households can be complex. Parents may weigh the potential benefits of schools in terms of future employment and earnings against the monetary cost of school fees and supplies. Traveling long distances from home is a common concern, particularly for girls, whose mobility they wish to control. The desire to instill proper values and mold youths into 'good

Muslims', 'good citizens' and 'good wives' who fulfill responsibilities to family and community is important. Studies highlight that parents may send children within the same family to different types of schools: one survey showed that among families with at least two secondary school-age children, 70% chose madrasa education for some and secular education for others (Asadullah et al, 2015).

A common assumption is that poor families send their children to madrasas motivated primarily by economic necessity. Both Alia and Quomi madrasas are often either totally subsidized or considerably less expensive than government or other private schools. Quomi madrasas function as boarding schools, providing food and lodging to students whose families might otherwise struggle to support them. Many Quomi madrasas market themselves as orphanages. Despite their low cost, potential earnings for madrasa graduates are lower overall than those who graduate from secular schools. A policy concern is that madrasa education can marginalize poor children by making them economically uncompetitive with their peers, particularly Quomi graduates, whose degrees are not officially recognized. Even if expected future earnings for madrasa graduates are lower, some parents assume that madrasa graduates will spend a higher proportion of their earnings to support their parents (Asadullah et al, 2015).

Particularly in rural areas, there is little difference in quality between the reformed Alia madrasas and government schools, and therefore the decision can often be between Alia madrasas and government schools on the one hand and Quomi madrasas on the other. If economic or career success is a goal, parents are more likely to choose an Alia madrasa or government school.

Religious knowledge and values are appreciated in Bangladeshi society, a major reason why parents choose madrasa education (Asadullah et al, 2015). Quranic literacy is highly prized in many communities, and having a child who is a Quran *Hafez* (able to recite the entire Quran from memory) can be a source of pride, conferring considerable blessings upon the family. The qualities that madrasa education aims to develop in youth – trustworthiness, moral fortitude, good judgment and submission to God – are seen as critical attributes for a leader in Bangladeshi communities. Because they treat Islamic scripture comprehensively, Quomi madrasas are seen as better equipped to impart these qualities. In rural areas in particular, community leadership still has strong religious associations, and madrasas serve a critical function. Higher religiosity on the part of the father is positively correlated with madrasa attendance. Madrasas also seem to be favored in more religiously conservative areas (Asadullah et al, 2009).

Since reformed Alia madrasas opened their doors to girls in the early 1990s, demand for girls' madrasas has increased dramatically. Issues related to *purdah* figure heavily in decisions on whether to send girls to school in many conservative communities (Asadullah & Wahhaj, 2012). *Purdah* involves restrictions placed on women's mobility in order to safeguard their purity and virtue, and these qualities are often seen as essential to ensure marriageability. An emphasis on *purdah* is seen as contributing to a girl's safety both in the classroom and in travel to and from school. Women's rights advocates see it as a severe restriction on the social agency of women. In contrast to government and non-profit schools, 85% of madrasas maintain a 'strict policy of *purdah*' in the classroom, while the figure is just 18% for secular schools (Asadullah & Wahhaj, 2012). Mobility restrictions on girls are at their most severe at secondary school age, which corresponds with the age of menarche. If a secondary madrasa is not available, families may choose not to send their daughters to school. In conservative contexts, if madrasas are available, girls are six times more likely to attend secondary school (Asadullah & Wahhaj, 2012). Madrasas are also seen as important for developing etiquette and manners (*abab*) in girls, to produce an ideal Muslim woman and cultivate the qualities of selflessness and dedication that make a good wife and mother (Begum & Kabir, 2012).

Demand for religious education, and particularly Islamic education, is also strong in Senegal, echoing the society's high religiosity. The word 'education' is often used in a holistic sense to mean instilling children with strong morals and good values, while preparing them to contribute to society. For many decades, Islamic and state schools were sharply separated, both in practice and in policy; few saw Islamic education and 'western' education as compatible and complementary. Rigorous analysis of parents' motivation for choosing either Islamic or secular education is limited, and debates tend to draw on anecdotal evidence.

As in Bangladesh, a family's financial situation can factor into decision-making around education. Parents may send their children to the *daaras* simply because they cannot afford to feed another child; these schools can be a lower-cost option for parents. Public schools do not feed and clothe children, and unofficial costs in addition to enrollment fees and charges for uniforms and supplies can be prohibitive for families. However, many Senegalese *talibés* do not come from impoverished families; families elect to send their children to the *daara* for the competencies they believe their children will gain there.

A significant motivation in selecting a school type is social and religious norms (Thorsen, 2012). Senegalese society values Islamic knowledge and Quranic memorization. Senegalese religious leaders are expected to have gone through Senegal's Islamic education system – a small number study in other Muslim-majority countries. The Sufi orders in Senegal have strong ties to Sufi communities in other countries (Nigeria, Mauritania), and parents from these countries also send their children to Senegal's *daaras* because of the quality Islamic education they believe their children will receive.

Both countries have seen protracted debates about Islamic education. Madrasas are controversial institutions in Bangladesh, with madrasa reform debated since independence in 1971. During the bitter Liberation War, Islamic tradition and political power were central issues, and the new government defined itself in its constitution and ethos as a secular nation. It thus viewed the madrasa system it inherited negatively; the network of religious institutions was suspected of harboring collaborators with pro-Pakistani militias that had sought to retain a unified Islamic state. In 1974, the Education Commission recommended the abolition of the madrasa system. This sparked widespread outrage among Bangladesh's orthodox Muslim community. The plan was abandoned, but mutual suspicion and distrust persist. The issue of madrasa education figures prominently in polarized discourse regarding the role of Islam in Bangladeshi society. Concerns that the madrasas contribute to radicalization and militarism, that they tend to perpetuate regressive gender norms, and that many madrasa students are poorly integrated in society are enduring issues.

The vision of madrasas as hotbeds of extremism should be seen in relation to broader national and international political contexts. Concerns arise partly from the closed nature of these institutions. Quomi are a largely unlit area in both development and scholarly literature. Widely held assumptions about the links between madrasas and terrorism were challenged by recent high-profile Islamic militant attacks, including the July 2016 Holey Bakery attack and killings of bloggers and secular thinkers, with many of the suspected militants captured or killed coming from middle- or upper-class backgrounds and having attended elite private schools in Dhaka. Madrasa students have been implicated in ongoing terrorism; for example, a weapons cache was discovered at a mosque run by a UK-based charity in 2009, but periodic raids on madrasas have turned up little in the way of weapons or militant literature (bdnews24, 2009). Likewise, the few studies of attitudes among Quomi madrasa teachers and students give little credence to fears of rampant radicalization.

Since a growing number of Quomi madrasa graduates struggle to find employment and face social alienation in wider society, fears remain that they will be highly susceptible to radical messages. Many Quomi madrasa teachers and students are involved in Hefazat-e-Islam, the coalition of orthodox madrasa teachers and students with highly socially conservative positions who advocate for the social Islamization of Bangladesh. In 2011, the group publicly opposed the National Women's Development Policy, which, among other things, granted equal rights to inheritance between male and female siblings, which members of Hefazat suggested was in direct violation of sharia law. Their largest and most violent demonstration came in 2013 in response to the anti-Islamist 'Shahbag' uprising. The group issued a list of 13 wide-ranging demands that included a ban on the public mixing of sexes, prosecution of atheists and imposition of the death penalty for blasphemy.

There is a growing divide in Bangladeshi society between more 'secular' social forces – this ideology particularly dominant within the nation's large NGO sector – and religious conservatives, most strongly represented by the Quomi madrasa system. Education has long been recognized as key to shaping values and social attitudes; consequently, it has been a major focus of social reformers. Madrasas are a particularly important ideological battleground in Bangladesh between religious conservatives and secular progressives. Some advocate reform or abolition of madrasas, concerned that these institutions inculcate youth with regressive social attitudes and perpetuate traditional patriarchal gender norms. There is evidence that madrasa graduates hold more conservative social attitudes, particularly with regard to gender. A recent study found that in comparison with students at secular schools, madrasa students are more likely to prefer larger families and believe that it is 'up to God' to decide the appropriate number of children. They are also more likely to view higher education as more necessary for boys than for girls and to prefer a greater integration of religion into governance (Asadullah & Chaudhury, 2010).

Tense debates in Senegal about education policies often hark back to the colonial era. Despite progress, especially in expanding enrollments, many educational indicators are disappointingly low. Senegal's Islamic schools vary widely in curriculum content, infrastructure and basic educational models; some issues are particular to the Islamic education system, while others are more broadly part of the education challenges that Senegal faces. Several key concerns are highlighted in policy debates. A common critique is that students coming out of certain types of schools are not equipped with the necessary skills to modernize Senegal (Human Rights Watch, 2010). There are limited data to suggest that graduates from any single category face worse job prospects (overall job prospects are poor) (Thorsen, 2012). *Daaras*, in particular, are subject to such critiques. Some students emerge without basic literacy and numeracy skills, which limits their options largely to the informal economy or to serving in religious positions, where numbers are fairly limited.

Although students at many Islamic schools study a wide variety of subjects, their language skills are often in Arabic rather than French; Arabic is not widely spoken in Senegal outside religious circles. Notwithstanding skills they have acquired, lack of French proficiency limits their higher education opportunities in Senegal and their ability to enter many fields, such as many civil service positions (as French is the official language in Senegal). Opportunities for arabophones are increasing, but they are far fewer than those for francophones.

Vocal critics of the pedagogical practices employed in the *daaras* focus on methodology, notably rote memorization. Defenders of the *daara* model are particularly concentrated in religious communities, seeing the schools as central to the formation of good Muslims, with, for example, an emphasis on core values of humility and respect. Proponents argue that the *daaras* have produced Senegal's foremost religious leaders and scholars. These leaders, past and present, are highly respected and are seen as contributors to Senegalese society. It is difficult, some Senegalese say, to argue with these visible results of a *daara* education (personal communication, May 2016).

Other concerns center on whether the curriculum and the approach of public schools align with Senegalese cultural and religious realities (COSYDEP, 2014). This perception is strong in some regions, notably in important religious cities, such as the Mourides' holy city of Touba. Residents of several regions point to the lack of religious education as their greatest concern with the current public education system; this is most common in rural areas, which tend to have fewer education options (COSYDEP, 2014).

The Ministry of National Education's current strategic plans highlight the need to adapt the public education curriculum to local realities and to include local communities in the process (Ministère de l'Education Nationale, 2014). This is seen as a way to increase equity in education and eliminate discrimination linked to gender, geographical location, instruction type or religious affiliation (Ministère de l'Education Nationale, 2014). A goal is to enroll more girls in school by addressing cultural concerns. Reforms provide new options to parents who do not wish to send their girls away to live in *daaras* but do not want their daughters to attend French-style schools; however, development of Franco-Arabic schools has been slow and has not kept up with public demand (Ministère de l'Education Nationale, 2014).

Many Senegalese children never attend school or drop out after a short period. Reasons include: girls leaving school to work at home or as domestics in urban areas to contribute to their family's income; insufficient infrastructure and sanitation facilities; and limited education options in rural areas. In 2012, about 590,000 primary school-aged children were out of school (43% girls), representing approximately 30% of that population (Ministère de l'Education Nationale, 2008; World Bank, 2016a,b). A cooperative approach involving Islamic education could be part of the solution.

The welfare of many *talibés* is a controversial topic. As many *daaras* relocated to urban areas, the nature and pattern of relationships between *talibés* and Quranic instructors changed. Many *talibés* in cities are sent into the streets to beg for money that goes to the Quranic instructors. Some organizations, including Human Rights Watch and Anti-Slavery International, contend that this is a form of child slavery, with gross human rights violations in certain *daaras*, including poor living conditions and allegations of physical abuse. Scholar Rudolph T. Ware III (Ware, 2014) maintains that most *daaras* employ the same practices that have been used for centuries. These practices are seen as central to raising a good Muslim and instilling religious knowledge and values – for example, begging instills humility. This view holds that outsiders misunderstand the *daara* system. Living conditions and practices differ widely among *daaras*, with most largely outside government regulation. Modernizing *daaras* is seen as a long-term solution.

Madrasa Reform Efforts in Bangladesh and Senegal: lessons?

Bangladesh and Senegal offer two illustrative cases with insights into the challenges and potential of addressing Islamic education in education policy in more purposeful ways. The two very different contexts illustrate shared dynamics that have relevance beyond the two countries. Education plays roles in retaining and transmitting 'traditional' knowledge and values, particularly in contexts of rapid development and economic and social transformation. Demand for religious or religiously infused education appears to be on the rise. Religiously provided and religiously focused education can be controversial for reasons that vary with context. As debates swirl around the roles of religious beliefs and institutions in society and in governance, these issues take on political dimensions.

In both Bangladesh and Senegal, Islamic schools fill critical gaps and reach key populations. This was the case when madrasas opened to girls in Bangladesh and when the Senegalese government responded to the demand for religious education in the public school curriculum and supported blended religious/secular school models. Concerns linked to Islamic education in both contexts are relevant to national education policies – for example, how Islamic schools serve as education providers while retaining traditional functions of training religious clerics and providing a moral education.

The Bangladesh and Senegal experiences are relevant for those engaged in leadership and management of education systems, including religious actors. Questions to explore further include the impact of reforms on the training of religious clergy and how this contributes to evolving traditions in contemporary Islam, including interreligious relationships. The broad issue of social norms – whether in terms of adapting to changes brought about by modernization, such as gender equality, approaches to child rearing and protection, and democratic and civic norms, or in relation to susceptibility to radical currents, especially those linked to violence – is a central concern in both countries. How to balance secular and religious approaches to governance and to education remains the topic of active debate in both Bangladesh and Senegal.

Notes

[1] Hefazat-e-Islam (Protectors of Islam), an alliance of orthodox madrasa teachers and students centered in Bangladesh's Chittagong region, claims to represent more than 25,000 Quomi madrasas, under the leadership of Shah Ahmad Shafi. While the group claims to have exclusively religious goals, it has engaged in high-profile protests and demonstrations against national legislation related to education and women's empowerment, issuing a list of 13 demands that include a ban on the public mixing of sexes, prosecution of atheists and imposition of the death penalty for blasphemy.

[2] The *Baccalauréat* is the exam that students take at the end of high school in order to gain entry to institutions of higher education.

References

Adams, N., Herzog, L. & Marshall, K. (2017) Modernizing Islamic Education: the cases of Bangladesh and Senegal. Case study. Berkeley Center for Religion, Peace and World Affairs, Georgetown University and World Faiths Development Dialogue.

Anti-Slavery International (2011) Time for Change: a call for urgent action to end the forced child begging of Talibés in Senegal. http://www.antislavery.org/includes/documents/cm_docs/2012/t/1_talibereporteng lish_medium.pdf

Asadullah, M.N., Chakrabarti, R. & Chaudhury, N. (2015) What Determines Religious School Choice?, Theory and Evidence from Rural Bangladesh, *Bulletin of Economic Research*, 67, 186-207. https://doi.org/10.1111/j.1467-8586.2012.00476.x

Asadullah, M.N. & Chaudhury, N. (2010) Religious Schools, Social Values, and Economic Attitudes: evidence from Bangladesh, *World Development*, 38, 205-217. https://doi.org/10.1016/j.worlddev.2009.10.014

Asadullah, M.N. & Chaudhury, N. (2013) Peaceful Coexistence? The Role of Religious Schools and NGOs in the Growth of Female Secondary Schooling in Bangladesh, *Journal of Development Studies*, 49, 223-237. https://doi.org/10.1080/00220388.2012.733369

Asadullah, M.N., Chaudhury, N. & Al-Zayeh Josh, S.R. (2009) Secondary School Madrasas in Bangladesh: incidence, quality, and implications for reform. http://documents.worldbank.org/curated/ en/2010/03/12765227/secondary-school-madrasas-bangladesh-incidence-quality-implications-reform

Asadullah, M.N. & Wahhaj, Z. (2012) Going to School in Purdah: female schooling, mobility norms and madrasas in Bangladesh. Forschungsinstitut zur Zukunft der Arbeit Discussion Paper Series. http://ftp.iza.org/dp7059.pdf

Bano, M. (2014) Madrasa Reforms and Islamic Modernism in Bangladesh, *Modern Asian Studies*, 48, 911-939. https://doi.org/10.1017/S0026749X12000790

bdnews24 (2009) UK Charity Body Probing Bangladesh Madrasa Arms Haul. http://bdnews24.com/bangladesh/2009/03/26/uk-charity-body-probing-bangladesh-madrasa-arms-haul1

Begum, M. & Kabir, H. (2012) Reflections on the Deobandi Reformist Agenda in a Female Quomi Madrasah in Bangladesh, South Asia. *Journal of South Asian Studies*, 35, 353-380. https://doi.org/10.1080/00856401.2012.659650

Bouche, D. (1974) *L'école française et les musulmans au Sénégal de 1850 à 1920*, *Revue française d'histoire d'outre mer*, 61, 218-235. https://doi.org/10.3406/outre.1974.1756

Coalition des organisations en synergie pour la défense de l'éducation publique (2014) *Pour la réfondation de l'éducation et de la formation au Sénégal*.

Duke Bryant, K.M. (2015) *Education as Politics: colonial schooling and political debate in Senegal, 1850s-1914*. Madison: University of Wisconsin Press.

Falkowska, M. (2013) *Girls' Education in Bangladesh: lessons from NGOs*. Leverkusen: Budrich UniPress.

Gellar, S. (2005) *Democracy in Senegal: Tocquevillian analytics in Africa*. New York: Palgrave Macmillan. https://doi.org/10.1057/9781403982162

Government of Senegal (2005) *Loi 2004-37 du 15 Décembre 2004, Journal Officiel*, 6202. http://www.jo.gouv.sn/spip.php?article2689

Government of Senegal (2015) *Plan Sénégal émergent*. http://www.gouv.sn/IMG/pdf/PSE.pdf

Hefner, R.W. (2009) The Politics and Cultures of Islamic Education in Southeast Asia, in R.W. Hefner (Ed.) *Making Modern Muslims: the politics of Islamic education in Southeast Asia*, pp. 55-105. Honolulu: University of Hawaii Press.

Human Rights Watch (2010) Off the Backs of the Children: forced begging and other abuses against Talibés in Senegal. https://www.hrw.org/sites/default/files/reports/senegal0410webwcover.pdf

Ministère de l'Education Nationale (2008) *Rapport national sur la situation de l'éducation en 2008*. http://www.men.gouv.sn/root-fr/upload_pieces/RNSE%202008.pdf

Ministère de l'Education Nationale (2013) *Rapport national sur la situation de l'éducation 2013*. http://www.education.gouv.sn/root-fr/upload_pieces/Rapport National 2013.pdf

Minstère de l'Education Nationale (2014) *Elaboration d'une politique d'éducation de base de dix ans diversifiée, articulée et intégrée*. http://www.men.gouv.sn/root-fr/upload_docs/Rapport%20d'Evaluation%20de%20l'Education%20de%20base %20au%20Senegal_Version%20mai%202014.pdf

Ministère de l'Education Nationale (2015) *Sénégal: Examen national 2015 de l'Éducation pour tous*. http://unesdoc.unesco.org/images/0023/002316/231652f.pdf

Thornton, H. & Thornton, P. (2012) *Institutional Assessment of Education in Bangladesh*. British Council.

Thorsen, D. (2012) Children Begging for Qur'ānic School Masters: evidence from West and Central Africa. http://www.unicef.org/wcaro/english/Briefing_paper_No_5_-_children_begging_for_Quranic_school_masters.pdf

UNICEF (2009) Quality Primary Education in Bangladesh. https://www.unicef.org/bangladesh/Quality_Primary_Education(1).pdf

van Nuland, S. & Khandlewal, B.P. (2006) Ethics in Education: the role of teacher codes: Canada and South Asia. http://unesdoc.unesco.org/images/0014/001490/149079e.pdf

Villalón, L.A. & Bodian, M. (2012) *Religion, demande sociale, et réformes éducatives au Sénégal*. http://www.institutions-africa.org/filestream/20120423-appp-research-report-religion-demande-sociale-et-r-formes-ducatives-au-s-n-gal-l-a-villal-n-et-m-bodian-avril-2012

Ware III, R.T. (2009) The *Longue Durée* of Quran Schooling, Society, and State in Senegambia, in M. Diouf & M. Leichtman (Eds) *New Perspectives on Islam in Senegal*, pp. 21-50. New York: Palgrave Macmillan.

Ware III, R.T. (2014) *The Walking Qur'an: Islamic education, embodied knowledge, and history in West Africa.* Chapel Hill: University of North Carolina Press.

World Bank (2013) Seeding Fertile Ground: education that works in Bangladesh. https://openknowledge.worldbank.org/bitstream/handle/10986/16768/806130ES W0BD0E00Box379859B00PUBLIC0.pdf

World Bank (2016a) World Development Indicators. Children out of School, Primary, Female. http://data.worldbank.org/indicator/SE.PRM.UNER.FE

World Bank (2016b) World Development Indicators. Children out of School, Primary, Male. http://data.worldbank.org/indicator/SE.PRM.UNER.MA

World Bank (2016c) World Development Indicators. Gross Enrollment Ratio, Primary, Both Sexes (%). http://data.worldbank.org/indicator/SE.PRM.ENRR

World Bank (2016d) World Development Indicators. Literacy Rate, Youth Female (% of females ages 15-24). http://data.worldbank.org/indicator/SE.ADT.1524.LT.FE.ZS

World Bank (2016e) World Development Indicators. Literacy Rate, Youth Male (% of males ages 15-24). http://data.worldbank.org/indicator/SE.ADT.1524.LT.MA.ZS

World Bank (2016f) World Development Indicators. Out-of-school Children of Primary School Age, Both Sexes (Number). http://data.worldbank.org/indicator/SE.PRM.UNER?locations=SN

World Bank (2016g) World Development Indicators. School Enrollment, Primary (Gross), Gender Parity Index (GPI). http://data.worldbank.org/indicator/SE.ENR.PRIM.FM.ZS

World Bank (2016h) World Development Indicators. School Enrollment, Primary (% net). http://data.worldbank.org/indicator/SE.PRM.NENR

CHAPTER 11

Faith-based Low-fee Private Schools in Kenya and Haiti: the paradox of philanthropy and enterprise

MALINI SIVASUBRAMANIAM
& STEVE SIDER

SUMMARY The rapid expansion of low-fee private schools (LFPS) has been controversial. However, what has been less examined is the motivation of entrepreneurs who start these schools, particularly from a faith persuasion. This chapter examines some of the complexities around faith-based LFPS in Kenya and Haiti. The authors distinguish between different types of entrepreneurialism evident in the operation of these schools and suggest that LFPS started from a faith motivation function within a curious paradox of philanthropy and enterprise. While these proprietors are committed to a business enterprise, they also view their service to the educational needs of marginalized communities as part of their vocational calling. As such, and in the contribution they make, these schools are uniquely situated within the discourse on private provision of education.

Introduction

The exponential growth of low-fee private schools (LFPS) in many countries in the Global South continues to generate a robust and often ideologically polarized debate. These private schools, catering specifically to lower-income households, charge very minimal fees and, in a number of countries, enroll as many pupils as the state sector, or more. In fact, one research study shows that up to 43% of children in the two urban Nairobi informal settlements of Korogocho and Viwandani were enrolled in these private low-fee schools (Oketch, Mutisya, Ngware & Ezeh, 2010). Similarly, in Haiti, a 2006 World Bank study on the role of private education in the country reported that 82%

225

of all primary and secondary school students attend private fee-based schools (World Bank, 2006).

However, the expansion of this sector has been contentious. On the one hand, this unprecedented growth is welcomed by some as extending choice to low-income households who have no other alternative other than public education of questionable quality or who have no access to public education (Andrabi et al, 2008; Tooley et al, 2008). On the other hand, others argue that such expansion has a 'ghettoising effect' on state schools because the more well-off households exit the state system (Härmä, 2016). More importantly, there is concern that these schools remain inaccessible to the poorest of the poor (Rose, 2002, 2009; Lewin, 2007; Srivastava, 2013; Härmä, 2011). However, others claim that these schools are contributing to global educational mandates and goals, including the Education for All (EFA) goals (Tooley & Dixon, 2006).

A wide range of non-state actors are involved in the provision of education within the low-fee school sector. LFPS may be started by 'NGOs, faith-based organizations, communities and commercially oriented private entrepreneurs ("edupreneurs"), each with different motives' (Rose, 2007, p. 2). However, this private provision of education is not new. Churches and other faith organizations have had a long history of involvement in the provision of healthcare, education and other social development goals in Kenya and Haiti. Unsurprisingly then, philanthropic and religious school providers are often regarded as effective partners in complementing state-provided education (Wales et al, 2015); however, as Rose (2010) points out, the relationship between religious providers and the state has not been given enough attention in the research. Given the preponderance of LFPS that have faith associations, this lack of research is unfortunate because it limits our understanding of their roles and the motivations of their proprietors. Building on our previous work (Sivasubramaniam & Sider, 2015) where we suggest a necessary distinction between faith-based and non-faith-based providers in the LFPS sector, here we focus on private entrepreneurs setting up fee-paying low-fee schools from a faith motivation.

Non-governmental organizations (NGOs) are often contrasted with private providers 'on the grounds of their philanthropic aims rather than being driven by profit' (Rose, 2010, p. 475), and similar claims can be made about religious providers. However, in the case of LFPS such distinctions are not so straightforward. These schools sustain their commercial viability by charging fees, but similar to low-fee schools in other research studies, they also offer a substantial number of free or concessionary places (Tooley & Dixon, 2005; Srivastava, 2007). Moreover, some schools may take in a profit, while others may struggle to break even. Thus, the blurring of boundaries between philanthropy, faith and enterprise makes it problematic to characterize these schools. Clearly, a purely profit or not-for-profit dichotomy is too narrow and does not sufficiently capture the diversity of these schools and their motivations. In a similar vein, Moschetti (2015) asserts the reasons for setting up a low-fee school may be varied: 'Thereby, personal or institutional reasons include aspects related to religion, philanthropy, commerce, and community engagement. If we narrow these reasons to commercial matters, we would be losing sight of a whole range of solutions that communities build to face the need for education' (p. 18). To compound the argument, there is a prevailing cynicism that philanthropy motivated by self-interest cannot truly benefit the poor, as Härmä (2016, p. 274) contends: 'Where profit, no matter how small, is a motivator, then there will be no incentive to ensure access for the marginalised.'

What many commentators find problematic with these schools is the profit-making or business entrepreneurialism aspect and whether this adversely impacts and undermines equity considerations. The concern is that these fee-charging schools may be exploiting the poor and providing education that may only be marginally better than the state provision, if at all (Srivastava, 2013). To address these concerns, we propose a more nuanced examination of the motivations of entrepreneurs of faith-based schools. As Walford (2011, p. 47) points out:

> There is a spectrum of reasons why LFPS have been established
> in developing countries, but emphasising the entrepreneurial
> profit-making part of the spectrum leads to particular proposals
> that aim to extend such provision.

To interrogate these entrepreneurial motivations that extend beyond a focus on 'profit-making' we use a typology of entrepreneurialism (Woods et al, 2007; see Figure 1 in this chapter) that allows us to distinguish between business, social, cultural and public entrepreneurialism.

In this chapter, we examine the extent to which these schools are able to reach the marginalized and low-income families underserved by the state schools. We consider whether these schools are differently positioned to meet the post-2015 education goals. We begin by reviewing the literature on LFPS and providing the country context for both Kenya and Haiti, situating LFPS within the broader educational context in each country. We follow this by describing the conceptual framework we use to analyze our findings and our methodology. Next, we present the narratives from our interviews with the low-fee faith-based school proprietors. We conclude by discussing the implications our findings have for examining the role faith-based low-fee schools are playing in meeting the needs of low-income families and advancing the global education agenda.

Positioning LFPS and Providers in Kenya and Haiti

The burgeoning growth of what have now come to be termed 'low-fee private schools' has been the focus of research in many countries in the Global South – for example, in India (Tooley & Dixon, 2006; Srivastava, 2007, 2010; Tooley et al, 2007; Härmä, 2009), Nigeria (Härmä, 2016), Ghana (Akaguri,

2014), Pakistan (Andrabi et.al, 2008), Argentina (Moschetti, 2015), Nepal (Joshi, 2014), among others. While there is considerably more literature on low-fee schools in Kenya (Tooley et al, 2008; Tooley, 2009; Oketch, Mutisya, Ngware & Ezeh, 2010; Oketch et al, 2012; Dixon et al, 2013; Stern & Heyneman, 2013), less is documented on Haiti (for exceptions, see e.g. Salmi, 2000; Sider, 2014).

This exponential growth in LFPS, even with free public education, has clearly impacted the educational landscape in Kenya and Haiti in terms of issues of access and equity. A number of recent studies have attempted to address this conundrum of why poor households are paying for education in low-fee schools when there is free provision in the government sector (see e.g. Tooley et al., 2008; Oketch, Mutisya, Ngware & Ezeh et al, 2010; Härmä, 2013; Akaguri, 2014; Joshi, 2014; Sivasubramaniam, 2014). While the reasons offered are as varied as the heterogeneity of the schools themselves, a number of the more commonly cited reasons include the perception of better quality, access, affordability and reliability (Phillipson, 2008; Day Ashley et al, 2014). Nonetheless, there continues to be conflicting and inconclusive evidence on the relative quality and efficiency of these schools (Tooley & Dixon, 2006; Srivastava, 2013; Day Ashley et al, 2014; Macpherson, 2014), as well as controversy over questionable practices that show LFPS are able to keep their fees at lower rates largely by paying their teachers lower wages (Andrabi et al, 2008; Phillipson, 2008; Härmä, 2009; Day Ashley et al, 2014).

Country Context: Kenya

Kenya, which became independent from British rule in 1963, is one of East Africa's more politically stable countries. Kenya (population 48,461,105 million) is predominantly Christian due largely to the influence of Christian missionaries in the country in the nineteenth century. Islam has the second largest following, with both Sunni and Shi'ite Muslim groups. The distribution of religions in the country is as follows: Christian-Protestant 45% (this includes the Anglican Church of Kenya); Roman Catholic 33%; Islam 10%, Indigenous religions 10%; and Other 2% (Republic of Kenya website).[1]

Several pressing challenges continue to plague the country, in particular that of poverty and corruption. About 57% of the population lives at or below the poverty level on less than $1 per day. Kenya's gross domestic product (GDP) is US$70.529 billion (World Bank, 2017b), whereas gross national income (GNI) per capita is US$1380 (World Bank, 2017b). Kenya's Human Development Index (HDI) ranking is 146th of 177 countries (HDR, 2016). Corruption is another constraining factor in Kenya's growth and development. In 2016, Kenya ranked 145 out of 176 countries in Transparency International's Corruption Perception Index (Transparency International, 2017b).

Since independence there have been several attempts at universalizing access to primary education. The first was in 1974 when school fees were abolished in two key stages: (1) in semi-arid areas and needy cases throughout the country; and (2) for the first four years in 1974 (Oketch & Rolleston, 2007). However, this loss of revenue meant schools resorted to collecting building levies (which were higher than fees). By 1978, enrollment rates had grown from less than 50% at independence in 1963 to about 85% by 1978 (Oketch & Rolleston, 2007).

The second attempt was in 1979, when building levies and tuition fees were abolished. By the 1990s Kenya had achieved near universal primary education with enrollment. However, these gains were very quickly eroded with the introduction of cost-sharing measures (Somerset, 2009). Consequently enrollment rates declined, and completion and transition rates stagnated between 1990 and 2000 (Oketch & Rolleston, 2007).

One of the key pre-election promises that brought the ruling party NARC to power in December 2002 was the provision of free primary education (FPE). In January 2003, NARC delivered on its election promise and waived user fees for primary education. A total of 1.3 million out-of-school children were absorbed in formal primary schools and the government increased its education recurrent budget to almost 40% of total government spending. Kenya's gross enrollment ratio for the primary level rose from 88.2% in 2002 to 104.8% in 2004 (MOEST, 2006).[2]

While the FPE policy initiative saw massive increases in net enrollment ratios, large numbers of children, particularly from marginalized areas and groups, continue to be excluded from this provision of state education (Oketch, Mutisya, Ngware & Ezeh, 2010). To the contrary, several researchers have shown that children in urban slums are still enrolled in fee-paying private schools (Tooley & Dixon, 2006; Oketch, Mutisya, Ngware & Ezeh, 2010; Oketch, Mutisya, Ngware, Ezeh & Epari, 2010; Oketch et al, 2012). Likewise, the World Bank (World Bank Education Statistics, 2010) reported that for Kenya, private enrollment as a percentage of total primary enrollments increased from 4% in 2005 to 11% in 2008. Tooley's 2004 study in Kibera, the largest slum in Africa, revealed that there were 76 LFPS catering to 12,000 slum children, while the five public schools in the vicinity only served about 8500 students, who were mostly from middle-class suburbs. He concluded that private schools were still serving a large majority of the poor slum children even after FPE. In a recent update to this study, Dixon et al (2013) found 116 low-fee schools operating in Kibera, an increase of 130%.

LFPS in Kenya are not homogeneous in their management or provision (Stern & Heynemann, 2013). In their study, Tooley et al (2008) reported that of the 76 LFPS they identified in Kibera, 30% were run by individual proprietors, 26% were managed by religious organizations, 38% were run by community groups and one was managed by a charitable trust. However, in an earlier study by EKW (2004) examining LFPS in Nairobi, it was reported that 67% of schools were managed by individual proprietors, 15% by faith-based organizations and the remaining 18% by community groups.

Country Context: Haiti

Haiti's population in 2016 was 10.85 million with a population density of nearly 400 people per square kilometre (World Bank, 2017c). Many Haitians have a strong connection with Christian faith groups: approximately 80% of the population is Roman Catholic, 10% Baptist and 4% Pentecostal (US State Department, 2003). The remaining portion of the population tends to align with other non-denominational Protestant Churches. There are small numbers of non-Christian faith groups, including Jews and Muslims. Voodoo is practiced by many Haitians and is aligned with some Christian practices despite not being accepted by Christian denominations. Voodoo was recognized as an official religion in 2003.

Haiti is considered the poorest country in the western hemisphere and one of the poorest in the world, with a GDP per person of $846 (World Bank, 2017a). Nearly 60% survive on less than $2.50 per day, the national poverty line, and 24% survive on just $1.23 or less per day (World Bank, 2017a). Haiti's GNI per capita in 2016 was $780 (World Bank, 2017c), its Gini coefficient in 2016 was 59.2, and it was ranked 168 in the world (HDR, 2016). Corruption and good governance continue to be challenges, with Transparency International ranking it 159 out of 176 countries in 2016 (Transparency International, 2017a). A history of political and social upheaval has contributed to this fragile context. More recently, Haiti has suffered numerous natural disasters, such as the massive earthquake in 2010 and Hurricane Matthew in 2016. The 2010 earthquake destroyed or badly damaged nearly 5000 primary and secondary schools and approximately 38,000 students were killed, as were 1300 teachers (Leeder, 2010).

These devastating factors account for some of the reasons why Haiti has not developed a strong public school system where universal primary education is assured. Ironically, in its inaugural constitution of 1805, Haiti declared universal primary education for all citizens. Yet, more than 210 years later, it is an unrealized goal where approximately 76% of children attend primary schools and only 22% attend secondary school (World Bank, 2012). Furthermore, nearly 90%, of children attend private schools (World Bank, 2017c).

Despite efforts at reform and commitments made in the past 20 years to universal primary education in Haiti, the education system remains highly fragile. The government has not been able to significantly increase the number of publicly funded schools. This is partially due to challenges with building the infrastructure required to support schooling, and with the significant number of marginalized communities in rural Haiti that are difficult to access. Given the limited availability of, and access to, public education, many religious groups have established schools to fill this gap

(Salmi, 2000). More recently, private entrepreneurs and for-profit organizations have started schools in more urban areas. As Salmi (2000) states, 'the Haitian private education system has grown by default, one could almost say by despair, rather than by deliberate intention of the State' (p. 165). Complicating the situation further is the fact that a staggering 85% of teachers in private and public schools are not certified to teach (World Bank, 2012). Efforts to even register private schools and the teachers within them have been fraught with challenges.

There are no reliable statistics that provide an overview of LFPS in Haiti. Salmi (2000) suggests that two-thirds of private schools in Haiti are religious schools, made up of Catholic, Baptist and Pentecostal groups with significant support from foreign groups or churches abroad. Community schools are rarer and are largely supported by NGOs and local associations. A third group of schools which Salmi calls 'commercial' schools are those that tend to be established for profit. Salmi states, 'These schools, called *ecoles borlettes*, are named after the local lottery, because it is assumed that children attending these schools have the same probability of graduating as winning the lottery' (p. 167). This speaks to the perceived poor quality of these private for-profit schools.

Previous work (e.g. Sider, 2014; Sider & Jean-Marie, 2014) has documented the teaching and leadership experiences in LFPS in Haiti, but there has been limited literature on these schools. While the Haitian government will occasionally inspect these schools, it does not keep any available statistics on them. Thus, we are limited in our understanding of the types of religious groups which sponsor these schools or the types of entrepreneurs who give direction to them.

Conceptualizing Philanthropic Engagement and Entrepreneurialism

To differentiate forms of entrepreneurialism found in faith-based LFPS in Kenya and Haiti, we use a typology of entrepreneurialism proposed by Woods et al, 2007 (see Figure 1). They used this typology to understand the entrepreneurial features of academy schools in England. Academies were established through a partnership between the government and sponsors from business, faith-based groups and local educational partners. Similar to the charter schools in the United States, the academy school program in England was initiated by the government as a means to encourage more private participation in the provision and governance of public education in order to address deep achievement gaps and structural inequalities between schools. Prime Minister Tony Blair argued as the rationale for this partnership:

> Let's be brutally honest ... In schooling, the better off do have
> choice and power over the system. If they are sufficiently wealthy,
> they can send their children to a range of independent, fee-paying

schools, which, by and large, provide excellent education. Or they can move house to be next to the best state school. Or they can buy private tuition. In other words, for the better off, the British education system is full of options. But for a middle or lower income family, whose local school is the option and which is underperforming, there is nothing they can do, except take what they are given. (Blair, 2005, as cited in Woods et al, 2007, pp. 237-238)

Business Application and advancement of commitment to change and innovation as framed by the values, principles and practices of the private sector	*Public* Application of entrepreneurial flexibility and creativity to sustain and advance public ethos, values and aims
Social Action and drive, originating outside the traditional public sector, which mobilises ideas, practices and resources and finds and translates into practices new ways of bringing about change that has social value	*Cultural* Innovation, driven by a vision to bring meaning, which mobilises resources to advance values and understanding of the deepest importance to personal and social development

Figure 1. Types of entrepreneurialism (Woods et al, 2007, p. 242).

Despite situational and contextual differences, the academy school context offers some similarities to the low-fee-school sector. Low-fee schools, or what James Tooley has now famously coincd 'private schools for the poor' (Tooley, 2009), have allowed lower-income parents to 'vote with their feet' (Tooley, 2009). It is argued by some that the private sector can increase efficiency and choice, and expand access to education services, particularly for households that tend to be poorly served by traditional delivery methods (Barrera-Osorio et al, 2009). Proponents of these low-fee schools argue that they perform better than state-run schools and have more accountability in terms of lower teacher absenteeism (Phillipson, 2008; Day Ashley et al, 2014). Increased participation of private actors is also impacting the governance of these schools, in what Srivastava and Baur (2016) term 'a new global philanthropy in education and philanthropic governance' (p. 434). Within this new global philanthropy, LFPS are increasingly being framed as public-private partnerships (PPPs), and there has been a rise in the involvement of philanthropists and private corporate investors and chain schools (e.g. Pearson Education's Omega Schools in Ghana, Bridge Academies in Kenya, among others).

However, our use of this typology differs from the original use by Woods et al (2007) in that we do not examine how these different forms of entrepreneurialism shape the ethos, values and focus of the schools. Instead, our interest is in how the individual proprietors embody these different entrepreneurial imperatives.

To examine forms of entrepreneurialism in low-fee, faith-based schools, we draw on field research we have completed in each country. In Kenya (Sivasubramaniam, 2014) data were collected through a preliminary mapping of 34 low-fee schools in two urban slum communities, Kibera and Mukuru Kwa-jenga, using cluster sampling. Semi-structured interviews with school proprietors and document analysis of school policies, field notes and attendance documents provided triangulation of data. Qualitative analysis of the data identified major themes.

In Haiti, between 2013 and 2015, we conducted multiple case analyses examining school leadership practices. Haitian participants, the vast majority of whom were principals and founders of low-fee, faith-based schools, were selected purposefully using chain sampling. Interviews with these school principals, as well as document analysis of school and Ministry of Education policy statements, supplemented by field notes, provided triangulation of data. The data were analysed for recurring themes (see Jean-Marie & Sider, 2014; Sider, 2014; Sider & Jean-Marie, 2014).

For this chapter, we report on data from both these larger data sets and focus specifically on low-fee, faith-based schools. As our framework to examine similarities and differences in the data we collected, we specifically examined documents and interview data which provided insight into Woods et al's (2007) types of entrepreneurialism.

Entrepreneurialism and Faith in Kenya and Haiti

In this section, we use the narratives of school entrepreneurs to illustrate four types of entrepreneurialism: business, public, social and cultural. We hope to provide a new understanding of how entrepreneurs of low-fee, faith-based schools in the Global South, specifically Kenya and Haiti, align with the types of entrepreneurialism that Woods et al (2007) report on in the Global North, specifically the United Kingdom.

Business Entrepreneurialism

Low-fee, faith-based school entrepreneurs in Kenya and Haiti demonstrate business entrepreneurialism in a number of ways. First, many of these entrepreneurs develop innovative business practices which facilitate them in opening and operating their schools. For example, one school founder in Haiti founded a low-fee, faith-based school in his community but could not attract qualified teachers because of the rural location of the school. Often, in rural communities, the owners of faith-based schools will resort to hiring those from the community who have the highest education. However, this often only equates to having completed elementary school. To overcome this challenge, the owner hired motorcycle taxis to travel up to 25 kilometers to the surrounding communities and bring teachers to his school. The better-quality teachers he was able to hire led to improved student outcomes. This eventually drew more families to his school as people in the broader community recognized the enhanced quality of the school.

Second, to be sustainable, low-fee school leaders have to develop multiple business streams. In Kenya, one school had a women's self-help group that made and sold jewellery as part of their income-generating activities to help support the school. Another school leader said, 'We have 9 income generating projects: Vegetables, seedlings, carpentry, computer (we run a cybercafé and renting a place as a business), making peanuts and soap.' A further example is illustrated by a faith-based school leader in Kenya who discussed his business acumen by describing the fact that his school had no sewage system so he began a project to build septic tanks. The current pit latrine they had was only being attended to by the city council infrequently. So he also came up with a design for a toilet that has three chambers which separates solid waste from liquid, treats the waste, and produces manure and biogas. This school leader is also growing bamboo and looking for other ways to expand similar projects to the broader community.

Third, many low-fee, faith-based school proprietors vie for external financial sponsorship as a way to support their business operations. There can often be fierce competition for foreign financial assistance, as illustrated by one Kenyan school leader who said, 'In low-cost schools there is more international interaction because the low-cost schools are seeking help from NGOs.' School founders in Haiti will often try and solicit funding and sponsorship from individuals or churches in North America. This is often because the low fees that they charge are not sufficient to cover the operating expenses of the school. Having sponsors in North America allows the founder to provide scholarships to those in financial need or to provide a means of paying for teachers' salaries and other expenses so that the tuition fees can be kept affordable.

Fourth, many low-fee, faith-based school leaders utilize their relationship with churches as a means to support their school operation. Schools may not always receive financial help from a church, but many do use the church building or land. Churches also offer support in other non-material ways. For example, in Kenya, a school the lead author has worked with was built within a church compound. It was started by a pastor with the original intention of running only a preschool centre so that pupils would not have to walk long distances to school. When the management decided to expand to include a primary school, initially they used the church premises for classrooms and an office. They now rent rooms in the neighbourhood which they use as classrooms.

Similarly, it is very common in Haiti to find a school adjacent to a church, having been established by the pastor of the church. Some pastors believe that the school can provide a second income stream in addition to what they may get from the tithes that are given through the church. One principal stated, 'Historically, directors [principals] would simply pocket excess funds at the end of the year. After all, many directors have started a school as a way to supplement their income.' Thus, the school founder, who is also the pastor of the adjoining church, views the school as a way to supplement his income.

Public Entrepreneurialism

Woods et al (2007) indicate that public entrepreneurialism involves advancing a public ethos or sense of community-based values. One way in which a school leader of a low-fee, faith-based school in Haiti represents this type of entrepreneurialism is by helping finance the graduates of his school to attend universities, both within Haiti and in other countries such as Cuba and the Dominican Republic. Graduates are provided with a scholarship with the understanding that they return and productively engage in the community after graduation. A particular focus is on medical training for nurses, midwives and doctors. In some cases, the school founder has fully funded the cost of medical training but with a reciprocal agreement that, upon graduation, the students must return to the community for at least five years to provide medical service in local hospitals. The quality of the local medical services has improved dramatically over the years that he has engaged in this initiative, and many of the former students help provide scholarships for others who agree to participate in the program. Thus, his leadership has led to the building of a public ethos which values building the social capacity of the community.

Similarly, in Kenya, many school leaders echoed this commitment to the community. One school which was sponsored by an organization in the United States said its vision was 'to raise children who are holistically trained to rightfully place every institution in its place and to be visionaries themselves. We want them to be asking, "What can I do? How can I empower someone else?"' A school in Haiti also looked to provide physical spaces that could serve the local community. The school leader built separate toilets for boys and girls, a computer space, and a community garden. He did this because he believed that his school served a public purpose and that the buildings and facilities of the school could enhance this public space. Another principal in Haiti built a library to serve the children of the community. In an interview, the principal stated, 'We invest in books and, although it's not the best library in the world, we certainly have resources to introduce children to reading. Even the little ones come to the library and the librarian reads to them and helps develop a love for reading.' There is a very clear commitment to the community and to building the social capital of others in the community.

A further illustration is provided by a school entrepreneur in Kenya. A pastor found that the children in the community did not have a school so he decided to start a school nursery just for a year as an experiment. He started it with money from his own pocket and provided lunches for the students. There were many difficulties to this process, but once the year was over, parents said there was no school to continue after the nursery year and wanted him to continue. A woman from Riyadh who heard about the school helped to raise money to partition the building for classes. Fund raising was also completed to buy tables. Parent participation was also key as they helped raised funds to buy food and pay teachers. The parents pay a minimal fee, but not all parents can afford this. The school founder indicates that the school has responded to this challenge by providing other options for parents who cannot afford to pay (e.g. work on the compound in exchange for reduced tuition fees). The school founder describes why he has gone to all these efforts despite many difficulties and challenges: 'My vision is to bring Godly change ... in [name of community]. Why should people live in slums? Children who are without hope, once given hope can become agents of change for their community. Children can use education as a tool to change their own community.'

Social Entrepreneurialism

Social entrepreneurs bring about change that has social value. Many of the school proprietors we have interviewed in Kenya and Haiti spoke of their work as school leaders as being a 'calling'. They did not set up a school just for the sake of making a profit: they want their schools to make a difference in building the capacity of the students to be change-makers.

When asked what makes their school successful, one school proprietor in Kenya said, 'We have teachers, students, textbooks. We are not bad academically. We have a lot to be thankful for.' Clearly, this school leader was not primarily interested in a profit motive but in ensuring students were able to receive an education. Similarly, when asked about needs, he said, 'It is not just funds, but, anything they want to give. The main target is the children. As long as the children benefit even spiritually, if they can come and share the word of God, that is good. Church is the backbone of every community. We are still very needy, also in terms of security – even books can be stolen. Fence and watchman is still needed, but spiritual is more important.'

These comments represent a common theme among low-fee, faith-based school entrepreneurs: their schools typically serve a very impoverished community. One Kenyan principal said, 'Most of our children – almost 99% – come from very humble, poverty-stricken homes and for some the school is the most comfortable place they can be.' Another stated, 'When students cannot pay fees we don't turn them away. We forgive fees. We don't want to deny them education. We want to see them do well.'

One Haitian principal started a low-fee, faith-based school in a rural area where no school existed. People in the rural community were extremely poor and could not afford the transportation costs to send their child to the closest public school. Recognizing the need, he left a government job, sold his car and mortgaged his house to raise the money he needed to establish the school. He built a school in 2012 and started with 60 students. In the early days of running the school, he would pay the teachers through the salary he earned by teaching sections of classes in other schools He stated, 'I cannot turn families away from the school. I know that many of them cannot afford to pay but without the school, what hope do the children have?'

School proprietors often talked about their faith motivation for setting up and operating the schools despite many hardships. One Kenyan school leader said, 'I work as unto the Lord. My faith creates a platform to work from. God gives me strength and wisdom.' Another stated, 'This school is a vision I had. Some do it for business, some do it because it is a burden, but this is a calling in my heart. I worked as a computer consultant for 15 years and made good money. I was working very hard for myself and my children. I was even constructing a house. I saw children coming by asking for food ... Some kids were sniffing glue. As a Christian I was moved. I had a vision. I wanted to preach the word and do just as Jesus went around doing good.'

One further example of social entrepreneurialism is provided through the work that low-fee, faith-based schools have done to meet the needs of students with special education needs. Traditionally, Haitian schools have not accommodated students with special needs, and often these children remain with their families with no formal educational opportunity. One principal of a faith-based school stated, 'We know that these children need our support because they will not receive it elsewhere. We cannot provide the types of programs that are in the United States but we can be creative in using our resources to meet their needs.' This school leader was demonstrating a commitment to providing an education for all students, one based on a higher calling than a profit motive. Similarly, social entrepreneurialism is illustrated by a Kenyan school leader who commented, 'This is not a business. We are involved in people's lives. Business is about how much profit I can make. It sees them [the children] as a commodity.'

Cultural Entrepreneurialism

Woods et al (2007) state: 'Cultural entrepreneurs have a mission to bring meaning' (p. 243). This heightened sense of personal and social development is illustrated through the school leaders we have worked with in Kenya and Haiti. Frequently, these leaders refer to their commitment to their faith as critical to their work as school entrepreneurs. The following comments from three different Kenyan school leaders reflect this commitment. One proprietor stated, 'I am here because of my faith in this school ministry. I was working in a good job but I wanted to do more. I saw the need to give something to society.' Similarly, another said, 'I am here because of my faith. I am working for God.' A third school founder illustrates this further by stating, 'I felt a serious conviction ... to give something to society. When I saw the need of the children on the street I wanted to show them God's love.' These Kenyan entrepreneurs saw their low-fee, faith-based school as a channel to bring meaning to children and their families. Similarly, in Haiti, the low-fee, faith-based school provides a place where children can develop basic literacy, thus serving as an opportunity for continued learning about the Bible and Christian values.

Another example of cultural entrepreneurialism speaks to the importance of supporting the ability of teachers within schools. This illustrates the fostering of social development within the teaching staff. One Haitian leader stated, 'The evidence from North America seems clear that when teachers plan together, they support each other's professional ability. Again, this may seem common sense to you but you have to understand our context. It is costly to provide planning time for teachers. It is not something normally done in Haiti.' Another principal stated in an interview that he 'recognized that the entire community benefited from enhanced teaching so I do not view these events [professional development workshops] as a way to gain a "competitive edge" but as a way to build the social capital of the entire community.' Another principal stated when interviewed, 'Our school has been successful because we invest in professional development for our teachers. Parents recognize that our teachers are good educators and want their children to experience this high quality of education.'

Several points need to be made about the findings. First, all four types of entrepreneurialism are apparent to varying degrees. We also find that rather than uniquely separate quadrants, these types of entrepreneurialism overlap in many ways, and may be more accurately described as parts of a continuum. This imprecision represents both the low-fee sector in general as well as the different actors positioned within the sector. Second, the faith-based, low-fee schools in our datasets were all Christian, specifically Protestant Christian. This is less surprising in the Kenyan context given the religious demographics of the country. In Haiti, although the majority of Haitians are Catholic, Catholic schools are perceived to provide a higher-quality education, and also to charge higher tuition fees, than the Protestant schools. Many Catholic schools have long histories in the country and are seen as elite schools. Thus, many families may choose to enrol in a low-fee, Protestant school because it is a comparatively inexpensive option to the Catholic schools. Third, many of the low-fee, faith-based schools charged a relatively low fee. These fees were comparable to, and in some cases a little lower than, that charged by other low-fee schools. While we acknowledge concerns raised around 'affordability for whom' (Srivastava, 2013, p. 28) when it comes to claims made about the cost-efficiency of low-fee schools, it was not our focus in this study to ascertain how accessible these faith-based low-fee schools were to households compared with other low-fee schools.

Examining the Paradox of Philanthropy and Enterprise

Debates around low-fee schools are premised on the contention that they offer inequitable outcomes for marginalized communities because there is commercial interest at play. What is problematic within these debates is the conceptualization of the motivations of low-fee schools, and the conflation of faith-based and non-faith-based providers. Our findings point to sharp differences in these low-fee schools.

We draw on the study findings to consider the extent to which faith-based LFPS are able to complement national policy commitment to achieve education for all, as well as the extent to which some of these aspirations may be in conflict with one another. We also consider the extent to which these schools may be limited in their ability to contribute to these national and international goals in education.

Complementarity

Our findings suggest that the motivations of the proprietors of these faith-based, low-fee schools complement that of the state in reaching the marginalized and under-served communities in the provision of education. In doing so, many of these schools are contributing to increasing access to schooling for those who may not be able to access state schools or other more costly private schools.

However, private provision of education that is motivated by profit continues to be contentious. Härmä (2016, p. 261, emphasis added) in her conclusion argues:

> The reasons that parents in urban areas are increasingly choosing private schools are compelling, and arguably governments should take on a more positive attitude towards the contribution of private providers, where these are operating. However, it is an inescapable truth that it is down to governments, the duty bearers of the human right to education, to be the providers of last resort to achieve access and quality for the poorest. *Business interests will never align with reaching the poor and remote, who will remain untouched and unaided by the market.*

While we do not dispute that the provision of basic education should primarily be the responsibility of the state, our findings point to a different conclusion with regard to faith-based, low-fee schools with business interests reaching the poor. We find that the poor are 'touched and aided' by these low-fee schools. We find that they have the potential to be complementary providers in the delivery of education and, in doing so, are able to extend access to marginalized pupils. Our findings also suggest that, in the case of Kenya and Haiti, these low-fee schools are currently meeting a demand for schooling.

Some scholars are critical and skeptical of philanthropic engagement in education in the Global South as they see it as a form of legitimizing the marketization of education (Ball & Olmedo, 2011; Robertson et al, 2012; Srivastava & Baur, 2016). We posit that the low-fee schools that are set up by faith-based entrepreneurs are differently positioned within the discourse. Unlike many for-profit schools that are commonly associated with neoliberalism and privatization, the individuals providing private religious schools in our research were differently motivated, and we have found that many of these schools were driven by a genuine compassion in responding to the needs they saw, not by self-interest. Driven by their deep faith commitment to serve the 'least of the least', many of these school leaders invest their own resources to start these schools. Their emphasis on their work as a calling shapes their motivation, as noted in Kurgat (2004): 'to the extent that people internalize this view it is likely to increase productivity. The individual worker may think along the following lines. "I am working for God, not just for my employer or for myself. Therefore, I would better put out a little more and do the best job possible"' (Johnstone, pp. 170-174, as cited in Kurgat, 2004, p. 84).

Many of the school proprietors see their work as a Christian vocational calling and an opportunity to serve God by giving back to the community. As many live in the same community as the families they serve, there is also a deep sense of kinship and extended social capital entailed in these relationships. Walford (2011) has made similar observations in comparing low-fee schools in the Global South with 'low-fee' Christian schools in England. Walford goes on to quote from Tooley's book, where Tooley describes a school he visits in Lagos:

> His motives for setting up the school seemed to be a mixture of philanthropy and commerce – yes, he needed work and saw there was a demand for private schooling on the part of parents disillusioned with the state schools. But his heart also went out to children in his community and from his church – how could he help them better themselves? (Tooley, 2009, p. 40, as cited in Walford, 2011)

Walford's point, and one that we concur with in our research, is that many of these faith-based schools were set up by entrepreneurs, not as means to generate profit, but rather in response to a need they saw within their community. A similar point is made by Moschetti (2015), who asserts: 'We have seen that the for profit/non-profit dichotomy is not always sufficient to describe the ways in which institutions can operate from an economic and financial perspective' (p. 17).

Faith-based, low-fee school entrepreneurs view the schools as an extension of community building. As one school proprietor in Kenya said, 'Parents view this school as a saviour to their situation ... as an "emergency school" ... easily available. My neighbour runs it. They have faith in this school. It is their school.' These low-fee schools, built along lines of kinship and social capital and run by those living within the community, demonstrate how these school proprietors have a deep and genuine understanding of the needs of their community members. As social entrepreneurs who live in the community, their motivations for setting up these low-fee schools suggest a mix of rationalities that could be best described as serving the needs of the community while balancing notions of profit. In our earlier work (Sivasubramaniam & Sider, 2015), we describe this configuration as negotiating the demands of profit, philanthropy and philosophy. In a similar vein, the low-fee, faith-based schools in our respective studies demonstrate an equally strong commitment to business viability as well as a pursuit of intrinsically driven faith commitment to 'doing good'.

Although several researchers acknowledge that LFPS are engaged in philanthropy towards the most disadvantaged households (Rose, 2002; Srivastava, 2007), philanthropic intent in low-fee schools is a contested notion. The objections are hinged on the equity implications of LFPS, and the perceived incompatibility between profit and philanthropy. Some claim that the act of philanthropy is no more than a marketing tool intended to retain and attract households (Rose, 2002; Srivastava, 2007), or that fee concessions are merely a consequence of schools inflating the fees and then relying on the outcome of households' ability to bargain for fees (Srivastava, 2007, 2013). On the other hand, citing evidence from their research in Nigeria and India, Tooley and Dixon (2005) assert that there is no conflict between the 'motivations for commercial gain' and a 'concern for the poor' (p. 21). Furthermore, they also suggest that without commercial gain many of these schools would not be motivated to express concern for the poor as they would not have a financial surplus to do so. Our findings would suggest a contrary conclusion: concern for the poor was the motivation regardless of commercial gain. Such altruism was not intended to 'raise the profile and reputation of the school' (Tooley & Dixon, 2005, p. 24), or for 'client retention and profit maximisation' (Srivastava, 2007, p. 183), but to share God's love and to live out a personal commitment to biblical social action. LFPS with a commercial interest are criticized for excluding those who cannot pay, as Macpherson (2014, p. 296) contends: 'yet monetising access, the *raison d'être* of LFPS, aggravates inequality through the structural exclusion of certain groups'; but we find, on the contrary, that the faith-based schools that are for profit, in that they charge fees, yet also driven by faith-based philanthropic intent, increase access. In doing so, they challenge traditional dichotomies in our understanding of these schools.

Finally, faith-based, low-fee schools that are rooted in the community have a unique position of influence. For example, Nishimuko (2009), in her work on faith-based organizations in Sierra Leone, notes that faith-based organizations (FBOs) are rooted in the communities they serve, have the trust of the communities and are able to sensitize them to issues such as the importance of education, while providing emotional, moral and spiritual support.

Faith-based LFPS are often small enterprises that allow them to be more innovative and responsive in their operation and pedagogy. Their vicinity also makes them an attractive option to many households who worry about their children walking long distances to the state school. However, many of these proprietors are also constrained and limited in what they are able to offer because of their limited material resources. Proprietors often reported the inability to pay teachers, or to provide sufficient teaching and learning material. Despite such limitations, many proprietors see their schools 'as a burden given by God to help the community and the children'. This motivation enables them to persist in spite of such limitations. Teachers similarly accept working without pay or for very little payment because they see their teaching positions as being inextricably tied to their service to God.

Contestation

Arguably, faith-based LFPS have the potential to be important partners to advance international development goals in education, particularly the Sustainable Development Goals (SDGs). However for this partnership to be successful, much depends on state support and commitment to such an engagement. Governments need to see these schools less as threats and more as allies in reaching pupils currently being underserved by state provision. Such posturing, drawing on what Bano (2010) points out on the basis of research concerned with expanding the reach and role of madrasas in Bangladesh, India and Pakistan, needs to be focused on building a 'trusting rather than adversarial or controlling relationship' (p. 564).

In both Kenya and Haiti, the schools did not see themselves in competition with the state. Rather, through the different entrepreneurialisms expressed, particularly social and cultural, they showed that their concern was simply to meet the needs they encountered as an expression of their faith. Using Woods et al's (2007) framework, we have demonstrated how the entrepreneurial imperative within low-fee schools started from a faith motivation offers more than just a business enterprise. It is deeply connected to the well-being of the community and transcends a purely profit mindset. In doing so, it is perhaps better positioned to offer equitable opportunities for low-income families. While several researchers have expressed skepticism that these low-fee schools are expanding access, particularly for the most marginalized (Lewin, 2007; Harma, 2011), our findings show otherwise, and echo more of Walford's (2011, p. 11) following observation:

> In general, these school owners and parents do not adhere to an
> ideology that believes that the private is always better than the
> public or that progress can only be made through privatisation of
> services. This local, bottom-up movement is far from the
> ideological underpinnings of most government-initiated
> privatisation policies. This is no private finance initiative or
> public-private partnership ... it is simply local people trying to do

the best they can for their own children and the children in their community.

The faith-based school proprietors in both Kenya and Haiti did not express a desire for an expanded role for the low-fee private school sector or for marketization of educational delivery. Rather, school proprietors repeatedly told us, 'We are starting a ministry not a school' or, 'I see my role as giving them hope. I am sharing bread with the needy.' Their motivation was driven neither by profit nor by an ideology based on private expansion but by a commitment to living out their faith.

However, faith-based, low-fee schools have also created a competitive pool for external funding, and this is sometimes exploited by other low-fee private schools. These schools may choose to adopt faith-inspired names, often not as a reflection of their faith commitment, but because this branding makes them far more amenable to attracting potential international faith-based donors and social capital (Sivasubramaniam & Sider, 2015). Tooley (2009) records a similar observation in his book *The Beautiful Tree*. Relating his visit to a low-fee school named Makina Baptist Church in Kibera, Tooley writes:

> And her school it turned out, just like similar schools elsewhere, had nothing to do with the church, but simply used the name for marketing purposes – 'Church schools have a very good reputation in Kenya,' Jane told me, 'so it's a good name to have for a school.' (Tooley, 2009, p. 107)

Such questionable practices contribute to the murkiness of the sector, and make it problematic to characterize these schools and to understand their contribution to marginalized communities.

Conclusion

We have documented ways in which the leaders of faith-based LFPS demonstrate the different forms of entrepreneurialism. However, we suggest that a framework that focuses solely on business, cultural, social and public entrepreneurialism does not fully capture the motivations of these entrepreneurs and that more attention needs to be given to a spiritual or vocational domain. We have seen frequent and significant examples of the commitment of these leaders to establishing and operating schools to benefit a Christian mission of serving the needs of those in the community and of providing support for Christian value and belief formation. We find the theological commitment to social action and evangelism similar to the world missions' statement of Christian universities described in Hwang's Chapter 3 in this book. While in some ways this is a form of social and public entrepreneurialism because it aims to impact a public ethos, it is clear that the motivation for this is not just to enhance the social capital of the students or the community but to live out a calling that exists beyond the temporal world.

We would encourage further research in this area to better understand whether these schools offer a comparative advantage to marginalized communities by documenting the practices and outcomes of these schools. We identify three areas for further research. First is the issue of quality. We have provided a descriptive overlay of the proprietors, but further research could provide a quantitative examination of the performance of these schools. This would complement other macro research that measures the quality of LFPS (Dixon et al, 2013) and address the issue of a lack of reliable data on private religious providers (Menashy, 2013). For example, how do these schools compare with for-profit private schools or public schools in relation to international standards such as the Programme for International Student Assessment (PISA) and the Trends in International Mathematics and Science Study (TIMSS)? What role do these low-fee, faith-based schools have in increasing literacy rates in the communities they serve? But we also want to understand other elements of quality beyond performance measures that, as Srivastava (2013) suggests, have not been the focus of research – for example, schooling processes and social outcomes.

Next is the issue of access. Most notably, our qualitative data suggest that school proprietors living out a faith missional statement strive to expand access to these traditionally excluded groups, particularly girls, those with special needs and other excluded groups. It would be important to understand these inclusions and possible exclusions better. Furthermore, it would be important to consider whether and how these schools are able to influence gender enrollment. These questions hold important implications for issues of equity.

Finally, our research has focused on leaders of Christian schools. In the interest of formulating evidence-based policy, future research needs to consider low-fee schools affiliated to different religions and in different geographical contexts in the Global South to compare the entrepreneurial motivations and dispositions of the founders of these schools. Such evidence will be required to test out assumptions of philanthropy, enterprise and faith, and to make broader generalizations about the potential of faith-based LFPS.

Our findings suggest that faith-based entrepreneurs may offer another form of state-community engagement that lies outside the contentious public-private debate. As new actors in the field of education they challenge the way we conceptualize philanthropic engagement in education. However, we are only at the beginning of the process of understanding the role or potential of these schools in reaching communities that are disadvantaged. More research is needed to help us unravel the paradox of philanthropy and enterprise in these schools.

Note

[1] http://republicofkenya.org/culture/religion/

[2] 'Gross' enrollment includes students of all ages. In other words, it includes students whose age exceeds the official age group (e.g. repeaters). Thus, if there is late enrollment, early enrollment, or repetition, the total enrollment can exceed the population of the age group that officially corresponds to the level of education – leading to ratios greater than 100%. (https://datahelpdesk.worldbank.org/knowledgebase/articles/114955-how-can-gross-school-enrollment-ratios-be-over-100

References

Akaguri, L. (2014) Fee-free Public or Low-fee Private Basic Education in Rural Ghana: how does the cost influence the choice of the poor? *Compare*, 44(2), 140-161. https://doi.org/10.1080/03057925.2013.796816

Andrabi, T., Das, J. & Khwaja, A.I. (2008) A Dime a Day: the possibilities and limits of private schooling in Pakistan, *Comparative Education Review*, 52(3), 329-355. https://doi.org/10.1086/588796

Ball, S.J. & Olmedo, A. (2011) Global Social Capitalism: using enterprise to solve the problems of the world, *Citizenship, Social and Economics Education*, 10(2 &3), 83-90. http://dx.doi.org/10.2304/csee.2011.10.2.83

Bano, M. (2010) Madrasas as Partners in Education Provision: the South Asian experience, *Development in Practice*, 20(4/5), 554-566. https://doi.org/10.1080/09614521003763129

Barrera-Osorio, F., Patrinos, H. & Wodon, Q. (2009) *Emerging Evidence on Vouchers and Faith-based Providers in Education: case studies from Africa, Latin America, and Asia.* Washington, DC: World Bank.

Day Ashley, L., Mcloughlin, C., Aslam, M., Engel, J., Wales, J., Rawal, S., Batley, R., Kingdon, G., Nicolai, S. & Rose, P. (2014) *The Role and Impact of Private Schools in Developing Countries: a rigorous review of the evidence.* London: Department for International Development.

Dixon, P., Tooley, J. & Schagen, I. (2013) The Relative Quality of Private and Public Schools for Low Income Families Living in Slums of Nairobi, Kenya, in P. Srivastava (Ed.) *Low-fee Private Schooling: aggravating equity or mitigating disadvantage*, pp. 83-103. Oxford: Symposium Books.

EKW (2004) *Rapid Assessment of Non-Formal Basic Education in Informal Settlements in Nairobi.* Nairobi: Elimu Kwa Wanavijiji Coalition.

Härmä, J. (2009) Can Choice in Primary Schooling Promote Education for All? Evidence from Private School Growth in Rural Uttar Pradesh, *Compare*, 39(2), 151-165. https://doi.org/10.1080/03057920902750400

Härmä, J. (2011) Low Cost Private Schooling in India: is it pro poor and equitable?, *International Journal of Educational Development*, 31(4), 350-356. https://doi.org/10.1016/j.ijedudev.2011.01.003

Härmä, J. (2013) Access or Quality? Why Do Families Living in Slums Choose Low-cost Private Schools in Lagos, Nigeria? *Oxford Review of Education*, 39(4), 548-566. https://doi.org/10.1080/03054985.2013.825984

Härmä, J. (2016) School Choice in Rural Nigeria? The Limits of Low-fee Private Schooling in Kware State, *Comparative Education*, 52(2), 246-266. https://doi.org/10.1080/03050068.2016.1142737

Human Development Report (HDR) (2016) http://hdr.undp.org/en/content/income-gini-coefficient

Jean-Marie, G. & Sider, S. (2014) Educational Leadership in a Fragile State: comparative insights from Haiti, *Comparative and International Education*, Special Issue on Leadership, 43(1), 1-16.

Joshi, P. (2014) Parent Decision-making when Selecting Schools: the case of Nepal. Prospects, 44(3), 411-428. https://doi.org/10.1007/s11125-014-9319-9

Kurgat, S. (2004) Religion: shaper of economic trends, in K. Onkware (Ed.) Looking at Religion in the Eye: essays in the sociology of religion, pp. 79-94. Eldoret, Kenya: Zapf Chancery.

Leeder, J. (2010) Teaching without Schools: Haiti after the earthquake. Professionally Speaking. http://professionallyspeaking.oct.ca/september_2010/features/haiti.aspx (accessed 2 July 2017).

Lewin, K. (2007) The Limits to Growth of Non-government Private Schooling in Sub-Saharan Africa. CREATE Pathways to Access Research Monograph No. 5. Brighton: University of Sussex.

Macpherson, I. (2014) Interrogating the Private-school 'Promise' of Low-fee Private Schools, in I. Macpherson, S. Robertson & G. Walford (Eds) *Education, Privatisation and Social Justice: case studies from Africa, South Asia and South East Asia*, pp.279-392. Oxford: Symposium Books.

Menashy, F. (2013) Private Sector Engagement in Education Worldwide: conceptual and critical challenges, *Annual Review of Comparative and International Education: international perspectives on education and society*, 20, 137-165.

Ministry of Education, Science and Technology (MOEST) (2006) Public Expenditure Review and Medium Term Expenditure Framework 2006/7-2008/9: delivering strategies of the Sessional Paper No. 1 of 2005 on education, training and research. http://siteresources.worldbank.org/INTKENYA/Resources/gok_eduction_sector_rpt.pdf

Moschetti, M. (2015) Private Education Supply in Disadvantaged Areas of the City of Buenos Aires and 'Low-fee Private Schooling': comparisons, contexts, and implications, *Education Policy Analysis Archives*, 23(126).

Nishimuko, M. (2009) The Role of Non-governmental Organisations and Faith-based Organisations in Achieving Education for All: the case of Sierra Leone, *Compare*, 39(2), 281-295. https://doi.org/10.1080/03057920902750525

Oketch, M., Mutisya, M., Ngware, M. & Ezeh, A.C. (2010) Why Are There Proportionately More Poor Pupils Enrolled in Non-state Schools in Urban Kenya in Spite of FPE Policy?, *International Journal of Educational Development*, 30(1), 23-32. https://doi.org/10.1016/j.ijedudev.2009.08.001

Oketch, M., Mutisya, M., Ngware, M., Ezeh A.C. & Epari, C. (2010) Free Primary Education Policy and Pupil School Mobility in Urban Kenya, *International Journal of Educational Research*, 49(6), 173-183. https://doi.org/10.1016/j.ijer.2011.01.002

Oketch, M., Mutisya, M. & Sagwe, J. (2012) Do Poverty Dynamics Explain the Shift to an Informal Private Schooling System in the Wake of Free Public Primary Education in Nairobi Slums?, *London Review of Education*, 10(1), 3-17. https://doi.org/10.1080/14748460.2012.659056

Oketch, M. & Rolleston, C. (2007) Policies on Free Primary and Secondary Education in East Africa: retrospect and prospect, *Review of Research in Education*, 31, 131-158. https://doi.org/10.3102/0091732X07300046131

Phillipson, B. (2008) *Low-cost Private Education: impacts on achieving universal primary education*. London: Commonwealth Secretariat.

Robertson, S., Mundy, K., Verger, A., et al (Eds) (2012) *Public Private Partnerships in Education: new actors and modes of governance in a globalizing world*. Cheltenham: Edward Elgar. https://doi.org/10.4337/9780857930699

Rose, P. (2002) Is the Non-state Education Sector Serving the Needs of the Poor? Washington, DC: World Bank. http://siteresources.worldbank.org/INTWDR2004/Resources/22485_roseWDR.pdf

Rose, P. (2007) Supporting Non-state Providers in Basic Education Service Delivery. CREATE Pathways to Access Monograph No.4. http://www.create-rpc.org/publications/pathwaystoaccesspapers.html

Rose, P. (2009) Non-state Provision of Education: evidence from Africa and Asia, *Compare*, 39(2), 127-134.

Rose, P. (2010) Achieving Education for All through Public-Private Partnerships?, *Development in Practice*, 20(4/5), 473-483. https://doi.org/10.1080/09614521003763160

Salmi, J. (2000) Equity and Quality in Private Education: the Haitian paradox, *Compare*, 30(2), 163-178. https://doi.org/10.1080/03057920050034101

Sider, S. (2014) Virtual School Leadership: professional development using digital technologies in Canada and Haiti, *On-line Journal of Distance Education and e-Learning*, 2(4), 177-186. http://www.tojdel.net/volume.php?volume=2&issue=4

Sider, S. & Jean-Marie, G. (2014) Educational Leadership in Haiti: a case study of innovative and exemplary leadership in a fragile state, *Planning and Changing*, 45(3/4), 261-284. https://education.illinoisstate.edu/planning/articles/vol45.shtml

Sivasubramaniam, M. (2014) Household Educational Decision-making in Low-fee Private Primary Schools in Kenya: an exploratory mixed-methods study. Unpublished Ph.D. dissertation, University of Toronto, Canada.

Sivasubramaniam, M. & Sider, S. (2015) Social Entrepreneurship and Change: challenges and opportunities, in G. Jean-Marie, S. Sider & C. Desir (Eds) *Comparative International Perspectives on Education and Social Change in Developing Countries and Indigenous Peoples in Developed Countries*, pp. 21-44. Charlotte, NC: Information Age Publishing.

Somerset, A. (2009) Universalising Primary Education in Kenya: the elusive goal, *Comparative Education*, 45(2), 233-250. https://doi.org/10.1080/03050060902920807

Srivastava, P. (2007) For Philanthropy or Profit? The Management and Operation of Low-fee Private Schools in India, in P. Srivastava & G. Walford (Eds) *Private Schooling in Less Economically Developed Countries: Asian and African perspectives*, pp. 153-186. Oxford: Symposium Books.

Srivastava, P. (2010) Public-Private Partnerships or Privatisation? Questioning the State's Role in Education in India, *Development in Practice*, 20(4/5), 540-553. https://doi.org/10.1080/09614521003763079

Srivastava, P. (2013) Low-fee Private Schooling: issues and evidence, in P. Srivastava (Ed.) *Low-fee Private Schooling: aggravating equity or mitigating disadvantage?* Oxford: Symposium Books.

Srivastava, P. & Baur, L. (2016) New Global Philanthropy and Philanthropic Governance in Education in a Post-2015 World, in K. Mundy, A. Green, B. Lingard & A. Verger (Eds) *The Handbook of Global Education Policy*, pp. 433-448. https://doi.org/10.1002/9781118468005.ch24

Stern, J.M.B. & Heyneman, S.P. (2013) Low-fee Private Schooling: the case of Kenya, in P. Srivastava (Ed.) *Low-fee Private Schooling: aggravating equity or mediating disadvantage?*, pp. 65-82. Oxford: Symposium Books.

Tooley, J. (2009) *The Beautiful Tree: a personal journey into how the world's poorest people are educating themselves.* Washington: Cato Institute.

Tooley, J. & Dixon, P. (2005) Is There a Conflict between Commercial Gain and Concern for the Poor? Evidence from Private Schools for the Poor in India and Nigeria, *Economic Affairs*, 25(2), 20-26. https://doi.org/10.1111/j.1468-0270.2005.00546.x

Tooley, J. & Dixon, P. (2006) 'De Facto' Privatisation of Education and the Poor: implications of a study from sub-Saharan Africa and India, *Compare*, 36(4), 443-462. https://doi.org/10.1080/03057920601024891

Tooley, J., Dixon, P. & Gomathi, S.V. (2007) Private Schools and the Millennium Development Goals of Universal Primary Education: a census and comparative survey in Hyderabad, India, *Oxford Review of Education*, 36(4), 517-520.

Tooley, J., Dixon, P. & Stanfield, J. (2008) The Impact of Free Primary Education in Kenya: a case study of private schools in Kibera, *Educational Management Administration and Leadership*, 36, 449-469. https://doi.org/10.1177/1741143208095788

Transparency International (2017a) Haiti. https://www.transparency.org/country/HTI

Transparency International (2017b) Kenya. https://www.transparency.org/country/KEN

US State Department (2003) International Religious Freedom Report: Haiti. https://www.state.gov/j/drl/rls/irf/2003/24496.htm (accessed 2 July 2017).

Wales, J., Aslam, M., Hine, S. et al (2015) *The Role and Impact of Philanthropic and Religious Schools in Developing Countries: a rigorous review of the evidence.* Education Rigorous Literature Review. London: Department for International Development.

https://www.gov.uk/government/uploads/system/uploads/attachment_data/file/482
337/role-impact-philanthropic-schools.pdf

Walford, G. (2011) Low-fee Private Schools in England and in Less Economically
Developed Countries: what can be learnt from a comparison? *Compare*, 41(3),
401-413. https://doi.org/10.1080/03057925.2010.542033

Woods, P., Woods, J. & Gunter, H. (2007) Academy Schools and Entrepreneurialism
in Education, *Journal of Education Policy*, 22(2), 237-259.
https://doi.org/10.1080/02680930601158984

World Bank (2006) Social Resilience and State Fragility in Haiti: a country social
analysis.
http://documents.worldbank.org/curated/en/533491468257084108/pdf/360690H
T.pdf (accessed 13 July 2017).

World Bank (2012) Haiti Improves Access to Education with a Targeted Government
Strategy. http://www.worldbank.org/en/news/feature/2012/11/21/haiti-education-
strategy (accessed 2 July 2017).

World Bank (2017a) Haiti Overview.
http://www.worldbank.org/en/country/haiti/overview (accessed 2 July 2017).

World Bank (2017b) http://data.worldbank.org/country/kenya?view=chart

World Bank (2017c) World Development Indicators Database: Haiti.
http://databank.worldbank.org/data/Views/Reports/ReportWidgetCustom.aspx?R
eport_Name=CountryProfile&Id=b450fd57&tbar=y&dd=y&inf=n&zm=n&coun
try=HTI (accessed 2 July 2017).

World Bank Educational Statistics (2010). Summary Education Profile: Kenya.
http://devdata.worldbank.org/edstats/SummaryEducationProfiles/CountryData/G
etShowData.asp?sCtry=KEN,Kenya

CHAPTER 12

Religious Education in the Israeli State School System

YAACOV J. KATZ

SUMMARY After the establishment of the State of Israel in 1948, the different Jewish educational streams which existed prior to the attainment of independence continued to function under the aegis of the Israel Ministry of Education. The political leadership continued negotiating the needs of the religious Jewish communities as well as the needs of the Arab communities. The National Education Act (1953) called for the establishment of a three-track system (state Jewish modern orthodox religious, state Jewish secular and state Arab), which was adopted by the majority within Jewish secular, Jewish modern orthodox religious and Arab populations. Jewish ultra-orthodox communities as well as a small minority of Arabs communities opted for non-state (private) education that is autonomous as well as unofficial.

Background

Israel is a unique country in that its population has increased tenfold since independence in 1948 and is composed of Jews and Arabs, veterans and immigrants hailing from over 100 countries throughout the world. As such, Israel has the trappings of both a traditional and a modern society at one and the same time, in addition to having an extremely heterogeneous population. The Israeli sociologist Eisenstadt (1996), in his comments on traditional and modern society, indicated that one of the major differences between traditional societies on the one hand and modern, and especially postmodern, societies on the other is the distinction between the striving for maximum cohesion and homogeneity in traditional societies as opposed to the promotion of individual communities and the tolerance of heterogeneity in modern and postmodern societies.

The first Israeli Prime Minister, David Ben-Gurion, and the other founding fathers of the independent Israeli state adopted a national policy whereby state institutions, such as the state educational system, serve as social melting pots and agents for the promotion of integration of the different religious, cultural and ethnic groupings in Israeli society. This policy was best suited to the traditional society of the 1950s and 1960s. However, since the 1960s, Israeli society began to move steadily away from social traditionalism, and the issue of individual civil rights rather than the rights of the collective became a major societal goal, and the development of different communities with unique religious, cultural and ethnic agendas became increasingly more tolerated, normative and acceptable in Israeli society. Since the late 1960s and the early 1970s, the different groupings in Israeli society have become increasingly determined to realize their unique needs, and this has led to the transformation of Israeli society from one where traditional values of unity and integration were accepted without question, to one where sectoral and group values are perceived as legitimate and even desirable.

As a result of this move away from traditionalism to modernism, and even postmodernism since the 1990s, it has become totally legitimate as well as socially acceptable to emphasize the different divides in Israeli society. The different sectors in Israeli society naturally emphasize the religious, ethnic, economic and cultural divides that characterize Israeli society in an attempt to enhance the realization of sectoral aims and goals without considering the ramifications of fragmentation and disaffection that have resulted from the pursuit of sectoral needs. The development of the state educational system, and especially religious education, is closely linked to the religious divide in Israeli society, to be discussed further on in this chapter.

Introduction to Modern Jewish Education in Israel

The roots of modern Jewish education go back to the eighteenth century in Eastern Europe, when the famous philosopher Moses Mendelsohn established the 'enlightenment' movement. This movement proposed that the Jewish communities throughout Central and Eastern Europe adopt the languages, customs, cultural values and educational goals of their local non-Jewish environments (Litvak, 2012). Thus, Jews belonging to the 'enlightenment' movement established schools in which secular subjects were taught alongside the traditional religious curriculum and where Jewish pupils were trained in the customs, vernacular and traditions of the non-Jewish surroundings as well as being instructed in traditional Jewish subjects. During the nineteenth century increasing numbers of Jewish schools in Europe adopted a model which incorporated the study of secular as well as traditional subjects within the modern school (Schumacher-Brunhes, 2012).

In Palestine the first serious attempts to integrate secular studies into the traditional religious curriculum were made towards the end of 1905. The 'Tahkemoni' and 'Netzah Yisrael' schools can be clearly identified as forerunners of the modern religious educational system in Palestine. Although the schools did not have a specific ethos, they both emphasized traditional religious studies as well as the modern secular curriculum. Both schools were guided by the 'Torah with Worldliness' stream in the Jewish world which stemmed from the philosophy underlying the German Jewish orthodox community of the latter half of the nineteenth century (Breuer, 1986).

Dror (2003) described how in the 1920s more methodical attempts were undertaken in order to increase the number of schools, pupils and teachers involved in the new style of religious education. A variety of institutions were founded (kindergartens, elementary schools, high schools, *yeshiva* [theological] high schools, teacher training seminaries and even a *yeshiva* [theological] agricultural high school), and between 1920 and 1948 many religious educational institutions were established throughout the length and breadth of Palestine.

Dror (2003) added that religious schools were granted full internal autonomy regarding instruction and learning and they gradually became united in an educational stream which was closely connected to the Mizrahi modern orthodox religious political party which undertook responsibility for and sponsored the newly established religious educational stream, which became known as the 'Mizrahi Stream'. Three other ideological educational streams were established during the same period, the secular 'General Stream' and 'Workers' Stream', and the ultra-orthodox religious 'Agudat Yisrael Stream', which, together with the above-mentioned 'Mizrahi Stream', made up the formal educational framework of the Jewish community in Palestine during the period of the British Mandate (1917-1948). The establishment of ideological educational streams was designed to ensure that the population groups ascribing to the diverse ruling political and religious ideologies would be given the opportunity to educate their children and youth according to their unique ideological beliefs. At first the 'Mizrahi Stream' did not have a crystallized educational philosophy, but as time passed, organizational and educational principles were developed and these later became the initial platform which characterized the state modern orthodox religious schools.

The ideological basis of the 'Mizrahi Stream' was developed by the leadership of the Mizrahi political party together with the educational leadership of the stream. Itzchak Raphael Etzion (1986), the then National Inspector of the 'Mizrahi Stream', stated that the 'Mizrahi Stream' integrated traditional religious Jewish education with modern secular themes which characterized the developed societies in Europe and the United States. Thus this stream provided the pupils with an opportunity to absorb religious traditions and values as an ideological basis for their daily lives as well to imbibe all the educational necessities vital in a modern society. In addition, the 'Mizrahi Stream' aspired to prepare its pupils to build the new Jewish homeland together with citizens adhering to other ideologies. At the time of the establishment of the State of Israel in 1948, the 'Mizrahi Stream' consisted of about 27,000 pupils, who made up 25.9% of the total number of Jewish pupils.

The ultra-orthodox 'Agudat Yisrael Stream' developed parallel to the other streams that existed in Palestine and provided education that was almost totally based on religious topics such as the Bible, oral law, and laws and customs. Rudimentary Hebrew and mathematics were provided in the ultra-orthodox curriculum but were perceived as being of secondary importance when compared with the religious topics that dominated the school curriculum (Zameret, 1999). This stream consisted of about 5000 pupils, which was about 5% of the total Jewish pupil population. According to Zameret, the leaders of the 'Agudat Yisrael Stream' were severely criticized by extremist elements within the ultra-orthodox community who perceived the association of this stream with the other educational streams as being traitorous and contrary to the religious and ideological beliefs of the ultra-orthodox community. Nevertheless, the educational leadership of the 'Agudat Yisrael Stream' cautiously ignored the criticism and continued loose and flexible cooperation with the Jewish community's educational authorities in pre-state days.

Introduction to Modern Arab Education in Israel

Abu-Saad and Champagne (2006) described the development of Arab education from Ottoman times (from the beginning of the sixteenth century) up to 1917 and indicated how the public educational system was established only during the latter part of the nineteenth century and was, in most cases, limited to the elementary level. It was not until 1869 that a public network of elementary and secondary schools modeled on the French system was established for the indigenous Arab population. Because of the relatively low educational level and the perceived irrelevance of French-styled education, the schools were not very successful in attracting the indigenous Arab population (Al-Haj, 1995).

In addition to the public schools, a number of private traditional Muslim schools were established in Arab towns and villages and their numbers increased toward the end of the Ottoman era. These schools concentrated on the teaching of reading based on the Quran and also taught some basic arithmetic. The curriculum was primarily religious and moral in content (Abu-Saad, 2006).

Abu-Saad and Champagne (2006) described how the establishment of church schools for Arab children became a common phenomenon at about the same time. The church schools were run by teachers belonging to different European Church denominations. The language of instruction in the church schools was mainly Arabic, but they also emphasized the European language (English or French or German) of the particular missionary society that ran the schools. These schools became increasingly popular and attracted many Arab pupils.

During the period of the British Mandate in Palestine (1917-1948) the educational system for Palestinian Arabs in Palestine continued to be based on schools administered by the mandatory authorities or by private governing bodies. The mandatory authorities took control of many of the private Muslim schools but allowed the church schools to continue to operate independently. The vast majority of schools provided education at the elementary level and only a few high schools were established during this period (Al-Haj, 1995).

The mandatory authorities well understood that Arab education under its responsibility was not succeeding and a number of attempts were made to rectify this situation. According to Mar'i (1978), the British began to establish public high schools in Palestine that, despite their limited numbers, represented a major step forward. As the number of high school graduates increased, high school education came to be associated with social mobility, which included the attainment of jobs, usually as civil servants who enjoyed not only economic prosperity and security but also a higher social status because of their association with the British administration. However, these educated youth soon became nationally aware and politically active. In many cases, they expressed their disappointment and frustration at the lack of Arab autonomy over the Arab educational system, which was administered and controlled by British officials. They were especially upset and frustrated when comparing the Arab educational system under the British Mandate with the Jewish educational system, which was better organized, more widespread and more independent of British influence (Tibawi, 1956).

The British attempted to rectify the situation and delegate some authority to the Arab leadership so that they could have influence over Arab education. The mandatory administration established successive Palestinian Arab advisory councils to participate in policy making regarding Arab education in Palestine. However, the members of the councils felt that they did not have enough power to bring about positive change and as a result the advisory councils often collapsed shortly after their establishment (Mar'i, 1978). These problems hindered the development of the Arab school system and school attendance remained low up to the end of the British Mandate in 1948. By the end of the British Mandate and the establishment of the State of Israel in 1948, about 34% of the Arab boys and 12% of the Arab girls of school-going age attended schools, with more than 50% of them studying in private schools run by Muslim or Christian organizations (Tibawi, 1956).

Establishment of State Education in Israel

The attempts to establish a unified state education system in Israel began immediately after the declaration of independence and the establishment of the State of Israel in May 1948. The Israeli government succeeded in uniting the different public service groups that operated separately under the British Mandate in Palestine and felt that this success could be attained in the field

255

of education as well. An example of this activity is the uniting of the various semi-underground military organizations which participated in the struggle for independence into the Israel Defence Force. However, the uniting of the different politically inspired educational streams which existed prior to the establishment of the state – namely, the 'General Stream', the 'Workers' Stream', the 'Mizrahi Stream' and the 'Agudat Yisrael Stream', each sponsored by a different political party – turned out to be a much more difficult challenge, which necessitated serious ideological and organizational preparations. In addition, serious preparation was necessary in order to bring Arab education into a unified state system.

It is imperative to understand the two major differences between the Jewish and Arab educational systems that had developed in the pre-state period regarding school attendance. Whereas in the Jewish sector there was almost universal participation in elementary schools and a high rate of participation in high schools, in the Arab sector only 20-30% of the school-going population actually attended schools, with only 5-7% of these pupils in high schools. In addition, whereas in the Jewish population, choice of school was highly related to religious or political ideology, in the Arab population, religion and political ideology were not significant motivating factors in the choice of schools despite the fact that many of the Arab pupils attended either Muslim or Christian schools. The major reason for this in the Jewish sector is that all schools maintained a reasonably high level of education and parents chose schools on the basis of their affinity for religious or politically oriented education. On the other hand, Arab parents chose Muslim and Christian schools because they maintained superior levels of education when compared with public schools and thus were more popular with the Arab population.

During the first five years of Israeli statehood, the different Jewish educational streams functioned under the aegis of the Israel Ministry of Education, with the different political parties serving as 'supervising committees' of each of the streams. Goldschmidt (1973) stated that a four-pronged educational structure in which educational streams exist side by side could be acceptable in times of normality; however, in the turbulent period which faced the state as a result of the mass influx of immigrants from Europe, North Africa and the Middle East, inter-stream competition led to much bitterness and a waste of precious resources. In addition, it was thought untenable by many that the state should shoulder the responsibility for the educational system without having any real say in the running of the different educational streams.

Prime Minister David Ben-Gurion led the struggle against the educational stream system and after lengthy negotiations, he succeeded in convincing the members of his own political party to support the call to do away with the 'General Stream' and the 'Workers' Stream' and to form a united state educational system. In addition, he managed to convince the leadership of the Arab community to agree that the Arab educational sector join a united educational system.

However, the major problem affecting the Israeli educational system was that of religious education. To some extent the Israeli problem somewhat resembled the 'religion vs secularity' struggle that has characterized many countries in the West, with the development of modern national educational systems that seemed to encroach on the educational hegemony of the Church.

The Religious Divide in Jewish Society in Israel

A major issue that motivated the Jewish religious political leadership to seriously address the status of religious education stemmed from the conspicuous religious divide in Jewish society. Guttman (1996) pointed out that in Israel the religious divide occurs on two axes, the first of which is Jewish versus Muslim or Jewish versus Christian, and the second of which is Jewish Religious versus Jewish Secular. From the social point of view, the Jewish Religious versus the Jewish Secular axis is far more crucial to the development of sectoriality in Israeli society than the Jewish versus Muslim or Jewish versus Christian axes, as the religious minorities usually perceive the cultural, ethnic and national issues rather than the religious issue as that which demarcates them from the Jewish majority (Abu Asba, 2007).

According to Katz (2010), the historical status quo which arranged for workable relations between the religious and secular sectors of the Jewish population in Israel has been under constant assault since the establishment of the State of Israel in 1948 and more especially during the 1970s and onward. Religious and secular demands have forced the Supreme Court to arbitrate on issues such as military service of *yeshiva* (theological academy) students, the closing of public roads on the Sabbath, and the importing of non-kosher meat, to mention just three such issues, that were previously solved by the consensual status quo, and that have brought inter-sector relations to the boil because of the acrimony accruing from legal and political debate on these issues.

In addition, since the late 1980s and the early 1990s public figures associated with the secular sector of the Jewish population have increasingly called for a change in Israel's Declaration of Independence regarding the definition of Israel as a Jewish state. These figures, backed by the Arab minority leadership, demand that Israel be defined as a state of all its citizens. Although this demand is not a religious issue per se, it has critically divided those Jewish citizens who are religiously observant or more religiously traditional from those who define themselves as being secularists, as well as from the Arab minorities who perceive the definition of Israel as a Jewish state as being discriminatory. Thus the demand by Jewish secularists as well as the Arab minority to have Israel defined as a state of all its citizens is perceived as an additional controversy present in the religious divide (Dwairy, 1997).

Educational Solution to the Religious Divide in the Jewish Population

Moshe Unna (1970), a Member of Knesset (MP) and Member of the Parliamentary Education Committee, who represented the 'Hapoel Hamizrahi' party, was the first modern orthodox religious leader to realize that unitary state education was becoming popularly accepted and that in any political struggle over the character of religious education, the religious minority would lose out to the secular majority. Thus, in the early 1950s, Unna suggested that the religious parties campaign for state education that would have two parallel tracks – religious and secular – and that both would be granted full state recognition. After much soul-searching and debate, the modern orthodox political leadership decided to opt for integration within the state educational system, while providing full legitimacy and rights for those preferring religious education as well as internal autonomy for the religious track. Although there were grave doubts as to whether this was to be the optimal solution for the modern orthodox community, because of the fact that the secular majority in the government were those in whom final authority was invested (Goldschmidt, 1984), the three-track state system (state Jewish modern orthodox religious sector, state Jewish secular sector, Arab sector) was preferred. Nevertheless, many misgivings were evident and there were those who said that despite the fact that they were prepared to accept governmental jurisdiction over security, economy, health, welfare etc., the issue of education was of such importance that only the authority of modern orthodox religious Jews who understood the educational needs of the modern orthodox religious community could be acceptable (Kiel, 1975).

Goldschmidt (1984) stated that the modern orthodox religious community perceived itself as being part of the general community and that the state was responsible for the provision of all their needs, including those in the areas of religion and education. Thus they opted for a state solution in which the state would be responsible for the needs of those requiring religious education. Modern orthodox religious education would not be perceived as an additional option with a number of weekly hours dedicated to religious subject matter, but as an integrated but autonomous track in the state system. Kiel (1975) asserted that full-scale religious education could not be undertaken by individuals or even sectoral groups; thus, only the state with its resources could undertake the establishment of a parallel state track of modern orthodox religious education. On the other hand, the ultra-orthodox school system opted for educational autonomy as an unofficial track, outside the jurisdiction of the Ministry of Education and totally independent in its choice of pupils, teachers and subjects to be taught in the school curriculum. Thus, the ultra-orthodox school system adopted a curriculum overwhelmingly religious in its nature, with basic Hebrew language and rudimentary mathematics being the only secular subjects taught in schools administered by the ultra-orthodox community.

Although the modern orthodox religious community opted for integration in a state school system, the question of autonomy of the state modern orthodox religious education track was one of paramount importance. Strict provisions were made within the framework of the National Education Act of 1953, which set out all the parameters and details relevant to state education, to ensure autonomy of the state religious system. The law defined the exact parameters regarding the definition of religious institutions: a religious curriculum; eligibility of teachers, school principals and inspectors for employment in the religious systems; and religious style of institutional functioning. Goldschmidt (1984) specified the legal mechanisms established to ensure the autonomy of religious schools. He stated that the curriculum in the state modern orthodox religious school would differ from that in the state secular school. Teachers would necessarily be observant and modern orthodox in their daily lives, irrespective of the subject matter taught. Only observant modern orthodox personnel would be allowed to serve as school inspectors. The schools would educate towards religious observance and a religious outlook. The supervision of the state religious educational system would not be left to the Minister of Education (even in the case of the minister being an orthodox Jew, as has been the situation on and off since 1977) or to the Director-General of the Ministry, but would be undertaken by a 14-member committee of government-appointed observant and orthodox Jews and by a civil servant appointed to the position of Director-General of the state religious educational system.

With regard to the state modern orthodox religious school system, each teacher, principal and inspector would be appointed by the 14-member committee. Without the committee's approval no person would be permitted to work in the religious system. In addition, any teacher, headmaster or inspector found to be non-observant or secular in their style of life would be disqualified from working within the religious system. The committee would have final say regarding the introduction of new curriculum material into religious schools. The Director-General of the religious educational system was invested with the authority to solve all pedagogical problems that could have any implications regarding the religious character of the institutions in the state religious system. Thus, the Director-General would need to be in constant contact with the inspectorate and with the institutional heads in order to guide them from the ideological, religious and pedagogical points of view. He or she would organize in-service training for teachers at all levels in the religious educational system and would cooperate with the Organization of Religious Teachers, a statutory body recognized by the Ministry of Education comprising all educators and teachers working in religious schools.

The ultra-orthodox religious Jewish community was extremely cautious and far more hesitant regarding the joining of forces with the other sectors in

Jewish society and decided against joining the other streams as part of a fledgling state national educational system. Friedman (1991) asserted that although the ultra-orthodox community recognized the leadership of the government on issues such as security, health and welfare, in the educational domain the community leadership demanded that its schools comply with the ultra-orthodox rabbinical edicts and that as little cooperation as possible be maintained between the 'Agudat Yisrael Stream' and the other educational streams making up the Jewish educational system. The ultra-orthodox community decided to maintain non-state (private) schools for the children of school age and opted out of joining the state educational system.

Thus, after five years of debate and deliberation (1948-1953), a three-track system consisting of state modern orthodox religious education, state secular education and state Arab education was adopted by the secular and modern orthodox parliamentary majority, with the Jewish ultra-orthodox religious minority and the Arab communities strongly favoring Muslim or church schools refusing to accept the situation. Those who sided with the incorporation of modern orthodox religious education into the three-track system under the umbrella authority of the Ministry of Education reluctantly accepted that state modern orthodox religious education would become a parallel partner to the already-existing secular education system (Unna, 1970). However, because of their total opposition to a sectoral solution to the educational problems of the modern orthodox religious community, the leaders of the modern orthodox Jewish community felt that a solution to their educational problems was justified within the broad framework of state responsibility.

Religion as an Educational Ideology

Thus we see that state modern orthodox religious education as a comprehensive system is perceived by the Ministry of Education to be motivated by an ideology that pervades all state modern orthodox religious schools and is inclusive in its accepting the different religious nuances in outlooks and behaviors of the religious community (Ron, 1977; Dagan, 2006). In order to overcome the potential problems that can arise from different religious nuances, the state modern orthodox religious education system legitimizes religious pluralism. Pupils willingly enter the system from diverse religious backgrounds ranging from those from families belonging to fundamentalistically religious hassidic (pious) sects to those from liberal modern orthodox families, as well as those from families where the parents are graduates of *yeshiva* (theological) high schools and tertiary academic institutions of learning to those from families where the parents are graduates of secular high schools affiliated to the state secular educational system. Dagan added that the common denominator of all pupils and teachers (and their families) studying in schools affiliated to the state modern orthodox religious educational system is a normative Jewish modern orthodox way of life in one of its multifarious forms. The common denominator which serves as the criterion for acceptance into a state modern orthodox religious school is the maintaining of an orthodox lifestyle, and it excludes conservative and reform Jews as well as those who do not accept traditional Jewish law (Halacha) as a basis for their everyday personal deportment and behavior.

During the first two decades of the existence of the state modern orthodox religious educational system, apparently out of exaggerated faithfulness to the policies of unified state education, the religious system attempted to crystallize the lifestyles of all its participants into one unitary pattern and serve as a religious melting pot (Schremmer, 1985). In fact, subtle attempts were made to dictate the Western Ashkenazi lifestyle to the Oriental Sephardi pupils, and especially to those who came from culturally disadvantaged family backgrounds and were a considerable subgroup in the religious system's pupil population at the time. This policy severely limited the declared pluralism of the religious educational system and also detrimentally affected the religious world of the Oriental pupils. These pupils were forced into a conflict which juxtaposed two different values systems (Ashkenazi and Sephardi) and resulted at best in feelings of frustration and inferiority and at worst in the alienation and resulting secularization of Oriental pupils and an emergence of anti-religious feelings (Ron, 1973; Dor-Shav & Rand, 1984).

As soon as the leadership of the state modern orthodox religious educational system realized the seriousness of the situation arising from the above-mentioned conflict, a positive change was adopted in the early 1970s. This change brought about widespread legitimization of the traditions, customs and beliefs of the Oriental section of the population and religious pluralism within the system became a reality. However, Katz (1988) described how this emerging religious pluralism within the state modern orthodox religious educational system caused tensions between the different groups whose levels of orthodoxy and observance were not homogeneous. Allegations were made about some population groups being less observant and too liberal in their religiosity. Counter allegations were made against other groups concerning their development of religious extremism. There were parents who perceived religious education to be a critical extension of synagogue and other faith-based activities, and those who viewed religious education as pedagogic and focused on traditional or cultural activities only. These tensions were not only pronounced in the struggle by the more fundamentalistically religious to establish schools for either boys or girls (uni-educational) or regarding the number of hours to be devoted to religious versus secular studies, but also centered around pressure brought to bear on the less orthodox to leave the religious school system. In addition, serious attempts were made by the more fundamentalistically religious community to establish elitist modern orthodox religious schools outside the state modern orthodox religious system (Liebman, 1982).

The tensions also influenced the ideology of the state modern orthodox religious educational system. There were those who increasingly demanded complete and extreme subservience to Jewish law (Halacha) and to the modern orthodox Rabbinate, and the employment of teachers with attitudes congruent to these principles (Katz, 2004), as opposed to those who increasingly demanded more freedom, flexibility and openness in accordance with the dynamic changes occurring in modern orthodox religious society as a whole (Shremmer, 1985). In order to deal with this potential conflict of interest within the modern orthodox religious community, the original agreement reached by all modern orthodox religious sectors concerning the entry point into the state religious education system – namely, that only those pupils and their families who accepted the Jewish law (Halacha) as the guide to their public as well as private behavior would be eligible for study in state religious schools – became more stringently enforced by the state modern orthodox religious educational authorities.

In addition to religious pluralism, the issue of the religious Jew and the tensions in his or her inner world became apparent. The religious Jew actually lives in two worlds (Katz, 2004): the world of holiness in which his or her belief and observances are consummated; and the secular world in which there is almost no religious symbolism and in which there are no signs of the existence of the creator of the world or of the creator's ritualistic commandments. In this secular world the modern orthodox religious individual works for a living and participates in general society. There is an attempt to totally differentiate between life as a modern orthodox religious Jew and life in a predominantly secular society in order to avoid or bypass conflicts between religion and secularity. The secular world does not serve as a location where God will be easily recognized (Ron, 1973). Thus Katz (2007) categorically stated that the modern orthodox religious educational system increasingly demanded that its pupils develop a more fundamental religious outlook in which they could view the secular world from a religious vantage point and understand its phenomena in the context of a totally modern orthodox Jewish perspective. This would serve as a bastion against secular influences that could undermine the ideology and religiosity of the state modern orthodox religious educational system.

Mention must be made of the fact that religion as an educational ideology does not figure as a prominent or controversial issue within the Israeli Arab community. Unlike the Jewish community in Israel, where religion is a major flashpoint which invoked the establishment of different educational streams in pre-state Jewish education, within the Arab community there is no such dilemma and little or no discussion. Students who attended Muslim or Christian schools did so because of their academic aspirations and not because of their religious beliefs or ideologies. According to Jabareen (2006), the vital problems facing the Arab educational system were related to improved study of the Arab language, national identity and history. Thus the political struggle that ensued regarding the status of religion in education in Israel was confined to the Jewish community, with the Arab community focusing on other issues of particular importance to their sector of the population.

Jewish Education in Twenty-first-century Israel

The Jewish educational system in Israel is highly developed and enjoys a large budget that allows for dynamic development of facilities, school-based technology, advanced teaching and learning methodologies, and varied extra-curricular programs for students at all levels in the school system (Gaziel, 1999). The level of teachers is satisfactory, with almost all teachers in the educational system in possession of a college degree and a teaching diploma. School facilities, such as classrooms, libraries, laboratories, computer rooms and sports facilities, are well developed; achievement of Jewish students in matriculation examinations is on a par with achievement in the average western country; the drop-out rate of students is fairly low and, in general, Jewish parents are involved in their children's education.

Jewish education in Israel caters to approximately 1.3 million students at the elementary, junior high and high school levels and is divided into two sectors (state secular and state modern orthodox religious) that exist side by side, with inspectors, who represent the two sectors, responsible for supervising the educational process in their particular sector. The Ministry of Education is responsible for the curriculum, examinations and teacher certification of all sectors and coordinates the educational processes that characterize the two sectors. The following sections provide a description of the present situation in the Israeli educational system (following Katz, 2004, 2010).

State Modern Orthodox Religious Educational System

According to Katz (2004, 2010), parents choose this sector mainly because their particular religious persuasion is modern orthodox. In this sector the emphasis is placed on achievement in subjects that are part of the core curriculum (Hebrew, English, mathematics, science, history, citizenship) in addition to a range of religious subjects (Bible, Talmud, Jewish philosophy, Jewish laws and customs) that are taught from a clear modern Orthodox point of view. Values that are concurrent with modern orthodox Judaism are imparted to the students and teachers are aware of the centrality of modern orthodox Judaism in the values presented to the students. Therefore teachers are intent on inculcating a modern orthodox way of life in their students and view western civilization and citizenship through the Jewish modern orthodox prism.

State Secular Educational System

Parents choose this sector mainly because they have no particular religious commitment and wish their children to experience an all-round education that emphasizes achievement in the core curriculum subjects (Hebrew, English, mathematics, science, history, citizenship) as well as humanistic values and citizenship (following Katz, 2004). In this sector the students are taught the different subjects from a pluralistic values point of view that does not have any intention of imparting to the students any particular ideology apart from humanistic and democratic values that characterize western civilization.

Additional Non-state (Private) Jewish Educational Subsystems

In addition to the two official Jewish state educational sectors described above, there are two unofficial private educational sub-sectors that are partially budgeted by the Ministry of Education. These are the recognized but unofficial educational sub-sector and the exemption educational sub-sector. Both these sub-sectors cater to the needs of the ultra-orthodox religious community.

Recognized but Unofficial Educational Subsystem

Katz (2004) described how parents who send their children to schools affiliated to this educational sub-sector usually are of ultra-orthodox persuasion and perceive the school as the long arm of the ultra-orthodox family. Thus the schools in this sub-sector perceive religious instruction to be the main goal of the school curriculum and the teachers feel beholden to impart religious knowledge to their students and to ensure that their students maintain their high standards of religious observance throughout their school careers. Achievement is perceived as a secondary goal of the schools in this sub-sector, with the major thrust directed to religious instruction and success. These schools receive 75-100% of their budgets from the Ministry of Education (depending on the proportion of the official curriculum taught), with the rest of their budget covered by parents' payments.

Exemption Educational Subsystem

Katz (2004) indicated that the National Education Act (paragraph 5) provides the ultra-orthodox community with the legal right to establish a sub-sector of schools that are not supervised in any way by the Ministry of Education but are licensed to operate as educational institutions and schools. The curriculum in the exemption institutions is not ratified by the educational authorities and each school has the legal right to teach according to its particular philosophy and belief. The lack of common philosophies and beliefs in the exemption institutions significantly contradicts the declared

264

policy of the Ministry of Education, which officially requires all schools to educate towards the enhancement of social cohesion and a broadly common perception of constructive citizenship (Ministry of Education, 1996). Because these exemption institutions receive only 35-55% of their budget from the Ministry of Education (depending on the proportion of the official curriculum taught in these schools), with the remaining portion of the budget paid by the parents, those in leadership positions in these schools are in actual fact not bound by the official policy of social cohesion and constructive citizenship.

Arab Education in Twenty-first-century Israel

The Arab educational system is administered by the Department of Arab Education within the framework of the Israeli Ministry of Education. Since the establishment of the State of Israel, the number of Arab children in the school system had grown to a total of over 300,000 in 2004. However, despite this numerical progress, Glaubman and Katz (1998) indicated that the Israeli educational authorities have not been able to close the vast quality gap that exists between the Arab educational system and the educational system that caters for Jews.

Glaubman and Katz (1998) further indicated that the Arab educational system is characterized by a number of serious limitations that militate against educational achievements and success. Despite the fact that Arab education is budgeted according to the same parameters that dictate the budget for Jewish education, benign neglect over the years by successive Israeli governments has led to a situation of inequality between Jewish and Arab schools. Arab schools are typified by a significant lack of physical facilities, such as classrooms, libraries, laboratories; a significant lack of qualified teachers; a significantly high student drop-out rate; a remarkably low rate of success in the Israeli matriculation examinations which serve as a major criterion for entry into education at the tertiary level; an almost total lack of extra-curricular activities offered to students by school authorities; and an almost total lack of parental interest in their children's educational future.

According to Glaubman and Katz (1998), the limitations that typify the Arab educational system are perceived by the Arab population as part of a planned governmental policy of neglect and are viewed as an extension of grievances held against the Israeli government. Thus the Arab minority feels grossly discriminated against on all fronts and most especially in the educational domain because of the inferiority of the Arab school system in comparison with schools attended by Jewish students in Israel.

All this has compounded feelings of frustration, anger and even hostility against the majority Jewish population and against the successive Israeli governments (which represent the Jewish majority) that have consistently failed to contribute to an improvement of Arab education. In marked contradistinction to the Jewish population, the Arab sector is dissatisfied with the standard of education provided for their children. Arab citizens are frustrated and unhappy with the poor achievement level of Arab school students and these feelings have major implications for Israeli society as a whole. The feelings of inequality and bitterness have given rise to the fomentation of anti-Israeli Islamic fundamentalism and a general wariness of the Israeli government, the Israeli municipal authorities as well as the general Jewish population (Ben-David, 1993).

As mentioned above, the Arab sector in the educational system is preoccupied with the urgent issue of raising achievement standards and closing the gap that exists between Jewish and Arab pupils and schools. Thus the Ministry of Education is undertaking different initiatives that will lead to significantly improved academic performance by Arab pupils as well as significantly upgrading Arab schools. Religious education is not perceived as being a priority of Arab education in Israel when compared with the urgent needs that have begun to receive more intensive attention from the relevant authorities in the Ministry of Education. Arab parents are rather indifferent to the issue of religious education in the school system and perceive private religious frameworks such as mosque- or church-based complementary educational centers to be the major providers of religious education to all who voluntarily feel the need for such education. Schools under the aegis of the Ministry of Education are perceived solely as places of learning where core curriculum academic subjects are studied towards providing students with a basis for entry into tertiary education or the workforce (following Abu Asba, 2006).

Majority and Minority Subsystems in Arab Education

Within the state Arab educational system there is a major system and a minority subsystem. The major system is that of state Arab education, which provides education for the vast majority of the Arab school-going population. Pupils are offered core curriculum subjects (Hebrew, Arabic, English, mathematics, science, history and citizenship) as well as rudimentary and basic religious education which is designed to deliver the basic tenets of Islam and Christianity. Contrary to religious education in the Jewish sector, which is totally faith based, in the Arab sector religious education is knowledge based. The Druze educational subsystem maintains close reciprocal relations with the Arab sector because of the fact that Arabic is the language of instruction in both the Arab and the Druze systems. The curriculum of the Druze educational subsystem is almost identical to that of the Arab educational system but deviates from it in the field of religious education, where the Druze religious heritage is emphasized. The problems regarding achievement, resources, neglect and disappointment that characterize the Arab population concerning the educational system that fails to cater to its pupils are less apparent in Druze schools, that maintain satisfactory achievement standards.

Because of prevailing dissatisfaction with the academic level of education provided in state Arab schools, there are numerous parents in the Arab community who send their children to non-state (private) Arab schools maintained by independent Muslim and Christian governing bodies. These schools incorporate the core curriculum, consisting of Hebrew, Arabic, mathematics, science, history and citizenship, with either Muslim or Christian religious studies. The majority of parents sending their children to Muslim or Christian non-state (private) schools belong to the upper-middle and upper social classes within the Arab population and prefer the superior academic level attained by non-state (private) schools over those totally regulated by the state.

Summary

The Israeli state educational system is a complex three-track system regulated by the Ministry of Education. The need for a three-track system derived mainly from the unique nature of the religious divide in the Jewish population, a situation that is highly exceptional and rare in most other national educational systems. In Israel, at the outset, the three-track system is regarded as a solution to diversity in the population and consciously allows different philosophies to motivate the educational policies of each of the three tracks, thereby limiting inclusiveness and universality of goals and allowing for sectoral interpretations of equality, citizenship and national goals. Religious education was developed as part of the unified state educational system but allows the educational leadership of the state modern orthodox religious sector much autonomy regarding the way modern orthodox religious education is implemented and who in the Jewish population is eligible for acceptance into the state modern orthodox religious educational system. Secular education allows parents who do not wish to have their children exposed to religious education to send them to state schools where religious education is not taught. The Arab educational system addresses the needs of the Israeli Arab population, which strives for improved academic achievement rather than education that is religiously oriented. The ultra-orthodox Jewish community chose to remain outside the state educational system for religious reasons, and ultra-orthodox pupils attend non-state (private) ultra-orthodox religious schools. Similarly, a minority of the Arab community chose not to join the state Arab educational system mainly for academic reasons, and pupils belonging to this minority attend non-state (private) Muslim or Christian schools.

The Israeli Ministry of Education over the years, under governments of different shades of political opinion, has unequivocally maintained that the ethos of the national educational system is to enhance common universal values, equality and constructive citizenship (following Ministry of

Education, 1996), with religious education left to the whims and fancies of the respective sectors. However, because of the inherent sectoral differences in the three-track system and the emphasis on sectoral definitions of values, of equality and of constructive citizenship, as well as of religious education, the declared ethos of the Israeli educational system has not been realized and remains an ongoing and persistent challenge in Israeli society.

References

Abu Asba, K. (2006) The Arab Education System and Equality, *Mifneh*, October, 43-50 (in Hebrew).

Abu Asba, K. (2007) *Arab Education in Israel: dilemma of a national minority.* Jerusalem: Florsheimer Institute for Policy Research (in Hebrew).

Abu-Saad, I. (2006) Bedouin Arabs in Israel: education, political control and social change, in C. Dyer (Ed.) *Education of Nomadic Peoples: current issues, future prospects*, pp. 141-158. Oxford: Berghahn. https://doi.org/10.1177/0002764205284717

Abu-Saad, I. & Champagne, D. (2006) Introduction: a historical context of Palestinian Arab education, *American Behavioral Scientist*, 49(8), 1035-1051.

Al-Haj, M. (1995) *Education, Empowerment and Control: the case of the Arabs in Israel.* Albany: State University of New York.

Ben-David, Y. (1993) *The Settlement of Bedouins in the Negev: reality and the need for improvement.* Jerusalem: Florsheimer Institute for Policy Research (in Hebrew).

Breuer, M. (1986) *Judischer orthodoxie im Deutschen reich 1871-1918.* Frankfurt am Main: Judischer Verlag bei Athenaum (in German).

Dagan, M. (2006) *State Religious Education in the Test of Time.* Jerusalem: Lifshitz Academic College (in Hebrew).

Dor-Shav, Z. & Rand, Y. (1984) Religious Ashkenazi Life Style in School and its Relationship with Level of Religiousness of Oriental Children, *Studies in Education*, 40, 151-166 (in Hebrew).

Dror, Y. (2003) The General Laborers' Organization during the Period of the British Mandate in Palestine: an educational movement and trade union, in A. Bareli & N. Karlinsky (Eds) *Economics and Society in the Days of the Mandate*, pp. 583-615. Sede Boker: Ben-Gurion University Press.

Dwairy, M. (1997) *Personality, Culture and Arabic Society.* Jerusalem: Al-Noor Press.

Eisenstadt, S.N. (1996) Comments on the Post-modern Society, in M. Lissack & B. Knei-Paz (Eds) *Israel towards the Year 2000*, pp. 19-27. Jerusalem: Magnes Press (in Hebrew).

Etzion, I.R. (1986) The Essence of Mizrahi Education, in M. Bar-Lev (Ed.) *Religious Education in Israeli Society*, pp.129-130. Jerusalem: Hebrew University Press (in Hebrew).

Friedman, M. (1991) *The Haredi Ultra-orthodox Society: sources, trends and processes.* Jerusalem: Jerusalem Institute for Israel Studies (in Hebrew).

Gaziel, H. (1999) Educational Policy in Israel: structures and processes, in E. Peled (Ed.) *Fifty Years of Israeli Education*, pp. 67-84. Tel-Aviv: Ministry of Defense Press (in Hebrew).

Glaubman, R. & Katz, Y.J. (1998) *The Bedouin Community in the Negev: educational and Community Characteristics* (Research Report No. 11). Ramat-Gan: Institute for Community Education and Research, School of Education, Bar-Ilan University (in Hebrew).

Goldschmidt, J. (1973) The Legal Status of State Religious Education, in H. Ormian (Ed.), *Education in Israel*, pp. 112-113. Jerusalem: Ministry of Education and Culture (in Hebrew).

Goldschmidt, J. (1984) State Religious Education in Israel, in A. Wasserteil (Ed.) *Philosophy and Education: letters of Joseph Goldschmidt*, pp. 69-72. Jerusalem: Ministry of Education and Culture (in Hebrew).

Guttman, E. (1996) The Religious Divide, in M. Lissack & B. Knei-Paz (Eds) *Israel towards the Year 2000*, pp. 61-73. Jerusalem: Magnes Press (in Hebrew).

Jabareen, Y.T. (2006) Law and Education: critical perspectives on Arab Palestinian education in Israel, *American Behavioral Scientist*, 49(8), 1052-1074. https://doi.org/10.1177/0002764205284718

Katz, Y.J. (1988) High School Headmasters' Evaluations of Teachers Trained at Universities and Theological Colleges, *British Journal of Religious Education*, 10(2), 102-107. https://doi.org/10.1080/0141620880100208

Katz, Y.J. (2004) State Religious Education in Israel: developmental trends in the Zionist era, in Z. Gross & Y. Dror (Eds) *Education as a Social Challenge*, pp. 73-83. Tel-Aviv: Ramot Publishing House, Tel-Aviv University (in Hebrew).

Katz, Y.J. (2007) Education for Peaceful Coexistence in the Israeli State Jewish School System, in J. Astley, L.J. Francis & M. Robbins (Eds) *Peace or Violence: the ends of religion and education?*, pp. 195-207. Cardiff: University of Wales Press.

Katz, Y.J. (2010) The State Approach to Jewish and Non-Jewish Education in Israel, *Comparative Education*, 46(3), 325-338. https://doi.org/10.1080/03050068.2010.503741

Kiel, Y. (1975) Uniqueness within Uniformity in the Ideology of State Religious Education. Paper presented at Training Course for Religious High School Social Education (in Hebrew).

Liebman, C. (1982) Neo-traditional Development Among Orthodox Jews in Israel, *Megamot*, 27(2), 231-250 (in Hebrew).

Litvak, O. (2012) *Haskalah: the romantic movement in Judaism*. New Brunswick, NJ: Rutgers University Press.

Mar'i, S. (1978) *Arab Education in Israel*. Syracuse, NY: Syracuse University Press.

Ministry of Education (1996) To be Citizens in Israel. Report of the Kremnitzer Commission. Jerusalem: Pedagogic Secretariat, Ministry of Education.

Ron, A. (1973) Philosophical Principles of State Religious Education, in H. Ormian (Ed.) *Education in Israel*, pp. 110-111. Jerusalem: Ministry of Education and Culture (in Hebrew).

Ron, A. (1977) On the Holistic Perception of Religious Education, in A. Ron (Ed.) *Studies in the Philosophy of Religious Education*, pp. 55-68. Jerusalem: Ministry of Education and Culture (in Hebrew).

Schremmer, O. (1985) State Religious Education: basic principles versus operational criteria, in W. Ackerman, A. Karmon & D. Zucker (Eds) *Education in an Evolving Society*, pp. 349-373. Jerusalem: Van Leer Institute (in Hebrew).

Schumacher-Brunhes, Marie (2012) *Enlightenment Jewish Style: the Haskalah movement in Europe*. Mainz: Leibniz Institute of European History.

Tibawi, A. (1956) *Arab Education in Mandatory Palestine*. London: Luzac.

Unna, M. (1970) *The Field of Religious Education*. Tel-Aviv: Kibbutz Dati Secretariat (in Hebrew).

Zameret, Z. (1999) Sanctioning the Fourth Stream: the Agudat Israel educational network, in Y. Rich & M. Rosenak (Eds) *Abiding Challenges: research perspectives on Jewish education*, pp. 121-143. London: Freund Publishing House.

SECTION THREE
Religion in Policy Processes and Conflict Resolution

CHAPTER 13

Religious Education in Northern Ireland: conflict, curriculum and criticism

L. PHILIP BARNES

SUMMARY The aim of this chapter is to examine the role of religious education in relation to the Conflict in Northern Ireland and to identify what contribution it has made to the ongoing 'peace process'. Attention is given to the social, political, religious and ideological forces that shape religious education and to the wider topic of the extent to which the Conflict is appropriately described as religious. The complexity of the issues ensures that the relationship of religious education to peace-building is both not easily identified and subject to different interpretations. The view that religious influences should give way to secular influences in education is questioned and the case is made for a more transparent and even-handed consideration of the relevant evidence.

The Conflict in Northern Ireland (often euphemistically referred to as 'the Troubles') has been the subject of intensive research. Every aspect of the Conflict's origins and causes, history and effects, and resolution has been investigated and interrogated from different theoretical and political perspectives (e.g. Brewer & Higgins, 1998; McKitterick & McVea, 2001). The issue of the role of religion has figured prominently (see Fulton, 1991; Barnes, 2005), given that Northern Ireland on most indices of religiosity is a religious society compared with most other Western European societies; and as a subsidiary theme within this, the role of religion in schools, where interest has focused on their religiously segregated nature. Limited attention has been given to religious education. While accepting that it cannot be easily differentiated from the larger issue of the role of religion in schools, this chapter aims to look closely and critically at the role and influence of religious education in Northern Ireland, principally with regard to its contribution to reconciliation and peace-building between the communities, though other theoretical and educational matters will be considered as well.

While some knowledge of the background to the Conflict is presupposed, a short introductory section is devoted to describing the emergence of segregated Catholic and Protestant schools and to explaining the historical role of religious education in the curriculum, before more recent developments are introduced and subjected to analysis and criticism.

Religion in Schools in Historical Context

The government of Northern Ireland in 1921 inherited a system of primary education that was, although substantially paid for by the state, under the control of the Churches. Education for the majority of children was received in schools which were parochially organised, denominationally segregated and clerically managed. The government had serious concerns about the degree of influence exerted by the Churches over education, believing that their influence encouraged sectarianism, and the first Minister of Education, Lord Londonderry, attempted to set up an integrated system of schools that would be attended by all pupils. His hope was that such a system would undermine the deep divisions between the two communities and contribute to social and political reconciliation. In pursuit of this aim, the Education Act of 1923 excluded religious education from the school curriculum, though it granted 'ministers of religion and other suitable persons' access to pupils for half an hour each day if the parents so desired. The Roman Catholic Church rejected the provisions of the Act, on the grounds that any system of education that did not yield complete control of education to the institution of the Church was incompatible with a Catholic understanding of the chief aim of education, which was to reproduce Catholic faith in the life of the pupil, an aim realisable only when the curriculum is controlled and determined by the Church, and managed by the clergy. Protestant opposition was more muted but also critical. The accusation was that an education system that appeared to position religion at its periphery was unacceptable to the Protestant Churches and their adherents, which numbered the majority of the population. Both Catholics and Protestants united in the conclusion that Londonderry's Act sought to establish a secular system of education that was inappropriate to the needs of society and contrary to public demands. The different Churches continued to provide education for their respective adherents (see Akenson, 1973, pp. 39-71; Farren, 1995, pp. 35-128).

The state educational system did, however, become acceptable to the Protestant Churches, but not to the Catholic Church, in 1930, when an Amending Act provided for religious education in the form of Bible instruction by teachers to be included in the school curriculum. As a result of this (and of certain rights of representation on school management committees), the Protestant Churches relieved themselves of the increasing financial burden of their schools and 'transferred' them to state control.

From the 1930s a dual system of education, comprising state schools (chiefly attended by Protestants) and Roman Catholic schools, developed at both primary and secondary levels. In the same year the state agreed to pay Roman Catholic schools 50% of capital expenditure and 50% of maintenance costs (the state has always covered the full cost of staffing). Over the years the level of funding to Roman Catholic schools has increased and since 1992 both capital and maintenance costs have been met entirely by the state, a provision that contrasts with the funding of 'faith schools' in other parts of the United Kingdom, where they do not receive full funding.

Following World War II the Northern Ireland Education Act of 1947 legislated for post-primary (state) schools to provide 'undenominational religious instruction based upon the Christian scriptures', thus essentially applying the earlier primary-level religious settlement to the newly emerging and expanding secondary level. What was new in the Act, much to the chagrin of the Protestant Churches, was the introduction of a conscience clause that allowed teachers in state schools to be excused from giving religious instruction or leading collective worship if they were conscientiously opposed to so doing (parents already had the legal right to withdraw their children from religious education classes): no such right applied or applies to teachers in Roman Catholic schools.

Up until the 1970s (and in some cases beyond this) it would have been appropriate to speak of religious education in state schools as providing an explicit form of Christian nurture. As society became more secularised, however, the aims of religious education in state schools were gradually modified to fit a less uniformly religious population. Religious education, under the influence of currents of thought emerging from England associated with such figures as Ninian Smart (1968), the philosopher Paul Hirst (1972), and John Hull (1984; brings together earlier essays), came to justify itself on strictly educational grounds and to focus narrowly on educational aims, such as the advancement of religious knowledge and understanding (though, given that the majority of religious education teachers in state schools were religiously committed, the advancement of religious knowledge and understanding was and in many cases still is pursued within the context of a generally positive attitude towards Christianity). By contrast, over this period and up to the present, religious education in Catholic schools (where the subject is named 'religion') is directed to the religious nurture of pupils. Schools regard themselves as faith communities charged by parents and by the Church with the responsibility of fostering discipleship and religious commitment to Catholicism. The problem for Catholic schools, from the 1980s onward, however, is that as the Catholic community becomes increasingly secularised in terms of church attendance and observance of the Church's sacraments, albeit to a lesser extent than the Protestant community, so the assumption that schools are coherent worshipping communities has become less convincing, both to parents and to the Church authorities.

Matters are not straightforward, however, for induction into Catholic faith is also induction into distinctively Irish traditions, beliefs and customs, perhaps in some sense induction into a distinctively Irish 'way of life', of which Irish nationalism is a part. Induction into such a way of life was and still is an important component of Catholic education and it is this that complicates attempts to discern the historical importance of and public support for religious education as a vehicle of 'religious' nurture, for nurture in this case includes nurture into Irish culture and in many cases Irish nationalism. Politics and religion traditionally go together in Northern Ireland: historically, Catholics have desired political union with the Republic of Ireland (though support for this is falling away, and in a poll conducted in 2015, only 25% expressed themselves as in favour of a 'united Ireland'; see *Belfast Telegraph*, 2015), whereas Protestants support the existing constitutional union with Britain. Religion does not exist independently of culture and society; religion is not only concerned with 'the after-life' but also with identity and with power and influence in this world. Support for religion may have little to do with commitment to distinctively religious beliefs and practices and more to do with belonging to a community and with advancing one's own interests in and through that community. Nevertheless, what can be said, with some degree of certainty, is that the traditional focus of Catholic education and of religious education in particular on religious nurture is challenged by a growing number of pupils who are more properly regarded as candidates for conversion ('evangelisation') to the beliefs of Catholicism than as candidates for nurture into an already accepted religious position (see Brennan, 2001).

The Religious Education Curriculum

This section will review the historical content of religious education, with particular attention given to those parts of the curriculum that focus on developing positive relationships between the 'two' communities.

Emphasis upon the Bible has been an enduring feature of religious education in state schools. Historically, religious education is equated with biblical instruction and the acquisition of biblical knowledge. Such a focus is entirely understandable, for whatever the divisions between the different denominations within Protestantism, all agree on the centrality of the Bible and acknowledge its authority: thus the Bible serves as a unifying theme for religious education. Right up to the present, the different programmes devised by the Protestant Churches in conjunction with professional religious educators reflect this emphasis. Interestingly, the one exception to this, a primary-level programme entitled *Themes in Religious Education*, produced in 1971 by the Religious Education Council (a then non-statutory body with representatives from the Protestant Churches and from education), that did attempt to shift the focus within religious education from explicitly biblical stories and characters to implicitly religious life themes, proved unpopular with teachers. It was soon superseded by a traditional biblically orientated programme produced by staff from Stranmillis University College, Belfast, which trains teachers mainly for the state sector.

The inspiration for a thematic, implicit approach to religious education in the 1970s came largely from those influenced by developments in British religious education, and its failure to be adopted by schools illustrates the conservative character of religious education in Northern Ireland, which endures up to the present. A further illustration of this is the way in which multi-faith religious education, which is characteristic of English religious education, has had limited influence in Northern Ireland, where Christianity continues to dominate the curriculum. Narrative material from the Bible is central to (state) primary-level religious education, though there is anecdotal evidence that the subject is much less frequently taught than one might presume or than the law requires. Much depends on the individual school and the support given to the subject by the principal, and in many cases much depends on the individual teacher.

Non-denominational, biblical Christianity also dominates secondary-level religious education in state schools, except in the upper stages of secondary schooling, where biblical material is complemented by a consideration of contemporary personal and social issues that are more relevant to pupils' experience and concerns. (The content can be different for those who pursue external qualifications at GCSE and A level, though Christian content is chiefly pursued, despite a range of other possibilities.) One weakness in the emphasis upon biblical stories and non-denominational Christianity in classrooms is that the doctrinal and theological beliefs of Christianity have tended to be neglected for fear that differences of opinion and conviction might emerge. Behind this lies the assumption (shared with Roman Catholic educationalists) that religious education should confine itself to religious matters on which there is community agreement and for the most part should exclude controversial issues from the curriculum. Traditionally, this has meant that state schools virtually ignore the subject of Roman Catholicism, while Roman Catholic schools virtually ignore the subject of Protestantism. In recent times this judgement requires qualification, as we shall see.

In 1964, in the context of an increasingly child-centred approach to education being pursued by schools in Northern Ireland, the Northern Dioceses of the Roman Catholic Church dropped the traditional catechetical programme of instruction and adapted with some revision the more experientially orientated *On Our Way* programme, which had been developed in the USA by Sister Maria de la Cruz. This, together with the influence of Vatican II, served as a stimulus and model for the production of new materials. In 1973 the Irish Bishops appointed a team to draw up a syllabus for primary schools based on the *General Catechetical Directory* (Sacred Congregation for the Clergy, 1971) and adapted to the Irish situation. The eight graded programmes of the *Children of God* series (see Hyland, 1989) were completed in 1978 and subsequently revised as *Alive-O*, and are currently being revised as *Growing in Love*. Teacher books both provide a clear rationale of the programme for each year group and set out the part to be played by parents, teacher and priest. Music, posters and audio-visual material were produced to augment teacher resources. Revisions reflect educational developments, take advantage of new resources and the emergence of online materials, and relate more to the changing life-world of pupils. The aim of the series is to nurture a distinctively Roman Catholic conception of faith; the series assumes a similar faith on the part of the teacher. In 1980 the original primary series was supplemented by a secondary programme entitled *The Christian Way* (subsequently revised as *New Christian Way* and more recently as *Fully Alive*). Although similarly confessional in orientation, this programme does make reference to the different Protestant denominations, and its latest revision includes a short introduction to non-Christian religions.

The idea may have been given so far in this chapter that state schools and Catholic schools pursue separate paths, approaches and strategies in the teaching of religious education. Historically, this has been the case, though the fact that both the Catholic and the Protestant traditions are variants of Christianity alerts us to the fact that some overlap of content was enjoyed, albeit presented in different ways. In the 1970s, however, against the background of increasing sectarian strife and violence a curriculum project was set up, chiefly on the initiative of Dr John Greer, an academic from the University of Ulster, Coleraine, with the aim of producing religious education resources that could be used by both Catholic and state schools. The aim of the project was for pupils 'to gain a sympathetic appreciation of the religious beliefs and practices of people who belong to traditions which are different from their own' and to challenge religious stereotypes and sectarian attitudes (Greer et al, 1977, p. 77). Certainly at this stage there was limited knowledge and understanding among pupils of the diversity of Christianity and of any tradition of Christianity, either Catholic or Protestant, other than their own. Eight different Units of Work were produced. There are two theoretical assumptions in the material that are worth noting: that knowledge can counteract negative attitudes and that and that belief in Christianity can serve as a unifying force within Northern Irish society. This last point is well illustrated in the Unit of Work on Irish Christianity (Greer, 1985a). It gave attention to distinctively Irish traditions of Christianity (as the title implies) and traced the origins of both Catholicism and Protestantism in Ireland to the Celtic Church: this common 'trunk' from which both branches of Christianity, in part, emerged is posited as providing the basis for a common Christian identity. The materials enjoyed some popularity, particularly among grammar schools, but their effectiveness and influence was constrained by the fact that Catholic schools tended to follow their own religious curriculum that was determined by the Irish bishops and implemented with support at the diocesan level.

The most significant piece of legislation in education over the last three decades has been the Education Reform Order of 1989, the main aim of which was to legislate for a new statutory Northern Ireland curriculum, modelled on the newly introduced National Curriculum for England and Wales in 1988. This legislation and the curriculum that developed in response to it were perceived by the Churches, with some justification, as marginalizing the role and importance of religion in schools. Seven compulsory areas of study were specified, and referred to as 'foundation subjects', among which religious education was not included; churchmen were not to have an automatic right to sit on the management committees of the newly constituted 'Integrated' Schools, where pupils of all religious persuasions or none could be educated together (see Moffatt, 1993; Dunn, 1989); provision was made for schools to develop secular programmes of Personal and Social Education, with separate timetable allocation from religious education; and responsibility for the production and introduction of the new curriculum was given to a central, publicly funded body with no formal religious associations (i.e. the [then] Northern Ireland Council for the Curriculum and Examinations). In effect, much of the influence that the Churches exerted over the curriculum was effectively removed. The Education Reform Order also introduced six mandatory cross-curricular themes, which included two complementary themes of Education for Mutual Understanding (see Smith & Robinson, 1996) and Cultural Heritage that aimed to foster respect for self and for the beliefs and values of others. As stated, these themes were cross-curricular, and although religious education regarded itself as making a contribution to them, their 'incorporation' (if that is the appropriate term to use) had little effect on existing provision in religious education.

The Churches naturally complained that the long-established partnership between them and the state had been reconfigured to the advantage of the state and to the disadvantage of the Churches and the cause of Christianity in schools. In reaction, the then Minister of Education attempted to ameliorate the situation by extending an invitation to the Churches to produce their own 'agreed' syllabus of religious education, the content of which would be made mandatory in schools. There are different readings of this action. On one reading it was an admission of the importance of the Churches to Northern Ireland education; on another, it served to accentuate the division between the religious and the secular aspects of education and to consolidate a largely secular curriculum, which, while purporting to contribute to the 'spiritual development' of pupils, did so by undermining the importance of religion across the curriculum. The syllabus produced by representatives of the Catholic Church and the main Protestant Churches (Drafting Group, 1993) was heavily biblical and ecclesiastical, implicitly confessional, and exclusively Christian. Core content that focused on Bible narratives, church beliefs and practices, and morality was prescribed, and freedom given for state schools and Catholic schools to complement the 'core' in different ways. The core required Catholic and Protestant pupils to study each other's religion, but only in the last two years of formal schooling. The syllabus was subjected to criticism by a number of commentators and at one stage a group representing a range of religions (the Inter-Faith Forum) threatened legal action on the basis of equality and human rights legislation, which it believed required a multi-faith religious curriculum. The legal challenge was not pursued, and in any case (as argued elsewhere; see Barnes, 2002) was unlikely to have been successful. A subsequent revision of the Core Syllabus in 2007 requires pupils to pursue a study of Islam and Judaism at some time during Key Stage 3 – that is, between the ages of 11 and 14.

It is clear that for the most part religious education in Catholic schools retains its distinctiveness from religious education in state schools, while overlapping in certain respects. Catholic schools still view Christian nurture as an essential aim, even if in some cases at secondary level realisation of this aim has had to take account of the nominal commitment of an increasing number of pupils. Religious education in state schools, which are required by law to accommodate pupils from diverse backgrounds, formally eschews confessionalism, although a positive attitude to Christianity is often implicit in what is taught and presented to pupils. Where religious education is taken to GCSE Level or A level, academic aims predominate and often Catholic and Protestant pupils pursue the same options.

Analysis, Interpretation and Criticism

The aim of this final section is to complement the preceding descriptive account of the nature and role of religious education in Northern Ireland with analysis and critical comments. Understandably, given the imposed lack of space, it is impossible to interact meaningfully with other interpreters and positions; consequently, conclusions are necessarily tentative and to some extent deliberately provocative.

On one reading, the subject of religious education remained aloof from educational efforts to challenge sectarianism and religious bigotry and to promote reconciliation between the Catholic and Protestant communities, at least in any direct sense. In fact a number of liberal educators have actually faulted religious education in this regard, and with some justification. Much criticism has focused on the Core Syllabus (for discussion, see Barnes, 1997) and its failure to focus more comprehensively on acquainting pupils with versions of Christianity other than their own and to do this at a much earlier stage of education. Equally, while the syllabus recognises the contribution that the teaching of Christianity can make to educational efforts to bring about reconciliation between the two communities, it is not pursued with sufficient vigour or seriousness. Too much emphasis is placed on the institutional and formal aspects of Christianity and not enough on its transformative potential for individuals and for communities. Finally, too much of the syllabus lacks relevance to the experience of pupils and too few connections are made with the moral challenges of our age, beyond the predictable subjects of abortion and euthanasia (which are traditional *bêtes noire* of Catholic education).

These are reasonable criticisms that illustrate the conservative nature of religious education in Northern Irish schools and of the Churches, which, in the latter case, invariably act in ways to protect their interests in education. The criticisms, however, can be exaggerated, and when accompanied by the negative judgement that the Conflict was essentially religious, can lead to unwarranted conclusions. Once religion is identified as a primary cause of the Conflict and recognised as one of the chief influences on social reality, there is a kind of logic that moves almost inevitably to the position that the influence of religion on education should be reduced; and this in a sense is equivalent to saying that Northern Ireland should 'progress' toward a more secular system of education. This position and its logic are less convincing than they initially appear.

To say that education should become more secular actually introduces a new conceptualisation: first, that of a distinction between the religious and the secular; and second, a distinction in which the latter term is privileged over the former. Secular education is equated with progress, with liberal attitudes and values, with respect for others, and so on, whereas religious forms of education are equated with opposition to change, backward attitudes and values, even intolerance and bigotry. It would be possible to analyse and to interpret the history of social institutions and social reality in Northern Ireland as a struggle between secular and religious forces in this way. But the assumption that secular influences are good and religious influences bad in society is not entirely convincing. One could adduce evidence to support the view that the conflict was largely ethnic (see Whyte, 1990) and that increasing violence was in part the result of the growing secularisation of Northern Irish society in the late 1960s and the removal of religion as a bulwark against violence and a force to minimise and curtail civil strife. Added to this is the recognition that traditional Republicanism, which initiated and perpetrated much of the violence, was inspired by orthodox Marxist (anti-religious) philosophy that regards violence as a legitimate (and necessary) means to the attainment of political ends (see Barnes, 2005). One may also point out that nationalism can be viewed as being in opposition to religion and regarded as a secular alternative to religion. Nationalism is a secular ideology, which, while happy to embrace religion and use it to advance its interests, as in the case of civil religion, nevertheless brooks no opposition and quickly divests itself of religion should the latter compete for the ultimate loyalty of citizens. Align this with the widely accepted evidence that the Churches and the churchmen and churchwomen were in the forefront of efforts to challenge violence, to correct past injustices and to engage in peace-building initiatives and to advance reconciliation, and a more positive picture begins to emerge of the role of religion, in this case

Christianity, in Northern Irish society and in its institutions (see Gallagher & Worrall, 1982; Brewer et al, 2011).

In this context, a focus on Christianity in schools, coupled with efforts within religious education to foster Christian attitudes, values and behaviour, may well have had positive effects both on pupils and on the wider society. These observations are not meant to defend religious influence in schools and in religious education or to exonerate religion from all blame; rather, they are to suggest that secular forces have also been at work in society and in schools in Northern Ireland and that their effect is not only equally ambiguous and contested, but, like that of religion, on occasions negative. The difference is that secular influences of a negative kind are frequently overlooked and undiscussed; this flawed diagnosis, which ignores much of the evidence, inevitably results in inadequate solutions that often simply spring from the 'prejudice' that religious influences should give way to secular influences. What is needed is a more critical approach to the role of religion in schools that is less partisan in assembling and evaluating the evidence and that is appreciative of the ideological force of both religious and secular influences.

The next aspect of our analysis focuses on the issue of confessionalism in schools. In broad terms religious education in Catholic schools is confessional, whereas religious education in state schools is (formally) non-confessional. Many view confessional religious education as indoctrinatory and not properly educational. Much of the opposition to Catholic schools in Northern Ireland reflects this opinion. But is it sustainable? There are a number of challenges facing those who construct a dichotomy between confessional and non-confessional religious education, to the disadvantage of the former (see Barnes et al, 2015, pp. 22-29). First, there is the challenge of defining indoctrination in a way that applies only to religious nurture and its associated practices in schools and not to other subjects and practices, which are regarded as educationally appropriate. Second, attempts to argue that religious nurture *necessarily* stifles the development of rational autonomy in pupils, which is one of the principal aims of liberal education, typically stall for lack of evidential support – namely, that there is little or no empirical evidence to show that confessional education somehow reduces one's capacity to engage in rational, self-critical, responsible life choices, which may even include moving from religious to a non-religious commitment. Elsewhere (Barnes, 2014, pp. 59-63) it has been argued that the appropriateness of confessional education is an entirely contingent matter (relative to a particular political and legal framework, the past and present involvement of religion in education, the accessibility of non-confessional education, and so on), while accepting that some forms of confessional education ought properly to be viewed as indoctrinatory and inappropriate to educational institutions. The critical question in Northern Ireland is not whether confessional education in Catholic schools is indoctrinatory (for should it prove to be in particular schools, the situation can be resolved in ways compatible with liberal education), but whether 'separate' schooling is defensible in the context of a society that remains, largely self-consciously, religiously divided.

In response, it may be argued, and with some degree of force, that parents have a right to an education of their choice for their children, and if they desire to send them to a school that reflects their beliefs and values, the state should facilitate (or clearly not forbid) this. It may even be that certain negative consequences follow for society from religious segregation in schools, but this does not provide an overriding reason for curtailing parental choice: in liberal societies all kinds of behaviour and choices are allowed to be exercised even though they produce negative effects for individuals and for society. Nevertheless, on a more personal note, I believe there to be good reasons, both religious and non-religious, for the Churches to come together to establish common schools with a Christian ethos that cater for both Catholic and Protestant pupils. Clearly religiously segregated housing in some areas complicates matters, and it is unrealistic to think that all schools should be such; however, even the existence of a small number of Christian schools of this form would be an interesting educational development that offers potential for the realisation of the moral and social aims of education.

Opposition to multi-faith religious education has been a feature of religious education in Northern Ireland, and understandably has attracted criticism from those influenced by post-confessional developments in England and Wales, where the study of a wide range of religions is characteristic of almost all locally produced 'agreed' syllabuses. The Northern Ireland Core Syllabus prescribes a short period of study of Judaism and Islam for all pupils at secondary level, between the ages of 11 and 14, but apart from this, Christianity is studied throughout; this is clearly not multi-faith religious education, as the term is most commonly understood. The strongest educational argument for a study of different religions by pupils is that religious beliefs and practices take different forms and that an understanding of the nature of religion is not adequately gained from a study of any one religion: understanding is gained only by acquaintance with religion in its diversity and variety in different cultural contexts. We are reminded of Max Müller's dictum that '[h]e who knows one [religion], knows none' (Müller, 1873, p. 16). The classic expression of this view, with direct application to educational practice and the curriculum, is to be found in Ninian Smart's *Secular Education and the Logic of Religion* (1968). His argument was widely influential in the 1970s in undermining exclusively Christian content for religious education in British schools and establishing the case for multi-faith (then phenomenological in form) religious education (see Barnes, 2000).

Another argument in favour of multi-faith religious education is that in our increasingly plural world pupils are exposed to religious diversity and to the challenge and the truth claims of different religions, and because some kind of response will necessarily be made toward the different religious and non-religious options, it is appropriate for pupils to be taught about these different options in school, so that they are able to make informed rather than uninformed choices. A further reason often advanced by supporters is that multi-faith religious education is effective in challenging racism, religious intolerance and bigotry. Unfortunately, this assertion lacks firm empirical support – admittedly, in part, because the research has not been undertaken. There is research, however, that seems to show that simple acquaintance with the beliefs and values of minority groups within an educational context will achieve little in terms of lessening prejudice towards them (see Malone, 1998, for example). More recently, Gerdien Bertram-Troost (2008), on the basis of an empirical research project in Holland, concluded that that 'getting knowledge about different religions as such, does not necessarily contribute to learning to have respect for everyone, irrespective of their religion ... the correlation between "At school I get knowledge about different religions" and "At school, I learn to have respect for everyone, whatever their religion" is not very high (r=.371)'. Interestingly, a major study of religious attitudes and prejudice among school pupils in Northern Ireland, conducted during the Conflict by John Greer (1985b, p. 275), found that there was 'a positive relationship between attitude to religion and openness: 'young people [in Northern Ireland] most favourably disposed to [the Christian] religion being most open to the other religious tradition'. Greer's research seems to give substance to the view that pupils who were confident of their own religious beliefs and commitments were more positive towards those with whom they differed religiously than those who had limited or negative attitudes towards religion.

More could be said on these matters, but what seems to be emerging is the view that multi-faith religious education, understood as a straightforward study of a wide range of religions, may do little to challenge intolerance and bigotry and that confidence in one's own religious commitment can facilitate openness to those with different commitments. To this may be added the point that prejudice and intolerance are attitudes and although attitudes may be influenced by education and increased knowledge, they are much more liable to be challenged and changed by personal experience and personal encounters, and by personal example. There is some research to show that intolerance is best challenged in schools that promote a positive view of minority groups across the different curriculum subjects, where teachers provide clear and consistent examples of positive attitudes to others, where teaching is inclusive and draws upon the values and wisdom of different communities, and where controversial issues are openly discussed in the classroom with sensitivity and care (Cheng & Soudack, 1994).

The debate on the effectiveness of multi-faith religious education in terms of its contribution to the moral and social aims of education will continue (see Barnes, 2014, pp. 10-24). Whatever the outcome of this, there remain educationally good reasons for study of a number of religions. This number should be determined by the cultural, historical, political, religious and demographic context of schools in particular societies. Given that the majority of the population in Northern Ireland profess to be Christian, that the religious divide in society is within Christianity, between Catholics and Protestants, and finally that non-religious adherents account for less than .05% of the population, there are good reasons for Christianity being central to the religious education curriculum. Certainly the current curriculum needs to relate much more effectively to the interests and needs of pupils, just as it needs to focus more explicitly on the positive role of Christianity in effecting reconciliation in society and in challenging religious intolerance and bigotry; it also needs to give more attention to other religions than the perfunctory study that currently obtains. This falls short of endorsing multi-faith religious education, where a wide range of religions is studied from the outset of a pupil's school career; it certainly fails to endorse current English forms of multi-faith religious education, where more than ten different traditions of belief and non-belief have been recommended for study by the Religious Education Council of England and Wales in its recent Framework document (Religious Education Council of England and Wales, 2013): such a proposal will inevitably result in superficial teaching and truncated and confused learning.

Conclusion

In one sense a review of religious education in Northern Ireland produces little that initially seems relevant to other places and to other contexts. In fact one of the important lessons to be learned is that religious education is always set in a particular historical, legal, political, religious and social context and this context determines the form it takes and the form to which it can aspire. There are no universal solutions to the challenges that educators face, particularly educators in divided societies, or if this is too strongly worded, a more circumspect statement is that there are no universal solutions that can be straightforwardly applied in different places, for all solutions require to be contextualised in order to take account of the 'local' situation.

Reconciliation between Catholics and Protestants and challenging religious intolerance have not been major themes in the religious education curriculum, and probably both need greater emphasis. Both themes, however, are related to themes that are prominent in the Core Syllabus, of forgiveness and repentance, the unconditional character of Christian love and the dignity of human beings, which is derived from the doctrine of men and women as bearing the image of God. If pupils accept these beliefs, hold attitudes based on them, and act in ways that give expression to them, it seems reasonable to conclude that religious education of this form has made, and will continue to make, some contribution to the creation of a peaceful and just society in Northern Ireland, in which respectfulness is extended to all.

Finally, a number of interpretive distinctions – the secular/religious distinction and the confessional/non-confessional distinction – have been subjected to critical analysis and scrutiny. Attention has been given to the way in which evidence is often skewed or ignored in order to favour one side of the constructed dichotomy over the other. In the case of Northern Ireland, interpreters often assume that the Conflict was essentially religious, and on this basis (with some degree of predictability) conclude that religious influence in society should give way to secular influence. What is overlooked is that religion is a multi-faceted reality (and concept) that relates to and incorporates other phenomena, thus making it difficult to determine its causal influence and significance. What is also overlooked is the negative influence secular forces can exert in societies and in schools. The negative consequences of religion in Northern Ireland are well known, the negative consequences of secularism in Northern Irish society and in schools are less well known and often overlooked.

References

Akenson, D.H. (1973) *Education and Enmity: the control of schooling in Northern Ireland 1920-50.* New York: Barnes & Noble.

Barnes, L.P. (1997) Reforming Religious Education in Northern Ireland: a critical review, *British Journal of Religious Education*, 19(2), 73-82. https://doi.org/10.1080/0141620970190204

Barnes, L.P. (2000) Ninian Smart and the Phenomenological Approach to Religious Education, *Religion*, 30(4), 315-332. https://doi.org/10.1006/reli.2000.0291

Barnes, L.P. (2002) World Religions and the Northern Ireland Curriculum, *Journal of Beliefs & Values*, 23(1), 19-32. https://doi.org/10.1080/13617670220125647

Barnes, L.P. (2005) Was the Northern Ireland Conflict Religious?, *Journal of Contemporary Religion*, 20(1), 55-69. https://doi.org/10.1080/1353790052000313918

Barnes, L.P. (2014) *Education, Religion and Diversity: developing a new model of religious education.* London: Routledge.

Barnes, L.P., Davis, A. & Halstead, J.M. (2015) *Religious Education: educating for diversity.* London: Bloomsbury Academic.

Belfast Telegraph (2015) Poll Finds Only 25% of Catholics Wants United Ireland Now. 5 November. http://www.belfasttelegraph.co.uk/news/northern-ireland/poll-finds-only-25-of-catholics-wants-united-ireland-now-34172038.html

Bertram-Troost, G. (2008) Learning to Live Together? The Impact of Religious Diversity or Homogeneity in Dutch Schools for Secondary Education. Unpublished paper, International Seminar on Religious Education and Values, Ankara, July 2008.

Brennan, O. (2001) *Cultures Apart? The Catholic Church and Contemporary Irish Youth.* Dublin: Veritas.

Brewer, J. & Higgins, G. (1998) *Anti-Catholicism in Northern Ireland 1600-1998.* London: Macmillan. https://doi.org/10.1057/9780333995020

Brewer, J., Higgins, G.I. & Teeney, F. (2011) *Religion, Civil Society and Peace in Northern Ireland*. Oxford: Oxford University Press.

Cheng, M. & Soudack, A. (1994) Education to Promote Racial and Ethnocultural Equality: a literature review, *Spectrum*, 12(4), 28-40.

Drafting Group (1993) *Core Syllabus for Religious Education*. Belfast: The Churches' Religious Education Core Syllabus Drafting Group.

Dunn, S. (1989) Integrated Schools in Northern Ireland, *Oxford Review of Education*, 15(2), 121-128. http://dx.doi.org/10.1080/0305498890150202

Farren, S. (1995) *The Politics of Irish Education 1920-65*. Belfast: Institute of Irish Studies.

Fulton, J. (1991) *The Tragedy of Belief: division, politics, and religion in Ireland*. Oxford: Clarendon Press.

Gallagher, E. & Worrall, S. (1982) *Christians in Ulster, 1968-80*. Oxford: Oxford University Press.

Greer, J. (1985a) *Irish Christianity: five units for secondary pupils*. Dublin: Gill & Macmillan.

Greer, J. (1985b) Viewing 'the Other Side' in Northern Ireland, *Journal for the Scientific Study of Religion*, 24(3), 275-292. https://doi.org/10.2307/1385817

Greer, J., McCullagh, J. & Rihan, A. (1977) Religion in Ireland: a school based curriculum development project, *Learning for Living*, 17(2), 75-78. https://doi.org/10.1080/00239707708556978

Hirst, P. (1972) Christian Education – A Contradiction in Terms, *Learning for Living*, 11(4), 6-11. https://doi.org/10.1080/00239707208556777

Hull, J.M. (1984) *Studies in Religion and Education*. Lewes: Falmer Press.

Hyland, M. (1989) *Children of God: priest's guide to the Veritas Primary Religious Education Programme*. Dublin: Veritas.

Malone, P. (1998) Religious Education and Prejudice among Students Taking the Course *Studies in Religion*, *British Journal of Religious Education*, 21(1), 7-19. https://doi.org/10.1080/0141620980210103

McKitterick, D. & McVea, D. (2001) *Making Sense of the Troubles*. Harmondsworth: Penguin.

Moffat, C. (Ed.) (1993) *Education Together for a Change: integrated education and community relations in Northern Ireland*. Belfast: Fortnight Education Trust.

Müller, M. (1873) *Introduction to the Science of Religion*. London: Longman, Green & Co.

Religious Education Council (1971) *Themes in Religious Education*. Belfast: Stranmillis College.

Religious Education Council of England and Wales (2013) *A Review of Religious Education in England*, REC. http://resubjectreview.recouncil.org.uk/media/file/RE_Review.pdf

Sacred Congregation for the Clergy (1971) *General Catechetical Directory*. Dublin: Veritas.

Smart, N. (1968) *Secular Education and the Logic of Religion*. London: Faber & Faber.

L. Philip Barnes

Smith, A. & Robinson, A. (1996) *Education for Mutual Understanding: the initial statutory years*. Coleraine: Centre for the Study of Conflict, University of Ulster.

Whyte, J.H. (1990) *Interpreting Northern Ireland*. Oxford: Clarendon Press.

CHAPTER 14

Mainstreaming Madrassas in India: resistance or co-optation?

HUMA KIDWAI

SUMMARY Within the broad framework of post-colonial critique, this chapter presents an educational application of co-optation theory that explains various ongoing transformations of and resistances within the madrassa system of education in India. It organizes observed patterns of findings concerning changes that emerged after policy interventions by the State to 'modernize' or mainstream madrassas in the Uttar Pradesh (UP) province of India. The chapter highlights ways in which various participating and non-participating madrassas adopt and resist State-suggested reforms, often leading to changes in internal practices and ideologies, as well as strategies to reinvent and localize policies they deem fit for their structural capacity and value system.

Introduction

The study of madrassas in India is particularly interesting. While in many countries madrassas are State-sponsored or purely private religious organizations, India's experience reveals a model in which State involvement seeks to reform primarily and historically religiously run institutions in a supposedly secular, non-Muslim majority country (Nair, 2008). Additionally, what makes India a unique case for this research is the history of social and political transformation in the institutional structure and ideology of madrassas during the colonial and post-colonial periods. Madrassas were once the prime institutions of learning in the region, with far-reaching socio-political influence across and beyond the subcontinent. Muslims represented one of the most educated and economically enterprising communities in the country. However, the situation at present is the contrary: Muslims have low levels of educational achievement and high levels of poverty. Madrassas are considered to be no longer relevant to present-day development needs and the agenda of the government. Given the existing abjectness of the community and its institutions in the country, what is the government trying to do with madrassa education? But, most importantly, why do many madrassas often decline any aspect of State interventions? What happens when madrassas do allow the State to intervene? These are some of the key questions that drive the research for this chapter.[1]

The purpose of this chapter is to organize observed patterns of findings on transformations that transpired after policy interventions by the State to 'modernize' or mainstream madrassas in the Uttar Pradesh (UP) state of India. Within these transformations the chapter highlights ways in which various participating and non-participating madrassas adopt and resist State-suggested reforms, often leading to changes in internal practices and ideologies, as well as strategies to reinvent and localize policies they deem fit for their structural capacity and value system. The theory of co-optation has been a particularly useful framework for interpreting and discussing the findings. The chapter begins by discussing the theory of co-optation, followed by a description of contemporary co-opting strategies and perceived intentions of the government in India and UP. I illustrate this relationship between policy and change in the form of three models, each based on a distinct purpose with which the government strategizes its policies for mainstreaming madrassas. Finally, I present key forms of transformations that have been observed in the institution of madrassas in response to the government's co-opting strategies.

The Theory and Politics of Co-optation

The process of 'modernization' and mainstreaming, I argue, can be likened to the course of co-optation. Co-optation, as described by one of its first analysts, Dr Philip Selznick (1949), is the process by which a group assimilates or subsumes a smaller group with related interests. In the process, one group gains converts from another group by attempting to replicate aspects they find appealing without fully adopting the ideals of the smaller group. Theorized from the perspective of the State, per Selznick, the defense of State legitimacy is the main political function of co-optation. This theory and its later modifications have mostly been applied to cases of military and political ascension. The concept has been employed widely to understand governance in the former Soviet States and Eastern Europe. It has been mostly devised as a tool to better understand the patterns of governance in conditions of uncertainty, and to explore and evaluate conditions and strategies that enable and constrain co-optation. There is a dearth of research from the point of view of those who are seemingly co-opted, which reveals the politics of power that guide the choice of perspectives in research. As will be evident in the description of some of the key features of this theory, I find that it applies well to the reality of madrassa mainstreaming in UP.

The following is an interpretation of the theory of co-optation and several of its modified versions that I find most relevant to the case of State-madrassa relationships. It draws from some of the common characteristics of the co-optation process, observed in strategies of policy-making bodies and social movement organizations, and theorized by proponents of the theory:

1. *Motivation:* The motivation to co-opt comes from the need to reduce environmental uncertainty or to mitigate threats to the survival or success of the co-opting group or organization (King, 2007).

2. *Process:* According to Shleifer and Treisman (2000), co-optation implies 'not dealing the stakeholders out of the game but dealing them new cards', and 'transforming stakeholders from opponents to supporters ... requires the creation of rents by the government that these stakeholders can be offered in exchange for their support' (pp. 8-9). Incentivizing collaborations, officially and unofficially, by offering material benefits such as social status, political power, security, monetary benefits, etc., is one of the most common strategies for co-optation.

3. *Probability of success:* According to King (2007), an organization's ability to co-opt or be co-opted is largely based on the internal structure of the organization as well as on the network of relationships in which it is rooted. Referring to observations of governance in Eastern European countries, she explains that those governments that have 'dense and overlapping' links to the body they wish to co-opt are more likely to be successful. In contrast, if the oppositional group has a high level of in-group solidarity and internal processes, policies, norms and procedures that disallow and discourage 'collaboration with nonaligned organizations', there is less likelihood for co-optation to occur or be sustained (King, 2007, p. 157).

4. *Outcome:* The outcome of co-optation depends on the relative strength of the co-opting and co-opted groups, the extent to which their interests are aligned, and the sincerity with which the members are willing to pursue those mutual interests. For example, if a large textile corporate takes over a small NGO concerned with local crafts and use of environmentally friendly materials, the resulting group might change only its name, mission and advertising, or might change the methods of production and profit margins. It is also possible that the smaller NGO gains more from this collaboration and can use the corporate label to expand the market for its product and its production philosophy.

Adoption of elements from opposing or rival groups can be symbolic, often having no significant effect on outcomes and processes. At the same time, co-optation can result in 'goal displacement', which may occur when group resources are deployed for purposes other than those for which they were originally intended (King, 2007, p. 157). For example, if the craftsmen from the small NGO are delegated with responsibilities for large-scale production of textile crafts, they may not have time to pursue their need for values-driven artistic expression, though that was the initial goal of the organization.

Another common outcome of co-optation that is often intended by the co-opting force is the creation of internal dissent. Members of the co-opted group may begin to disagree with each other in relation to adopting the new conditions and culture within the collaboration. The weakening of group solidarity and internal structures further facilitates the domination of the co-opting agency.

Co-optation, in the case of State-madrassa relationships, can be examined from two perspectives: the perspective of the State or policy-making bodies, and the perspective of madrassa representatives or networks challenging the viewpoint of the State. Typically, from the perspective of the State, co-optation is seen as a rational and adaptive process that allows the sustained domination of State leadership. On the other hand, much of the literature on social movements reveals that smaller groups, as I argue in the case of madrassas, gain access to the State or co-opt it in their own ways to meet their interests, often against the expectations of the State. The resulting outcome of the process is a mix of co-optation, social control, institutionalization and policy change.

Madrassa 'Modernization': a model of co-optation or resistance?

Co-optation, as observed in this study, involves inducement offers to some, but not all, members of the nonconformist group, thereby assuming the form of a 'divide and rule' tactic (Gamson, 1968). In this regard, co-optation theory is reminiscent of the expansionist policies of British and French colonizers of the Indian subcontinent (Morrock, 1973). To govern Indian provinces and prevent large-scale revolutions and conflicts, colonists brought several Indian states under their management, backed them during conflicts with other (not yet but soon to be co-opted) states, created 'rents' for a class of elite Indians who were 'subsumed' within the colonial society, and weakened the possibilities of unified retaliation against their rule for over three centuries. In the post-colonial context, divide and rule is still an important political and conflict resolution strategy of governing bodies seeking to maintain their position of power. If we are to acknowledge that the State's current policies to maintain stability and strength are reminiscent of colonial policy, we must recognize the existence and possibilities of resistance that emerge either during the process or as a result of co-optation.

The history of India's national movement for independence is replete with examples of resistance during the process of colonization, when the rulers of various princely states fought wars independently and in alliance with other rulers, as well as with examples of resistance that emerged as a direct result of colonization. For instance, most of the key leaders of the national movement, such as Gandhi, Nehru and Jinnah, were products of western education in England who interpreted British values of liberalism towards the cause of their own independence. I notice stark similarities between the pattern of colonial rule leading to explicit and implicit resistance in the Indian community, and the pattern of State co-optation of madrassas leading to a mix of co-optation, compromise, resistance and reinterpretation. Figure 1 is a simple model designed to illustrate the dynamics of co-optation processes as discussed by Bertocchi and Spagat (2001) in their analysis of post-Soviet privatization policies. It is modified to adapt to the general context of policies engaging the State with madrassas in India.

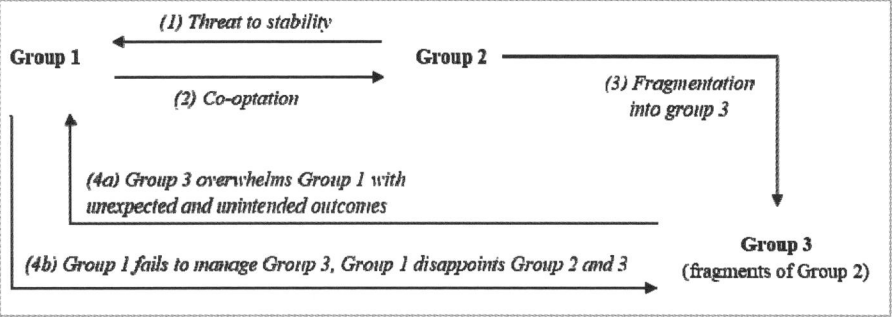

Figure 1. An illustrative model for the process of co-optation.

The model in Figure 1 consists of three groups. Group 1 holds political power and authority. Group 2 is an independent body that threatens the power of Group 1 by not conforming to its ideology and values, or by presenting itself as a potential political rival. Group 1 expects to decrease the probability of disorder by co-opting some agents of Group 2 into a more non-threatening and dependent third group. However, an opposite or less-than-desired effect takes place when the fragmentation of Group 2 leads to an even larger and more diverse Group 3. This group overwhelms Group 1. Group 1 fails to manage and satisfy the diverse needs of Group 3 and as a result, members of Group 3 and the initial Group 2 feel disappointed with Group 1. Sentiments of mistrust and difference of opinion grow deeper than before.

This model is a simplification of a process that is highly intricate and multi-dimensional. For the purpose of interpreting broad relationships between the two institutions, the model momentarily assumes homogeneity of identities and relationships within each group. Group 1 represents the *government* and Group 2 represents the broad category of *madrassas*. It is widely acknowledged in this text that the principle of homogeneity is particularly inapplicable to the case of the Indian government, which entails multiple actors across different levels. It was concluded, on the basis of interviews and focus groups with diverse madrassa groups and government officials, that institutional affiliation does not necessarily determine a common ideology and identity, and the immense hierarchy within the structure and the diversity of socio-political values make the group intensely differentiated. Intra-group differentiation of madrassas is far more penetrating. There is no simple basis for classifying madrassas, given the multiplicity of ideologies, regional histories, institutional structures, national and international networks, etc. One reason there is a severe lack of any credible research that attempts to create a typology of madrassas in the region is the sheer impossibility of the task. Realizing the complexity of the context, I created certain feasible suppositions and chose to deal with two broad groups – State as Group 1, madrassas as Group 2 – and the fragmentation of Group 2 caused because of Group 1's attempt to co-opt Group 2, as Group 3. To compensate for the potential oversights based in these assumptions, I will now turn to a discussion of the multidimensionality of the State's motivation to co-opt.

In my data I notice three motivations behind the State's attempt to modernize or mainstream madrassa education in UP. The three factors are: (a) educational ideology based on modern education and outcomes; (b) political interests of the ruling and opposition parties; and (c) perceived threats to security under national majoritarian rule and western international pressure. These factors work in tandem and simultaneously to give multiple dimensions to the process and outcomes of official state intervention (or co-optation) strategies. The following sections outline the overlapping dimensions of these three factors in the given model.

Co-optation Motivated by Educational Ideology

The first factor leads us to consider a process of co-optation driven by the government's ideology for education and modern values for development that do not see madrassas as credible, progressive institutions of learning. The government wants to expand educational access to all citizens and believes that madrassa education is a departure from the national standards of education and associated goals and practices. The government thus devises a scheme to modernize madrassas by offering to pay salaries for teachers teaching secular subjects. This comes as a significant incentive to teachers, who had been earning half the amount the government just offered to pay. However, there is widespread resistance to accepting this offer, as the madrassa community suspects this intervention will give the government a stronger hold on their traditionally autonomous institutions. Different stakeholder groups get divided on the issue. While some madrassas remain private, others apply for full aid. At the same time, many feel that partial aid is a more agreeable, middle-ground option. Over time, as the dependency on aid gets stronger, more madrassas apply for aid, thereby adopting an *applicant-to-aid* status. There is a seemingly increased demand for madrassa education as organizations and groups of individuals begin to create employment for themselves by opening and registering new madrassas with the government. There are examples of private schools registering themselves as madrassas since the recognition norms of madrassas are simpler than those for general private schools. This leads to the creation of a category of schools that are called 'madrassas' but have nothing to do with Islamic education. They are unintended outcomes of a 'false' sense of demand created under the policy programs.

As the network of madrassas begins to enlarge and complicate, the government finds it difficult to manage this group. This outcome is different from the initial objectives of the government. There are delays in teacher salary disbursements. This leads to mass discontentment among teachers, giving rise to teacher-led movements and activism against the State. Activists create teacher and madrassa unions that advocate for the rights of the teachers, often getting politicized in the process. Overall, this effort to co-opt certain teachers within madrassas (modeled in Figure 2) leads to the expansion of madrassa networks – an outcome quite the opposite of the initial goals.

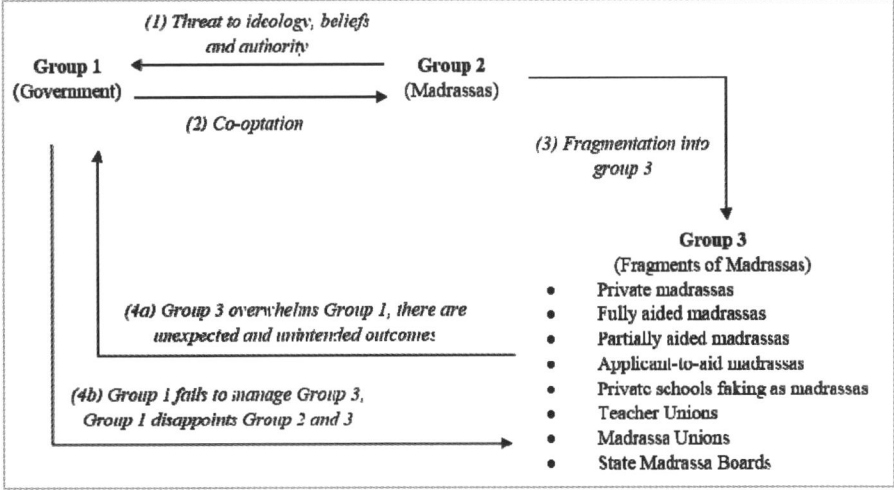

Figure 2. Co-optation based on educational ideology.

Co-optation Motivated by Political Interests

Figure 3 shows a model where the goals of co-optation are driven by political interests of local parties, the second factor we will consider. The strategy for co-optation in this model is to offer madrassa managers certain material benefits – connections with political leaders, higher social standing, access to the use of party property such as a car, phone, computer, etc. – in exchange for support during election campaigns to mobilize support in the Muslim community. Madrassa teachers and managers command high respect in their local communities and are attractive allies for political parties. By co-opting these individuals, political parties aspire to increase their electoral base in the

295

region. The relationship has often been found to be mutually beneficial. In working with the political parties, ally madrassas enter the domain of public madrassas and get partially or fully funded by the government.

Having being exposed to political processes and having realized their social status in the community, certain madrassa teachers and managers may develop political aspirations of their own. Furthermore, they develop a workers' union and command a much higher level of political force as a collective. This was certainly not the outcome sought by political parties when they first looked for support. The creation of multiple and often conflicting power groups is destabilizing for the political parties, which become overwhelmed by the response their co-optation strategy yielded.

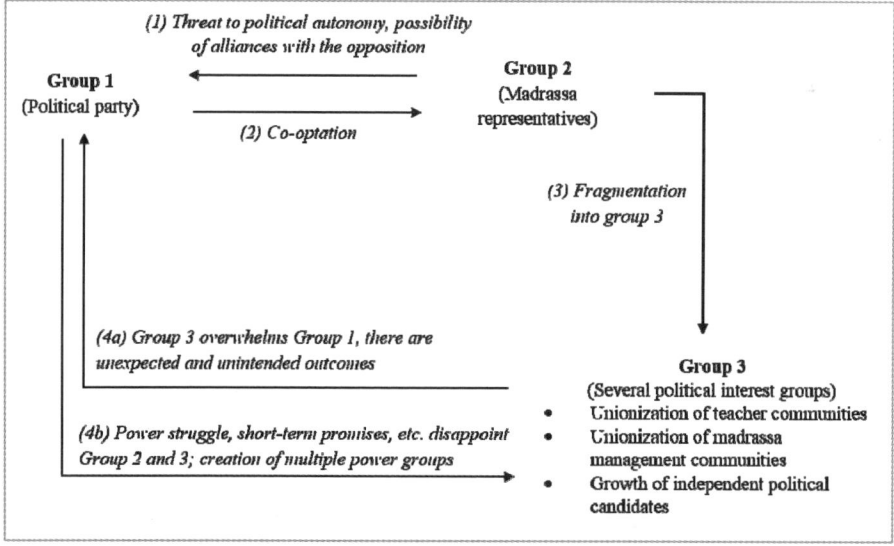

Figure 3. Co-optation based on political interests.

Co-optation Motivated by Perceived Threat of Terrorism

Figure 4 shows a model of co-optation based on the perceived threat of supposedly extremist madrassas to the national and international vision of peace and security. Motivated by the need to monitor and regulate madrassas and their 'suspicious' activities, governments may use educational programs as a pretext to intervene in the system. This strategy to form internal allies yields certain unexpected outcomes similar to the outcomes shown in Figure 2.

Differences in opinion regarding whether to work with the government lead to further fragmentation among Muslims. While division of large groups into smaller ones may seem like a successful outcome of this co-optation process, in due course each fragmented madrassa, in order to survive and perpetuate its ideology, pulls together a group of followers and initiates more madrassas, perhaps explaining in part the rise of madrassas in India. This was also the outcome of colonial policies for madrassas that led to numerous factions, separating moderate voices from extreme views on the subject of education and society for Muslims in India.

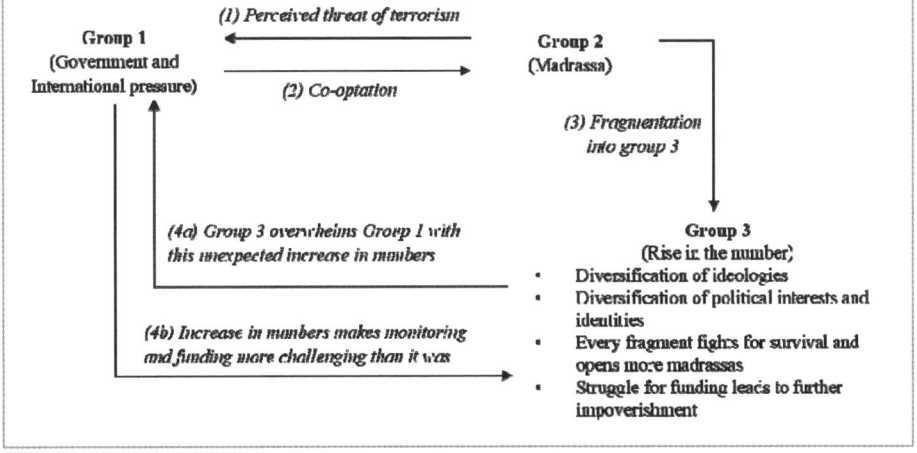

Figure 4. Co-optation based on perceived threat to peace and security.

Co-optation Strategy: conditioning psychology and increasing participation

Co-optation, according to most literature from the point of view of the State and policy making, is an effective mechanism through which the State's legitimacy is enhanced (Siegler, 1982). Co-optation, according to Siegler's analysis of Soviet State policies, contributes to systematic support by bringing different stakeholders into the established policy-making framework of the State. However, it is important to consider, as data in this study indicate, changes in the behavior and attitude of co-opted individuals and institutions as they begin to see the State from within.

According to Andrei Amalrik (1970), after individuals from dissenting groups are co-opted to participate in the affairs of the State, they develop a 'State-psychology' that further serves to induce support for the system (p. 19). He points out that the psychology of the State worker is oriented around the status quo and lacks any kind of independent thinking and action. Once an individual from a dissenting group begins to work under State supervision, the character of his or her disagreement with the State takes the form of 'the dissatisfaction of a junior clerk [towards] the attitude of his superior' (p. 19). According to the leaders and members of madrassa teachers' unions, over 2500 written complaints have been submitted by teachers in UP who have not been receiving their salaries on time, or who have not received any salary

297

for the last two to three years. Yet, they continue to work within the system, using the existing bureaucratic procedures to redress their issues. Critics of State-madrassa partnerships for education, particularly those coming from private or independent madrassa bodies, often refer to this bureaucratization of madrassa teachers as an example of the loss of educational spirit and democracy in State-funded madrassas. A senior teacher from a private madrassa in Barabanki said:

> We know teachers who used to be active participants of our
> movement against the government's discriminatory policies. The
> Government of India favors Hindus across the board, be it
> education, employment, justice system, or distribution of social
> schemes. Many of us [teachers] used to often write articles for
> [Urdu] newspapers questioning the government's unjust practices.
> But ever since they started receiving a government salary, they
> have changed. I believe they still feel for their Muslim brethren,
> but they do not get any time. They are busy running after clerks to
> get their salaries on time. They no longer have time for the
> community. (Teacher, private madrassa, interview, Barabanki,
> January 2014)

This shift in expression of dissatisfaction is similar to Amlrik's (1970) description of the 'petty clerk' mentality where an individual may protest, not against the office or the department, but against his rather low salary or against his rude supervisor. The co-optee sees himself/herself as too insignificant to change anything, as the system appears to be too overwhelming, especially when seen from the inside. The process of changing what now seems a law-like, immutable structure seems too painful and strenuous, and the co-optee may become content working within the system rather than against it (Siegler, 1982). This sense of helplessness within the system was expressed by study respondents from both the groups – the government officials and the recently co-opted madrassa teachers.

Government officials seemed overwhelmed with the daily routines of maintaining records and documents to report to their superiors. In my observation of interactions between bureaucrats of different levels, never did I see a lower authority figure question or stand up to his superior officials, even when the latter made seemingly unreasonable demands. District-level officials are closest to the realities of madrassas and the community they work for. However, they do little to pass on their experience to their superiors or to question the usefulness of seemingly flawed policy instructions that are passed down to them for execution. By bringing in madrassa teachers within the domain and control of State bureaucracy, the government alters the goals of these individuals.

Another form of co-optation strategy that appears to be found effective in the context of State programs for madrassas is, ironically, the inclusion or participation of madrassa representatives in policy-making committees, state and local advisory bodies, and various programs to design and implement new policies. As evident from policy meeting minutes over the last three years, a prescribed number of madrassa activists, including religious leaders and union representatives, is included in limited institutional decision making and power sharing. However, no groundbreaking discussion takes place. According to Coy and Hedeen (2005), this is the 'paradox of collaboration', where the continued participation of key resisters or challengers to any particular government program may become a goal in and of itself and 'other movement objectives may be subsumed by the goal of ongoing access in the bodies that are beginning to regulate the partial policy changes that the movement has won' (p. 14). The paradox of collaboration suggests that most members of the group will increasingly identify with the process due to their participation in it, and that their 'ownership' of the policy-making process and even of policy implementation will also increase. Gradually, minority activists and teacher union leaders move from the position of outside critics to that of inside defenders of the critique.

The inclusion/participation component of co-optation relies on a principle that is well known in conflict resolution theory and practice: participation in decision making and policy making tends to increase ownership in the policies and decisions, even when the policies do not undergo substantive change or even when the specific outcomes are not actually very satisfactory to the included participant (Coy, 2003; Mansbridge, 2003). Over time, the organizing energy of protestors is transferred from suggesting alternative initiatives to the existing ineffective policies, and redirected toward the maintenance or, at best, the reform of established processes and institutions (Morrill, 1998). This participation, in turn, tends to increase movement ownership in the status quo. This paradox is visible in the platforms aiming to bring the State and madrassa representatives together in one place. Being invited to state-level discussions in Lucknow or in Delhi becomes an indication of recognition of a teacher union leader or a local religious leader. In this regard, according to a religious scholar in Lucknow:

> So many people have gained political power by interacting with the government on the pretext of 'modernizing' and 'reforming' madrassas. What kind of reform requires travelling first class in trains to attend meetings, and then spending long days chatting in air-conditioned rooms of the ministry offices? By getting these so-called supporters of reform used to such luxuries and attention the government has created divisions within groups. These union leaders represent themselves and their interests over their followers and often stand with the government to support their decisions. (Religious scholar, interview, Lucknow, January 2014)

Reportedly, the government seeks participation from individuals and groups that are likely to support its decisions, thereby creating an 'illusion' of legitimate democracy in its policy-making processes. Several respondents complained of the lack of true representation of the community of respected scholars of religious and minority issues in policy meetings. Additionally, they feel the media does a poor job of describing the situation to the world. In the words of a teacher from a partially aided madrassa:

> as soon as a religious leader gives his opinion against the government's program for modernization of madrassas, the media issues headlines like 'Madrassas reject modernization' or 'Dark ages continue for madrassas'. English and Hindi media are complicit with the government and have caused so much harm to the image of madrassas and its students in the country and abroad. (Teacher, partially aided madrassa, Saharanpur, April 2014)

Staying away from such allegations about 'rejecting modernization', according to some aided madrassas, has been one of the many factors for accepting State aid. The media repeatedly presents the 'regular' participants of State-madrassa meetings as 'moderate' and 'secular' Muslims, thereby reinforcing a certain character of voice and outlook that is supportive of the State view of reform and mainstreaming.

Transformation *of* and *by* Co-optees

One interest of this study is in the field of contestation tactics: how and when do madrassas resist the government and contest its power? It can be easily generalized from my findings across the state of UP and from relevant informants at the national level that the better established and older madrassas are seen as adopting a stance of resistance towards political parties that approach them. These madrassas largely refuse to interact with any government agency or political party member and remain independent, and are thus less available to be co-opted. Such an independent position is natural, given the undesirable outcomes of numerous cases where madrassas did permit the government to intervene with madrassa functions and allowed political relationships with local party members. Most independent madrassa representatives who participated in the study believed that they can maintain an independent voice and stand up to injustice of any sort only if they stay out of the government's control. They clearly prefer to exert pressure from below and not risk co-optation.

The case of madrassas in India, I propose, is a case of common co-optation of a social movement by a ruling party, with significant but short-term gains for both sides in the process. With regard to State-madrassa interactions in UP, these arrangements represent the classic trade-off of co-optation. Co-opted madrassa representatives get tangible and immediate benefits, while the government or the political party gains a measure of social stability. These outcomes of co-optation have been well established in political science literature on social movements and governments in Latin

America (Prevost et al, 2012), the Soviet Union (Bertocchi & Spagat, 2001) and several Middle Eastern countries (Khatib et al, 2012).

In discussing the three motivations behind the State's attempt to modernize or mainstream madrassa education in UP, I have described ways in which new interpretations of policy are made locally. As presented in the description of the first motivating factor – the government's ideology for education – a common transformation resulting from the co-opting strategies has been an increase in the perceived demand for madrassa education in UP. Since the government collects data only on 'recognized' madrassas, the rise in numbers of recognition applications each year can be misleadingly interpreted as a rise in the actual number of madrassas or madrassa students in the state.

On the other hand, there has been an evident rise in the number and size of teacher unions and madrassa unions across the state. This has also led to greater political power in the hands of madrassa teachers. New forms of corrupt practices are taking hold in the system. Recognition certificates to madrassas are often released without necessary inspections, in exchange for monetary enticements. An area of complaint regarding State intervention into the madrassa sector has concerned a rise in low-quality education systems that are neither fulfilling the objectives of madrassa education nor meeting the educational standards prescribed by the national education policy. Since the recognition procedures for madrassas are simpler than those for general private schools, many private schools are registering themselves as madrassas. They continue to offer their original curriculum and may add a class or two on Islamic studies. One such case was explored in Bareilly district:

> Until four years ago our school name was 'Little Flower Public [2] School.'[3] We had been trying to get our school recognized for many years but it was so difficult. So much paperwork to do, so many school facilities to show, and hence a big bribe… Then we found that the government was recognizing madrassas and giving aid to teachers to teach English, math, and science. We had already been teaching these subjects. Most of our students are Muslims. We thought why are we any different from a madrassa? Isn't madrassa just a place of learning? We changed our name to 'Madrassa Little Flower' and filed for recognition as a madrassa. Within a year we were [government] recognized. We follow the same curriculum as before but we had to add a subject on Islamic studies where we teach children basic things about the religion. We changed the school uniform of children to replace skirts with *kurta-salwar* for girls and replace shorts with pants for boys. Now, we are a recognized school and three of our teachers get their salary from the government. (Teacher, recognized private madrassa, Bareilly, interview, March 2014)

'Madrassa Little Flower' is one of the newly emerging crop of madrassas that have nothing much to do with the system or Islamic education. The curriculum follows the basic guidelines prescribed by the national framework and barely teaches any core subjects pertaining to the religion or the Urdu language. These new 'madrassas', being primarily driven by profit-making, charge students a fee and other costs.

From a distance, this situation is interpreted in different ways. According to a low-level bureaucrat, senior officials who visit from the capital and do not know enough about the history and context of these *naqli*, or fake madrassas, think that madrassas are modernizing and, as a result of their minority welfare programs, giving up old traditions for 'modern and more relevant education'. At the same time, this situation presents itself as a 'mockery' of the madrassa system to the opponents of State intervention. In the words of a manager of a private madrassa:

> They [the government] have made a joke out of madrassas. Now any 'road-side school' can call itself madrassa for aid and the government has no care ... they just do their daily paperwork. Had they cared for good quality education for Muslims they would have improved the condition of government schools being run in Muslim localities. Instead, they choose to support poor quality madrassas that produce students who are neither educated in *deen* [faith] nor in *duniya* [world/worldly] ... Now, students graduating from these fake madrassas will be certified as madrassa students. They are such poor-quality students, cannot even write their names in Urdu, leave alone interpreting religious texts. They will ruin the *martaba* [eminence] and *waqaar* [dignity] of good madrassa education that we had been trying so hard to protect.
> (Manager of private madrassa, interview, Saharanpur, April 2014)

It is a widely held belief among the private madrassa community that instead of supporting poor-quality madrassas, the government should allow them to perish with time. 'Why fund an institution that has no vision or means for providing meaningful education for Muslims?' is a question raised by one of the many similarly opinioned madrassa teachers in Azamgarh district (management committee, focus group, Azamgarh, February 2014). They feel that the government, as a part of a larger 'non-Muslim' conspiracy, is set to bring down the quality of education among Muslims by promoting sub-par education institutions run by 'ignorant' and 'thoughtless' Muslims. Such concerns have added vigor to the ongoing internal debates to re-invent madrassa education in ways that do not compromise the sanctity and entirety of the curriculum. A major part of these discussions is to consider the possibilities of reviving the pre-colonial character of madrassas, before they fell into the British 'trap' of dividing knowledge into separate streams of religious and rational sciences. At the same time, a component of the discourse focuses on providing an educational alternative to Muslim students who do not wish for specialized education in religion. Many argue that they should be educated in a medium that is mainstream but not Hindu dominated.

One of the prominent action-oriented outcomes of this discourse is a movement led by certain like-minded, progressive but anti-State intervention members of the Deeni Taleem Council. This organization was initially formed in 1959 with a view to arrange technical support for *maktabs* (primary grades) of madrassas so that they do not have to rely on State support for curricular reforms. This movement got revived during the early 2000s with the rise of Hindu nationalist groups in the politics of UP and the associated 'saffronization' [4] of culture and schooling in the region. The Council aimed to curb the entry of Muslim children into 'Hindu-run' government schools that practice a 'one-sided curriculum'. Critique of the disproportionate references to literature from Hindu mythology and of the lack of reference to Muslim contributions to the national movement of independence forms the basis of their anti-government school argument.

The Council's office, according to its general secretary, interviewed in Lucknow, presently supports over 7000 unrecognized *maktabs*, mostly located in UP, by: (a) conducting examinations and facilitating students' transition to mainstream schools or larger madrassas; (b) prescribing syllabi and providing textbooks up to the level of Grade 5 that have been designed to match the requirements of the state Board of Education but 'from a Muslim point of view'; and (c) conducting research and analysis of government school textbooks and advocating for 'secularization' of content to remove elements that create bias against Muslims. The main argument of the Council is that unless the State provides its citizens with 'fair' and 'truly secular' content, Muslim institutions should not seek government support and Muslim children should be provided with an alternative education scheme that fairly represents different religious standpoints.

More silent but salient forms of resistance can be seen at the level of individual madrassa teachers and their classroom activities. It is an explicit effort of the madrassa management committees to hire teachers who can teach 'secular' subjects from within the local community or who are previous graduates of a madrassa system. Having come from similar backgrounds with regard to education and beliefs, these teachers cover the 'secular' syllabus provided by the government in a manner that is a combination of their ability and their ideological judgments. It was found through observing classrooms and reviewing student textbooks and workbooks that teachers employ selection bias while picking from the chapters to be taught in their classrooms. For example, topics related to Hindu festivals and practices would be conveniently skipped over in favor of a culturally neutral subject. Similarly, a teacher may skip certain sections of a mathematics syllabus that she finds difficult to teach. Another example is the subject of human evolution in science. It is common knowledge that teachers across madrassas, whether private or public, do not teach Darwin's theory of evolution, as it stands contrary to the principles of evolution understood within the Islamic interpretation. They do refer to the theory in higher-grade levels, albeit with a strong emphasis that it is a 'western theory' and not a 'universal fact'.

Inclusion of fine arts and performance arts is another example where madrassa teachers exercise their ideological judgment. By tradition, most forms of creative arts such as music, painting and dance have been discouraged within Islamic education. However, these forms of knowledge and expression occupy a central place in the National Curriculum Framework of India. Most activities at the end of each textbook chapter entail the use of some form of visual or performance art. Madrassas almost never stress these sections of the textbooks, or modify them into activities more in line with their pedagogic traditions. For example, the recitation of *naat* (musically composed poetry in praise of the Prophet) is a way in which many madrassas of the region integrate the art of music and poetry into their curriculum. Most madrassas participate in inter-school *naat* competitions, and recitation often forms part of the daily cultural activity during morning prayers or on special occasions.

These activities are more common in girls' madrassas, as *naat* recitation is part of the folk traditional and local household culture among Muslims in UP, often led by female congregations in each neighborhood. As discussed earlier, girls' madrassas have clearly risen in numbers due to a multiplicity of factors, of which one is undeniably a response to government aid. Increase in participation of girls in education has been a nationwide phenomenon. However, there is a strategic acceptance of this change at the level of schools and madrassas. In girls' madrassas, it is found that, despite apparent similarities with the curricula of boys' madrassas, a policy of selective emphasis is practiced locally. At the expense of certain subjects like mathematics, logic and Islamic jurisprudence (*fiqh*), girls are trained in more domestic areas of knowledge such as cooking, sewing, embroidery, etc. Clearly, access has not ensured opportunities of the same kind, and locally defined aspirations for educational outcomes dominate the State's view of common standards for education.

These were some examples of ways in which aided madrassas selectively localize and often reinterpret the nationally designed curriculum for their institutions. While on the surface it may seem that the policies for modernization are creating a common standard of learning and culture, there exist many contextual variations of the common curriculum. This finding challenges the broad assumptions of convergence theories that schools around the world are becoming more similar over time (Anderson-Levitt, 2003). It was found that most participating madrassas were already teaching some secular subjects and did not see the policy bring in any drastic changes to their curricular foci. Nevertheless, they 'pretended' to employ the policy for economic and political motivations (Steiner-Khamsi, 2008).

In the words of a madrassa manager from one of the earliest state-funded madrassas in Barabanki, 'the government may not be, but the money is "secular"'. According to him, as long as madrassas stick to their traditional mission and zeal there is no harm in receiving government aid as 'it is the right of all children'; it is, however, the responsibility of madrassas, he suggests, to ensure that this aid is used for the benefit of the community and does not distract the madrassa from its religious and social duties.

Concluding Remarks

Social exclusion, economic deprivation and physical oppression determine part of the Muslim community's situation in India and influence the group's political imagery. Its outlook is also informed by sociopolitical dynamics within the community in response to the rise of majoritarian politics in India, negative perceptions of Islam and Muslims in the international media post-9/11, and growing opportunities for cultural exchange with wealthy Arab countries in the Middle East. The community is constantly transforming itself and both actively and passively adapting to the environment by adopting certain attitudes. Common responses to the current political climate include the reassertion of a religious identity that is threatened, distancing themselves from mainstream politics, building transnational linkages and developing sentiments of empathy with the plight of Muslim communities internationally. These reactions underscore a 'shared subaltern identity' that further isolates Muslims from the wider political processes in their environment (Riaz, 2012, p. 166). Transformations of madrassas, as educational spaces for young Muslim girls and boys in India, must be understood from a broader development lens aimed at promoting social, political and economic equity in the region and beyond.

I have pursued this research with an understanding that there is a forced estrangement between faith and development in the name of a secular and non-ideological modern vision of development (Marshall, 2004). I argue for the relevance of better understanding of patterns of relationship between faith institutions and governments, as the two represent significant agents of development, particularly the educational development of their communities and citizens, respectively. This conceptual understanding of the faith-development linkage, in the form of State-madrassa relationships in India, forms the underlying rationale for the study, as well as an area of development literature that this research aims to contribute to. However, findings from this research and from that of others in this book (see chapter 15 by Elena Lisovskaya) offer a word of caution; the forced separation of religion from the development dialogue, as well as its reinsertion into it, need to be regarded more critically and historically. This chapter has attempted to critically analyze how this development dialogue plays out in the field through the theoretical lens of co-optation.

Co-optation, as defined in previous research, is a process by which an organization with greater authority and power tries to subsume smaller organizations in order to remove potentially threatening and destabilizing elements from its environment. I see a strong colonial undertone to this political strategy, which becomes apparent in the ways the government processes of co-optation have come to be designed. These strategies are characterized by the principles of divide and rule; the creation of materialistic enticements for key community representatives; increasing the base of participation in policy making without any effective policy changes; and, most importantly, bureaucratizing the environment of the co-opted member, who undergoes an increasing shift of attitude-behavior in favor of the co-opting body. However, in applying the concept of co-optation to understanding policy processes, I was more interested in the 'undesired' and counter-intuitive outcomes.

Among the various transformations madrassas and the minority education community have undergone in response to State policies, several examples show the influence of the collective and individual agency of madrassa organizations and teachers. The emergence of a new institutional variety of schools-faking-as-madrassas is a local response to the aid environment created by State bureaucracy that was neither expected nor desired by either the State or the madrassas. With the rise of seemingly large numbers of ill-equipped institutions under government support, several prominent Islamic scholars and leaders have come together to raise the voice of internal reforms and to restrain the entry of Muslim children into poor-quality and Hindu-oriented government-aided schools. At the same time, the individual attempts of teachers at aided schools to modify and reinterpret reforms in line with their beliefs and practices are found to be the most implicit yet prominent response to the policy.

Overall, it seems that the way the co-optation has been carried out is presently incomplete, owing to the diverse responses it has generated in the community to be co-opted. There is wide variation in the lived experiences of madrassas and teachers that overwhelm the standardization agenda of reform policies. However, it must be acknowledged that the policies have created certain common structures, such as increased enrollment of girls, recruitment of female teachers, introduction of school uniforms, etc., that are likely to be internalized over time. Looking back into the colonial policies of institutionalizing education in India, we find that despite strict resistance to the westernizing influences of the British curriculum, over time madrassas could not resist selectively adopting certain characteristics, such as the principle of classrooms and grades, the classification of knowledge groups, and use of examinations and certifications. Over time, greater clarity will emerge as to the outcomes of the present reform policies and the sustenance of responses generated for and against the 'modernization' program.

This research offers policy implications for the national policy on education in India. It challenges broad policy and process assumptions about the purpose of education. With a country as diverse and complex as India, the notion of common goals and standards of development is limited in scope and practice. These assumptions are based on the 'myth' of modernity, progress, change and success for the meritorious individual in a competitive society – which clash with the lived experiences of many Muslims in India and with the very ideas upon which Islamic education is founded (Ahmad, 2003, p. 27). At the same time, madrassa education based on assumptions and beliefs in 'cultural superiority' and unity and strength in the notion of Islamic fraternity often place students at a distinct economic disadvantage, with limited options for social mobility (p. 27). In dealing with the dilemma madrassa education presents for Indian Muslims and the State, it should be acknowledged that madrassas cannot be wished away and that the madrassa system of education plays an important educational and cultural role in the lives of millions of people.

Notes

[1] This chapter is drawn from my dissertation 'Postcolonial Challenges to Madrassa Education Reform in India: bureaucracy, politics, resistance, and cooptation', submitted at Teachers College, Columbia University in May 2015. It is based on an extensive qualitative study of the state-madrassa relationship for educational reform in India. Data about policy processes were collected at the national level in New Delhi, at the provincial level in Uttar Pradesh, and at the district level in Barabanki, Azamgarh, Bareilly and Saharanpur. Twenty-eight madrassas were sampled to capture a classification of madrassas based on their relationship with government funding as well as their sectarian ideology for religion and education. In the process, a total of 148 interviews, 25 focus groups and 32 sessions of non-participatory observations were conducted.

[2] In India, it is common practice to use the word 'public' to denote private schools. Government-aided schools are called government schools.

[3] The name has been modified to maintain anonymity.

[4] According to renowned Indian historian and educationist Romila Thapar, *Hinduization* (or *saffronization*) refers to a process of social change in India characterized by an inculcation of the ideology that argues that a particular form of Hinduism, a much more narrowly defined form, is what should motivate the development priorities of the country because Hindus technically constitute the majority. Further, this ideology supports upper-caste opinion. Thapar posits that, from her historian perspective, this ideology seeks to redefine the past. Politically, the supporters of this often hidden agenda are trying to suggest that the only history, civilization and cultural forms that matter are Hindu. Thapar insists that this ideology is not just confined to academic discourse; it affects the everyday lives of people through day-to-day politics, school teaching and national curricula (BBC News, 2002).

307

References

Ahmad, I. (2003) Muslim Educational Backwardness, in A.H. Chaoudhury (Ed.) *Education of Muslim Children in Assam: problems and prospects*, pp. 13-33. Guwahati: Government of Assam.

Amalrik, A. (1970) *Will the Soviet Union Survive until 1984?* New York: Perennial Library.

Anderson-Levitt, K. (2003) *Local Meanings, Global Schooling: anthropology and world culture theory*. New York: Palgrave Macmillan. https://doi.org/10.1057/9781403980359

BBC News (2002) Historian Professor Romila Thapar [Audio file: Real Player]. May. http://news.bbc.co.uk/2/hi/south_asia/1977246.stm

Bertocchi, G. & Spagat, M. (2001) The Politics of Co-optation, *Journal of Comparative Economics*, 29(4), 591-607. https://doi.org/10.1006/jcec.2001.1734

Coy, P.G. (2003) Negotiating Danger and Safety under the Gun: consensus decision making on Peace Brigades International teams, in P.G. Coy (Ed.) *Consensus Decision-making, Northern Ireland, and Indigenous Movements*, pp. 85-122. Greenwich, CT: Elsevier Science/JAI.

Coy, P.G. & Hedeen T. (2005) A Stage Model of Social Movement Cooptation: community mediation in the United States, *Sociological Quarterly*, 46(4), 405-435. https://doi.org/10.1111/j.1533-8525.2005.00020.x

Gamson, W.A. (1968) *Power and Discontent*. Homewood, IL: Dorsey Press.

Khatib, L., Lefèvre, R. & Qureshi, J. (2012) *State and Islam in Baathist Syria: confrontation or co-optation?* St Andrews: University of St Andrews Centre for Syrian Studies.

King, M. (2007) Cooptation, in M. Bevir (Ed.) *Encyclopedia of Governance*, pp. 157-158. Thousand Oaks, CA: SAGE.

Mansbridge, J. (2003) Consensus in Context: a guide for social movements, in P.G. Coy (Ed.) *Consensus Decision-making, Northern Ireland, and Indigenous Movements*, pp. 229-253. Greenwich, CT: Elsevier Science/JAI.

Marshall, K. (2004) Faith Perspectives for Development Institutions: new faces of compassion and social justice, *International Journal*, 59(4), 893-901. https://doi.org/10.1177/002070200405900413

Morrill, C. (1998) Institutional Change and Interstitial Emergence: the growth of alternative dispute resolution in American law, 1965-1995, in W. Powell & D. Jones (Eds) *Bars of the Iron Cage: institutional dynamics and processes*. Chicago: University of Chicago Press.

Morrock, R. (1973) Heritage of Strife: the effects of colonialist 'divide and rule' strategy upon the colonized peoples, *Science & Society*, 37(2), 129-151.

Nair, P. (2008) The State and Madrasas in India. Working paper, Non-governmental Public Action Programme. Birmingham: University of Birmingham.

Prevost, G., Campos, C.O. & Vanden, H.E. (2012) *Social Movements and Leftist Governments in Latin America: confrontation or co-optation?* London: Zed Books.

Riaz, A. (2012) *Faithful Education: madrasahs in South Asia*. Piscataway, NJ: Rutgers University Press.

Shleifer, A. & Treisman, D. (2000) *Without a Map: political tactics and economic reform in Russia*. Cambridge, MA: MIT Press.

Siegler, R.W. (1982) *The Standing Commissions of the Supreme Soviet: effective co-optation*. New York: Praeger.

Steiner-Khamsi, G. (2008) Towards a Contextualized Comparison of European Post-bureaucratic States: a commentary.
http://knowandpol.eu/IMG/pdf/o1.integration.steiner-khamsi.pdf

CHAPTER 15

Religion's Uneasy Return to the Russian School: a contested and inconsistent desecularization 'from above'

ELENA LISOVSKAYA

SUMMARY This chapter generalizes and theorizes a quarter-of-a-century-long process of religion's return to the Russian school and its ideological outcomes. It builds upon the argument that this return represents a case of inconsistent and contested desecularization 'from above'. The desecularization process is described as a multi-stage 'social drama', propelled by the struggles among the top political and religious elites, whose educational orientations have oscillated between a secularist, a neo-traditionalist and, ultimately, a neo-imperial paradigm in a background of apathetic public support and participation. The religious education course established in 2012 is a product of the Church-State alliance, which promotes this paradigm. It is shown that the ideologies promoted by the course textbooks are congruent with a neo-imperial orientation.

Problem and Main Arguments

When the Soviet regime collapsed in 1991, it left behind a state-run school system that had been hostile to any religion and promoted the official doctrine of 'scientific atheism'. The demise and discredit of Soviet atheism made it possible, for the first time in decades, to change the Russian school's stance towards religion. This new opportunity generated much enthusiasm among early post-communist reformers. Religious and secular leaders of the 1990s broadly accepted the idea that bringing religion back into the school would alleviate the moral crises of post-communism.

Yet, how does one bring religion back into the school of a constitutionally secular state? And how can this be accomplished in a multiethnic and multi-confessional society in such a way that minority rights are not violated? Should students learn the fundamentals of religion or of science about religion? Should religion-related courses be required or elective? What religions should be taught, and should the traditionally dominant Russian Orthodoxy receive preferential treatment?

It took almost a quarter of a century to develop and implement a formula for introducing religion to schools which would address these fundamental questions. This process went through a series of stages and in 2012 eventually culminated in introducing a mandatory course in the *Fundamentals of Religious Cultures and Secular Ethics.*

The structure of the course has already been described by many observers, including the author of this chapter (Lisovskaya, 2016), and I will return to the details of the course later in this chapter. In brief, it has become the first course within the curricular area of *Spiritual-Moral Education of Russia's Citizens* established in 2007. It consists of six modules, from which a student's parents must select one. Five of them focus on religions, and one is on secular ethics. Four modules are dedicated to four religions that in Russia are deemed 'traditional'.[1] These are Orthodoxy, Islam, Buddhism and Judaism. One surveys multiple religions, with a strong emphasis on the four traditional ones.[2] One textbook for each module has been approved by the Ministry of Education Coordinating Council and published by *Prosveshchenie,* the largest state-controlled publishing house. Although the course is now mandatory for only the fourth-graders, plans have been made to extend its reach to high school students. Existing literature dealing with the process of implementation of religious education in Russia has focused on specific facets and stages of this process. Yet, little has been done to understand and theorize its general social dynamics. Now that we have over twenty-five years of observations of the development of religious education in Russia, generalizations are both feasible and much needed. This chapter is an attempt to generalize and theorize this process and its political-ideological outcomes.

In my previous research, it was argued that the introduction of religion to Russia's schools represents a case of 'inconsistent and contested desecularization from above', which has been a prevalent pattern of religion's return to Russian society (Lisovskaya & Karpov, 2005). Within this pattern, desecularization of Russia's education has been centered on the state-run schools from the very early years of post-communism instead of, let's say, parish (*Sunday*) or private religious schools. It has been carried out from above by the ruling religious elites (primarily of the Russian Orthodox Church of Moscow Patriarchate [ROC MP hereafter]) in collaboration with secular political and educational elites at the federal level of administration. Moreover, resistance to these attempts has also typically come from above. In this chapter, I build upon this argument and provide an overview of the history of these struggles as a 'social drama', to borrow Victor Turner's term (Turner, 1974), which consisted of six acts or stages and was surrounded by intense struggles, political debates and intrigues.[3] I show how, in the course of these struggles and stages, educational policies had oscillated between a *neo-traditionalist* and, ultimately, *neo-imperial* orientation (in Turner's terms, 'paradigm') that favors a privileged status of Orthodoxy, and a *secularist* orientation (paradigm) that acknowledges the importance of religion, yet emphasizes the need for its separation from the state-run school. While the neo-traditionalist orientation embodied in the religious course prevailed, I suggest that the struggle between these two tendencies is far from over.

It is further shown that the social dynamics of this drama had been largely between segments of top secular and religious elites whose attitudes towards religious education reflected their situational political, economic and broader cultural interests. Meanwhile, the conflict surrounding the issue of religious education did not involve significant mass mobilization (even though activists and 'paradigm-bearers' from below were occasionally involved). This argument finds its support in official statistics and survey data, which demonstrate that attempts to desecularize education have lacked broad popular support. The idea of religious instruction has been supported by a minority of the Russian public, and even of the Orthodox believers. Given the limited space of this chapter, this argument will not be developed in detail here.

In the last section I briefly summarize the outcomes of this drama in terms of the course content and form. It is argued that the introduction of the religious culture course clearly represents a radical turnabout within the official ideology of Russian education after seventy years of forced atheism and the uncertainty of the transitional period. Even a brief look at today's textbooks in this new course shows that religion is no longer represented as a 'sigh of the oppressed creature, the heart of a heartless world' and as 'the opium of the people', according to Marx (1992, p. 244), or as 'ideological necrophilia', according to Lenin (1976, pp. 121-124). On the contrary, the course has come to replace the former Soviet disdain of religion with its positive evaluation and especially focuses on Russia's four 'traditional' religions. As it is said in the opening lesson, common to all six textbooks, religious traditions represent Russia's 'cultural treasure', a repository of moral norms and values, grounded in 'eternal values of the good, the honorable, fairness, and mercy', and the spiritual foundation of Russia's people (e.g. Kuraev, 2012, p. 5). At the same time, a big question that my analysis raises is whether the goal of acculturating young Russians into these treasures is just a façade, a smokescreen covering up a hidden and a less benign political-ideological curriculum associated with this course.[4] Indeed, given the history and legacies of using culture-oriented courses for ideological indoctrination in Soviet schools, one would expect that the course in religious cultures has come to replace the outdated ideology of atheism and to fill the 'ideological vacuum' left after the collapse of communism with some other ideology or ideologies (Lisovskaya, 1999; Lisovskaya & Karpov, 1999).

Therefore, my final argument in this chapter is that the course structure and ideological content reflect the nature of the prevalent pattern of Russia's desecularization from above. Thus, along with teaching about religious traditions proper, the course promotes ideologies which are congruent with the interests of the ruling political and religious elites. These ideologies legitimize the power of the elites and existing institutional order. I use my analysis of religious culture textbooks to specify the core elements of these ideologies. The chapter concludes that religion's return to Russia's education, which represents a case of desecularization from above, is unlikely to profoundly change the ethos of Russian schooling or the religious beliefs and attitudes of the younger generation. Despite the victory of neo-traditionalist tendencies, Russian schools are likely to retain their largely a-religious ethos. The established formula for religious education may well turn out frail and shaky in the face of local and global socio-economic and political pressures and changes to come.

Theoretical Framework

I interpret my findings in the context of theoretical discussions of secularization and desecularization (or counter-secularization) processes. These debates point to desecularization trends as no less influential in the contemporary world than the secularization tendency that has long been emphasized by sociologists (Berger, 1999; Davie, 2000; Greeley, 2003). The important point for this discussion is that secularization is not a self-propelled and unavoidable modernizing trend (Smith, 2003). According to Karpov (2010), desecularization is not an automatic and inevitable outcome of the collapse of atheist or secularist regimes either. Rather, counter-secularization is a result of actions by specific social actors, and the resurgence of religion's influence on the public sphere is contingent on these actors' power and influence in society. Furthermore, depending on the location of relevant social actors and activists in the social structure, desecularization can develop from below (when it involves grassroots-level initiatives) and/or from above (when it is largely driven by ruling religious and secular elites). From this point of view, in the case of Russian education, both the initiatives to bring religion to schools and resistance to them have clearly emanated from secular and religious elites. Therefore, the quarter-century-long change in Russian education is described as a case of desecularization from above.

Next, it is proposed that this process has been contested and inconsistent. It has been *contested* because of the tensions and contradictions in elites' interests, goals and visions of the outcomes of religion's entry into education. This contestation showed in debates and struggles among the segments of these elites. It has been *inconsistent* because inconsistency is an integral characteristic of desecularization as a transitional process. Theoretically, religious resurgence is a lengthy transitional process, which develops unevenly in different social domains and levels of analysis. As a result, we may see inconsistencies and contradictions between persistent (or even growing) secularism in some domains and a resurgence of religion's influence in others (Karpov, 2010). In Russia, in particular, dramatic and speedy changes occurred in terms of religion's return to the public arena (de-privatization), including to education, in the rapprochement between formerly secularized institutions and religious norms, and in the proliferation of ordinary people affiliating with religions. At the same time, research has shown that an increase in the number of religiously affiliated has not been associated with a parallel increase in religious belief and its practice on the individual level (Karpov et al, 2012). From this perspective, the process of bringing religion back into Russian education can be understood as inconsistent desecularization, where prominent developments at the macro level of social institutions, organizations and top echelons of secular and religious actors and activists (elites) were not accompanied by corresponding changes in mass beliefs, attitudes and practices.

Furthermore, the pattern of desecularization from above has been consolidated in a 'desecularizing regime', as a 'politico-normative mode, in which desecularization is carried out, expanded, and sustained' (Karpov, 2010, p. 24). This mode is a product of a rapid and spirited rapprochement between Church and State, and a reflection of the converging interests, goals and visions of desecularization of religious and administrative elites (primarily members of the ROC MP). These interests and visions have been embodied in particular institutional arrangements, which required ideological support and legitimization. Given this agenda, a focus on the state-run schools as one of the primary 'ideological state apparatuses' (Althusser, 1971, pp. 127-186) and as a tool capable of efficiently disseminating these ideologies among the mass public is understandable. Moreover, the focus on the development and implementation of a course in religious cultures proper may be viewed as an attempt to find a model to replace the former, communist-style courses in social studies used to fulfill this ideological function. From this perspective, a critical look at the ideological content explicitly and implicitly promoted by the course textbooks gives us clues for understanding the nature of these ideologies. Indeed, as is well known from critical sociology of education, school textbooks are an ideal empirical object for a study of ideological discourse in education. Their ideological function was characterized as telling 'children what their elders want them to know' (FitzGerald, 1979, p. 47), and as representing 'to each generation of students a sanctioned version of human knowledge and culture' (De Castell, 1991, p. 78). Textbooks in religious culture courses may be expected to represent such a version, and as such are ideal material for research on ideologies of desecularization in education.

The 'Social Drama' of Desecularization of Russian State-run Schools: historical predispositions

What follows is a brief account of major developments and landmark events in the process of bringing religion into the schools, initiated and pushed forward from above. The focus is primarily on the history of the relationships between two principal agencies of desecularization of the school, Russia's federal government and the ROC MP's leadership, which have undergone considerable changes since the early 1990s. Roughly, one could specify *six stages* in the development of their relationships, described below. At the same time, these relationships developed in the context of pre-Soviet and Soviet historical legacies, which should be considered in order to better understand the struggles around the issues of religion in education and the dynamics of the Church-State interaction. Before going into the post-communist developments, at least the following three historical patterns of Church-State-school relations in Russia need to be briefly highlighted.

First, within the framework of the Church and State symbiotic relationships in pre-communist Russia, the ROC MP was not an independent player in the arena of education, and its educational impact had been mostly through state-controlled structures. However, the foundational role of Orthodoxy was consistently affirmed by the State as one of the pillars of the Russian empire, and challenges to the ROC domination were often harshly suppressed.

Second, the dependency of the Church on the State was further strengthened under communism, when, following the nearly complete suppression of religion, Stalin had opted to re-establish a fully controlled Church in 1943. This change allowed the elites of the ROC MP and other officially permitted confessions to live in what the religious dissident Zoya Krakhmal'nikova (1989) once called 'the sweet captivity' – that is, a complete surrender to the Soviet state control in exchange for privileged (even if unofficially) status and comfortable living. Importantly, the upper echelons of the ROC MP's current hierarchy are still mostly the people who rose to positions of influence in the Church under communism and have cooperated closely with the State (including, among its other branches, security services).

Third, while mandatory religious instruction existed in pre-Soviet schools, it never was part of a system of mass compulsory and universal schooling. Such a system was fully developed only under communism, and official atheism was its inalienable element. Thus, unlike some European nations, Russia lacks historical experience of religious instruction in its state-run system of mass compulsory schooling. At the same time, the Soviet school included a thoroughly developed system of indoctrination into the official ideology of the State. It is reasonable to expect that this system has developed considerable inertia, manifest in the persistence of the pedagogy and practices of indoctrination, even though the official ideology has changed. As some commentators suggested, this inertia results in the attempts to replace the Soviet-era atheist indoctrination with compulsory religious instruction (Bunimovich, 2004).

The reference to these legacies is not to suggest a rigidly deterministic path dependency model of the development of Russian education. However, as shown below, these historical patterns have re-emerged in the course of educational reforms in Russia.

Towards State-School-Church Rapprochement: stages, struggles and main actors

Stage 1

From the end of communism to the mid-1990s was the time of romantic and enthusiastic experimentation with religious education by Yeltsin's government in the spirit of the newly acquired freedom and openness. At this stage, a legal framework was put in place providing for a secular state, secular education in its schools, and freedom of religion in society. This framework was reflected in the 1990 Law on Religion, the 1993 Constitution and the 1992 Law on Education. The liberal provisions of these laws strongly resemble the US model of Church-State-school relations.

Moreover, reform ideology swung from notorious Soviet atheism to enthusiastic proclamations of the positive role religion should play in the upbringing of post-Soviet youth (Halstead, 1992). Russian education was proclaimed 'open for Christian values' and western Christian (primarily American Protestant) leaders were invited to Russia for assistance without the ROC MP's agreement (Van Den Bercken, 1994; Glanzer, 1999; Deyneka, 2004). The Church leadership perceived these developments as an intrusion of western churches into its 'canonical territory' (Glanzer, 1999, pp. 300-303), and already in the early 1990s, the Church began slowly but steadily preparing to expand its educational influence on society. In 1990, the Department for Religious Education and Catechization was established, and in June 1992 and the first big conference on religious education was organized, where the question of religious education in state-run schools was first raised (Van Den Bercken, 1994, pp. 174-176).

Stage 2

From 1995 to 1998-1999, Russian society lived through the times of declining economic expectations and trust in the government, which allowed the ROC MP to significantly consolidate its power over state and educational institutions. By the mid-1990s, communists and nationalists asserted their political influence in the Russian parliament. The democratic euphoria of the early 1990s was over, and attempts to emulate western institutions were confronted by the ROC MP. A landmark victory for the ROC MP at this stage was the ratification of the 1997 Law on the Freedom of Conscience and Religious Associations that restricted religious freedom for 'non-traditional' religions (including most Protestant denominations), while granting a privileged status to Orthodoxy, Islam, Buddhism and Judaism as 'traditional' confessions. The law also included provisions for religious instruction by religious organizations in state schools outside of the framework of the required curriculum, which de facto opened their doors to religious intervention. Needless to say, this provision put most western churches out of school reach, while privileging 'traditional confessions', of which the ROC MP claimed to be the 'first among equals', to use a Soviet-era euphemism.

Stage 3

From 1998-1999 to 2004, the Church-State-school rapprochement developed in full swing. In 1998, a profound economic crisis shook Russia, wiping out the remnants of confidence in pro-western reforms and reformers, and reinforcing mass nostalgia for the good old times. Putin's ascent to power in 1999-2000 marked the end of the decade of radical reforms, including those in education.

As a reputed Orthodox believer, Putin remarked that the State must remove the wall of Church-State separation (*Prepodavanie osnov*, 2002). The culmination of the Church-State-school rapprochement at that period was the broadly debated 2002 decision by the Minister of Education, Filippov (in office 1998-2004), to offer a Fundamentals of Orthodox Culture (*Osnovy Pravoslavnoi Kul'tury*) course in the upper grades of secondary state-run schools. Formally, the course was supposed to be an elective and culture-oriented. Yet, as many critics noted, this course and its first textbook by Borodina (2002) did amount to de facto introduction of mandatory Orthodox religious instruction.

The ROC MP leadership fully supported the government's efforts to reinstate instruction in the Orthodox faith, and argued that teaching religion did not contradict the Constitution and the laws on secular education and/or freedom of religious expression (Mitropolit Kirill, 2002).

Stage 4

From Spring, 2004 to 2007, thinly veiled desecularization attempts at the federal level seemed to be abruptly abandoned in favor of a secularist view of religion's place in the state-run schooling. Thus, the new Minister of Education and Science, Fursenko (in office 2004-2012), proclaimed that students should study history of world religions rather than a particular religion. While noting that Orthodoxy's special role in Russian history should be acknowledged, Fursenko insisted that teaching exclusively the Orthodox culture course was out of the question (*Ministr Fursenko*, 2004), and charged a group of scholars from the Russian Academy of Sciences with the task of preparing a new textbook in the history of world religions (Agranovich & Shits, 2004).

Although at this stage a secularist tendency seemed to prevail at the federal level, previously made decisions had already had serious consequences at the regional level. Thus, while the Ministry of Education and Science in Moscow was promoting a course in the history of various religions as part of the overall secular curriculum, 26 out of Russia's 89 regions had already introduced the Fundamentals of Orthodox Culture course (Bunimovich, 2004). Thus, since 2006, it was taught in 11,184 schools of 15 regions of Russia as part of their regional curricular standard (*K dvadtsatiletiju*, 2011), which in practice often turned into blatant instruction in the Orthodox faith.

These developments on the regional level had been systematically supported by the ROC MP leadership, and strongly opposed by the non-Orthodox, especially Muslim leaders (*Mir Religii*, 2002; Lisovskaya & Karpov, 2005, pp. 292-295). These disagreements often took the form of heated public debates. The atmosphere was getting tense and the time to make the 'final decision' regarding religious coursework had come.

Stage 5

2007 to September 2012 stage was characterized by intense struggles between the advocates of teaching religion in schools and its opponents, who construed their opposition as resistance to 'clericalization' of Russian society (*Presidentu Rossiiskoi Federatsii*, 2007). In this debate, President Putin lined up with the ROC MP and the traditionalists in their support for religious culture courses. At the same time, he chilled out the ROC's hegemonic claim to an exceptional role in the religious curriculum. Thus, in 2007 he made a public statement that all traditional religions were as important for Russia's security as its nuclear shield, elevating the status of religious education to the level of a matter of national security (*Putin schitaet*, 2007). It was also the time of curtailing the regional educational and religious administrations' freedom and initiative in shaping the religious education curriculum. All further deliberations regarding the expediency of religious education in secular schools were brought to an end. Under Putin's rule, regionalism has been effectively replaced with the Soviet-style centralized structure of administrative and ideological control of education, and the State-Church-school relationships were both strengthened and centralized. Thus, in 2007, by amendments to the education law, local and regional curricular standards within general secondary education were eliminated, leaving the state-run schools bound exclusively by the federal curricular requirement. A new curricular division labeled *Spiritual-Moral Development of Russia's Citizens*, developed in collaboration between the Ministry of Education and Science and the Department of Religious Education and Catechization of the ROC MP, was added to this federal curricular requirement. In 2009, the first course within this area, called the Fundamentals of Religious Cultures and Secular Ethics (FRCSE), was included as a mandatory component within this federal requirement for general secondary education. The course was approbated in 21 regions in 2009-2011, and in 2012 it was launched in all state-run schools in Grade 4 for one hour per week.

Stage 6

Since September 2012, after the course had been introduced, the Church-State-school alliance has continued to develop and strengthen. Thus, the ROC MP started actively lobbying for expanding religious education to the whole course of secondary education (i.e. Grades 1 through 11) (Orthodox 'Bomb' for Russian School, 2016). These efforts were supported by the government. Thus, the Minister of Education and Science, Livanov (in office 2012 to August 2016), who opposed such an expansion, was replaced by Olga Vasilieva, a high-ranking functionary in Putin's administration responsible for the development of the program of patriotic education, and a historian of Church-State relationships. Not surprisingly, her appointment was welcomed with great enthusiasm by the leaders of the ROC MP (Putin Chooses Religious Studies Scholar, 2016).

*****

As shown by this brief historical account, until recently, the 'social drama' of desecularization of schooling has been developing gradually, from stage to stage. It was contested and propelled by the struggles among the top political and religious elites, whose educational orientations oscillated between a secularist and a neo-traditionalist paradigm. The primary actors in this drama included the Putin government, the ROC MP leadership, regional secular and religious bureaucracies, influential educational administrators, and some non-Orthodox, primarily Muslim, leaders. The elites' struggles were associated with their conflicting interests, goals and visions of desecularization, briefly addressed in the next section of the chapter. At the same time, in the course of these struggles, the common interests and goals of both elites have been clarified and subsequently crystallized in particular institutional arrangements. The course in religious cultures established in 2012 represents the end product of this process as an institutional arrangement congruent with the intersection of the interests, goals and visions of desecularization of the school.

The approval of the course has crowned the history of the State and the Church coming together again, after a brief period of independence from each other in the early 1990s, and forming an alliance, similar to the pre-Soviet and Soviet history of these relationships, when the Church was the State's ally and also at its mercy. The rebuilt Church-State alliance seems functional for both players and may be expected to survive for a while. In this case, the State will continue doing favors to the Church while keeping the upper hand over it and the Church will continue to serve as the State's handmaid as long as their interests coincide.

Now let us briefly discuss the core interests, goals and visions of desecularization of education, which guided the efforts and policies of the key players involved in this process.

Elites' Interests, Goals and Visions of Desecularization

As was already mentioned, secular and religious proponents of religious education in state-run schools expressed their hopes that bringing the younger generation of Russians closer to their spiritual and cultural heritage would help overcome the moral crisis of post-communism. Although such hopes may have been true on the part of politicians and religious activists, more pragmatic latent and less idealistic interests and motivations that incited the key political and religious actors to join their efforts in bringing religion back to the state schools should not be disregarded in the context of our discussion. Certainly, these interests and motivations have not been explicitly articulated in the ROC MP official documents or declarations of Putin's administration. However, within the Weberian tradition of understanding (*Verstehen*) or interpretation of social action, the likely motivations behind these actors' moves can be discerned, and reconstructed.

First, for the ROC MP's national and regional leadership, the introduction of religious education was a way to resolve some of its most urgent and closely intertwined problems at the taxpayers' expense. These included preservation and expansion of its flock in the context of growing competition for influence on the newly opened and diversifying religious market. Indeed, sociological studies have consistently shown that while the Church as a government-supported organization grew considerably since the collapse of official atheism, this growth was not matched by a similar development of parishes as communities, capable of effective religious education of their members. Thus, in 2005, fifteen years after the collapse of official atheism, regular church attendance ('at least once a month') was in single digits (Mitrokhin & Sibireva, 2007) and did not exceed 10% of Russians (Karpov et al, 2012). This precluded the formation of vibrant parish life and any sizable growth of Sunday schools. When, in a country that boasts a deeply Orthodox culture and spirituality, most parents do not show up for services (even once a month), it is unrealistic to expect their children to learn the fundamentals of their ancestral faith. Under these circumstances, the state-run schools should have been viewed by the ROC MP as a 'free' instrument for the upbringing of the new generations of its members. In addition, let us not forget that, historically, the ROC MP did not develop a culture of independent educational initiatives. Thus, in a sense, by seeking to use the state-run schools, the Church re-established a traditional political pattern. Moreover, this focus on the state-run schools was an effective way for the ROC MP to also win the competition with Protestant newcomers, and with some dissenting Orthodox groups, many of whom became politically radicalized and challenged the privileged status of the Moscow

Patriarchate (Papkova, 2011). In this regard, the case of the ROC MP fits into a trend common for other dominant churches in post-communist European societies described by Ramet (2014), when they chose to rely upon the State and its schools to win the competition on the newly opened religious market and secure their influential position.

For Putin and his team, the ROC MP represented a valuable lever for legitimization and consolidation of their power. He emphasized the inseparability of the links, mutual national interests and interdependence among Russia's State and its traditional religions in multiple declarations and speeches at the meetings with the leaders of these religions (e.g. *Stenogramma*, 2012; Putin, 2013a). Among these religions, he 'habitually emphasized the centrality of Orthodoxy to Russia's historical, spiritual and political development' (Knox, 2005, p. 129). It was already mentioned above that the State has historically used Orthodoxy to consolidate its control of society. Putin's formulation that religious education is a matter of national security is telling in this respect (e.g. Archbishop Ioann et al, 2005; *Putin schitaet*, 2007). Additionally, in the context of conservative-nationalist reorientation of the ideology and politics of the Russian State under Putin's rule, promoting Russian nationalism and loyalty to the State by means of religious studies in its schools could have been perceived as a substitute for the Soviet-era ideological indoctrination. Moreover, the view of religious education as a highly promising tool for endorsing neo-imperialist and chauvinist ideologies could have been adopted by Putin's administration after his ambitions to rebuild the Russian empire had been revealed in Moscow's ruthless suppression of the Chechen independence movement, the 2008 war against Georgia, the annexation of Crimea and the military assault on eastern Ukraine (Karpov, 2013).

After all, the ROC MP, like most Orthodox Churches, has historically emphasized its national identity and inseparable link to the imperial State, be it that of pre-revolutionary Russia or the Bolshevik Soviet Empire. The desire to re-create the imperial pattern of the privileged status of Orthodoxy among Russia's other faiths with the State's help already showed in the ROC MP's pushing for the 1997 Law. Perhaps even more importantly, about half of all parishes of the ROC MP are in Ukraine, and any loss of control of Ukraine would dramatically shrink the size of the Church and drastically reduce its standing in global Orthodoxy (Chapnin, 2016). Thus, the Putin regime's neo-imperial aspirations resonated with the ROC MP's ecclesial interests. In this sense, attempts to bring Orthodoxy back to the state-run school could have been perceived by Putin's government as the restoration of a valuable historical tradition and a tool for legitimating its rule and policies. From the ROC MP's perspective, an alliance with the State and assistance in its neo-imperial aspiration and policies could have been viewed by the Church leadership as a sure path to its prosperity and stability.

At the same time, as the history of State-Church relations in Russia has shown for centuries, Putin and his allies were probably apprehensive about giving the Church too much influence in society. Such an approach was rooted in the centuries-long tradition established by pre-Soviet and Soviet governments that used to hold the Church as one of their 'branches responsible for Orthodox confession' (Kyrlezhev, 2004). Religious associations have never entertained a status independent from the State in Russia, including after the collapse of communism and their formal liberation from state control. For example, to be legitimate, all religious associations, including Russian Orthodox parishes, were required to register with the Ministry of Justice since the 1997 Law (Knox, 2005). According to Mitrokhin, a renowned scholar of the Russian Orthodox Church, 'Russia's politicians and statesmen do not mind viewing the ROC MP as part of the country's cultural heritage and even as one of the symbols of Russia's statehood. ... However, when making personnel decisions or developing socially significant projects hardly any of the state officials would consider the opinions of the Church representatives' (Mitrokhin, 2004, p. 235).

After having secured their control of the parliament (*Duma*), media and business, Putin's administration needed an influential Church, but only if it was fully under the State's control; they needed the Church as an instrument of their power, not as a parallel center of power. It is not surprising, therefore, that once Putin's re-election for the second term in 2004 was certain, his government's support shifted abruptly from teaching Orthodox culture to teaching history of religions. This, however, as we have seen, changed again once the regime sought further consolidation and geopolitical expansion (2007-2012). In addition, Putin's administration had to pay attention to western reactions to its activities, at least until the occupation of Crimea in 2014. It did not like to create the impression that it was willing to violate its own constitution by desecularizing the state school and violating ethnic and religious minorities' rights (Lisovskaya & Karpov, 2010).

Also, Putin's administration had to consider the Islamic factor in Russia and the possible consequences of its underestimation. Muslims have been too large and politically too important a minority in Russia to have their right to teach Islam in the predominantly Muslim regions disregarded (Putin, 2013b). Given the rise of a radical Islamist wing in Chechen resistance and elsewhere in the North Caucasus, denying this right might have been a greater risk for Putin and his team than granting it. Finally, Putin's government had to respond (at least initially) to pressures coming from human rights groups and journalists sympathetic to their causes who publicly expressed concerns regarding the clericalization of education.

Thus, the outcomes of the struggles surrounding the introduction of religious education largely depended on the intersection of major interests and goals of Putin's government and the ROC MP's leadership. Of these, Putin's government represented the strongest player and the ROC MP its strongest ally. The final decision on the establishment of the course in its present shape was made within a narrow circle of both state and religious elites whose interests, goals and visions of how the school should be desecularized had largely converged. The main point of convergence was in filling the ideological void created by the collapse of communism with an ideology that would strengthen political power and secure the status of both the State and the ROC MP. Based on these considerations, the core elements of this ideology may be expected to include the values of Russian nationalism, imperial greatness, privileged status of the ROC MP and control of religious minorities. As shown in the last section, analysis of textbooks in religious cultures supports these expectations.

At the same time, the topic of religious education did not seem to have concerned parents, and there were not many signs of their mobilization on this front despite the growing presence of religions and their influence on Russian society. Studies and official enrollment statistics (e.g. Palkin, 2002; Lisovskaya & Karpov, 2010; *Rossijane vysskazalis'*, 2013) show that popular support for teaching the religious cultures course, and for Orthodox culture in particular, has been weak. It has been in steady decline since the course was launched. A little more than half of Russia's students took any religious cultures course module in 2009-2013, and steadily increasing numbers of them have been selecting secular ethics. Thus, in Russia, unlike in some post-communist countries (e.g. Poland), desecularization of education has not been initiated or driven by the grassroots movements of parents or teachers. It has never gained popular support and there are no signs that it will. Despite massive religious propaganda and pressure on parents to select the Orthodox culture module, the majority of them retain a secular conception of state education and resist indoctrination of their children into Orthodoxy. Given this, the process of desecularization of the state schools has not only been contested, it has also been inconsistent. In other words, an incessant promotion of religious education by political and religious hierarchs existed side by side with an apathetic and uninvolved general public.

The outcomes of the elites' struggles are reflected in the ideological content and structure of the school course briefly outlined below. Despite the lack of public engagement with these struggles, a sizable proportion of Russian children has been already exposed to religious studies courses, and the pressure is mounting to expand the courses' reach. Thus, the innovations are bound to have a lasting impact on the nation's future, while the Russian people remain, as they so often have throughout their history, silent.

Ideological Content of the Course

The argument above suggests that the course established in 2012 came to replace the ideology of official atheism with some other ideology or ideologies. Furthermore, I theorized that the new ideology would have the function of legitimizing the new desecularizing regime and its institutional arrangements. Thus, I hypothesize that the course was meant to instill a constellation of ideological beliefs and orientations into the impressionable minds of the new generations of Russians, which would back up the current political and religious elites' interests and goals and their struggle to maintain, strengthen and expand their power. To restate, the analysis was supposed to answer the following question: what are those ideological symbols and value-ideas which are explicitly, and, most importantly, implicitly promoted by the new subject area in *Spiritual-Moral Education of Russia's Citizens*, and by its first course on the Fundamentals of Religious Cultures and Secular Ethics? To answer the question, I conducted discourse analysis of five modular textbooks in the fundamentals of Orthodox, Muslim, Judaic, Buddhist and world religious cultures. The textbook in secular ethics was not included in this analysis. The following value-ideas (Krippendorf, 1980) and ideological constructs implicitly promoted by these textbooks have been identified.

A central role within the textbooks' representations belongs to the symbols of Russian *nationalism*. The textbooks glorify the Russian nation and instruct students to feel patriotic and loyal to it. Strengthening patriotic feelings of belonging and loyalty to a nation understood as an 'imagined community' (Anderson, 1991) has been a common practice around the world. However, much depends on what particular symbols, values and ideas a nation is going to be shaped and united by. What kind of community is 'imagined' indeed, to use Benedict Anderson's definition of a nation? What image is created and instilled by the schools? What are the boundaries and who is included and excluded from this image? How is patriotism defined and what should students learn to love and be loyal to? What are those cornerstone ideas and values, based on which the community of people should come together and act? Finally, how does a religious education course contribute to creating this imagined community?

The limits of this chapter do not allow me to go into detail about each of these questions. However, they have been examined in detail elsewhere (Lisovskaya, 2016). In a nutshell, the ideology of nationalism promoted by the textbooks is built around the following core ideas: (1) loyalty to the State and its causes; (2) identification with the common spiritual heritage rooted in Orthodoxy; (3) nostalgia for Russia's imperial past and implicit support for the re-establishment of the empire within its pre-1917 borders; and (4) support for the privileged status of Orthodoxy among all other faiths and the corresponding relegation of their status to the level of ethno-religious minorities at the outskirts of Russia, as was the case in the former empire. Now let us briefly discuss each of these ideas.

First, the textbooks emphasize patriotism and a strong feeling of belonging and loyalty to a community, which is construed as an inseparable family of peoples unified by a shared heroic past and a common glorious spiritual tradition. Through the stories about the heroism of believers during various military campaigns led by the state rulers, students learn to feel patriotic and loyal to the community often referred to as their Fatherland or Motherland. They learn that being patriotic means being at service to this community and ready to sacrifice life for its causes. According to Anderson's definition, nation is not only an imagined but also a *sovereign* community (1983, p. 7). What form of sovereignty is at the core of the nationalism promoted by the textbooks? Analysis suggests that they emphasize loyalty to the Russian State first and foremost. For example, throughout the textbooks, the word 'State' is used interchangeably with the words 'Fatherland' or 'Motherland', to whom students should feel patriotic.

Second, students are also taught to identify and share a spiritual tradition represented as a foundation of the Russian nation and common to all Russians. Anderson emphasized that a common mythology must be in place to create a nation (1983, pp. 187-206). According to the textbooks' interpretations, and especially those of the Orthodox and world religious cultures textbooks, this tradition is unquestionably Orthodox in its nature and origins, and is rooted in a highly idealized imagery of 'The Holy Rus'', 'the presumed golden age of faith and a paradise lost' (Karpov, 2013, p. 23). In a multi-religious Russia, such an idea is potentially controversial. However, none of the textbooks on non-Orthodox cultures challenges it. It may be concluded that these emphases on the ideology of nationalism built upon the symbols of love and loyalty to the State, and identity with a common, Orthodox-based spiritual tradition are in congruence with the goals of consolidating the nation around its state and religious leaders (primarily, the ROC MP). As the ROC MP's social doctrine states, the Church and the State must consolidate their efforts against unwanted internal and external 'spiritual and cultural intervention' (Mchedlov, 2002, p. 390), or, to use Putin's words, to enhance Russia's 'spiritual security' (*Putin schitaet*, 2007).

Third, the ideology of nationalism is saturated with the symbols of imperialism, which are in congruence with the neo-imperialist expansionism of Russia's current leadership and its ideology. The neo-imperial facets of the ideology of nationalism show in how the textbooks construe the limits and boundaries of the contemporary Russian nation. Interestingly, the textbooks do not use the word 'nation' [*natsiia* -нация] proper. Instead they use the Russian word *narod* [народ], which has multiple meanings in the Russian language: it can be translated as a 'nation,' 'people' or an 'ethnic group'. Thus, saying 'Russian *narod*' may mean Russian nation, Russian people or Russian ethnicity. Therefore, it is not clear what the textbooks mean when they declare that *narod* is one of the objects of patriotic love and loyalty. Instead, students are instructed to love what is described as 'our country' or 'our land' or simply Russia. As is known to the students of nationalism, an important aspect of Anderson's definition of a nation is that it is a community imagined as inherently *limited* (1991, p. 7). In this respect, it is interesting to notice that the textbooks in religious cultures construe the limits and boundaries of the land in a very peculiar way. Thus, throughout the textbooks, 'our country' or 'our land' is modelled as an entity outside specific historical context and beyond the geographical details of the contemporary Russian Federation. Thus, the textbooks in Orthodoxy and in world religious cultures tend to blur the distinctions between ancient Rus' (which nowadays is the territory of independent Ukraine), the Russian Empire (which used to include Poland and Finland), the Soviet Union (which included such presently independent states as the Baltic republics), and the contemporary Russian Federation, referring to either one as '*our country*' or '*our* land' [emphases mine]. By this discursive fuzziness, the textbooks ideologically appropriate the territories that are no longer part of Russia, and aim at generating a distorted image of the actual map of the nation in the students' minds. The image created is one of Russia as a legitimate owner of such lands as Ukraine (and not just Crimea or eastern Ukraine), the Baltic States, Moldova and Georgia. Such a representation implicitly justifies Russia's present or future claims on these territories.

Finally, the last set of ideological symbols promoted by the textbooks deals with the issue of religious diversity in Russia. As I explained in detail elsewhere (Lisovskaya, 2016), the course structure and its content perpetuate an imperial pattern of state domination and toleration of Russia's religious minorities. They also promote the notion of the hierarchy of religions, with the ROC MP at the top of this hierarchy. What pattern is this? In the Russian empire, religious minorities were tolerated by the State and could co-exist along with the dominant Orthodox Church only to the extent that they practiced their religions within clearly defined geographical boundaries, did not claim any privileged status, and did not create any trouble to the central powers. Within this ethno-religious-territorial structure, the ROC continued to exercise its dominant role and did not have to worry about religious competition for the souls of its existing or potential adherents. All ethnic Russians were assigned to the Orthodox Church by default as all other religious minorities were confined to their respective ethnic and territorial entities. Tatars and Chechen were to be Muslims, Kalmyks were, as if by birth, Buddhists, and so on. In imperial Russia, this structure guaranteed relative security and stability to the ROC and to the religious minorities – it conferred the geographically limited right to exist and practice their faith, including opening religious schools. In the officially atheist Soviet Union, all religions were suppressed and the issue of religious diversity lost its importance. Furthermore, the legacy of the imperial ethno-territoriality of religions was considerably undermined by the geographic and social mobility fueled by communist industrialization and the politics of forced migration. Yet, after the collapse of communism, the ROC MP opted for a neo-imperial model of toleration that would restore a privileged status to Orthodoxy (Karpov, 2013).

Analysis shows that the textbooks promote ideologies which support neo-imperial toleration of religious diversity and the ROC MP's privileged status. Thus, the Orthodox, Islamic and world religious cultures textbooks instill the ideology of ethnodoxy, which rigidly links religious and ethnic identities (Karpov et al, 2012). Students receive a message that being Russian means being an Orthodox, and that being a Tatar or a Chechen, for example, means being a Muslim. There is no mention of a possibility of crossing these ethno-religious borders. These assumptions are promulgated matter-of-factly, almost in passing, and usually through stories about individuals and through the textbooks' illustrations. Moreover, by offering the choice of only four modules in the so-called traditional (for Russia) religions, the course also propagates the view that some religions belong to Russia and others do not. The latter, for example, include Roman Catholics or Lutherans, who established their presence in the country long before communism and played a significant role in the development of Russian culture and society. Furthermore, only particular, sanctioned versions of Orthodoxy or Islam are included in the textbooks, excluding those which are not in agreement with the dominant trends within these respective faiths. Thus, by including some and excluding other religions or their versions, the course effectively suppresses external and internal religious pluralism, indicating to the students that there are right and wrong religions. By teaching the ideology of ethnodoxy (a rigid fusion of religious and ethnic identities), the course provides ideological support to the (neo)imperial mode of toleration of religious minorities by the State, and by so doing continues to strengthen the privileged status of the ROC MP among all faiths.

Conclusion

After more than two decades of intense political struggles and deliberations that followed the collapse of official atheism, Russia's approach to religious education's place in state-run schools has ultimately crystallized. The Fundamentals of Religious Cultures and Secular Ethics course became part of a required curriculum in 2012. This chapter has offered a generalized historical overview and a theoretical interpretation of this quarter-of-a-century-long process and its outcomes. We have seen that the process unfolded as an intense 'social drama' in which participant actors developed, promulgated and acted upon competing visions of religion's place in the school. This change was initiated and propelled primarily by the top political, administrative and religious elites (mainly the ROC MP), who went through a process of gradual, multi-stage rapprochement and clarification of their common interests, goals and visions of desecularization of Russian society and education. Thus, in terms of contemporary sociological theory, religion's re-entry into Russian state schools is a case of *contested* desecularization from above. The chapter has shown that the elites' orientations and policy choices oscillated between a neo-traditionalist and, ultimately, neo-imperial paradigm that privileges Orthodoxy, and a secularist one that seeks to distance education from any religion. The inauguration of the new course and the current efforts to expand its reach to the full course of general secondary education have heralded the supremacy of the neo-traditionalist and neo-imperial paradigm.

Furthermore, the reintroduction of religion into the Russian school is a case of *inconsistent* desecularization. This means that, while the aforesaid elites actively promoted desecularization, the masses remained relatively inert and uninvolved.

In terms of political-ideological outcomes of desecularization of Russian schools, my discourse analysis of five textbooks in religious cultures shows that the content of the course reflects the nature and functions of Russia's prevalent pattern of desecularization from above. Thus, along with teaching about religious traditions proper, the course promotes an ideology which is congruent with the interests and goals of the ruling political and religious elites and legitimizes the new political regime and its symbiosis with the Church. Analyses show that the core ideology promoted by the textbooks is *nationalism*, as loyalty to an 'imagined community', to use Anderson's definition of a nation (1983). Granted, schools all over the world are routinely used to teach loyalty to national values. However, the political, social and moral outcomes of such an education depend on the ideas and beliefs promoted by the school as the foundation of that nation which students are encouraged to love and be loyal to. In the case of Russia, textbook nationalism is saturated with symbols of imperialism, the cult of the State, loyalty to its policies, and the mythology of 'Holy Russia' without borders, and, as such, it is congruent with the neo-imperialistic expansionism of Russia's current political regime and its ideology. The course also perpetuates the notion of a neo-imperial, state domination of religious minorities, and the hierarchy of religions, with the ROC MP at its top. It promotes the ideology of ethnodoxy, which rigidly fuses ethnic and religious identities, and creates a negative perception of ethnically 'alien' faiths. These ideological symbols form a hidden curriculum of the 'spiritual-moral' development of future citizens of Russia. It seems that the system of indoctrination into the official ideology of the State practiced within Soviet education for seventy years has returned. Judging by the content of this hidden curriculum, the course in religious cultures is unlikely to contribute to the goals of facilitating inter-cultural peace and providing equitable and inclusive quality education for all students as envisioned by the Sustainable Development Goals (SDGs) set by the United Nations. If successful, the indoctrination of students into loyalty to the current State and its neo-imperialistic policies would shape a citizen of Russia who supports state expansionism and militarism. Indoctrination into the ideas of state domination of religious minorities and relegating them to a low social status while privileging Orthodoxy against other faiths would effectively exclude the minority students from active social participation and inhibit their equitable development. If the idea of ethno-religious fusion is instilled in students' consciousness, the outlook in terms of conciliation and prevention of inter-ethnic and inter-religious conflicts in Russia will be bleak.

From a comparative perspective, the case of Russia's desecularization from above shows that political, social, ideological and moral outcomes of providing religious education in state schools depend on the socio-political and moral context in which such an education is developed and implemented. As the experience of liberal European democracies has shown, establishment of religious studies in the context of respect for international law, human dignity and minority rights may be in congruence with the goals of peaceful and inclusive education. This is not the case, however, when the introduction of religious education, even from above, takes place in the context of an increasingly authoritarian political system and degradation of civil society.

Notes

[1] The term 'traditional religions' has been used in Russia to refer to Orthodoxy, (official) Islam, Buddhism and Judaism, that were given a privileged status *vis-à-vis* other religions by the 1997 Law on the Freedom of Consciousness and Religious Associations.

[2] The textbooks include: *Fundamentals of Orthodox Culture* (Kuraev), *Fundamentals of Islamic Culture* (Latyshina & Murtazin), *Fundamentals of Judaic Culture* (Chlenov, Mindrina, & Glotser), *Fundamentals of Buddhist Culture* (Chimitdorzhiev), *Fundamentals of World Religious Cultures* (Beglov, Saplina, Tokareva, &Yarlykapov) and *Fundamentals of Secular Ethics* (no author).

[3] The 'social drama' approach has already been creatively applied to the analysis of desecularization in Russia by Schroeder and Karpov (2013) and Schroeder (2016).

[4] This chapter is based only on the analysis of five textbooks on the Fundamentals of Religious Cultures. The sixth textbook, on the Fundamentals of Secular Ethics, was not included in the analysis.

References

Agranovich, M. & Shits, M. (2004) Malankara vera [Little faith], *Rossiiskaia Gazeta*, 30 June, 3514. http://www.rg.ru/2004/06/30/istoria-religii-printable.html

Althusser, L. (1971) *Lenin and Philosophy and Other Essays*, trans. B. Brewster. New York: Monthly Review Press.

Anderson, B. (1991) *Imagined Communities: reflections on the origin and spread of nationalism*. New York: Verso.

Archbishop Ioann (Popov), Voz'mitel', A. & Khvylia-Olinter, A. (2005) *Dukhovnaia Bezopasnost'*. Moscow: RAN.

Berger, P.L. (1999) The Desecularization of the World: a global overview, in P.L. Berger (Ed.) *The Desecularization of the World: resurgent religion and world politics*, pp. 1-18. Grand Rapids, MI: W.B. Eerdmans.

Borodina, A.V. (2002) *Osnovy pravoslavnoi kul'tury* [Fundamentals of Orthodox culture]. Moscow: Pokrov.

Bunimovich, E. (2004) Pedagog: Vsio te zhe grabli [Pedagogue: all the same rake], *Roditel'skoe Sobranie*, 2. http://www.yabloko.ru/Publ/2004/2004_05/040515_rs_bun_pravoslavie.html

Chapnin, S. (2016) Tserkov' budet meniatsia v storonu prostoty [Church will change in the direction of simplicity]. 5 January. http://www.rosbalt.ru/moscow/2016/01/05/1476536.html

Davie, G. (2000) *Religion in Modern Europe: a memory mutates.* Oxford: Oxford University Press.

De Castell, S. (1991) Literacy as Disempowerment: the role of documentary texts, in D.P. Ericson (Ed.) *Philosophy of Education.* Normal, IL: Philosophy of Education Society.

Deyneka, A. (2004) The Russian Connection, in P. Johnson (Ed.) *The CoMission*, pp. 153-165. Chicago, IL: Moody.

FitzGerald, F. (1979) *America Revised: history schoolbooks in the twentieth century.* New York: Vintage Press.

Glanzer, P. (1999) Teaching Christian Ethics in Russian Public Schools: the testing of Russia's Church-State boundaries, *Journal of Church and State*, 41, 285-305. https://doi.org/10.1093/jcs/41.2.285

Greeley, A. (2003) *Religion in Europe at the End of the Second Millennium: a sociological profile.* New Brunswick, NJ: Transaction.

Halstead, M. (1992) Recent Development in Religious Education in Russia, *British Journal of Religious Education*, 14, 99-106. https://doi.org/10.1080/0141620920140206

Karpov, V. (2010) Desecularization: a conceptual framework, *Journal of Church and State*, 52(2), 1-39. https://doi.org/10.1093/jcs/csq058

Karpov, V. (2013) The Social Dynamics of Russia's Desecularization, *Religion, State, and Society*, 41(3), 254-283. https://doi.org/10.1080/09637494.2013.821805

Karpov, V., Lisovskaya, E. & Barry, D. (2012) Ethnodoxy: how popular ideologies fuse religious and ethnic identities, *Journal for the Scientific Study of Religion*, 51(4), 638-655. https://doi.org/10.1111/j.1468-5906.2012.01678.x

K dvadtsatiletiju uchrezhdeniia Otdela religioznogo obrazovaniia i katekhizatsii Russkoi Pravosloavnoi Tserkvi [To the twentieth anniversary of the establishment of the Department of Religious Education and Catechization] (2011) *Russkaia Pravoslavnaia Tserkov'*, 1 February. http://www.patriarchia.ru/db/text/1399119.html

Knox, Z. (2005) *Russian Society and the Orthodox Church: religion in Russia after communism.* London: Routledge.

Krakhmal'nikova, Z. (1989) *Gor'kie plody sladkogo plena* [Bitter fruits of sweet captivity]. Montreal: Monastery Press.

Krippendorf, K. (1980) *Content Analysis: an introduction to its methodology.* Beverly Hills, CA: SAGE.

Kuraev, A. (2012) *Fundamentals of Orthodox Culture.* Moscow: Prosveshchenie.

Kyrlezhev, A. (2004) *Russkaia pravoslavnaia Tserkov' pered problemoi modernizatsii* [Russian Orthodox Church in front of modernization problem]. 17 February. http://www.sova-center.ru/religion/publications/state-confessional/2004/02/d1736/

Lenin, V. (1976) Letter to Maxim Gorky, *Collected Works*, vol. 35, pp. 121-124, trans. A. Rothstein. Moscow: Progress Publishers (original work published 1924).

Lisovskaya, E. (1999) The Dogmatism of Ideology: a content analysis of communist and postcommunist Russian textbooks, in N. McGinn & E. Epstein (Eds) *Comparative Perspective on the Role of Education in Democratization, Part I: Transitional States and States in Transition*, pp. 367-395. New York: Peter Lang.

Lisovskaya, E. (2016) Religious Education in Russia: inter-faith harmony or neo-imperial toleration?, *Social Inclusion*, 4(2), 117-132. https://doi.org/10.17645/si.v4i2.509

Lisovskaya, E. & Karpov, V. (1999) New Ideologies in Postcommunist Russian Textbooks, *Comparative Education Review*, 43(4), 522-543. https://doi.org/10.1086/447582

Lisovskaya, E. & Karpov, V. (2005) *La religion dans les écoles russes: une désécularisation contestée* [Religion in Russian schools: a contested desecularization], in J.-P. Willaime & S. Mathieu (Eds) *Des maîtres et des dieux: écoles et religions en Europe* [*Masters and gods: religion and schools in Europe*], pp. 181-192. Paris: Belin.

Lisovskaya, E. & Karpov, V. (2010) Orthodoxy, Islam, and the Desecularization of Russia's State Schools, *Politics and Religion*, 3(2), 276-302. https://doi.org/10.1017/S1755048310000040

Marx, K. (1992) *Early Writings*. London: Penguin.

Mchedlov, M.P. (2002) *O social'noi concepcii Russkogo Pravoslaviia* [On social conception of Russian Orthodoxy]. Moscow: Respublica.

Ministr Fursenko otdelil Tserkov' ot gosudarstva [Minister Fursenko separated Church from State] (2004) *Gazeta Kommersant*, 6 October. http://www.kommersant.ru/doc/477679

Mir Religii (2002) 15 November. http://www.religio.ru/news/4728_print.html

Mitrokhin, N. (2004) *Russkaia Pravoslavnaia Tserkov': Sovremennoe Sostoyanie I Aktual'nye Problemy* [Russian Orthodox Church: contemporary state and current problems]. Moscow: Novoe Literaturnoe Obozrenie.

Mitrokhin, N. & Sibireva, O. (2007) *'Ne boisia, maloe stado!' Ob otsenke chislennosti pravoslavnykh veruiushchikh na mteriale polevykh issledovanii v Riazanskoi oblasti* ['Do not be afraid, little flock!' About estimating the number of Orthodox believers based on field research in Ryazan region], *Neprikosnovennyi Zapas*, 51. http://www.krotov.info/history/21/61_statistika/2007sibireva.htm

Mitropolit Kirill [Metropolitan Kirill] (2002) *'Pust' blagoslovenie Bozhie prebyvaet so vsemi nami'* ['Let God's blessing be with all of us'], *Izvestiia*, 24 December. http://izvestia.ru/news/271101

Orthodox 'Bomb' for Russian School (2016) *Krym.Realii*, 9 August. http://ru.krymr.com/a/27910724.html

Palkin, A. (2002) *Uroki pravoslaviia* [Lessons in Orthodoxy]. http://www.caesarion.ru/warrax/w/warrax.net/60/ortolessons.html

Papkova, I. (2011) *The Orthodox Church and Russian Politics*. New York: Oxford University Press.

Prepodavanie osnov religii: Kak delo obstoit seichas [Teaching the fundamentals of religion: how things are now] (2002) *Tema Dnia*, 24 November. http://www.temadnya.ru/spravka/24nov2002/1915.html

Presidentu Rossiiskoi Federatsii V. V. Putinu [To V. V. Putin, the president of Russian Federation] (2007) *Portal Credo.ru*, 23 July.
http://www.portalcredo.ru/site/?act=news&id=55762

Putin, V. (2013a) Speech at a Meeting of Valday Discussion Club, *Rossiiskaia Gazeta*, 19 September. http://www.rg.ru/2013/09/19/stenogramma-site.html

Putin, V. (2013b) Speech at a Meeting with Muftis from Russia's Muslim Spiritual Administrations, 22 October.
http://en.kremlin.ru/events/president/transcripts/19474

Putin Chooses Religious Studies Scholar to Head Education Ministry (2016) *Russia Religious News*, 19 August.
http://www2.stetson.edu/~psteeves/relnews/160819b.html

Putin schitaet odinakovo vazhnymi sostavliaiushchimi bezopasnosti strany eio traditsionnye religii i iadernyi shchit [Putin considers traditional religions and the nuclear shield equally important components of the country's security] (2007) *Interfax Religiia*, 1 February. http://www.interfax-<change>religion.ru/?act=news&div=16417

Ramet, S. (2014) Religious Organizations in Post-communist Central and Southeastern Europe: an introduction, in S. Ramet (Ed.) *Religion and Politics in Post-socialist Central and Southeastern Europe: challenges since 1989*, pp. 1-4. Basingstoke: Palgrave Macmillan.

Rossijane vysskazalis' po povodu religioznogo obrazovaniia v schkolakh [Citizens of Russia expressed their opinion about religious education in schools] (2013) *Newsru.com Religiia*, March.
http://www.newsru.com/religy/01mar2013/umfrage.html

Schroeder, R. (2016) Rising against the 'Enemies of the Church': the dynamics of Russian desecularization and the making of its punitive regime. Unpublished doctoral dissertation, Western Michigan University, Kalamazoo, MI.

Schroeder, R. & Karpov, V. (2013) The Crimes and Punishments of the 'Enemies of the Church' and the Nature of Russia's Desecularizing Regime, *Religion, State and Society*, 41(3), 284-311. https://doi.org/10.1080/09637494.2013.837705

Smith, C. (2003) Introduction: rethinking the secularization of American public life, in C. Smith (Ed.) *The Secular Revolution: power, interests, and conflict in the secularization of American public life*, pp. 1-96. Berkeley: University of California Press.

Stenogramma vstrechi predsedatelya Pravitel'stva RF V. V. Putina so Svyateishim Patriarkhom Kirillom i liderami traditsionnykh religioznykh obschin Rossii [A stenographic record of the meeting of the President of the government of the Russian Federation V. V. Putin with His Holiness Patriarch Kirill and leaders of traditional religious communities of the Russian Federation] (2012) 8 February. www.patriarchia.ru/db/print/2005767.html

Turner, V. (1974) *Dramas, Fields, and Metaphors: symbolic action in human society*. Ithaca, NY: Cornell University Press.

Van Den Bercken, W. (1994) The Russian Orthodox Church, State and Society in 1991-1993: the rest of the story, *Religion, State and Society*, 22(2), 163-181. https://doi.org/10.1080/09637499408431635

CHAPTER 16

The Role of Religious Education in Countering Religious Extremism in Diverse and Interconnected Societies

RATNA GHOSH & W.Y. ALICE CHAN

SUMMARY Despite the pre-eminent role of schools in the socialization of youth, and the significant function of education in the development of a peaceful and inclusive society, little attention has been paid to the role of education in relation to religious extremism. This chapter discusses the use of religious education (RE) as a form of *soft power* in countering violent (religious) extremism (CVE), as opposed to the *hard-power* measures of surveillance, policing and machinery promoted in counter-terrorism policies. We show that RE can be effectively used for CVE but only when infused with critical pedagogy, dialogue and an understanding of religion as an aspect of human development. When RE is devoid of this, it has been used to advance religious extremism instead.

Introduction

In the final chapter of this volume, Collet and Bang illustrate the third wave of multiculturalism. This is presented through examples of school policies in western countries that have changed in the past 20 years to incorporate the recognition and accommodation of religious identities, some with more success than others. This growing need for recognition of religious identities in a globalizing world marked by international migrations and religious diversity has also led to a rise in religious extremism.

From January 2016 to May 2016, 10,000 people have died as a result of extremists or counter-extremist efforts (Tony Blair Faith Foundation, 2016). During this five-month period, Al-Shabaab was the most active extremist group, the self-proclaimed Islamic State of Iraq and Syria (ISIS) killed the

335

most people, an increase in violent extremism was seen in East and Southeast Asia, and a religious extremist attack was reported for the first time in South America (Tony Blair Faith Foundation, 2016). To counter the occurrence of such events, policy-makers and the public need to understand the root of religious extremism and address it where possible.

Religious extremism is the complete rejection of ideas that appear to contradict or oppose a specific set of exclusive religious beliefs held by extremists (Davies, 2009). It implies intolerance of other religions but also other interpretations of a religion. The progression from religious fundamentalism to religious extremism and then to religious radicalism involves the assertion of extreme positions, such as a turn to ideologically motivated violence based on socio-economic and political objectives (Mirahmadi et al, 2015) which are justified on moral grounds (Davies, 2009). This moral aspect sets violent extremism apart from other forms of violence. The final progression to terrorism involves acts of violent religious extremism that cause fear in others (Moghaddam, 2005). To respond to such events, several government policies focus on the use of intelligence tactics, force and weaponry in hopes of protecting the security of a nation by dissuading future occurrences. The Canadian Counter-Terrorism Strategy, for example, focuses on preventing, detecting, denying and responding to terrorist threats in a 'multi-pronged' approach that includes 'diplomacy, intelligence, security and law enforcement, customs and immigration, transportation, justice and finance expertise' (Government of Canada, 2016). Although governments are spending trillions of dollars on these forms of intelligence and coercive actions, these are reactive measures and do not go to the root of radicalization. Furthermore, de-radicalization is an expensive and difficult process. In this chapter, we discuss the proactive and sustainable role that religious education (RE) can play in countering religious extremism.

Education's role is long sighted and long lasting. Wilner and Dubouloz (2010) suggest that radicalization sets off a transformation in the individual's psycho-cognitive processes, leading to the construction of new identities and consequent behaviour changes. Since both mental and emotional processes are involved in preparing and motivating an individual to pursue violent behaviour, education can and should play a major role in countering the possibility of such psycho-cognitive changes. Moreover, since violence is justified on moral grounds by extremists, religious and moral education are an essential component of education in countering violent extremism (CVE). Religious extremist groups spread ideology through education and media to attract potential extremists and use moral and psychological inducements to manipulate youth. Counter-terrorism strategies have not used moral or psychological appeal to destroy the extremist ideas. As religious extremism is a progression from one lens of exclusivity into another, religious education can be a means to arrest this progression and prevent its escalation. RE is an important subject through which students learn to be ethical and resilient citizens and is a significant way to counter extremist beliefs.

However, since various forms of RE exist globally, the most appropriate form for countering religious extremism needs to be considered. This chapter discusses how education can fulfill a proactive role in CVE and asks: how can religious education develop resilience against violent behaviour and/or radicalization in diverse societies, and what form of religious education is needed? To answer this, our chapter elaborates on the complexity of religious education in confessional and non-confessional settings and the potential of RE both to indoctrinate and to counter religious extremism. In considering the paradoxical role of RE, we first present examples that illustrate its ability to promote religious extremism. We then present an exemplary model and pedagogical approach through which RE can counter religious extremism.

Education

The Importance of Education for Moral Development, Resilience and Citizenship

Educational strategies aim to accomplish objectives that only develop over time. Research indicates that while it is difficult to make generalizations on how one is radicalized because of the varied characteristics among extremists, two factors stand out: resentment against society, and the need for recognition (Butler, 2015). Both these factors are developed during the socialization process in schools. Resentment arises when students feel alienated and marginalized, lack a historical understanding of discrimination and social inequalities, and are not recognized or are misrecognized (Taylor, 1994). All these triggers require the long-term development of values and understanding (Ghosh et al, 2016). As a form of *soft power*, education can make knowledge relevant for students, encouraging an attitude of respect for diversity that is embedded in citizenship education, and it can develop the skills of critical thinking (that includes analysis and reflection) and an understanding of social justice. This development guides students to expand the affective domain and instills a value system through dialogue and relational thinking on alternate world views (Ross, 2003). This aspect of personal development in relation to one's social environment and its value system can produce engaged and critical citizens. Our conception of citizenship education is based on Kymlicka's (2012) conception of *citizenization* – the process whereby individuals' autonomy, agency, consent, trust, participation and self-determination are respected.

Through a long-term development of these attitudes and skills, education is able to cultivate the resiliency of students to question and critique the ideologies with which extremists attempt to entice them. However, education is a double-edged sword as it can be used both to promote critical individual development and to indoctrinate youth.

Education and Indoctrination

The difference between education and indoctrination lies in how and what is taught: both deal with information and knowledge. However, indoctrination occurs when there is no opportunity to question, discuss and analyse, but information is handed down as exclusive content and students learn by rote. Education, on the other hand, refers to the development of both the cognitive and the affective domains. Knowledge is constructed by the student from the variety of sources that are consulted, and teaching is dialogical and critical and focuses on the relational aspect of human identity, since identity is formed through relationships (Ross, 2003). When knowledge learnt in schools is relevant to the student's experience it becomes meaningful. Thus, the content and method of education is very important in determining whether it aims to force and indoctrinate students with a particular ideology or whether it aims for personal and social development. Similarly, RE can also be used both to indoctrinate individuals and to promote individual development.

Religious Education

From the perspective of education, the issue of religion is rather complex because it raises a variety of issues dealing with policy, process, practice and outcome in relation to religion as a school subject as well as in mandatory school subjects (such as science education, in which the theory of evolution may be contradictory to creationism). Nonetheless, the overall question is: how effective is religious education in developing resilience against violent behaviour and encouraging the development of strong values of critical citizenship? What kind of narratives can counter the lure of media messages and what narratives could mitigate conflicting viewpoints in societies (Ghosh, 2016)? Due to its complexity, the school plays a crucial role in informing students about religion through RE.

In 'Religious Education as Encounter', John Hull (2009) explains that children and teachers encounter another world when they learn about the religion of other people (p. 21). For Hull, it is fundamental for RE to instill the recognition of the other and respect the fact that one's perspective encompasses a specific world view that may differ from that of other members in society. For CVE, the understanding of the existence of alternate world views and the empathy one has towards an individual of a differing world view is the most significant aspect that RE can provide. When one's world view can be perceived as normal or totalizing, it is difficult to see the perspective of others, and this can be an educational barrier to dialogue (Hull, 2009).

The term 'religious education' can mean various things, and as an encounter it can take three forms (Grimmitt & Read, 1975; Hull, n.d.). First, the teaching *of* religion or 'learning religion' occurs during confessional religious instruction where one is taught about a religion as a follower of the religion by teachers who are expected to be members of the religious community. In this form, religious texts are analyzed for their meaning and application to one's life in hopes of strengthening the religious commitment of the individual. Curriculum is often established by religious leaders. This form of RE limits the opportunity to encounter other world views within a pluralistic society (Hull, n.d.).

Second, the learning and teaching *about* religion is a non-confessional content-based approach that focuses on teaching the descriptive and historical aspects of a religion. Teaching *about* religion also includes the teaching of scriptures, religious texts and rituals, but it is taught as information to be understood and analyzed rather than as something that is to be accepted and believed. An example of this is learning about the Bible as literature in parts of the United States, and not learning its content for religious meaning. The American Academy of Religion (AAR) describes teaching *about* religion as a format that needs to convey that religions are internally diverse and dynamic, and are embedded in culture (AAR Religion in the Schools Task Force, 2010). This form of RE is used often in the United States and most European settings and aims to teach religion in a non-confessional form. While this form of RE is valuable in that it teaches students the skills to analyze and critique religious teachings and stereotypes and break down intolerance, Hull (n.d.) finds this form of RE limiting as it omits a discussion of the lived experience of members of the religious groups, thereby limiting the development of students' moral and spiritual values. In some examples, this form of RE has been used to promote other non-religious aims. In Japan, Fujiwara (2007) found that a non-confessional teaching *about* religion promoted Shinto ethno-centrism implicitly. In Indonesia, Baidhawy (2007) found that the government included the four official religions in RE (Islam, Christianity, Buddhism and Hinduism), only to marginalize Confucianism as a result. In both examples, teaching *about* religion imposes certain beliefs and values despite its non-confessional stance.

Third, in learning or teaching *from* religion, the focus is placed on students as learners who are taught to make sense of the world based on learning from religious beliefs, symbols or practices. This form of RE aims to foster empathy and respect for people of other world views as well as understanding how others may perceive the world that students co-habit. 'At its best, however, "learning from religion" is a unique resource for the advancement of human freedom' (Hull, n.d., para. 27). It 'might offer a stimulation to the curiosity of the children, challenge their values, deepen their distinctive sense of identity, and impart empathy for others' thereby offering students the opportunity to make sense of their lived experience on their own (Hull, n.d., para. 17). Therefore, it addresses the very issues of identity and relevance of school knowledge that exclude and turn youth to oppositional behaviour.

Values that are common among cultures and religions, such as empathy, honesty, equality and belief in human dignity, for example, are important to develop in children, and this is done optimally through religious literacy (discussed later in the chapter).

Religious Education Used to Promote Extremist Beliefs

Extremist groups have used religious education very successfully to indoctrinate young minds (through a particular interpretation of their religious text). Soft power, through the use of narratives and ideas in both non-formal and formal educational programs as well as media, has been used systematically to promote extremist ideologies. Some countries use RE to indoctrinate youth in order to subjugate their citizens or to stir up nationalistic sentiments.

RE that promotes extremist beliefs lacks the development of critical thinking, dialogue and respect for diversity. Through indoctrination it often promotes an extremist and narrow form of citizenship education that omits the process of *citizenization*. An indoctrinating form of learning and teaching *of* religion is currently established by different ministries of education worldwide, such as the state educational department in Saudi Arabia, and religious extremist organizations globally, such as ISIS.

Saudi Arabia

In a study entitled 'Ten Years On: Saudi Arabia's textbooks still promote religious violence', Shea (2011) found that Saudi textbooks from middle and high school grades included messages that promote violence and extremism. The examined textbooks, largely from the government's religious curriculum, were from courses in the upper grades that constitute a major focus of the Saudi school day. The following are excerpts from some of their textbooks:

1. 'In Islamic law, (jihad) has two uses: 1. specific usage: which means: Exerting effort in fighting unbelievers and tyrants' (Hadith and Islamic Culture: Management, Social, Natural, and Technical Sciences Section, Twelfth Grade. Ministry of Education, Kingdom of Saudi Arabia, 1431-1432; 2010-2011, p. 71).
2. 'The Islamic world today faces the problem of Muslim minorities that are spread in non Islamic states. Muslim minorities in many countries of the world are subjected to the threat of genocide or threats of Christianisation and conversion from their religion or planting atheist ideas and destructive principles in their minds' (Geography of the Islamic World, Eighth Grade. Ministry of Education, Kingdom of Saudi Arabia, p. 116).
3. 'The temptation of the sons of Israel remains in women for they have attempted in this era to corrupt women and get them out of their houses and make them a means for seduction and corruption' (Hadith, Eighth Grade, Ministry of Education, Kingdom of Saudi Arabia, p. 36).

These excerpts were translated into English in Shea (2011) and depict the promotion of Wahhabi extremist ideology in Saudi textbooks that are used in Saudi Arabia and distributed to many Muslim countries globally where they are part of the school curriculum. Wahhabi religious education was found in every subject's textbook and included a specific perspective towards Jewish people and gay individuals (see Shea, 2011, for more examples).

ISIS

In ISIS territory, religious education is taught formally and informally. Informally, *ashbal* – young children and teens referred to as lion cubs – are religiously educated by watching ISIS videos, distributing ISIS religious materials and attending beheadings of hostages, among many other activities (Khayat, 2014). Violence is taught to be morally justifiable and considered a righteous act to avenge the immorality of the West. Boys are required to study religion until the age of 14, when they join the ISIS military or its governing bodies, while girls attend schools to study religion and home economics until the age of 18 (Meir Amit Intelligence and Terrorism Information Center, 2014). The ministry of education and higher education, called 'Diwan of Knowledge', teaches Salafi ideology that includes gender segregation and the removal of topics related to citizenship and patriotism, music, art, philosophy, sociology, psychology, history and the religions of religious minorities – this religious curriculum is influenced by Saudi curricula. Other curricular subjects include physics, chemistry, mathematics, English and Arabic languages, and 'sharia sciences', which excludes ideology that conflicts with the Salafi ideology, such as Darwin's theory of evolution (Mamouri, 2014).

Religious education and training play a crucial role for ISIS. Riad, a former ISIS child soldier in Syria, told a Human Rights Watch interviewer: 'The leader of the camp said [ISIS] liked the younger ones better... He told me, "Tomorrow they'll be a stronger leader or a stronger fighter"' (HRW, 2014, p. 21). With respect to his training, Riad reported:

> It was a very difficult camp. They gave us a very severe training.
> We would wake up, pray, after prayer maybe around 9 a.m. we
> did exercises, then rest in the room, then sharia courses, then
> military study, then more sharia courses, then some rest, prayer.
> [Between afternoon prayers], they didn't let us sleep; they would
> come in our tent and fire into the sky and [send us] to guard a
> trench. Many times we fell asleep in this trench because we were
> so tired. (Human Rights Watch Skype interview with Riad,
> location in Syria withheld, 4 April 2014; HRW, 2014, p. 22)

This educational and training regimen in ISIS schools reveals their systematic and strategic use of religious education as a means to indoctrinate their recruits: there is no place for questioning. To counter this use of soft power, an opposing form of critical, dialogic and respectful religious education is needed to equip students who encounter extremist ideology in person and online.

Religious Education for Countering Violent Extremism (CVE)

The Need for Religious Literacy

Moore (2007) conceptualizes religious literacy as the ability to discern and analyze the role of religion in the social, economic and political spheres of society throughout history and today. To be religiously literate, an individual is aware of the diversity between and within the world religions, is familiar with the basic tenets of the world religions, and understands that the contemporary state of religious traditions arose from historical conditions and will continue to be shaped by cultural, social and political conditions today (Moore, 2007). RE that incorporates this form of religious literacy can foster resiliency by equipping students with the skills to understand and analyze religious traditions. As a result, it is dialogic and respectful, thereby fostering critical citizenship. Corresponding to this conception is Quebec's Ethics and Religious Culture (ERC) program – a highly developed form of RE in a North American non-confessional setting.[1]

The ERC in Quebec

Quebec's Ministry of Education offers a form of religious literacy through the Ethics and Religious Culture (ERC) program. We consider it a model that should be reviewed and expanded on by others as it aims to include dialogue, respect for others, citizenship and critical thinking, although the development of this skill is not explicitly stated. As it promotes dialogue about differing religious cultures and perspectives, and citizenship education through its course objectives, it has the potential to counter religious extremism.

Unique in Canada, the ERC is taught in all private and publicly funded schools and is mandatory for all elementary and secondary grades, with the exception of Grade 9 students (equivalent to Secondary Year 3). The course aims to promote the recognition of others and the pursuit of the common good through students' ability to fulfill the competencies of: (1) reflecting on ethical questions, and (2) demonstrating an understanding of the phenomenon of religion (MÉES, 2016). Foundational to these two competencies is the ability to dialogue about both ethical questions and the phenomenon of religion. These competencies are taught thematically so that various ethical perspectives are reviewed and similarities and differences within and across religious and non-religious beliefs can be discerned. Moreover, teachers are required to teach all ethical situations and aspects of religious and non-religious beliefs in an impartial manner at every level. Although not stated, the ERC program objectives promote *citizenization* as it is a course categorized within the subject area of personal development alongside physical education and health.

However, similar to the Indonesian example shared by Baidhawy, the non-confessional approach to teaching about religious and non-religious beliefs in Quebec can also marginalize certain members of the society. Based on Quebec's cultural heritage, the ERC requires the teaching of Catholicism, Protestantism, Judaism and First Nation spirituality each school year. Other world religions and non-religious beliefs are expected to be taught at least once every two years, but the primacy that the four religions and beliefs are given over others implicitly marginalizes the lived experiences of others in the province. To supplement the current curriculum and pedagogy for the purposes of CVE, we encourage the incorporation of Jackson's interpretive approach.

Robert Jackson's Interpretive Approach and Dialogue

Jackson's interpretive approach is a pedagogy proposed for non-confessional schools with religiously and non-religiously diverse student groups and promotes an analysis of representation, interpretation and self-reflection on religious beliefs among students and teachers (Jackson, 2015, p. 35). Jackson's approach was originally developed for a discussion of religious beliefs; however, we believe that a similar analysis of representation, interpretation and self-reflection can be conducted on non-religious beliefs as well.

In *Rethinking Religious Education and Plurality* (Jackson, 2004), where Jackson does not offer his own conception of religious literacy explicitly, he states that the aims of RE should be 'to help children and young people to find their own positions within the key debates about religious plurality' (p. 87). This suggests that his conception of religious literacy includes an outright focus on the personal aspect of religious literacy in the midst of religion in the social realm. For Jackson, the purpose of RE and religious literacy is social cohesion, which makes it a significant method for creating an inclusive and plural classroom and society.

In bridging the personal and public domains, Jackson (2012) asserts that a secular approach – one that is methodologically impartial to any particular belief and is inclusive – should be instituted in all RE, and that a secularist approach that may hold a specific methodological approach in presenting religious claims as false or meaningless is problematic. This is so because such a secularist approach would counter Jackson's goal of social cohesion and religious understanding altogether. Instead, Jackson emphasizes the need to present religious claims in a manner that would allow students to interpret and consider it themselves, and they may come to the conclusion that religion is meaningless. Thus, Jackson's approach echoes our call for a form of RE that fosters an understanding that religion can be an aspect of human development and that accepts atheism as another aspect of diversity.

To guide students through personal development, Jackson's interpretive approach incorporates an overarching consideration of the 'parts' and the 'wholes' of religions (i.e. an individual narrative of a religious believer and the narrative given from a broader perspective). This discussion of the parts and the whole is embedded in an analysis of the varying representations and interpretations of these narratives, and of one's self-reflection of them. Through this process, Jackson aims for students to advance their: (1) *self-awareness* by understanding how one's world view can be shaped by one's multi-identities; (2) *empathy* by understanding others; and (3) *edification* as students learn about themselves and attain a better understanding of the cultures around them. These goals acknowledge the 'parts' and carefully consider their representations. Thus, in recognizing the 'parts', the process of representation is taught carefully. Jackson's teaching materials include (Jackson, 1997, pp. 108-110):

1. *Reconsidering the character of 'religions'*, focusing on individual student narratives which pose various representations based on geographic, historical and social bearings. We believe this practice can be considered for non-religious beliefs as people who profess to be atheists, for example, express different narratives and lived experiences as well.

2. *Recognizing 'religions' and 'cultures' as dynamic and changing, with a content and scope which is negotiated and sometimes contested, and which may be delineated differently by different insiders and outsiders.*

3. *Avoiding or exercising great caution in projecting assumptions from one religious tradition onto other religious traditions.* The focus is on 'insider' knowledge and understanding through its own language and perspectives. Contrary to this idea, the ERC is taught thematically.

Based on these three aspects of representation, the process of interpretation occurs when teachers and students:

1. understand a religion from the three levels of tradition, membership group and the individual; and

2. compare and contrast the overlapping similarities and differences among insiders and outsiders of a tradition through a dialogical approach.

This dialogical method is pivotal to Jackson's interpretive approach and is crucial in fostering understanding between the three levels of individual, group and tradition. Despite not detailing a specific dialogical approach to take, Jackson encourages engagement in another's perspective in order to understand the other's subjective motives and actions, especially as a means to understand something that may seem irrational at first (Dillon, 2011). He promotes three forms of dialogical approaches that emphasize reflexivity and action through the values of democracy, social justice and human rights (Jackson, 2004) – namely, the approaches stipulated by Leganger-Krosgstad

(2011) in Norway, Weisse and Knauth (1997) in Germany, and Ipgrave (2003) in the UK. Each approach is valuable for different contexts: the Norwegian approach promotes students' independent reflection and dialogue that varies across three key age groups; the German approach engages in a philosophical discussion about religion; and the British approach uses dialogue as a means for students to voice their own notions about religious beliefs separate from that of their parents.

Jackson's review of varying representations through dialogue informs the process of interpretation in his interpretive approach. Understanding the varying representations of a religion invites students to understand religious individuals in a different way and encourages students and teachers through a self-reflection of their previous biases and updated understandings of individuals and their religious narrative.

Critical Thinking and Relationality

Both the ERC as a program and Jackson's approach develop critical thinking that requires analysis and critique of ideas based on evaluative criteria. This is fundamental in preparing students to critique the ideas and practices from different religious and non-religious individuals and groups. Such an analysis can support students in identifying and articulating the values that oppose extremist ideology.

Critical thinking is an essential component of the ERC program and the interpretive approach. Within the ERC's first competency, 'to reflect on ethical questions', the teaching of critical thinking is needed to help students analyze ethical situations, relate knowledge to their life experiences and consider possible perspectives in a given situation. Within the ERC's second competency, 'to demonstrate and understand the phenomenon of religion', critical thinking helps students situate the beliefs, practices and perspectives of religious cultures across different spheres of society and in their context. In Jackson's approach, critical thinking is taught and practiced through the analysis of the parts and the whole of religions, the interpretation of them, and the self-reflection that is expected by both teachers and students as they critique their own biases.

Fostering critical-thinking skills and offering the opportunity for critical thinking to occur is vital in allowing students the autonomy to understand the situatedness of the idea itself and determine the meaning certain ideas hold for themselves and others. Education that involves knowledge of the other involves a moral and ethical position.

Understanding Religion as an Aspect of Human Development

Religion is a fundamental aspect of most cultures (Fraser, 1999). Kymlicka (2010) considers religion the most controversial aspect of pluralistic societies today. Where religion may not have been a primary aspect of one's identity, individuals in religiously diverse societies are associating themselves primarily with their religious identity as others recognize them based on this aspect of their identity. For example, some Muslim youth in Canada are identifying themselves primarily with their religious identity as a response to governments in the western world where, as a result of 9/11, prejudicial profiling has corralled Muslim individuals despite their ethnic and cultural differences (Kymlicka, 2015). Many youth who have left their countries to join violent religious extremist groups identify more with a Pan-Islamic Ummah than with the countries in which they were born. Similarly, extremists indignant at the injustices incurred by western governments in other regions of the world are coalescing on the basis of religious identities as well.

Today, the increase in religious-ideological fundamentalism offers some individuals an opportunity to correct what they perceive as structural violence imposed upon them and others in a dualistic universe of Good and Evil (Galtung, 2015). Although violent extremism emerges with a religious justification, religion is often not the trigger and statistics indicate that in France, for example, one quarter of the extremists are converts (Butler, 2015). The form of RE discussed in this chapter can reframe the identity needs of youth and the ease with which they accept violence against innocent civilians as morally acceptable. This need to recognize an individual's religious identity and moral development is considered explicitly in Miedema's religious and/or world view education that includes citizenship education (2012).

Miedema's conception of RE is framed by the Dutch word *Bildung*, used to describe personhood education (2012) or religious edification (2014) – what Miedema considers an essential focus for all schools. On this basis, he believes that 'all domains of human potentiality and ability (be it cognitive, creative, moral, religious, expressive, etc.), that is, the development of the whole person, should be taken into account by the schools' (2012, p. 2). As a result, any discussion about religions and other world views in education is done with the understanding that it contributes to an aspect of human development. This personhood development occurs within citizenship education and so Miedema connects the two forms of education into one.

Other conceptions of RE, such as that of Jackson, do not incorporate citizenship education as Jackson points out that citizenship education cannot be value free (Jackson, 2004). In this respect, we agree that citizenship education is not value free because education is never value free and is always political. The RE curricula among nations and terrorist groups that promote religious extremism are also promoting a citizenship education, but a very specific kind. As a result, we argue that citizenship education which includes human rights and moral and ethical values such as in international documents needs to be an aspect of RE as it can counter the soft-power narratives of extremists. In doing so, both RE and the understanding of religion as an aspect of human development can develop resilient individuals through critical thinking and offer a specific form of citizenship that respects autonomy, agency and core civic values in society to counter violent religious extremism.

Looking Forward

Youth are being radicalized by soft power – the ideas, ideology, narratives and propaganda – very efficiently used in the education and propaganda spread by extremists. Can the use of hard power through military responses by governments adequately counter the appeal to the psychological, intellectual and emotional states of young people? This chapter suggests that education is indispensable to the long-term impact of countering violent extremism (CVE), but that the type of education is important. Given its paradoxical role, education can indoctrinate as well as develop engaged critical citizens who will work towards social justice and peace. Religious education needs to be a component of education in order to focus on critical thinking, ethical citizenship and respect for diversity, which are vital for CVE (Ghosh et al, 2016).

Since religion plays a very important role in people's lives, in religiously diverse secular societies the trend is to focus on values and talk about religion objectively rather than focusing on subjective terms of belief, in order to retain a neutral attitude towards a rich variety of beliefs and to develop respect for different belief systems. An education that inculcates values and respect for religious diversity rather than promoting absence of religion is likely to develop resilience as a necessary, if not sufficient, condition for peace and security in our conflict-ridden world.

Note

[1] In 1867, the British North America Act, the first Constitution of Canada, made education confessional – dividing it into Catholic and Protestant systems to accommodate the religions of the French and English population. While a version of this system remains in other provinces today, the Quiet Revolution in Quebec revolted against the domination of the Church in the 1960s. In the late 1960s and early 1970s secularization of the province established an educational system where a Ministry of Education replaced the governing roles that religious and local leaders had previously held over school affairs. In 2000, the confessional system was replaced by linguistic-based English and French school boards. The deconfessionalization of all school systems removed religious education from public schools, and the ERC is a response to the secular and diverse nature of what Quebec is today.

References

AAR Religion in the Schools Task Force (2010) Guidelines for Teaching about Religion in K-12 Public Schools in the United States. American Academy of

Religion. https://www.aarweb.org/sites/default/files/pdfs/Publications/epublications/AARK-12CurriculumGuidelines.pdf

Baidhawy, Z. (2007) Building Harmony and Peace through Multiculturalist Theology-based Religious Education: an alternative for contemporary Indonesia, *British Journal of Religious Education*, 29(1), 15-30. https://doi.org/10.1080/01416200601037478

Butler, D. (2015) Why Europeans Turn to Jihad, *Nature*, 528(20).

Davies, L. (2009) Educating against Extremism: towards a critical politicisation of youth people, *International Review of Education*, 55, 183-203. https://doi.org/10.1007/s11159-008-9126-8

Dillon, M. (2011) A Sociological Approach to Questions about Religious Diversity, in C. Meister (Ed.) *The Oxford Handbook of Religious Diversity*, pp. 21-28. Oxford: Oxford University Press.

Fraser, J. (1999) *Between Church and State: religion and public education in a multicultural America*. New York: St Martin's Press.

Fujiwara, S. (2007) Problems of Teaching about Religion in Japan: another textbook controversy against peace?, *British Journal of Religious Education*, 29(1), 45-61. https://doi.org/10.1080/01416200601037494

Galtung, J. (2015) *World Politics of Peace and War: geopolitics in another key: geography and civilization*. New York: Hampton Press.

Ghosh, R. (2016) How Education, Not Surveillance, is Most Effective in Countering Violent Extremism. OpenCanada. https://www.opencanada.org/features/how-education-not-surveillance-most-effective-countering-violent-extremism/

Ghosh, R., Chan, W.Y.A., Manuel, A. & Dilimulati, M. (2016) Can Education Counter Violent Religious Extremism? *Canadian Foreign Policy Journal*.

Ghosh, R., Manuel, A., Chan, W.Y.A., Dilimulati, M. & Babei, M. (2016) Education and Security: a global literature report on countering violent religious extremism (CVE). Tony Blair Faith Foundation. http://tonyblairfaithfoundation.org/foundation/news/education-and-security

Government of Canada: global affairs Canada (2016) Terrorism. 1 April. http://www.international.gc.ca/crime/terrorism-terrorisme.aspx?lang=eng

Grimmitt, M. & Read, G. (1975) *Teaching Christianity in RE*. Great Wakering, Essex: Mayhew.

Hull, J.M. (2009) Religious Education as Encounter: from body worlds to religious worlds, in S. Miedema (Ed.) *Religious Education as Encounter: a tribute to John M. Hull*, pp. 21-34. Münster: Waxmann.

Hull, J.M. (n.d.) Three Models of Religious Education. International Association for Religious Freedom. https://www.iarf.net/REBooklet/Hull.htm

Human Rights Watch (HRW) (2014) 'Maybe we live and maybe we die.' Recruitment and Use of Children by Armed Groups in Syria. http://www.hrw.org/sites/default/files/reports/syria0614_crd_ForUpload.pdf

Ipgrave J. (2003) Dialogue, Citizenship and Religious Education, in R. Jackson (Ed.) *International Perspectives on Citizenship, Education and Religious Diversity*, pp. 131-149. London: RoutledgeFalmer.

Jackson, R. (1997) *Religious Education: an interpretive approach.* London: Hodder & Stoughton.

Jackson, R. (2004) *Rethinking Religious Education and Plurality: issues in diversity and pedagogy.* London: RoutledgeFalmer. https://doi.org/10.4324/9780203465165

Jackson, R. (2012) Religious Education and the Arts of Interpretation Revisited, in I. Avest (Ed.) *On the Edge: (auto)biography and pedagogical theories on religious education,* pp. 57-68. Rotterdam: Sense.

Jackson, R. (2015) *Signposts: policy and practice for teaching about religions and non-religious world views in intercultural education.* Strasbourg: Council of Europe.

Khayat, M. (2014) Indoctrination of Children in the Islamic State Caliphate (ISIS). The Middle East Media Research Institute Jihad and Terrorism Threat Monitor. http://www.memrijttm.org/indoctrination-of-children-in-the-islamic-state-caliphate-isis-.html

Kymlicka, W. (2010) *The Current State of Multiculturalism in Canada and Research Themes on Canadian Multiculturalism, 2008-2010.* Ministry of Public Works and Government Services Canada. Ottawa: Citizenship and Immigration Canada.

Kymlicka, W. (2012) Responsible Citizenship, *Trudeau Foundation Papers,* 4(2), 56-87. https://www.academia.edu/4486454/Responsible_Citizenship_2012_

Kymlicka, W. (2015) The Three Lives of Multiculturalism, in S. Guo & L. (Eds) *Revisiting Multiculturalism in Canada,* pp. 17-36. Rotterdam: Sense.

Leganger-Krogstad, H. (2011) The Religious Dimension of Intercultural Education: contributions to a contextual understanding. Berlin: LIT Verlag.

Mamouri, A. (2014) Iraq Pulse: IS imposes new rules on education in Syria, Iraq, *Al-Monitor,* 21 October. http://www.al-monitor.com/pulse/originals/2014/10/islamic-state-impose-education-program-iraq-syria.html#ixzz3Z0uCm1Du

MÉES (2016) The Ethics and Religious Culture Program. Quebec, Canada: Gouvernement du Québec. http://www.education.gouv.qc.ca/en/ethics-and-religious-culture-program/

Meir Amit Intelligence and Terrorism Information Center (2014) Spotlight on Global Jihad. 24-31 December. http://www.terrorism-info.org.il/en/article/20752

Miedema, S. (2012) A Plea for Inclusive Worldview Education in All Schools: original research, *Koers: Bulletin for Christian Scholarship = Koers: Bulletin Vir Christelike Wetenskap,* 77(1), 1-7. https://doi.org/10.4102/koers.v77i1.35

Miedema, S. (2014) 'Coming out Religiously!' Religion, the Public Sphere, and Religious Identity Formation, *Religious Education,* 109(4), 362-378. https://doi.org/10.1080/00344087.2014.924753

Mirahmadi, H., Ziad, W., Farooq, M. & Lamb, L. (2015) Empowering Pakistan's Civil Society to Counter Global Violent Extremism. Washington: Center for Middle East Policy at Brookings. January. http://www.brookings.edu/~/media/research/ les/papers/2015/01/ us-islamic-world-forum-publications/empowering-paki- stans-civil-society-to-counter-violent-extremism-english. pdf

Moghaddam, F.M. (2005) The Staircase to Terrorism: a psychological exploration, *American Psychologist,* 60(2), 161-169. https://doi.org/10.1037/0003-066X.60.2.161

Moore, D. (2007) *Overcoming Religious Illiteracy: a cultural studies approach to the study of religion in secondary education.* New York: Palgrave Macmillan. https://doi.org/10.1057/9780230607002

Ross, H. (2003) Rethinking Human Vulnerability, Security, and Connection through Relational Theorizing, in W.C. Nelles (Ed.) *Comparative Education, Terrorism, and Human Security: from critical pedagogy to peace building?*, pp. 33-46. New York: Palgrave Macmillan.

Shea, N. (2011) Ten Years On: Saudi Arabia's textbooks still promote religious violence. Center for Religious Freedom, Hudson Institute. http://www.investigativeproject.org/documents/testimony/386.pdf

Taylor, C. (1994) The Politics of Recognition, in D. Goldberg (Ed.) *Multiculturalism: a critical reader.* Cambridge, MA: Blackwell.

Tony Blair Faith Foundation (2016) What We Know about Global Extremism in 2016. May. http://tonyblairfaithfoundation.org/foundation/news/what-we-know-about-global-extremism-2016

Weisse, W. & Knauth, T. (1997) Dialogical Religious Education: theoretical framework and conceptual conclusions, in T. Andree, C. Bakker & P. Schreiner (Eds) *Crossing Boundaries: contributions to inter-religious and intercultural education.* Münster: Comenius Institute.

Wilner, A.S. & Dubouloz, C. (2010) Homegrown Terrorism and Transformative Learning: an interdisciplinary approach to understanding radicalization, *Global Change, Peace and Security* (formerly *Pacifica Review: Peace, Security and Global Change*), 22(1), 33-51.

CHAPTER 17

A Multicultural Analysis of School Policies on Religion in 20 Western Democracies, and Their Challenges for Accommodating Migrant Religions: a cluster analysis

BRUCE A. COLLET & HYEYOUNG BANG

SUMMARY This chapter examines public school policies regarding religion across 20 western democracies, and how these policies impact the faith traditions of migration populations. The project identifies, per country studied: (1) major migrant groups; (2) public school policies regarding religion; and (3) the level of commitment to multiculturalism. School policies examined include dress codes, prayer space, religious holidays and confessional and non-confessional instruction. Using hierarchical cluster analysis, the study groups the countries into five clusters: *High religious freedom providers* (Australia, Canada and Sweden); *Moderate religious freedom providers* (Austria, the Netherlands, Portugal, Spain and Denmark); *Christian-focused religious freedom providers* (Finland, Germany, Greece, Ireland, Italy, Norway, Switzerland, the United Kingdom); *Committed secularists* (France and Belgium); and *Sensitive religious freedom providers* (New Zealand and the USA). Through contextualizing its findings within a broader discourse on the global diffusion of multicultural norms and policies, the chapter contributes to the field unique cross-cultural and cross-national understandings of the intersection of migration, religion and education.

Introduction

The ways in which public schools in liberal democratic states treat their religious minority students may be one of the most significant barometers for measuring states' commitment to multiculturalism. Indeed, as Will Kymlicka notes, over the past twenty years religion as a basis for multicultural claims has risen to the fore. This is true not only in Canada, Kymlicka's home country, but more generally within the western world. The French headscarf controversy (*l'affaire du voile islamique*) dating back to 1989 is likely the most well-known (and well-publicized) example of this, but there are certainly others, and they involve not only Muslims. Working from Kymlicka's (2007, 2010, 2012) framing of immigrant multiculturalism as part of a larger human rights revolution combining antidiscrimination measures with positive forms of recognition and accommodation, in this study we conduct a 'multicultural analysis' of public school policies and practices in 20 western democracies as they pertain to the recognition of and accommodation to the religions of migrant students. These policies and practices include school dress codes, the opportunity for prayer in school, confessional and non-confessional instruction, and the recognition of religious holidays. Concomitantly, we examine data concerning states' admission of immigrants as well as asylum seekers. Finally, we incorporate data from the Multicultural Policy Index (MPI, 2010), co-authored by Will Kymlicka and Keith Banting, and hosted by Queens University in Kingston, Ontario.

Using hierarchical cluster analysis, our study groups the 20 countries we examine into five clusters, and we provide the clusters with descriptive names based on our analysis. Cluster 1 (Australia, Canada, and Sweden) is denoted as *High religious freedom providers*, while Cluster 2 (Austria, the Netherlands, Portugal, Spain and Denmark) is denoted as *Moderate religious freedom providers*. Cluster 3 (Finland, Germany, Greece, Ireland, Italy, Norway, Switzerland, the United Kingdom) is titled *Christian-focused religious freedom providers*, and Cluster 4 (France and Belgium) is dubbed *Committed secularists*. Finally, Cluster 5 (New Zealand and the USA) is denoted as *Sensitive religious freedom providers*. In our analysis, we provide a discussion of each of the clusters, noting their measure scores and relating these scores to the migrant populations they are host to.

We find that while all of the clusters face challenges with respect to recognizing and accommodating the religions of their migrant students, Clusters 3 and 4 face the highest number of challenges. This is due to a number of historical, social, cultural and political factors which differentiate these states from others within the study. We try to capture these factors through providing two cross-country comparisons (Norway and Greece, and Canada and France). These comparisons draw attention to particular country contexts as they influence public school policies and practices. The comparisons also help to nuance our thinking about the internal dynamics of the clusters, as well as about how we differentiate between the clusters.

Multiculturalism as a Conceptual and Analytical Frame

Liberal Multiculturalism

'Multiculturalism' may be variously described. The term may be taken up descriptively, wherein it simply denotes the existence of diversity present in society. However, descriptive definitions of multiculturalism will not take us very far by way of analysis. The term may also be taken up, as it often has within much of the post-multicultural literature, as a kind of 'feel-good celebration of ethnocultural diversity' (Kymlicka, 2012) that directs primary attention to acknowledging and embracing an array of differing customs, traditions and other material aspects of culture. Yasmin Alibhai-Brown has coined this particular framing as the 3S model: 'saris, samosas, and steel drums' (Alibhai-Brown, 2000). Yet saris, samosas and steel drums, engaging as they might be, tell us very little about the issues we probably should be most concerned with when it comes to recognizing the identities and accommodating the needs of immigrant groups. As Kymlicka (2012) notes, the 3S model ignores issues of economic and political inequality, risks trivializing cultural differences and ignoring the very real challenges that differences in cultural and religious values might raise, encourages a conception of cultural groups as 'hermetically sealed' and static, and may in fact end up reinforcing rather than challenging or disrupting power inequalities and cultural restrictions within minority groups.

An alternative is to frame multiculturalism as a political philosophy undergirded by actual and meaningful public policies. Here, multiculturalism is conceptualized as a set of policies that attempt to reformulate relations between ethno-cultural minorities and the state through the creation of new laws, policies and institutions (Kymlicka, 2012). These new laws, policies and institutions are meant to reduce the barriers and stigmas that have limited the ability of individuals to freely explore and express their identities. Hence, in Kymlicka's view, multiculturalism is a way of expanding rather than reducing the scope of individual autonomy, as it tackles the relations of hierarchy, stigmatization and oppression 'that had precluded or penalized particular life choices' (Kymlicka, 2015, p. 20). The post-war human rights revolution has thus acted as an inspiration for multicultural movements. Simultaneously, however, human rights norms also act as a constraint. Here Kymlicka writes: 'Insofar as historically excluded or stigmatized groups struggle against earlier hierarchies in the name of equality, they too have to renounce their own traditions of exclusion or oppression in the treatment of, say, women, gays, people of mixed race, religious dissenters, and so on. Human rights, and liberal democratic constitutionalism more generally, provide the overarching framework within which these struggles are debated and addressed' (Kymlicka, 2012, p. 6).

Liberal Multiculturalism and Religion

It might appear from the above that Kymlicka's framework of liberal multiculturalism seems concerned first and foremost with ethnicity and culture. So why look at religion? Critics of Kymlicka's theorizing, such as Dwight Newman (2003) and Erik Anderson (2001), have in fact accused Kymlicka of over-emphasizing the potentially oppressive nature of religion without giving adequate attention to the (potential) compatibility between fidelity to a religious community and the development of autonomy. Religion, they argue, is far too crucial a dimension of many people's cultural identities to ignore, and even where religion is attended to within liberal thinking about autonomy, it may be argued that it is far too crucial a dimension of identity to give secondary status in favor of culture. Kymlicka has stated that in the 1980s and 1990s religion had not been central to debates about multiculturalism.[1] Rather, the types of groups discussed were predominantly ethnic, and then later racial.

Kymlicka discusses a shift from ethnicity, to race, to religion in a 2015 essay, 'The Three Lives of Multiculturalism' (Kymlicka, 2015). He notes a number of reasons for the increased prominence of religion as a basis for political participation and claims-making, including global trends towards the (re-)politicization of religion as well as the ethnicization of Muslim identities, and heated concerns among governments in the post-9/11 era to ascertain 'what "the Muslims" think and feel', and whether or not they are becoming radicalized. This has effectively created new mechanisms for young Muslims to self-organize and participate along the lines of religious affiliation (Kymlicka, 2015, p. 27). In recognition of religious identity as a meaningful social category within multicultural thinking and policy-making, Kymlicka writes that the essential goals of multiculturalism still apply, and it is now clear that he recognizes religion as a meaningful category of group identification within multicultural societies.

Addressing the 'Backlash' Against Liberal Multiculturalism

Interestingly, three years prior to authoring his 'Three Lives' essay, Kymlicka and his colleague Keith Banting took on what ostensibly may have been seen as a more pressing issue at the time – namely, the apparent 'backlash' against multicultural policies that began to circulate in much of the western world, and particularly Europe, a decade into the twenty-first century. This backlash was captured in such announcements as that made by Chancellor Merkel in Germany, stating in 2010 that multiculturalism had 'utterly failed', and British Prime Minister David Cameron's claim in 2011 that state multiculturalism had led to the segregation of different cultures rather than to their integration into the mainstream. Kymlicka (2012) counter that this shift has been more complete at the level of discourse than at that of policy, and that retreat from multiculturalism in fact has not been the dominant pattern. Here, Banting and Kymlicka draw upon their ongoing study, the

'Multiculturalism Policy Index' (MPI). This project monitors the evolution of multiculturalism policies in 21 western democracies [2] across the span of three decades, from 1980 through 2010, and provides an index for each of three types of minorities: immigrant groups, historical national minorities, and indigenous peoples (Multiculturalism Policy Index [MPI], 2010). Using MPI data, Banting and Kymlicka find that in many countries, civic integration programs (the approach popularly touted by several European states as a better alternative to multiculturalism) are being 'layered' over multiculturalism initiatives rather than replacing them. Such processes have led to a multicultural version of civic integration. Kymlicka (2012) writes that in fact the record of multicultural policy within Europe is one of modest strengthening rather than weakening, when average scores from 1980 through 2010 are examined. He writes further that MPI evidence suggests that countries combining civic integration and multiculturalism policies 'are doing comparatively well on many dimensions', including levels of trust and social cohesion, political participation, and prejudice and far right xenophobia.

Method

Countries Examined

This study takes its cue from Banting and Kymlicka's Multiculturalism Policies Index (MPI), and the MPI has guided our selection of countries.[3] Banting and Kymlicka's multiculturalism policy index for immigrant minorities involves eight indicators:

1. constitutional, legislative or parliamentary affirmation of multiculturalism, at the central and/or regional and municipal levels; the adoption of multiculturalism in school curriculum;
2. the inclusion of ethnic representation/sensitivity in the mandate of public media or media licensing;
3. exemptions from dress codes, either by statute or by court cases;
4. allowing of dual citizenship;
5. the funding of ethnic group organizations to support cultural activities;
6. the funding of bilingual education or mother tongue instruction;
7. affirmative action for disadvantaged immigrant groups.

For each indicator, countries receive a score as 0 (no such policy), 0.5 (partial) or 1.0 (clear policy). The component scores are then aggregated, producing a total country score ranging from 0 to 8 (MPI, 2010).

Recognizing the increasing importance of religion as a basis for identity and claims-making among migrant groups, we wanted to explore what it might look like to expand the kinds of questions Banting and Kymlicka look at within the immigrant minorities index toward specific public school issues pertaining to religion. We also wanted to incorporate Banting and Kymlicka's 2010 total scores for each country within the index into our data and analysis, as these scores could serve as indicators of how strong the country is overall regarding immigrant multicultural policies. We could also compare our findings with Banting and Kymlicka's total scores to see the degree to which our data corroborate the total index scores (referred to hereafter in this study as Immigrant Minority Multicultural Policy Index, or IMMPI, scores). We chose not to incorporate *each* of Banting and Kymlica's eight indicators within this index as we thought it would overly complicate the research.

Multiculturalism Policies Scoring

The scoring areas given below were theoretically determined, as influenced by Kymlicka's (2007, 2010, 2012) articulation of liberal multiculturalism and multicultural citizenship. While Kymlicka's work does not explicitly address each of the areas below in relation to immigrant multiculturalism, we believe that our rationales for selecting them and coding them as we did are consistent with the principles of recognition and accommodation that undergird the theory. Our coding and rationale are also consistent with similar types of indices, such as Olsen's (2013) tolerance indicators.

We consulted a wide range of sources to determine country scores in the indicators listed below. These included four excellent edited volumes covering religion and education in international contexts: *International Perspectives on Education, Religion and Law*, edited by Charles Russo (Russo, 2014); *The Routledge International Handbook of Religious Education*, edited by Derek H. Davis and Elena Miroshnikova (Davis & Miroshnikova, 2013); *Religion and Education in Europe: developments, contexts and debates*, edited by Robert Jackson, Siebren Miedema, Wolfram Weisse, and Jean-Paul Willaime (Jackson et al, 2007); and *International Migration and the Governance of Religious Diversity*, edited by Paul Bramadat and Matthias Koenig (Bramadat & Koenig, 2009) Additionally, we consulted two key research reports: *Teaching about Religions in European School Systems: policy issues and trends*, by Luce Pépin and produced by the Network of European Foundations (Pépin, 2009); and *Assessing Tolerance in Everyday School Life*, by Tore Vincents Olsen and produced by the European Commission European Research Area (Olsen, 2013). We also drew upon data featured in the Multiculturalism Policies Index. Finally, we consulted the education ministries or education departments of each of the countries examined so as to access documents pertaining to school practices and policies. In the section below we describe and offer rationales for each of our scoring areas.

Allowable school dress (School dress codes). In this study we view the wearing of religious clothing and religious symbols as important parts of self-expression and the expression of faith. Public school dress codes that allow students to wear their religious garb both recognize the existence of multiple faiths and accommodate students in expressing their faiths. Hence we view school dress codes that are permissive in this manner as promoting multiculturalism. Our coding of public school dress policies in each country consisted of whether there exists a prohibition against the wearing of any kind of religious clothing or symbol in the public school, whether some types of clothing and symbols are permitted and others are not, and whether all kinds of religious clothing or symbols are allowed. We also examined particular types of religious clothing and symbols unique to particular religious groups. Here we focused on major migrant faiths as well as the dominant religions of migrant countries of origin. We also examined the types of religious dress that have most often been issues within public schools in the states we examined as guided by our sources noted above. These include the *hijab* and the *niqab* for Muslims (treated as two separate categories), the turban and *kirpan* for Sikh students (also treated as separate categories), the *kippah* for Jewish students, and Christian symbols for Christians. For each of the clothing or symbol categories, we investigated whether there exist explicit prohibitions against wearing them, whether they were allowed, or whether there exists variance across regions within the country regarding school prohibitions or allowances. Finally, we provided composite scores (up to 7) for each country, adding up their scores in each of the above areas. The higher the composite score, the greater the country exercised recognition of and accommodation to students' freedom to wear religious clothing and religious symbols.

Prayer space. The provisions for prayer space within public schools, so long as the spaces do not infringe upon the education of other students and do not result in a school's endorsement of any particular religion, are also important for the exercise of religious identity, and, like the wearing of clothing and symbols, may be important parts of the expression of faith. Providing space for students to pray during the day is different from requiring either individual or collective prayer as part of the formal or informal school curriculum or culture. In the name of equality, prayer spaces must be open to all students, and cannot privilege one religious tradition over the other. School policies that provide spaces for students to pray both recognize the existence of multiple faiths and accommodate students in exercising their faiths. Hence we view school policies that are accommodating in this manner as promoting multiculturalism. Our coding of prayer space policies in public schools in each country consisted of whether there exists an explicit prohibition against providing any type of prayer space for students, whether prayer spaces are open to all students, or whether some types of prayer spaces are permitted and others are not. Because prayer space issues have most often arisen around the needs of Muslim, and to a lesser extent Christian, students (Levey & Modood, 2009; Russo, 2014), we also examined whether spaces were allowed for these specific religious groups, again coding whether all schools allow such spaces, whether none do, or whether there exists variation across regions. Finally, we provided composite scores (up to 4) for each country, adding up their scores in each of the above areas. The higher the composite score, the greater the country exercised recognition of and accommodation to students' freedom to pray in a separate space.

Religious holidays. Religious holidays provide students with opportunities to freely associate with their religious and cultural groups and/or to exercise their faith. All of the countries that we examined already privilege Christian students by including Christian holidays within their official school calendars. The argument here is that, in the name of fairness and equality, minority religious groups should be extended the same privileges. Doing so both recognizes the existence of minority religious holidays and accommodates students who wish to celebrate or honor those holidays, and hence promotes multiculturalism. Our coding of school policies regarding holidays in each country consisted of determining whether students could not be excused for any religious holiday, whether there were some religious holidays for which students could be excused and others for which they could not, or whether there were no limitations regarding the kinds of religious holidays for which students could be excused. Because of the particular presence of Christianity within the school policies we examined on this topic, we also investigated whether the official school calendar included only Christian holidays, or whether it included Christian as well as other religious holidays. We also provided composite scores for each country, adding up their scores (up to 3) in each of the above areas. The higher the composite score, the greater the country exercised recognition of and accommodation to various religious holidays.

Confessional instruction. In this study, we define confessional instruction as teaching 'in' or 'of' a religion, and teaching (a particular) religion as truth. Confessional instruction provided in the public school, particularly if is mandatory and has no opt-out provision, is by nature antithetical to the secular dimension of public schooling within liberal democratic societies, which must protect students' rights to freely identify (or not identify) with the belief system they choose. Schools which offer confessional instruction but allow students to opt out taking it at least recognize the existence of other faiths, or the possibility that students may not be religious at all. We regarded such schools as more strongly multicultural than those which required students to attend confessional instruction and had no opt-out provisions. Our coding of school policies regarding confessional instruction in each country consisted of determining whether schools offered or did not offer confessional instruction, and whether, in the former case, the instruction was mandatory, or whether students could opt out. We also examined whether there existed variation across regions regarding these policies. We provided composite scores (up to 3) for each country, adding up their scores in each of the above areas. The higher the composite score, the greater the country exercised recognition of and accommodation to various religious (or non-religious) identities.

Non-confessional instruction about religion. Schools can teach about religion without teaching 'in' religion. In this study, we define non-confessional religious instruction as teaching about religion in an objective and non-biased manner. We regard the provision of non-confessional instruction as an opportunity to expose students to multiple perspectives and religious world views. Hence we see it as more conducive to recognizing the multiple faith traditions that migrants might represent. Given Kymlicka's (2015) recognition of religious group belonging as constituting a third stage of multiculturalism, we believe that non-confessional instruction is critical for understanding and living in a world of diversity and religious pluralism. Hence we view this type of instruction as promoting multiculturalism. Countries were scored on whether they do or do not offer non-confessional instruction.

Official religion. A state religion or an established state Church is a religious body or creed that is officially endorsed by the state. State Churches may have undue influence on public school policies and practices, and when they do, we see this as compromising multiculturalism. We scored countries on whether they do or do not have established state Churches. Given the above, we also recognized that having an established Church does not necessarily mean that such states do not take measures to recognize and accommodate differing migrant faiths in their public schools. We provide additional discussion and qualifications for these cases in our data presentation and analysis below.

Immigrant percentage and asylum applications in 20 countries. In this study we used the number of immigrants as a percentage of the total resident population of each country, as well as submitted asylum applications to the 20 countries we examined (see tables in Appendix).

Data Analysis Plan

Hierarchical cluster analysis. Hierarchical clustering is used as an explorative analytic tool that allows the grouping of cases of data based on the degree of association with respect to target characteristics/variables (Antonenko et al, 2012). We employed hierarchical clustering as we wanted to look at similar characteristics among the 20 countries in terms of their IMMPI total score, and among the educational policies and practices described above. Because clustering algorithms group cases based on the variables of interest rather than variables across cases, it is an appropriate tool to examine similarities and differences in terms of their policies and practices among the 20 countries.

The hierarchical clustering method is used in this study with three cluster analyses: hierarchical, K-means, and two-step clustering. It starts with each case as a separate cluster, and then sequentially combines clusters to construct a hierarchy of nested clusters, reducing the number of clusters at each step until all cases are combined into one cluster. By inspecting the progression of cluster merging, one can isolate clusters of cases with high similarity. Also, because it allows use of Ward's minimum variance clustering (Ward, 1963), it is useful for exploratory work when researchers do not have a hypothesized idea about the likely number of clusters. Finally, it is appropriate for small data sets ($N = 20$) (Antonenko et al, 2012), such as those used in this study.

ANOVA, post hoc and descriptive statistics. After obtaining clusters using hierarchical cluster analysis with Ward's minimum variance clustering, we conducted ANOVA analysis to see the significance of differences among the variables and to see if the clusters were correctly grouped. We then further examined the group differences using post hoc (Tukey's Honest Significant Difference [HSD]) and a descriptive analysis to see the characteristics of each cluster.

Once we identified the characteristics of clusters, we named each cluster as well as providing more descriptive data to examine in depth the scale of variables such as dress code, prayer space, religious holiday and confessional instruction in school. We also examined non-confessional instruction and official religion. After we named and identified characteristics of the clusters, we also looked at asylum application numbers in 2014 and immigrant percentages in 2015 in each cluster to identify particular challenges of these countries. In addition, we also conducted cross-national comparisons both within and across clusters to provide in-depth examination of particular social and cultural contexts, and to bring to the fore a more nuanced understanding of how the countries in our study demonstrate both similarity and difference.

Results and Discussion

Descriptive Analysis

Table I shows descriptive statistics. The country with the highest IMMPI score is Australia (8) and the one with the lowest is Denmark (0). The countries with the lowest dress-code composite score are Belgium and France (0), and countries with the highest scores are Australia, Austria, Canada, Finland, Greece, New Zealand and Norway (7). Countries receiving the lowest score on providing prayer space are France and Italy (0), and countries with the highest score are Canada and Denmark (4). The countries with the highest score on religious holidays, allowing not only Christian holidays but also other religious traditions' holidays, are New Zealand, the United Kingdom and the USA (3). A higher score on confessional instruction indicates that a country is sensitive to other religions and religious groups and provides choices rather than forcing students to take confessional instruction. The countries with the highest score are Australia, the United Kingdom, Germany, Italy and New Zealand (3). The country with lowest score is Finland (0.5). Regarding non-confessional instruction, Greece is the only country which does not teach about other religions in its public schools. Greece, Norway and Denmark are the only countries that have official religions or established state Churches. Regarding immigrant populations, in 2015 the USA had the highest (46,627,102) and Finland had the lowest (315,881).[4] However, the percentage of immigrants in relation to their total population shows that Switzerland has the highest (29.39%) and Finland has the lowest (5.74%). Regarding the asylum application numbers for 2014, Germany had the highest (65,659) and the USA had the second highest (52,835), while New Zealand (140) and Portugal (166) had lower numbers of applications submitted.

	n	Range	Minimum	Maximum	Mean	SD
MPI 2010	20	8.0	.0	8.0	3.800	2.3022
Dress code composite	20	7.0	.0	7.0	5.375	2.1575
Prayer space composite	20	4.0	.0	4.0	2.025	1.3424
Religious holiday composite	20	1.5	1.5	3.0	2.000	.4867
Confessional instruction composite	20	2.5	.5	3.0	1.975	.8656
Non-confessional instruction	20	1.0	.0	1.0	.950	.2236
Official religion	20	1.0	1.0	2.0	1.850	.3663
Immigrant percentage 2015	20	23.65	5.74	29.39	15.0525	6.25719
Number of immigrants in country as of 2015	20	46311221	315881	46627102	5781777	10207595
Asylum applications 2014	|20	65519.0	140.0	65659.0	13952.050	17968.4200
Valid n (listwise)	20					

Table I. Descriptive statistics.

Hierarchical Cluster Analysis

Utilizing hierarchical clustering with Ward's method (Ward, 1963), we obtained five clusters based on MPI scores and other school policies for religion and religious practice (dress code, prayer space, religious holiday and confessional instruction). Figure 1 shows a dendrogram using the Ward linkage. The figure shows how members (countries) in each cluster are close to each other, and how five clusters are obtained. Once we obtained the clusters, we examined other variables (specifically, whether an official religion exists, and the mean scores of immigrant percentage in 2015 as well as asylum applications in 2014 in each cluster). Table II shows ANOVA tests for showing statistical significance of variables/characteristics within each cluster, and the group means and standard deviations arrayed by clusters.

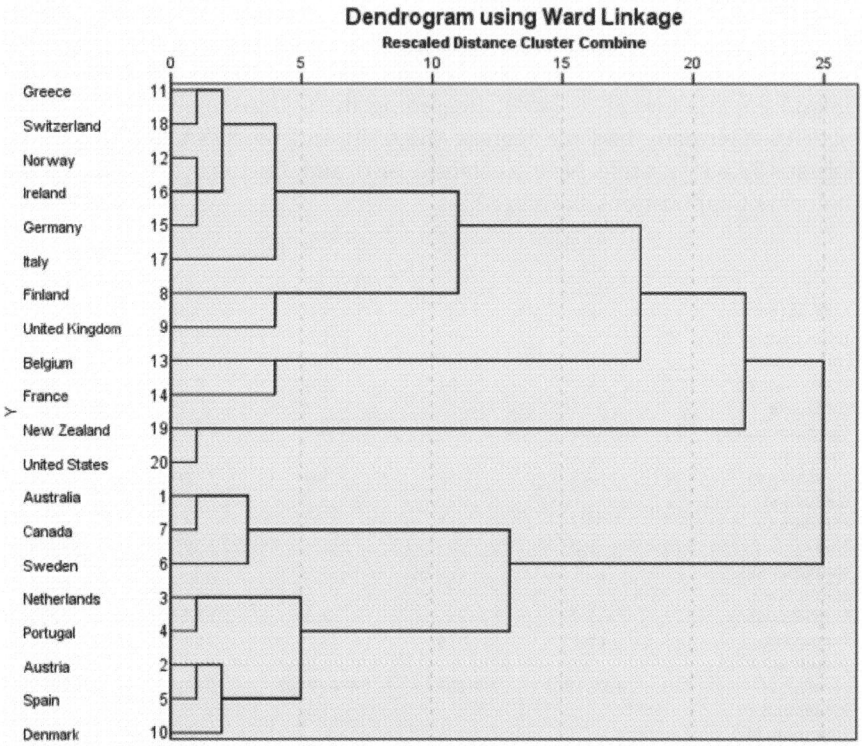

Figure 1. Dendrogram using Ward linkage.

Four one-way analysis of variance (ANOVA) tests showed that all determining variables (independent variables) of five clusters (as a dependent variable) reached statistical significance (MPI 2010: F [4, 15] = 5.179, p = .008; dress code: F [4, 15] = 13.257, p = .000; prayer space: F [4, 15] = 7.519, p = .002; religious holiday: F [4, 15] = 5.571, p = .006; and confessional instruction: F [4, 15] = 2.186, p = .004). Further post hoc analysis (Tukey HSD) was conducted to determine how clusters differed. Cluster 1 (C1) has significantly a higher MPI score (7) compared with C2 (2.1) and C3 (3.3). Cluster 4 has significantly lower score (0) on dress code composite mean score compared with C1 (6.5), C2 (6.0), C3 (5.5) and C5 (7.0). Cluster 1 (3.0) has a significantly higher prayer space score compared with C4 (0.5) and C5 (0.25), and Cluster 2 (3.3.) has a significantly higher prayer space score compared with C3 (1.69), C4 and C5. Cluster 5 (3.0) has significantly a higher religious holiday score compared with the rest of the clusters (C1-C4; see Table II). Cluster 3 (1.25) has a significantly lower confessional instruction score compared with C1 (2.83) and C5 (3.0).

	Cluster 1 (n=3) Group mean (SD)	Cluster 2 (n=5) Group mean (SD)	Cluster 3 (n=8) Group mean (SD)	Cluster 4 (n=2) Group mean (SD)	Cluster 5 (n=2) Group mean (SD)	Total mean	F	Sig.
MPI in 2010	*7.5 (.50)*	2.1 (1.48)	3.3 (1.79)	3.8 (2.48)	4.5 (2.12)	3.8	5.18	.008
Dress code	*6.5 (.87)*	*6.0 (1.06)*	*5.5 (1.39)*	*0 (0)*	*7 (0)*	5.38	13.26	.000
Prayer space	*3.0 (1.32)*	*3.3 (.45)*	1.69 (.96)	.5 (.71)	.25 (.35)	2.03	7.52	.002
Religious holiday	*1.8 (.29)*	1.7 (.27)	2.1 (.42)	1.75 (.35)	*3.0 (0)*	2.00	5.57	.006
Confessional instruction	*2.83 (.29)*	2.1 (.74)	*1.25 (.54)*	2.25 (1.06)	*3.0 (0)*	1.98	5.97	.004
Non-confessional instruction	Yes	Yes	Yes except Greece	Yes	Yes			
Official religion	No	Denmark	Greece & Norway	No	No			
Immigrant percentage 2015 (%)	22.26 (5.74)	12.01 (3.51)	14.05 (6.96)	12.19 (.13)	18.73 (5.99)	15.05 (6.26)		
Asylum applications 2014	12,960 (13481)	5,379 (4714)	15,733 (21635)	17,215 (16680)	26,488 (37261)	13,952 (17968)		
Countries	Australia Sweden Canada	Austria Netherlands Portugal Spain Denmark	Finland UK Greece Norway Germany Ireland Italy Switzerland	Belgium France	New Zealand USA			

Note: Bold type indicates significance.

Table II. Group means and standard deviations.

Characteristics of the Clusters and Applications

After examining between-cluster differences using IMMPI scores, dress code policies, prayer space policies, religious holiday practices and confessional instruction policies, we describe countries in Cluster 1 as *High religious freedom providers*, those in Cluster 2 as *Moderate religious freedom providers*, those in Cluster 3 as *Christian-focused religious freedom providers*, those in Cluster 4 as *Committed secularists* and those in Cluster 5 as *Sensitive religious freedom providers*.[5] Using these names, we also examine asylum application numbers in 2014 and immigrant percentage in 2015 in each cluster to see any challenges faced by countries in each cluster, and to provide suggestions for future policy and practice. In addition, we also make cross-national comparisons, within as well as across clusters, to provide in-depth examination so as to bring to the fore important contextual issues as well as to nuance our comparative evaluations. Table AI in the Appendix shows asylum application numbers in 2014 and immigrant percentage in 2015 in each of the countries.

In the section below we provide a discussion of each of the clusters, noting their Table II scores and relating these scores to the migrant populations they are host to. The latter draws upon information provided in Table AI in the Appendix, as well as in the additional tables provided in the Appendix (Table AII: top five migrant groups by country of origin and receiving state (mid-2013 estimates); and Table AIII: top five nationalities of asylum applicants by country of asylum (second quarter 2014).

Cluster 1: High religious freedom providers (Australia, Canada and Sweden). It is perhaps ironic to have Sweden, arguably the most secular country in Europe, join a club entitled 'high religious freedom providers'.[6] Yet these three countries (15% of the countries examined) are united by their very high scores in our all our measures. They also have high migrant percentages (average 22.26). Examined at a global level, the three countries form a kind of lopsided right-angled triangle, with a long hypotenuse extending from Sweden down to Australia. We might look at this shape as representing three global corners of refuge for religious migrant students who have non-Christian faiths. All three countries enjoy high IMMPI scores (Australia 8; Canada 7.5; Sweden 7). They are also accommodating in their dress codes (6.5) and school prayer space policies (3.0), they do not enforce confessional instruction (2.83), and they offer non-confessional instruction about other religions. Part of the explanation for this particular grouping is that 'they' mainly reside outside of Europe. This grouping is thus able to avoid some of the dominant patterns that unite other European countries and that have also mitigated the recognition of and accommodation to religious minorities (as particularly evident in Cluster 3 below). This is not to say that this cluster does not reflect Europe at all, or that there are not some internal differences within the cluster. Sweden, for instance, prohibits confessional instruction in its public schools, but in its (mandatory) non-confessional instruction about major world religions, there is a special focus on Christianity (Friedner, 2013). Nonetheless, Sweden is quite proactively multicultural, as evidenced by the Swedish Constitution, which enshrines principles related to multiculturalism (MPI, 2010).

The high scores within our study are important for Cluster 1, as a significant number of their migrants (the highest number in all the clusters), and in particular their asylum applicants, come from non-Christian-majority countries. Collectively, these countries include not only Muslim-majority states, such as Syria, Iraq, Pakistan and Afghanistan, but also countries such as Vietnam and India.

Cluster 2: Moderate religious freedom providers (Austria, the Netherlands, Portugal, Spain and Denmark). Capturing 20% of the countries we examined, Cluster 2 demonstrates moderate levels of recognition and accommodation. However, unlike Cluster 3, these countries have low migrant percentages (average 12.01). The individual country IMMPI scores are also low, ranging from Portugal (3) and Spain (3) to the Netherlands (2) to Austria (1.5) to Denmark (0). While they are more accommodating in their dress codes (6.0) and school prayer space policies (3.3) than Cluster 3, this is less the case with respect to religious holidays (1.7) (the public school holiday calendar for Denmark, for instance, includes only Christian holidays). Cluster 2 scores for confessional (2.1) and non-confessional instruction (1) are comparable to scores within Cluster 3, although the influence or presence of Christianity does not appear to be as forceful.

Perhaps the most important difference between Cluster 2 and Cluster 3 is that migrants are not flocking to Cluster 2 countries in significant numbers. For the migrants who do come, there are some challenges to be faced, particularly in the area of honoring religious holidays. This is because both with respect to migrants and with respect to asylum applicants, states within Cluster 2 are attracting people from non-Christian-majority countries. These countries are not only Muslim majority, most notably Syria and Turkey, but also mixed Muslim and Christian, such as Eritrea, as well as mixed between indigenous beliefs and Christianity, such as Angola.

Cluster 3: Christian-focused religious freedom providers (Finland, Germany, Greece, Ireland, Italy, Norway, Switzerland, the United Kingdom). Representing 40% of the countries we examined, Cluster 3 is our largest grouping. The cluster is characterized by mid or moderate levels of recognition and accommodation, but mid to high migrant percentages (average 14.05). The individual IMMPI scores range from a score of 6 (Finland) to a score of 1 (Switzerland). However, with the exception of the United Kingdom (5.5), the rest of the countries score 4 or below (Germany 2.5, Greece 2.5, Ireland 4, Italy 1.5, Norway 3.5). On our specific school measures, the countries are united in that they allow considerable freedoms with respect to dress codes (5.5) and recognizing the religious holidays of diverse traditions (2.06), but they are rather restrictive when it comes to prayer space (1.69), confessional instruction (1.25), and particularly non-confessional instruction (0.875). Perhaps the most significant thread that draws these states together is that their national identities are presently tied to an established religion, or have been in the not-so-distant past. Within our study, only three countries – Norway, Greece and Denmark – have an established Church, and two of them, Norway and Greece, are within this cluster. Even those countries that no longer have state religions still maintain very close relationships with a dominant faith. Ireland comes immediately to mind in this regard. The 'Christian-focused' component of this cluster comes out most strongly in the area of confessional instruction, where the states as a whole are least apt to recognize and accommodate minority religious (or non-religious) identities. The in-cluster comparison of Norway and Greece below provides an examination of the contexts within which these policies and practices are rooted.

If Cluster 1 represents global spots of refuge for migrant students with non-Christian faiths, the countries in Cluster 3 represent something of the opposite. While the dominant pattern regarding immigration in this cluster appears to reflect migration within greater Europe (for instance, Swedes moving to Finland, or Italians moving to Switzerland), the dominant pattern concerning country of origin for asylum applicants is very clearly non-European, and more particularly, non-Europeans from non-Christian-majority countries. These countries are predominantly Muslim majority, such as Iraq, Syria, Afghanistan, Mali and Nigeria. This poses a challenge for countries in Cluster 3, particularly in the areas of prayer space, confessional instruction and non-confessional instruction.

Cluster 4: Committed secularists (France and Belgium). Although they represent only two countries within our study, France and Belgium are rather exceptional. While Belgium scores far higher than France on the 2010 immigrant minorities index (Belgium scored 5.5 while France scored 2), on two of our specific school measures both countries scored quite low, particularly in the areas of school dress (0), prayer space (0.5) and religious holiday (1.75). The confessional instruction average score (2.25) was rather surprising, but we attribute this to a contrast between France and Belgium (wherein the former expressly forbids it, and the latter permits it, with qualifications). Both countries offer non-confessional instruction. By far the strongest thread connecting the two countries on our measures is the enactment of *laïcité* (secularity) in the public schools (discussed further below).

France and Belgium combined have mid-level percentages of migrants (12.19). However, they have the second-highest number of asylum applicants (combined average of 17,215), falling only behind Cluster 5. This latter figure poses a challenge given the low scores in school dress, prayer space and religious holiday, as their top asylum applicant countries include Syria, Eritrea and Bangladesh. The cross-cluster comparison of France and Canada below provides an examination of the contexts within which these policies and practices are rooted.

Cluster 5: Sensitive religious freedom providers (New Zealand and the United States). Cluster 5 represents the only entirely non-European grouping. We title this cluster 'sensitive' religious freedom providers because they score well on nearly all of our measures: dress code (7), religious holidays (3), confessional instruction (3) and non-confessional instruction (1). The surprising score concerns prayer space (0.25), and we attribute this in part to fears of Establishment Clause violations in the USA.[7] Like Cluster 1, the overall high scores are important for Cluster 5, again as a significant number of their migrants, and in particular their asylum applicants, come from non-Christian-majority countries. These countries include China, India, Sri Lanka and Turkey.

Cross-national Comparisons: within and across clusters

In the section below we provide two different types of cross-country comparisons. The first, a comparison between Norway and Greece, is a 'within-cluster' comparison, which helps us develop a more nuanced picture of important variations within our groupings. The second, a comparison between Canada and France, represents a 'cross-cluster' comparison of countries at opposite ends of the cluster spectrum when it comes to recognizing and accommodating the religious identities of their public school students. This second comparison highlights differences between two contrasting clusters, and therein also sharpens our understanding of school practices within the two respective countries. Both types of comparison draw out particular context conditions in terms of how they influence public school policies and practices. In describing the comparison countries, we draw upon the group means and standard deviations data featured in Table II, as well as upon migrant numbers and countries of origin data featured in the three tables in the Appendix.

A within-cluster comparison: Norway and Greece in Cluster 3 (Christian-focused religious freedom providers). Norway and Greece make for an interesting pairing. In terms of their aggregate IMMPI scores, Norway received a 2010 score of 3.5, while the score for Greece was 1 point lower at 2.5. Based on these figures alone, one might say that Norway is overall stronger than Greece in terms of multicultural public policies, but further investigation into our data reveals some interesting details.

Norway is officially a constitutional monarchy and has a parliamentary system of government. About 80% of the country's population belong to the Church of Norway, and Article 2 of the country's constitution refers to Evangelical-Lutheranism as the state's official religion. While not a constitutional monarchy, Greece is a parliamentary republic, and its constitution also establishes an official religion (or the 'prevailing religion'), in this case the Greek Orthodox Church, which is in larger communion with the Eastern Orthodox Church. The majority of Greeks are baptized within this Church (Maghioros, 2013).

Reflecting the strong role that a dominant religion plays in their respective societies, both states have had a tradition of providing confessional instruction in their public schools. In some very important respects, Greece has maintained a firmer grip. Religious education in this country is an obligatory subject in both public and private schools. Furthermore, religion is interwoven more generally within the culture and ethos of its public schools. For instance, yearly benedictions at school buildings are a common practice, and it is also common for classrooms to have icons of Jesus Christ as well as the Virgin Mary. Furthermore, a common prayer is made every day before the start of school at a joint gathering of students and teachers in the schoolyard (Maghioros, 2013).

Characteristic of other Protestant northern European countries, Norway by contrast has gradually become more pluralistic in its religious education (Willaime, 2007). This is reflected, for instance, in changes to the title of the subject as taught in the schools, moving from 'Christian Knowledge with Orientation to Religion and Life Stances', to 'Christian, Religious, and Life Stance Education', to the present 'Religion, Philosophies of Life and Ethics'. Nonetheless, these changes have not been easy, and a preferential treatment of the majority religion remains. Furthermore, the schools have maintained a limited right to exemption from the course, granting release only in cases where parts of the subject may, from the point of view of the student's own religion or life philosophy, be considered as amounting to the practice of another religion or adherence to another philosophy of life (Plesner, 2013).

With respect to the other ways in which we examine religious recognition and accommodation, the official school holiday calendars for both Norway and Greece honor Christian as well as other religious holidays, although this is generally common across most countries we examined (France being the notable exception). With respect to school dress codes in Norway, our data indicate that there exists variation across the schools regarding accommodations made for migrant faiths. This variation includes whether schools allow Muslims to wear the *hijab* and/or the *niqab*, Sikhs to wear the turban or carry the *kirpan*, Jews to wear the *kippah*, and Christians to wear a cross. Interestingly, Greece is more permissible than Norway in this area, as we did not find any evidence of public schools prohibiting the above religious dress or symbols. This, however, may partly be due to where we are likely to find concentrations of minority faiths in the two countries. For instance, in Western Thrace there are 194 'minority schools' set up specifically for children from the Muslim minority. In these schools teaching takes place in both the Turkish and Greek languages, following a special program entitled 'Education of Muslim Children' (Maghioros, 2013). We are not aware that any such parallel set of schools exists in Norway. Hence it may be that public schools in Greece outside of Thrace have dealt less with religious dress issues than have public schools in Norway.[8]

The above conditions paint an interesting and rather complex picture for migrants entering these two countries. In 2015, Norway had an immigrant population of 741,813 (Migration Policy Institute [MPI], 2016). In 2013, the top three countries of origin for immigrants to Norway came from majority Christian states; Poland (87% Catholic), Sweden (87% Lutheran) and Germany (34% Protestant and 34% Roman Catholic) constitute the top three countries of origin (CIA, 2016; Migration Policy Institute [MPI], 2016). However, in 2014 the majority of asylum cases in Norway represented traditionally Muslim countries, where Syria (74% Sunni Muslim) and Somalia (majority Sunni Muslim) constituted the top three countries of origin (CIA, 2016; UNHCR, 2016). Hence we could surmise here that while children from immigrant households are likely to have their religions recognized and, at least at a general level of faith, accommodated within Norway, children from asylum-seeking families are likely to run into some issues in terms of religious education and school dress codes, depending on the school they attend.

In contrast to Norway, Greece had a greater immigrant population (1,242,514) in 2015, and in 2014 had fewer asylum applicants (5063) (MPI, 2016). However, the country profiles of these migrant populations are a bit different, with a less clear religious demarcation between immigrants and asylum seekers, and also less religious uniformity with respect to immigrant countries of origin. Most current immigrants to Greece come from Albania (57% Muslim), Bulgaria (59% Eastern Orthodox) and Romania (82% Eastern Orthodox), while Afghanistan (approximately 85% Sunni Muslim and10% Shia), Pakistan (approximately 85% Sunni Muslim and 10% Shia) and Albania constituted the top countries of origin of asylum seekers in 2014 (CIA, 2016; MPI, 2016). We might surmise that in Greece, children from Christian immigrant households are more likely to have their religions recognized and accommodated, while children from Muslim immigrant households, unless they make their way to Western Thrace, are even more likely than Muslim children in Norway to experience religious marginalization in the public schools, particularly with respect to confessional instruction. The same of course also holds for Muslim children from asylum-seeking families.

A Cross-cluster Comparison: Canada (High religious freedom providers) and France (Committed secularists). Canada and France make for another interesting comparison. Our data corroborate the IMMPI total scores for the two countries with respect to policies related to immigrant minorities. Here, Canada had a 2010 score of 7.5, the highest of all countries in the index for that year, while France had a score of 2, one of the lowest. Indeed, Canada's commitment to multiculturalism is embodied in the constitution of the country, and specifically within Section 27 of the Canadian Charter on Rights and Freedoms. Furthermore, the Canadian Multiculturalism Act of 1988 affirms a policy of multiculturalism at the federal level, and also provides for the establishment of programs and policies in support of the act (MPI, 2010). In rather stark contrast, Article 1 of the French constitution affirms France's position as an indivisible, secular, democratic and social republic. The Article states that all citizens will be equal before the law without distinction of origin, race or religion. This has been interpreted that France does not recognize minorities, whether they are religious, ethnic, linguistic or other. Rather, under French law all citizens have equal rights and the law is not meant to accord specific rights to groups as defined by their community of origin, culture, beliefs or whatnot (Dericquebourg, 2013). Even though cultural diversity with France is not ignored entirely (integration is recognized as a two-way process, involving both migrants as well as the host society), France has been quite outspoken in its opposition to embracing a multicultural model (MPI, 2010).

The above points are interesting in light of the fact that religious identity, and Catholicism in particular, has historically tied the two countries. France has historically been a strongly Catholic country, and until 1950, 80% of the state's population was Roman Catholic. Under the monarchy and until the French Revolution, all schools were in fact under the authority of the Catholic Church (Dericquebourg, 2013). In Canada, French-speaking Roman Catholics constituted a powerful religious community (along with English-speaking Protestants) prior to the country's official founding in 1867, and Roman Catholics continue to enjoy political power. Within education, this is nowhere more apparent than in the full public support Catholic schools receive in four out of ten Canadian provinces (see further below). The fact that France has cleansed itself, as it were, of any religious influence in its public schools and that Canada has not, or at least has not entirely, says as much about French secularism as it does about Canadian multiculturalism.[9] On this count, the French appear to be better at being French than the Canadians at being Canadian.

With respect to our data, Canada predictably scores higher than France in terms of school dress codes as well as accommodations for prayer. While we found that public schools in Canada have no prohibitions against the wearing of the *hijab* and/or the *niqab*, the turban, the *kirpan*, the *kippah* or a Christian cross, France has banned nearly all religious symbols in its public schools. The French stance regarding religious garb in its public schools came to global attention through the well-publicized *l'affaire du voile*, or 'veil affair', involving Muslim school girls, and the prohibition against wearing the *hijab* in public schools. The highly contentious debate within French society resulted in the 2004 formation of Law 2004-228, which bans the conspicuous display of religious signs (Dericquebourg, 2013).[10] On the issue of providing prayer spaces for students, we found that public schools in Canada have no prohibitions against this, while French public schools, under the banner of complete secularization, do not allow any form of formal prayer on school premises.

On the matters of school holidays, confessional instruction and non-confessional instruction, we found further variance between the two countries, although not in as striking terms as for dress codes and prayer. In a rather ironic twist, the holiday calendar for French schools includes one religious holiday: Christmas. All other holidays are marked as seasonal breaks (that is, Winter Holiday, Spring Break, Autumn Break). The school holiday calendar in Canada, on the other hand, includes both Christian as well as other religious holidays. Neither of the countries provides confessional instruction in its public schools, although confessional instruction is a component of publicly funded Catholic schools in the Canadian provinces of Ontario, Alberta and Saskatchewan (Young, 2013). Finally, public schools in both Canada as well as France offer instruction about various religions, although presently in France, education about religion is taught from a 'religious facts' perspective through subjects deemed to be relevant, including history, literature, geography and civic education (Pépin, 2009). Public schools in Canada in turn may offer courses such as World Religions, or Ethics and Religious Cultures.[11] The most interesting and in many ways telling difference between the two countries on the matter of teaching about religions concerns the stated arguments for doing so. Canada seems to have taken a more proactive and positive stance towards offering instruction about religions, referencing such organizations as the US National Council for Social Studies, and their assertion that knowledge about religion is both a characteristic of a well-educated person as well as vital for understanding and living in a world of diversity (Young, 2013). France too is justifying public school instruction about religious facts for these sorts of purposes, but according to Dericquebourg (2013), the arguments are also just as much defensive. For instance, according Dericquebourg, people worry that instruction about religious cultures, if 'abandoned' to religious movements, will pave the way for instruction about irrational phenomena or esotericism. Further, a lack of teaching about religions in the public schools may open a clear path for radical and fundamentalist views. Dericquebourg thus concludes that these types of arguments are the result of an overall negative perception of religion, and that teaching about religions is therefore considered as a type of prophylaxis.

From the above, we can see that migrants to Canada and migrants to France thus enter two very different countries, and the religious persuasions of these migrants will matter. By 2015, Canada had a population of 7,835,502 immigrants (MPI, 2016). The top three countries of origin for immigrants to Canada are the United Kingdom, China and India. These states represent a spectrum of religious as well as non-religious traditions. The United Kingdom is a Christian-majority state (Anglicans, Roman Catholics, Presbyterians, Methodists), while India is majority Hindu, although it also has a Muslim presence (14%). China in turn is officially an atheist state, although there exists a sizable Buddhist population in the country (18%) (CIA, 2016; MPI, 2016). In 2014 Canada had 5781 new asylum applicants. The top three states representing these cases were China, Pakistan and Afghanistan, again showing some variation with respect to the dominant religions in the country of origin (CIA, 2016; UNHCR, 2016). The numbers and profiles of migrants coming to France present a different picture. By 2015 France had an immigrant population similar to Canada (7,784,418) (MPI, 2016). However, their countries of origin differed. The top three countries of origin for immigrants to France are Algeria, Morocco and Portugal. Both Algeria and Morocco are strongly Muslim states (both are 99% Muslim, and both mostly Sunni), while Portugal is majority Christian (81% Catholic) (CIA, 2016; MPI, 2016). In 2015 France had 75,750 new asylum applicants. The top three countries representing these cases were Sudan (majority Sunni Muslim with a small Christian minority),

Syria (87% Muslim, mostly Sunni) and Kosovo (96% Muslim) (CIA, 2016; UNHCR, 2016).

As noted, Canada's progressive policies regarding school dress codes and prayer accommodations are fitting for the kinds of religious diversity its migrants represent, and our data indicate that migrant students will benefit from these particular provisions equally. This being said, Canada's Christian and in particular Catholic migrants will still continue to enjoy the choice of attending publicly supported parochial schools, at least if they resettle in Ontario, Alberta or Saskatchewan. France's ardently secular policies regarding public school dress codes as well as accommodations for prayer continue to run a high risk of clashing with the religious demands of many of its migrant students, particularly as high numbers of both its immigrants and its asylum applicants come from strongly Muslim countries (Morocco, incidentally, is one of the most religious countries in the world). Fortunately, in neither of the countries will migrants be subject to confessional instruction within a particular religious tradition, and in both states migrants may have the opportunity to learn about other religions and perspectives through non-confessional classes. However, the purposes for migrants being in such classes appear to differ; in Canada, it is in the name of honoring and living with diversity, while in France at least part of the rationale seems to be geared toward managing diversity so that diverse actors do not get the upper hand.

A Way Forward

The above discussions highlight a range of challenges, many of which may be translated into recommendations. In summary fashion, we would first point toward Sweden taking a more neutral stance with regard to its non-confessional instruction about other religions and world views. Sweden is grouped within the *High religious freedom providers* cluster, scoring well on most of our measures. Yet the specific focus on Christianity within non-confessional religious instruction would seem to compromise students' ability to freely learn about and evaluate differing religious traditions. This we see as antithetical to schooling within the liberal democratic state. Second, we would suggest that countries in Cluster 2 (Austria, the Netherlands, Portugal, Spain and Denmark) expand their school calendars to include other non-Christian holidays. As noted, Cluster 2 involves *Moderate religious freedom providers*. In the name of fairness and equality and in the interest of promoting multiculturalism, Cluster 2 countries could advance beyond the designation of 'moderate' by extending to minority religious groups the same holiday privileges as those already enjoyed by the majority religion.

Third, regarding the countries in Cluster 3 (Finland, Germany, Greece, Ireland, Italy, Norway, Switzerland, the United Kingdom), we would recommend greater accommodations with respect to prayer space, re-examining policies of providing confessional instruction, and providing non-confessional religious instruction within more neutral atmospheres. Cluster 3 involves *Christian-focused religious freedom providers*, and as previously noted, national identities within these states have presently or at least historically been tied to an established religion. Yet the fact that many migrants in these countries are now from non-Christian states calls into question whether schools are doing enough to help their migrant students feel recognized and accepted. With respect to Cluster 4, the *Committed secularists* (France and Belgium), we would direct attention to policies regarding school dress, prayer space and religious holidays. We do recognize that taking a multicultural approach to such matters would be viewed as deeply contradicting the principle of *laïcité*. This is a challenge in particular for France. Perhaps we can only look over the long term to see whether the French model will be more successful than the multicultural model in integrating non-Christian, and in particular, Muslim, migrants into the society.

Finally, regarding Cluster 5, *Sensitive religious freedom providers* (New Zealand and the USA), we would direct attention to providing greater accommodations for prayer space. As noted, this may raise concerns regarding religious establishment, but we believe it is possible for schools to provide spaces for prayer so long as such spaces do not infringe upon the education of other students and do not result in a school's endorsement of any particular religion. In carrying forward a major thread within this volume, we would say that fulfillment of all the above recommendations advances the UN Sustainable Development Goal 4 of ensuring an inclusive and quality education for all and promoting lifelong learning, and particularly the target of advancing appreciation of cultural diversity.

Our study is not without its limitations. Cross-national studies have a rather succulent allure within the field of comparative and international education by offering the promise of broad declarations about schooling within regions of the world, and of grouping countries into convenient categories for theory and analysis. Methodological nationalism arises as a concern, and it is not obvious that nation-states are our best units of analysis for our study. We try to account for this by including measures of variation within states, as well as through our in-cluster and cross-cluster comparative examinations, where attention to context is paramount. Other limitations to our study are more intimate to our investigation. We do not, for instance, examine the role of teachers, although clearly some immigrants and refugees do become teachers in their hosting societies. Nor do we examine the role of religious organizations serving migrant communities, and the manners in which they might materially aid migrants through such secular matters as economic opportunity, political activity and the promotion of educational achievement (Alba et al, 2009). We also do not examine private religious schools. Our reasoning is that the public school is probably the most reliable educational constant across the countries we examine, and it is a perfect stage for examining multiculturalism 'at work' because it potentially draws so many kinds of communities together, and because, at least in theory, it is guided by core liberal democratic principles. There are other limitations involving the kinds of questions we ask, and whether we could have asked more (for instance, about the celebration of religious festivals in schools, or the display of religious images within schools). Finally, our study makes the assumption that migrants represent the majority religion of their country of origin, and this does not account for people representing minority religions within their countries (including those seeking asylum based on religious grounds), as well as people who simply have no religion at all. All we can say at the moment is that such questions are best reserved for future examinations and studies, an endeavor we believe is highly warranted.

Notes

[1] Personal interview, 17 December 2015.

[2] The states Banting and Kymlicka examine are Australia, Austria, Belgium, Canada, Denmark, Finland, France, Germany, Greece, Ireland, Italy, Japan, Netherlands, New Zealand, Norway, Portugal, Spain, Sweden, Switzerland, United Kingdom and the USA.

[3] Banting and Kymlicka also include Japan in their project. We chose, however, to drop this particular country because multicultural policies for immigrants in Japan are non-existent. Aside from this, our project looks at every country that the MPI examines.

[4] These figures should not be confused with numbers of immigrants who entered the country in 2015.

[5] The reader will note that four out of five of the cluster titles employ the term 'religious freedom'. We felt that 'freedom' was a better noun to use here than 'accommodation', as we wanted to describe the degree to which cluster countries allowed students to act, speak or think of their religions without unlawful constraint.

[6] According to the *Washington Post*, 76% of Swedes claim to be either not religious or atheist (see 'Map: these are the world's least religious countries', *Washington Post*, 14 April 2015).

[7] That is, the clause in the First Amendment of the US Constitution that prohibits the establishment of religion by Congress.

[8] It should be noted that parents in Norway have the right to establish private schools offering religious or philosophical education. According to Plesner (2013), private schools that fulfill the formal criteria as well as criteria on the quality of education 'have the right to receive state funding calculated on the basis of how many pupils they have' (p. 244).

[9] Public funding of religious schools in Canada continues to be a contentious issue. While constitutionally provided for in Section 93 of the Constitution Act, it is still an election sore point, particularly with increasing religious diversity in the provinces (notably Ontario).

[10] The French law still permits discreet signs of faith, such as a Star of David, a small cross or a Hand of Fatima.

[11] See also Ratna Ghosh and Alice Chan's chapter in this volume (Chapter 16). This varies by province. Not all public schools in Canada have such courses.

References

Alba, R., Raboteau, A. & DeWind, J. (2009) Introduction: comparisons of migrants and their religions, past and present, in R. Alba, A. Raboteau & J. DeWind (Eds) *Immigration and Religion in America: comparative and historical perspectives*, pp. 1-24. New York: New York University Press.

Alibhai-Brown, Y. (2000) *After Multiculturalism*. London: Foreign Policy Centre.

Anderson, E. (2001) Group Rights, Autonomy, and the Free Exercise of Religion, in C. Sistare, L. May & L. Francis (Eds) *Groups and Group Rights*, pp. 267-280. Lawrence: University Press of Kansas.

Antonenko, P.D., Toy, S. & Niederhauser, D.S. (2012) Using Cluster Analysis for Data Mining in Educational Technology Research, *Education Technology Research Development*, 60, 383-398. https://doi.org/10.1007/s11423-012-9235-8

Bramadat, P. & Koenig, M. (Eds) (2009) *International Migration and the Governance of Religious Diversity*. Montreal and Kingston: McGill-Queen's University Press and School of Policy Studies, Queen's University

Central Intelligence Agency (CIA) (2016) *The World Factbook*. https://www.cia.gov/library/publications/the-world-factbook/docs/contributor_copyright.html

Davis, D. & Miroshnikova, E. (Ed.) (2013) *The Routledge International Handbook of Religious Education*. New York: Routledge.

Dericquebourg, R. (2013) Religious Education in France, in D. Davis & E. Miroshnikova (Eds) *The Routledge International Handbook of Religious Education*, pp. 113-121. New York: Routledge.

Friedner, L. (2013) Religious Education in Sweden, in D. Davis & E. Miroshnikova (Eds) *The Routledge International Handbook of Religious Education*, pp. 343-348. New York: Routledge.

Jackson, R., Miedema, S., Weisse, W. & Williame, J.P. (Eds) (2007) *Religion and Education in Europe: developments, contexts and debates*. Münster: Waxmann Verlag.

Kymlicka, W. (2007) *Multicultural Odysseys: navigating the new international politics of diversity*. Oxford: Oxford University Press.

Kymlicka, W. (2010) The Rise and Fall of Multiculturalism? New Debates on Inclusion and Accommodation in Diverse Societies, *International Social Science Journal*, 61(199), 97-112. https://doi.org/10.1111/j.1468-2451.2010.01750.x

Kymlicka, W. (2012) *Multiculturalism: success, failure, and the future*. Washington, DC: Migration Policy Institute.

Kymlicka, W. (2015) The Three Lives of Multiculturalism, in S. Guo & L. Wong (Eds) *Revisiting Multiculturalism in Canada*, pp. 17-35. Rotterdam: Sense.

Levey, G.B. & Modood, T. (Eds) (2009) *Secularism, Religion and Multicultural Citizenship*. Cambridge: Cambridge University Press.

Maghioros, N. (2013) Religious Education in Greece, in D. Davis & E. Miroshnikova (Eds) *The Routledge International Handbook of Religious Education*, pp. 130-138. New York: Routledge.

Migration Policy Institute (MPI) (2016) International Migration Statistics. http://www.migrationpolicy.org/programs/data-hub/international-migration-statistics

Multiculturalism Policy Index (MPI) (2010) Immigrant Minorities. http://www.queensu.ca/mcp/

Newman, D. (2003) Liberal Multiculturalism and Will Kymlicka's Uneasy Relation with Religious Pluralism, *64 Bijdragen International Journal of Philosophy & Theology*, 64, 265-285.

Olsen, T. (2013) *Applying Tolerance Indicators: annex to the report on assessing tolerance in everyday school life*. San Domenico di Fiesole, Italy: European University Institute.

Pépin, L. (2009) *Teaching about Religions in European School Systems: policy issues and trends*. London: Alliance Publishing Trust.

Plesner, I.T. (2013) Religion and Education in Norway, in D. Davis & E. Miroshnikova (Eds) *The Routledge International Handbook of Religious Education*, pp. 243-250. New York: Routledge.

Russo, C. (Ed.) (2014) *International Perspectives on Education, Religion and Law*. New York: Routledge.

United Nations High Commissioner for Refugees (UNHCR) (2016) Asylum Trends 2014. http://www.unhcr.org/551128679.pdf

Ward, J.H. (1963) Hierarchical Grouping to Optimize an Objective Function, *Journal of American Statistical Association*, 58(301), 236-244. https://doi.org/10.1080/01621459.1963.10500845

Willaime, J. (2007) Different Models for Religion and Education in Europe, in R. Jackson, S. Miedema, W. Weisse & J.-P. Willaime (Eds) *Religion and Education in Europe: developments, contexts and debate*, pp. 57-66. Münster: Waxmann Verlag.

Young, J. (2013) Religious Education in Canada, in D. Davis & E. Miroshnikova (Eds) *The Routledge International Handbook of Religious Education*, pp. 69-75. New York: Routledge.

APPENDIX

Receiving state	Asylum seekers in 2014	Total immigrant population in 2015	Immigrant percentage (%)
Australia	4,589	1,492,374	28.22
Austria	8,395	6,763,633	17.47
Belgium	5,420	1,387,940	12.28
Canada	5,781	7,835,502	21.80
Denmark	3,870	572,520	10.10
Finland	1,407	315,881	5.74
France	29,009	7,784,418	12.09
Germany	65,659	12,005,690	14.88
Greece	4,863	1,242,514	11.34
Ireland	591	746,260	15.92
Italy	24,481	5,788,875	9.68
Netherlands	12,289	1,979,486	11.70
New Zealand	140	1,039,736	22.96
Norway	5,063	741,813	12.24
Portugal	166	837,257	8.09
Spain	2,174	5,852,953	12.69
Sweden	28,511	1,639,771	16.77
Switzerland	9,515	2,438,702	29.39
United Kingdom	14,283	8,543,120	13.20
United States	52,835	46,627,102	14.49

Table AI. Immigration percentage (2015) and asylum seekers (2014).
Source: Migration Policy Institute. http://www.migrationpolicy.org/programs/data-hub/international-migration-statistics

Receiving state					
Australia	UK (1,277,000)	New Zealand (583,000)	China (447,000)	India (365,000)	Italy (232,000)
Austria	Germany (200,000)	Serbia (174,000)	Turkey (165,000)	Bosnia & Herzegovina (139,000)	Romania (63,000)
Belgium	Italy (189,000)	France (156,000)	Netherland (148,000)	Morocco (91,000)	Spain (50,000)
Canada	UK (674,000)	China (640,000)	India (518,000)	Philippine (364,000)	USA (317,000)
Denmark	Germany (35,000)	Turkey (33,000)	Poland (31,000)	Iraq/ Sweden (22,000)	Norway (20,000)
Finland	Russia (68,000)	Sweden (36,000)	Estonia (34,000)	Somalia (10,000)	Iraq/China/ Thailand (9,000)
France	Algeria (1,456,000)	Morocco (928,000)	Portugal (644,000)	Tunisia (395,000)	Italy (380,000)
Germany	Turkey (1,544,000)	Poland (1,147,000)	Russia (1,008,000)	Kazakhstan (718,000)	Italy (433,000)
Greece	Albania (575,000)	Bulgaria (56,000)	Romania (39,000)	Georgia (38,000)	Pakistan (25,000)
Ireland	UK (254,000)	Poland (125,000)	Lithuania (38,000)	USA (25,000)	Latvia (22,000)
Italy	Romania (1,008,000)	Albania (450,000)	Morocco (425,000)	Germany (231,000)	Ukraine (213,000)
Netherlands	Turkey (203,000)	Suriname (191,000)	Morocco (173,000)	Indonesia (139,000)	Germany (127,000)
New Zealand	UK (314,000)	China (115,000)	Australia (81,000)	Samoa (65,000)	India (56,000)
Norway	Poland (76,000)	Sweden (53,000)	Germany (31,000)	Denmark/ Lithuania (26,000)	Iraq (25,000)
Portugal	Angola (161,000)	Brazil (139,000)	France (94,000)	Mozambique (73,000)	Cape Verde (61,000)
Spain	Romania (798,000)	Morocco (746,000)	Ecuador (451,000)	UK (381,000)	Columbia (359,000)
Sweden	Finland (167,000)	Iraq (130,000)	Poland (77,000)	Iran (67,000)	Bosnia & Herzegovina (58,000)
Switzerland	Germany (357,000)	Italy (261,000)	Portugal (203,00)	France (150,000)	Serbia (128,000)
United Kingdom	India (756,000)	Poland (661,000)	Pakistan (476,000)	Ireland (413,000)	Germany (311,000)
United States	Mexico (12,951,000)	China (2,247,000)	India (2,061,000)	Philippine (1,999,000)	Puerto Rico (1,685,000)

Table AII. Top five migrant groups by country origin and receiving state (mid-2013 estimates).
Source: Migration Policy Institute. http://www.migrationpolicy.org/programs/data-hub/international-migration-statistics

Receiving state					Total no. of asylum seekers
Australia	China (398)	India (275)	Pakistan (198)	Viet Nam (133)	Malaysia (124)	4,589
Austria	Syria (1221)	Unknown (787)	Afghanistan (743)	Somalia (403)	Russia (355)	8,395
Belgium	Syria (365)	Ukraine (201)	Eritrea (186)	Guinea (147)	Russia (142)	5,420
Canada	China (225)	Pakistan (170)	Afghanistan (134)	Columbia (124)	Nigeria (119)	5,781
Denmark	Syria (902)	Eritrea (238)	Somalia (215)	Russia (208)	Stateless (174)	3,870
Finland	Iraq (174)	Somalia (64)	Ukraine (48)	Nigeria (39)	Afghanistan (39)	1,407
France	Congo (1,390)	Russia (807)	Bangladesh (730)	Serbia (668)	China (662)	29,009
Germany	Syria (6,705)	Serbia (3,342)	Eritrea (2,961)	Albania (1,911)	Afghanistan (1,716)	65,659
Greece	Afghanistan (431)	Pakistan (404)	Albania (185)	Bangladesh (140)	Syria (139)	4,863
Ireland	Afghanistan (875)	Syria (514)	Serbia (319)	Palestinian (65)	Somalia (58)	591
Italy	Mali (3,169)	Nigeria (2,274)	Gambia (1,848)	Pakistan (1,521)	Senegal (1,038)	24,481
Netherlands	Eritrea (3,146)	Syria (2,300)	Stateless (580)	Somalia (202)	Iraq (160)	12,289
New Zealand	China (10)	Fiji (8)	India (7)	Sri Lanka (6)	Turkey (5)	140
Norway	Eritrea (1,370)	Syria (417)	Somalia (208)	Stateless (160)	Sudan (115)	5,063
Portugal	Ukraine (16)	Sierra Leone (7)	Morocco (7)	Angola (7)	Sri Lanka (7)	166
Spain	Syria (279)	Mali (184)	Ukraine (111)	Algeria (43)	Palestinian (40)	2,174
Sweden	Syria (6,839)	Eritrea (3,406)	Stateless (1,595)	Somalia (869)	Afghanistan (574)	28,511
Switzerland	Eritrea (1,652)	Syria (1,042)	Somalia (198)	Nigeria (170)	Sri Lanka (159)	9,515
United Kingdom	Pakistan (881)	Eritrea (746)	Iran (555)	Syria (440)	Albania (391)	14,283
United States	China (3,440)	Mexico (3,318)	El Salvador (2,004)	Guatemala (1,987)	Honduras (1,238)	52,835

Table AIII. Top five nationalities of asylum applicants by country of asylum. Second quarter 2014.
Source: United Nation High Commissioner for Refugees.
http://www.unhcr.org/5423f9699.html

Notes on Contributors

Nathaniel Adams is a PhD candidate in anthropology at Johns Hopkins University, USA. His research explores agrarian transformation in the Chittagong Hill Tracts region of Bangladesh; more specifically, how animist beliefs enter into negotiations around agricultural practice. He was previously program coordinator at the World Faiths Development Dialogue (WFDD), where he worked on projects in Bangladesh and Cambodia. He is the author of several reports and working papers for WFDD on topics including Buddhist activism. He joined WFDD in 2010 as a research fellow in Cambodia looking at 'spirit forests' and land rights in highland indigenous communities and the development work of engaged Buddhist clergy. From 2013 to 2016, he worked in Bangladesh with BRAC University coordinating a multi-year research project exploring a broad set of issues around religion and international development. He holds a BA in Anthropology from Virginia Commonwealth University and an MSc in International Development from Lund University.

Art-ong Jumsai Na Ayudhaya is the director of the Institute of Sathya Sai Education in Thailand. He is also the official trainer of teachers for the Ministry of Education in Human Values Education. He holds a BA and MA in Mechanical Sciences from the University of Cambridge, a PhD in Communications from Imperial College London, and a PhD in Education from Chulalongkorn University, Thailand. Previously, he has been a lecturer at the faculty of Engineering, Chulalongkorn University, an elected member of the House of Senate, and a member of the Parliament as Deputy Chairman of the House Committee on Education. He has also participated in NASA's Viking Space Project in the design of an automatic landing device.

Hyeyoung Bang, PhD, is an associate professor in the School of Educational Foundations, Leadership and Policy at Bowling Green State University, USA, where she teaches educational psychology and (cross-cultural) human development. Her main research focus concerns wisdom and self-development, and related topics such as resilience, emotional development (empathy), prosocial behaviour, motivation, spirituality and religion. She also researches refugee and immigrants' acculturation issues, including post-traumatic and acculturation stresses and their impact on schooling. Her latest project, supported by the Templeton Religion Trust, is about 'Self, Virtue, Moral Motivation, and Wisdom: a cross-national and cross-faith study'.

L. Philip Barnes is Emeritus Reader in Religious and Theological Education at King's College London. He has published widely within the fields of religious studies, theology and philosophy of education and contributed articles to such journals as *Modern Theology, Religious Studies* and the *Journal of Philosophy of Education*. His recent books include *Education, Religion and Diversity: developing a new model of religious education* (2014); (with Andrew Davis & J. Mark Halstead), *Religious Education: educating for diversity* (2015); and (with James Arthur) *Education and Religion* (2016), a four-volume edited collection.

W.Y. Alice Chan is a PhD candidate studying the potential connection between religious bullying and religious literacy, and is a research assistant on two projects led by Dr Ratna Ghosh, titled 'Countering Violent Extremism through Education in Multicultural Canada' and 'Educational Trajectories of Radicalized Females in Montreal'. She has co-published on this topic with Dr Ghosh. She will also be a lead author on a forthcoming guide on this topic commissioned by UNESCO and the Mahatma Gandhi Institute of Education for Peace and Sustainable Development. Her overall research interests include religious literacy, inclusive and multicultural education, student identities, and teacher education.

Bruce A. Collet is an Associate Professor in Educational Foundations and Inquiry in the College of Education and Human Development at Bowling Green State University, USA. He teaches courses in the social foundations of education, comparative education and the philosophy of education, and serves as Coordinator for Bowling Green's Master of Arts in Cross-Cultural and International Education program. His research focus concerns migration, religion and public schooling, with particular interests in liberal multiculturalism as well as critical security studies. Dr Collet is the author of *Migration, Religion, and Schooling within Liberal Democratic States* (Routledge, forthcoming), and he is Chief Editor of the journal *Diaspora, Indigenous, and Minority Education*.

Ratna Ghosh is James McGill Professor and William C. Macdonald Professor of Education in the Faculty of Education, McGill University, Canada. A member of the Order of Canada, Officer of the Order of Quebec and Fellow of the Royal Society of Canada, she was Dean of Education at McGill University. Since 2013, she has focused on the role of education in countering violent religious extremism and has published on this topic in the *Canadian Foreign Policy Journal* and in a global report commissioned by the Tony Blair Faith Foundation (TBFF). Other contributions include invited presentations and a course on Religion and Global Politics co-hosted by McGill University and TBFF in 2016.

Ruth Hayhoe is a professor at the Ontario Institute for Studies in Education of the University of Toronto, Canada. Her professional engagements in Asia included foreign expert at Fudan University (1980-82), Head of the Cultural Section of the Canadian Embassy in Beijing (1989-91) and Director of the Hong Kong Institute of Education, now the Education University of Hong Kong (1997-2002). Recent books include *Portraits of 21st Century Chinese Universities: in the move to mass higher education* (2011), *China Through the Lens of Comparative Education* (2015) and *Canadian Universities in China's Transformation: an untold story* (2016).

Christina Hwang is a doctoral candidate in Higher Education in the Department of Leadership, Higher, and Adult Education and Comparative, International and Development Education programme at the Ontario Institute for Studies in Education, University of Toronto, Canada. She holds an MA in Bilingual/Bicultural Education from Teachers College, Columbia University. Her doctoral research focuses on the internationalisation policies and programmes in faith-based Christian higher education institutions in South Korea and Canada and how they relate to Christian world mission. She has also held teaching, administrative and research positions in schools and tertiary institutions in Canada, the USA and South Korea.

Lauren Herzog is a program coordinator at the World Faiths Development Dialogue (WFDD), where she led an effort to strategically examine the religious dimensions of development in Senegal. She currently coordinates a project supporting an interfaith group of religious leaders in Senegal working to advance family planning. She has authored several reports and briefs for WFDD on various aspects of faith and development in the Senegalese context. She has been the recipient of two Department of Education grants to study the Wolof language, and she has lived and worked in Senegal and Congo-Brazzaville. She holds a bachelor's degree from Kalamazoo College, USA and a master's degree in French and International Development from the University of Wisconsin-Madison, USA.

Yaacov J. Katz is Professor Emeritus at the School of Education, Bar-Ilan University in Israel as well as President of Michlala – Jerusalem Academic College. He specialises in research on religious education and values, affective education, social attitudes in education, and ICT use in education. He served as Head of the School of Education at Bar-Ilan University, as Chairperson of the Israeli UNESCO Education Commission, and as Chief Pedagogic Officer at the Israel Ministry of Education, where he was responsible for all subject matter taught in the Israeli school system.

Huma Kidwai is an education consultant at the World Bank, in Washington, DC, USA, supporting projects ranging from early childhood and basic education to higher education and skills development in sub-Saharan Africa and the East Asia and Pacific region. She has a doctoral degree from Teachers College, Columbia University; her research focused on the relationship between the state and madrassas in India. Her other professional experiences include projects with the Poverty Reduction Group of the World Bank; projects related to health and social equity at the Praxis Institute for Participatory Practices in New Delhi; and education programmes and research at the Earth Institute's Global Center in Mumbai on their Model District Education Project.

Jun Li is Professor of Educational Leadership and Policy at Western University, Canada, Former Deputy Director of the Education Policy Unit of the University of Hong Kong (2015-17), Past Chairman of the Hong Kong Educational Research Association (2014-17), and Past President of the Comparative Education Society of Hong Kong (2012-14). He is currently serving on the the World Council of Comparative Education Societies' Research Standing Committee and Editorial Committee of *Global Comparative Education: Journal of the WCCES*. Dr Li was originally trained as a historian of Chinese education and later as a policy analyst of international education and development, each with a PhD. He has accumulated wide experiences in Canada, China, Japan and the USA, in addition to Hong Kong and Africa. His recent publications include *Quest for World-Class Teacher Education? A Multiperspectival Study on the Chinese Model of Policy Implementation* (Springer, 2016) and 'Ideologies, Strategies and Higher Education Development: a comparison of China's university partnerships with the Soviet Union and Africa over space and time' (2017, *Comparative Education*, 53[2], 245-264).

Elena Lisovskaya is Professor of Sociology at Western Michigan University, USA. She specialises in comparative sociology of education and religion. Her core research interests include institutional and ideological changes in post-communist education. She has published on privatisation, dogmatism and new ideologies in textbooks. Since the 2000s, she has been engaged in comparative research on desecularisation and religious education in state-run schools, and most recently published *Religious Education in Russia: inter-faith harmony or neo-imperial toleration?* She co-authored *Religious Intolerance among Orthodox Christians and Muslims in Russia* (2008); *Orthodoxy, Islam, and the Desecularization of Russia's State Schools* (2010); *Ethnodoxy: how popular ideologies fuse religious and ethnic identities* (2012) and many other works.

Shujuan Luo received her PhD from the Cultural Foundations of Education program at Kent State University, USA, where she also gained her MA in Education. She has a BA in English from Wuhan University of Technology,

China and a BSc in Psychology from Huazhong Normal University, China. Her main research interests are women's education and empowerment, informal learning of life skills, the capability approach, and entrepreneurial education.

Katherine Marshall, a Senior Fellow at the Berkley Center for Religion, Peace and World Affairs, is Professor of the Practice of Religion, Development and Peacebuilding in the School of Foreign Service, Georgetown University, USA, and heads the World Faiths Development Dialogue (WFDD), that bridges the worlds of development and religion. She has worked for four decades on international development, and was a senior officer for many years at the World Bank. She sits on several non-profit boards. Her most recent books are (with Susan Hayward) *Women, Religion, and Peacebuilding: illuminating the unseen* (USIP, 2015) and *Global Institutions of Religion: ancient movers, modern shakers* (Routledge, 2013).

Ya Na is a PhD student at Kent State University, USA. She grew up as part of the Mongolian minority ethnic group in Inner Mongolia, China. Her research interests include migrant girls' education in urban China and education of ethnic minority students in China. Currently, she is assisting in a study on ethnic Mongolian students' education in the Inner Mongolia Autonomous Region of China.

Prapapat Niyom has a background in architecture and holds an honorary doctorate in education for local development from the Rajapat Phranakorn University in Bangkok, Thailand. She founded Roong Aroon School in 1997 and the Arsomsilp Institute in 2006. She is currently President of the Arsomsilp Institute of the Arts in Bangkok. She is well versed in applying holistic education in schooling based on Buddhist principles. She has previously served as a member of the national reform council on education and as advisor to the Minister of Education and has also served as the deputy governor for the Bangkok Metropolitan Authority.

Sarfaroz Niyozov is an associate professor in comparative education, curriculum studies and teacher development at the Ontario Institute for Studies in Education, University of Toronto, Canada. He was the former founding head of the Central Asian Studies Unit at the Institute of Ismaili Studies, co-director of the Comparative, International Education Centre (CIDEC), University of Toronto, and the editor of *Curriculum Inquiry*. He is currently on a three-year period of unpaid leave to serve as the director of the Institute for Educational Development, Aga Khan University, Karachi (AKU-IEDP). His research interests include educational change, teacher development and religious education in post-socialist and Muslim societies.

Witit Rachatatanun is currently director of Panyaprateep School, Thailand, a private boarding school which has an emphasis on Buddhist education in its curriculum development. He holds an EdD and EdM from Harvard University, an MA in Sociology from the University of Essex, and a BSc in Economics from the London School of Economics. He also holds a graduate diploma in Curriculum and Instruction from STOU, Thailand. Previously, he has served as the Assistant Secretary-General, National Economic and Social Development Board (NESDB), Office of the Prime Minister, Thailand.

Vilma Seeberg is Associate Professor for International/Multicultural Education at Kent State University, USA in the College of Education, Health and Human Services. She studies the role of human agency, education and empowerment in social change, focusing on two marginalised peoples: rural girls in globalising China, and Black American students in predominately White schools in the USA. She has published two books on Chinese literacy policy and effects, numerous articles on a continuing long-term study of village girls' schooling and urbanisation (e.g. in *Comparative Education Review* in 2014), and has a forthcoming book on Black American students' achievement in the suburbs.

Steve Sider has a PhD from Western University, Canada and is an associate professor in the Faculty of Education at Wilfrid Laurier University in Waterloo, Canada. He teaches courses in global education, school leadership and special education. His research interest is in educational leadership in international contexts. He currently holds a national research grant examining inclusive leadership practices of Canadian school principals. Recent publications have included a co-edited book which provides comparative and international perspectives on education as well as articles in *International Studies in Educational Administration*, the *Canadian Journal of Education* and *Comparative and International Education*.

Malini Sivasubramaniam completed her PhD at the University of Toronto, Canada with a specialisation in Comparative, International and Development Education. Her dissertation examines household decision-making in low-fee private schools in Kenya. She is currently a visiting scholar with the Comparative, International and Development Education Centre at the Ontario Institute for Studies in Education (OISE/UT) as well as an independent research consultant. Her research interests include the privatisation of education, school choice and equity for marginalised communities, and faith-based non-state actors in education.

Benjamin Vokes currently teaches English at Panyaprateep School, Thailand, a private boarding school which has an emphasis on Buddhist wisdom education and curriculum development. He holds a BA from the

University of Teeside, UK. He has had prior teacher training in EFL at Chiangmai (Lanna) School in Chiangmai.

Keith Watson is Emeritus Professor of Comparative and International Education, University of Reading, United Kingdom. He was educated at the universities of Edinburgh, London and Reading. He has worked for the British Council in Poland, Pakistan, Thailand and, briefly, Iran. From 1976 to 2001 he was a lecturer, then reader, and finally Professor of Comparative and International Education and director of the Centre for International Studies in Education and Management at the University of Reading. In addition, he was also editor in chief of the *International Journal of Educational Development* from 1990 to 2006. He has written or edited about 16 books and over 120 articles. He was also variously secretary, chairman and president of the British Association of International and Comparative Education.

Mei-Yee Wong is an assistant professor in the Department of Social Sciences at the Education University of Hong Kong. Her research focuses on power relations, values and moral education in primary and secondary schools and universities, and teacher professional development. Her recent publications include her book, *Teacher-Student Power Relations in Primary Schools*, and her article, 'Teacher-Student Power Relations as a Reflection of Multileveled Intertwined Interactions', published in the *British Journal of Sociology of Education*. She is currently engaged in a values education project, exploring the use of portfolio and circle time for values learning.

Xinyi Wu is a lecturer at the Joseph H. Lauder Institute of Management and International Studies at the University of Pennsylvania, USA. She received her PhD in Comparative and International Development Education from the University of Minnesota-Twin Cities. Her research interests include economics of education, cultural foundations of education, and language and education. She is particularly interested in the issues of ethnicity, ethnic identity, and their relationship with educational equality and quality. She has conducted fieldwork in north-western China on the rural Chinese Muslim population. She also participated in projects for disadvantaged youth in Africa. Her recent publications include comparative studies of educational policies for China and Vietnam, Chinese ethnic minority students' access to higher education, and the effects of globalisation on development aid. Her most recent publication is a book entitled *Educational Journeys, Struggles, and Ethnicity: the impact of state schooling on Muslim Hui in rural China* (Palgrave Macmillan, 2017).

Oxford Studies in Comparative Education

GENERAL EDITOR: DAVID PHILLIPS

Aspects of Education and the European Union
DAVID PHILLIPS

Aspects of Education in the Middle East and North Africa COLIN BROCK & LILA ZIA LEVERS

Can the Japanese Change Their Education System?
ROGER GOODMAN & DAVID PHILLIPS

The Career Trajectories of English Language Teachers
PENNY HAWORTH & CHERYL CRAIG

The Challenges of Education in Brazil
COLIN BROCK & SIMON SCHWARTZMAN

The Changing Landscape of Education in Africa
DAVID JOHNSON

Comparing Standards Internationally
BARBARA JAWORKSI & DAVID PHILLIPS

Cross-national Attraction in Education HUBERT ERTL

Developing Schools for Democracy in Europe JOHN SAYER

Education and Change in the Pacific Rim KEITH SULLIVAN

ROGER GOODMAN, TAKEHIKO KARIYA & JOHN TAYLOR

The InstitutionS of Education K. CUMMINGS

International Schools MARY HAYDEN & JEFF THOMPSON

Internationalisation of Higher Education and Global Mobility BERNHARD STREITWIESER

Key Issues in Educational Development
TERRY ALLSOP & COLIN BROCK

Knowledge and the Study of Education
GEOFF WHITTY & JOHN FURLONG

Lessons of Cross-national Comparison in Education
DAVID PHILLIPS

Low-fee Private Schooling PRACHI SRIVASTAVA

New Approaches to Vocational Education in Europe
REGINA H. MULDER & PETER F.E. SLOANE

Opening Windows to Change JOHN SAYER

Partnerships in Educational Development
IFFAT FARAH & BARBARA JAWORSKI

PISA, Power, and Policy
HEINZ-DIETER MEYER & AARON BENAVOT

Political and Citizenship Education STEPHANIE WILDE

Politics, Modernisation and Educational Reform in Russia DAVID JOHNSON

Private Schooling in Less Economically Developed Countries PRACHI SRIVASTAVA & GEOFFREY WALFORD

Full details of all volumes in this series can be found at
www.symposium-books.co.uk
and can be ordered there, or from
Symposium Books, PO Box 204, Didcot,
Oxford OX11 9ZQ, United Kingdom
orders@symposium-books.co.uk